HERITAGE OF WESTERN CIVILIZATION

—— VOLUME II ——

From Revolutions to Modernity

NINTH EDITION

John L. Beatty ♦ Oliver A. Johnson
John Reisbord ♦ Mita Choudhury

PEARSON

Prentice
Hall

Upper Saddle River, NJ 07458

Library of Congress Cataloging-in-Publication Data

Heritage of Western civilization/edited by John L. Beatty, Oliver A.
   Johnson.—9th ed./[newly edited by] John Reisbord, Mita Choudhury.
   p.   cm.
   ISBN 0-13-034127-4 (v. 1)—ISBN 0-13-034128-2 (v. 2)
   1. Civilization, Western—History—Sources. 2. Civilization—
History—Sources. I. Beatty, John Louis. II. Johnson, Oliver A.
III. Reisbord, John. IV. Choudhury, Mita.
CB245.H428   2004
909'.09821—dc21   2002044570

Acquisitions Editor: Charles Cavaliere
Editor-in-Chief: Charlyce Jones Owen
Associate Editor: Emsal Hasan
Editorial Assistant: Adrienne Paul
Marketing Manager: Heather Shelstad
Marketing Assistant: Jennifer Bryant
Production Editor: Laura A. Lawrie
Manufacturing Buyer: Tricia Kenny
Cover Design: Kiwi Design

Cover Illustration/Photo: Mass emigration from Europe: Emigrants on board a ship en route to the United States./Library of Congress
Composition: This book was set in 10/12 Palatino by Preparé Inc.
Printer/Binder: Interior printed by Courier Companies, Inc. The cover was printed by Coral Graphics.

Credits and acknowledgments borrowed from other sources and reproduced, with permission, in this textbook appear on appropriate page within text.

Pearson Education LTD.
Pearson Education Singapore, Pte. Ltd.
Pearson Education Canada, Ltd.
Pearson Education—Japan

Pearson Education Australia PTY, Limited
Pearson Education North Asia, Ltd.
Pearson Educación de Mexico, S.A. de C.V.
Pearson Education Malaysia, Pte. Ltd.

10 9 8 7 6 5 4 3 2 1

ISBN 0-13-034128-2

In memory of John W. Olmsted

Contents

THE CONTEMPORARY WORLD

Preface

The editor assigned to a work entering its Ninth Edition takes on a special obligation. Since 1958, John Beatty and Oliver Johnson's *Heritage of Western Civilization* has proved a valuable tool for countless students and instructors. Our revision of the Eighth Edition was carried out with full knowledge and respect for the fact that we were working on a book that has stood the test of time. Still, no work such as this reaches a Ninth Edition unless its editors are constantly on the lookout for ways to improve on past efforts.

In a sense, our challenge was very much like that facing any teacher of Western Civilization. Given limited time, or in our case limited space, what should the instructor include and what must he or she leave out? The latter task was at least as difficult as the former. A strong argument could be made for the retention of every selection in the Eighth Edition. However, our mandate was to broaden the range of topics and authors included in this anthology without increasing its length and, in service of that goal, tough choices had to be made. We hope that the inclusion of authors such as the Muslim warrior and courtier Usāmah Ibn-Munqidh, the Italian matriarch Alessandra Strozzi, and the Dominican witch hunters Heinrich Kramer and James Sprenger will provide readers with a richer, more complex picture of Western history.

Changes to the Ninth Edition:
The most important change to the Ninth Edition of the *Heritage of Western Civilization* is the inclusion of fourteen new selections, six of which were authored by women. New sources include:

Volume I
• Esarhaddon, "Second Inscription of Esarhaddon"
• Xenophon, "The Character of Cyrus"
• Aristotle, "The Care of Infancy"
• Plutarch, "The Insurrection of the Gladiators"
• Hildegard of Bingen, *Letters*
• Usāmah Ibn-Munqidh, "An Appreciation of the Frankish Character"
• Laura Cereta, *Letters*
• Alessandra Strozzi, *Letters*

Volume II
• *Malleus Malificarum*
• Olympe de Gouges, "Declaration of the Rights of Women"
• Henry Mayhew, *London Labour and the London Poor*
• Catherine Booth, "God of Education"
• W. E. B. Du Bois, *The Souls of Black Folk*
• Gusta Dawidson-Draenger, *Justina's Diary*

In addition, the introductions to every source in both volumes of *Heritage* have been revised with an eye to providing students with the necessary context to explore the selection in question, while avoiding the imposition of any particular analytical framework on the material. Finally, in an effort to help facilitate students' close reading and critique of the selections, questions for consideration have been added to the introduction to each source and at the end of the general introduction to each major section.

John Reisbord

Mita Choudhury

Heritage
of Western Civilization

The title page of Leviathan by the British philosopher Thomas Hobbes depicts a giant king towering above his kingdom. Close examination of the king reveals that his body is made up of his subjects.

EARLY MODERN EUROPE

The century and a half from the Treaty of Westphalia (1648), which ended the Thirty Years' War, to the Napoleonic Wars, at the beginning of the nineteenth century, marked a period of great changes—political, economic, religious, intellectual, social, and technological—in European history. Some of these are now referred to as "revolutions"—the Scientific Revolution, the French Revolution, the American Revolution (America being considered an extension of European civilization), and the Industrial Revolution. All of the changes were to have profound effects on Western and, later, world civilization.

The Thirty Years' War, which ravaged much of central Europe, generated a curious but historically important anomaly. The war had its origins in religious animosities, pitting Catholics against Protestants. But, because the Catholics were led by the Hapsburg dynasty of Austria and Spain, which was contending for political domination of Europe against France, the French political strategist, Richelieu, even though himself a cardinal of the Catholic church, brought his country into the conflict on the side of the Protestants. The demands of national power, thus, were given precedence over religious convictions. Europe was witnessing the rise of the nation-state. As nation-states consolidated, centralizing their power, this power increasingly became concentrated in the person of the monarch. France offers a striking example of the concept of royal sovereignty, particularly under the "Sun King," Louis XIV, the most powerful European monarch of the seventeenth century. With an arrogance whose frankness betokened innocence Louis blandly proclaimed "*L'état, c'est moi.*" But the royal right to rule was not accepted simply de facto; rather, political theorists of the time offered complex arguments to justify it. Usually these had their basis in religion. Writers like Bishop Bossuet and Sir Robert Filmer (whose arguments John Locke was to lay waste in his *First Treatise of Civil Government*), turned to the Scriptures to establish the legitimacy of royal rule, developing the notion of the "divine right of kings." But another defender of royal absolutism, Thomas Hobbes, took a quite different line; according to him, a monarch's "right" to rule rested solely on his ability to gain and hold his power and to preserve the peace.

However the various monarchs might justify their rule, the central political fact of the period was the development of the European nation-state. Centralization of power was not narrowly political but extended into almost every area of life. Of special importance was the economic realm, which was brought under the supervision of the state, following a theory and practice known as *mercantilism*. In all its ramifications mercantilism deployed the economic activities of the country to enhance the power of the state, particularly in rivalry with the other states of Europe. One way to accomplish this end was to establish colonies that would import the manufactures of the mother country and export raw materials to it for processing and exportation to rival states, the controlling concept being the idea that the power of a state depended on its acquisition of precious metals at the expense of its rivals. This aspect of mercantilism led to a race by the European powers to acquire colonies in the "new world." Since these required large increments of cheap labor to farm the fields, the slave trade was born. In the case of North America, the taxes imposed by England on its colonies there led to increasing discontent, becoming a major factor causing the American Revolution. Nevertheless, whatever its defects, mercantilism contributed to the growth of the modern nation-state, as well as to the rapid industrialization of Europe.

While Europe was undergoing these political and economic changes, another kind of change was also going on—the rise of modern science. Begun as early as the Renaissance period by the astronomers, with Copernicus (1473–1543) leading the way, the scientific revolution, dominated by towering figures like Bacon, Kepler, Galileo, Descartes, Leibniz, and Newton, reached its zenith in the seventeenth century. Most of the major scientific advances of the time, like Newton's theory of universal gravitation, have become so much a part of our intellectual heritage that it would be superfluous to detail them here. However, something should be said of an equally important aspect of modern science—its method. Although scientific methodology was not invented in this period, earlier applications had been sporadic and only minimally articulated and put into practice. Modern scientific method is composed of two main constituents. First is the appeal to empirical evidence. If a scientific theory is to be considered seriously, its originator must be able to produce evidence in its support observable and confirmable by any qualified investigator. Considered a commonplace now, this requirement is a result mainly of the success of science itself; in the seventeenth century, it was a bold and, to some, a dangerous innovation. The second major component of scientific method is the use of mathematics. Mathematics guarantees precision, facilitates the prediction of future events, and gives scientists a powerful tool with which to develop new theories. The seventeenth century saw the birth of analytic geometry, which was the discovery of the French philosopher, René Descartes, as well as the emergence of calculus, independently developed by Newton and the German mathematician and philosopher, G. W. Leibniz.

Perhaps the most important consequence of the scientific revolution was the development of modern technology, first evidenced in the Industrial Revolution that got under way in the eighteenth century. Although technology had made a few advances during the Middle Ages, these were minor and most of the energy needed to accomplish work had the same source as it had had from time immemorial—animal and human muscles. But, building on previous scientific discoveries, inventors of the eighteenth century found in steam a new and enormous source of power. Steam engines were developed that could be put to work in innumerable ways—for example, to power looms that produce cloth. In the burgeoning industrial cities, like Manchester in England, mills were constructed that processed the raw cotton and other fibers that came mainly from the colonies, turning these into clothing and other finished products. With the development of railroads and, later, of steamships, these products could be distributed quickly and economically throughout the world.

In its transformation of European technology, the scientific revolution gave rise to more than the Industrial Revolution. Intellectual leaders, aware that the changes the scientists had wrought resulted from the application of human reason to an understanding of nature, argued that, through a similar application of reason to all areas of life—social, economic, political, and others—humanity could resolve its problems and civilization advance to a higher level than ever before. Led by people like Voltaire and the French *philosophes*, the eighteenth century proclaimed the "Age of Reason." In place of "superstition" which, they believed, had controlled society for millennia, they would liberate it through rationality.

But rationalism was not without its detractors. As the eighteenth century wore on, the Scottish philosopher and historian David Hume questioned the ability of reason to solve any problems whatsoever and maintained that humanity would be well advised to turn its affairs over to the control of feeling. And the Swiss-French writer Jean Jacques Rousseau rose up against the sophistication and artificiality of Enlightenment society to champion a return to nature, glorifying "the noble savage" whom Europeans believed they had discovered in the original inhabitants of the "new world." Enlightenment rationalism gave way before a movement that was to sweep through Europe toward the close of the century, particularly in literature and the arts—romanticism.

LOOKING AHEAD

As you learn about Early Modern Europe, consider the following questions.

1. What factors contributed to the rise of modern science in the sixteenth and seventeenth centuries? How would you describe the new scientific method?

2. Compare and contrast the medieval and early modern state. What goals were shared by most early modern monarchs?

3. What were the causes of the French Revolution? In your opinion, were the most important roots of revolution social, economic, or idelogical?

Witchcraft

Belief in witchcraft did not begin in the sixteenth century. In the early modern period, however, fear of witchcraft intensified and with this fear came an increased willingness on the part of Europeans to identify, try, and convict their friends and neighbors as witches. Nor was the belief in witchcraft limited to the poor and uneducated. Across the spectrum of society, from kings to commoners, most people were certain that individuals existed who could call on dark powers to carry out their evil wishes. In fact, witchcraft trials depended on the shared beliefs of accusers, prosecutors, and judges.

The *Malleus Malificarum*, or "Hammer of Witches," was an attempt to codify witchcraft beliefs: to explain the nature of the relationship between the witch and the devil, to define the things that witches could and could not do, and to provide a guide for the detection and trial of witches. Written in 1486 by Heinrich Kramer and James Sprenger, two Dominican monks, the *Malleus* became a handbook for inquisitors and a starting point for early modern discussion of the problem of witchcraft. The section included here focused on the gender of witches. Over 90 percent of accused witches were women. The authors took it for granted that this could be explained with reference to some particular qualities in women that made it more likely that they would form alliances with the devil. Kramer and Sprenger, therefore, set out to identify those qualities. As you read the passage, pay particular attention to the assumptions the authors make. What, for example, is the source of most of their information about the nature of women?

Consider the following questions as you study the text below.

1. What role did female sexuality play in Kramer and Sprenger's view of female weakness? How would you explain their emphasis on a connection between lust and witchcraft?

2. What explains the surge of witchcraft trials in the early modern period? How might the ideas expressed by Kramer and Sprenger have been interpreted in the context of the social, political, and religious upheaval of the sixteenth and seventeenth centuries?

Malleus Malificarum

Why Superstition Is Chiefly Found in Women

Others again have propounded other reasons why there are more superstitious women found than men. And the first is, that they are more credulous; and since the chief aim of the devil is to corrupt faith, therefore he rather attacks them. See *Ecclesiasticus* xix: He that is quick to believe is light-minded, and shall be diminished.

The second reason is, that women are naturally more impressionable, and more ready to receive the influence of a disembodied spirit; and that when they use this quality well they are very good, but when they use it ill they are very evil.

The third reason is that they have slippery tongues, and are unable to conceal from their fellow-women those things which by evil arts they know; and, since they are weak, they find an easy and secret manner of vindicating themselves by witchcraft. See *Ecclesiasticus* as quoted above: I had rather dwell with a lion and a dragon than to keep house with a wicked woman. All wickedness is but little to the wickedness of a woman. And to this may be added that, as they are very impressionable, they act accordingly.

There are also others who bring forward yet other reasons, of which preachers should be very careful how they make use. For it is true that in the Old Testament the Scriptures have much that is evil to say about women, and this because of the first temptress, Eve, and her imitators; yet afterwards in the New Testament we find a change of name, as from Eva to Ave (as S. Jerome says), and the whole sin of Eve taken away by the benediction of MARY. Therefore preachers should always say as much praise of them as possible.

But because in these times this perfidy is more often found in women than in men, as we learn by actual experience, if anyone is curious as to the reason, we may add to what has already been said the following: that since they are feebler both in mind and body, it is not surprising that they should come more under the spell of witchcraft.

For as regards intellect, or the understanding of spiritual things, they seem to be of a different nature from men; a fact which is vouched for by the logic of the authorities, backed by various examples from the Scriptures. Terence says: Women are intellectually like children. And Lactantius (*Institutiones*, III): No woman understood philosophy except Temeste. And *Proverbs* xi, as it were describing a woman, says: As a jewel of gold in a swine's snout, so is a fair woman which is without discretion.

Trans. Montague Summers (London: John Rodker, 1928).

But the natural reason is that she is more carnal than a man, as is clear from her many carnal abominations. And it should be noted that there was a defect in the formation of the first woman, since she was formed from a bent rib, that is, a rib of the breast, which is bent as it were in a contrary direction to a man. And since through this defect she is an imperfect animal, she always deceives. For Cato says: When a woman weeps she weaves snares. And again: When a woman weeps, she labours to deceive a man. And this is shown by Samson's wife, who coaxed him to tell her the riddle he had propounded to the Philistines, and told them the answer, and so deceived him. And it is clear in the case of the first woman that she had little faith; for when the serpent asked why they did not eat of every tree in Paradise, she answered: Of every tree, etc.—lest perchance we die. Thereby she showed that she doubted, and had little faith in the word of God. And all this is indicated by the etymology of the word; for *Femina* comes from *Fe* and *Minus*, since she is ever weaker to hold and preserve the faith. And this as regards faith is of her very nature; although both by grace and nature faith never failed in the Blessed Virgin, even at the time of Christ's Passion, when it failed in all men.

Therefore a wicked woman is by her nature quicker to waver in her faith, and consequently quicker to abjure the faith, which is the root of witchcraft.

And as to her other mental quality, that is, her natural will; when she hates someone whom she formerly loved, then she seethes with anger and impatience in her whole soul, just as the tides of the sea are always heaving and boiling. Many authorities allude to this cause. *Ecclesiasticus* xxv: There is no wrath above the wrath of a woman. And Seneca (*Tragedies*, VII): No might of the flames or of the swollen winds, no deadly weapon, is so much to be feared as the lust and hatred of a woman who has been divorced from the marriage bed.

This is shown too in the woman who falsely accused Joseph, and caused him to be imprisoned because he would not consent to the crime of adultery with her (*Genesis* xxx). And truly the most powerful cause which contributes to the increase of witches is the woeful rivalry between married folk and unmarried women and men. This is so even among holy women, so what must it be among the others? For you see in *Genesis* xxi how impatient and envious Sarah was of Hagar when she conceived: how jealous Rachel was of Leah because she had no children (*Genesis* xxx): and Hannah, who was barren, of the fruitful Peninnah (I. *Kings* i): and how Miriam (*Numbers* xii) murmured and spoke ill of Moses, and was therefore stricken with leprosy: and how Martha was jealous of Mary Magdalen, because she was busy and Mary was sitting down (*S. Luke* x). To this point is *Ecclesiasticus* xxxvii: Neither consult with a woman touching her of whom she is jealous. Meaning that it is useless to consult with her, since there is always jealousy, that is, envy, in a wicked woman. And if women behave thus to each other, how much more will they do so to men.

Valerius Maximus tells how, when Phoroneus, the king of the Greeks, was dying, he said to his brother Leontius that there would have been nothing lacking to him of complete happiness if a wife had always been lacking to him. And when Leontius asked how a wife could stand in the way of happiness, he answered that all married men well knew. And when the philosopher Socrates was asked if one should marry a wife, he answered: If you do not, you are lonely, your family dies out, and a stranger inherits; if you do, you suffer perpetual anxiety, querulous complaints, reproaches concerning the marriage portion, the heavy displeasure of your relations, the garrulousness of a mother-in-law, cuckoldom, and no certain arrival of an heir. This he said as one who knew. For S. Jerome in his *Contra Iouinianum* says: This Socrates had two wives, whom he endured with much patience, but could not be rid of their contumelies and clamorous vituperations. So one day when they were complaining against him, he went out of the house to escape their plaguing, and sat down before the house; and the women then threw filthy water over him. But the philosopher was not disturbed by this, saying, "I knew that the rain would come after the thunder."

There is also a story of a man whose wife was drowned in a river, who, when he was searching for the body to take it out of the water, walked up the stream. And when he was asked why, since heavy bodies do not rise but fall, he was searching against the current of the river, he answered: "When that woman was alive she always, both in word and deed, went contrary to my commands; therefore I am searching in the contrary direction in case even now she is dead she may preserve her contrary disposition."

And indeed, just as through the first defect in their intelligence they are more prone to abjure the faith; so through their second defect of inordinate affections and passions they search for, brood over, and inflict various vengeances, either by witchcraft, or by some other means. Wherefore it is no wonder that so great a number of witches exist in this sex.

Women also have weak memories; and it is a natural vice in them not to be disciplined, but to follow their own impulses without any sense of what is due; this is her whole study, and all that she keeps in her memory. So Theophrastus says: If you hand over the whole management of the house to her, but reserve some minute detail to your own judgement, she will think that you are displaying a great want of faith in her, and will stir up strife; and unless you quickly take counsel, she will prepare poison for you, and consult seers and soothsayers; and will become a witch.

But as to domination by women, hear what Cicero says in the *Paradoxes*. Can he be called a free man whose wife governs him, imposes laws on him, orders him, and forbids him to do what he wishes, so that he cannot and dare not deny her anything that she asks? I should call him not only a slave, but the vilest of slaves, even if he comes of the noblest family. And Seneca, in the character of the raging Medea, says: Why do you cease to follow your happy impulse; how great is that part of vengeance in which

you rejoice? Where he adduces many proofs that a woman will not be governed, but will follow her own impulse even to her own destruction. In the
same way we read of many women who have killed themselves either for
love or sorrow because they were unable to work their vengeance.

S. Jerome, writing of Daniel, tells a story of Laodice, wife of Antiochus
king of Syria; how, being jealous lest he should love his other wife, Berenice,
more than her, she first caused Berenice and her daughter by Antiochus to be
slain, and then poisoned herself. And why? Because she would not be governed, but would follow her own impulse. Therefore S. John Chrysostom
says not without reason: O evil worse than all evil, a wicked woman,
whether she be poor or rich. For if she be the wife of a rich man, she does not
cease night and day to excite her husband with hot words, to use evil blan-
dishments and violent importunations. And if she have a poor husband she
does not cease to stir him also to anger and strife. And if she be a widow, she
takes it upon herself everywhere to look down on everybody, and is in-
flamed to all boldness by the spirit of pride.

If we inquire, we find that nearly all the kingdoms of the world have
been overthrown by women. Troy, which was a prosperous kingdom, was,
for the rape of one woman, Helen, destroyed, and many thousands of Greeks
slain. The kingdom of the Jews suffered much misfortune and destruction
through the accursed Jezebel, and her daughter Athaliah, queen of Judah,
who caused her son's sons to be killed, that on their death she might reign
herself; yet each of them was slain. The kingdom of the Romans endured
much evil through Cleopatra, Queen of Egypt, that worst of women. And so
with others. Therefore it is no wonder if the world now suffers through the
malice of women.

And now let us examine the carnal desires of the body itself, whence
has arisen unconscionable harm to human life. Justly may we say with Cato
of Utica: If the world could be rid of women, we should not be without God
in our intercourse. For truly, without the wickedness of women, to say nothing of witchcraft, the world would still remain proof against innumerable
dangers. Hear what Valerius said to Rufinus: You do not know that woman
is the Chimaera, but it is good that you should know it; for that monster was
of three forms; its face was that of a radiant and noble lion, it had the filthy
belly of a goat, and it was armed with the virulent tail of a viper. And he
means that a woman is beautiful to look upon, contaminating to the touch,
and deadly to keep.

Let us consider another property of hers, the voice. For as she is a liar
by nature, so in her speech she stings while she delights us. Wherefore her
voice is like the song of the Sirens, who with their sweet melody entice the
passers-by and kill them. For they kill them by emptying their purses, con-
suming their strength, and causing them to forsake God. Again Valerius says
to Rufinus: When she speaks it is a delight which flavours the sin; the flower
of love is a rose, because under its blossom there are hidden many thorns.

See *Proverbs* v, 3–4: Her mouth is smoother than oil; that is, her speech is afterwards as bitter as absinthium. [Her throat is smoother than oil. But her end is as bitter as wormwood.]

Let us consider also her gait, posture, and habit, in which is vanity of vanities. There is no man in the world who studies so hard to please the good God as even an ordinary woman studies by her vanities to please men. An example of this is to be found in the life of Pelagia, a worldly woman who was wont to go about Antioch tired and adorned most extravagantly. A holy father, named Nonnus, saw her and began to weep, saying to his companions, that never in all his life had he used such diligence to please God; and much more he added to this effect, which is preserved in his orations.

It is this which is lamented in *Ecclesiastes* vii, and which the Church even now laments on account of the great multitude of witches. And I have found a woman more bitter than death, who is the hunter's snare, and her heart is a net, and her hands are hands. He that pleaseth God shall escape from her; but he that is a sinner shall be caught by her. More bitter than death, that is, than the devil: *Apocalypse* vi, 8, His name was Death. For though the devil tempted Eve to sin, yet Eve seduced Adam. And as the sin of Eve would not have brought death to our soul and body unless the sin had afterwards passed on to Adam, to which he was tempted by Eve, not by the devil, therefore she is more bitter than death.

More bitter than death, again, because that is natural and destroys only the body; but the sin which arose from woman destroys the soul by depriving it of grace, and delivers the body up to the punishment for sin.

More bitter than death, again, because bodily death is an open and terrible enemy, but woman is a wheedling and secret enemy.

And that she is more perilous than a snare does not speak of the snare of hunters, but of devils. For men are caught not only through their carnal desires, when they see and hear women: for S. Bernard says: Their face is a burning wind, and their voice the hissing of serpents: but they also cast wicked spells on countless men and animals. And when it is said that her heart is a net, it speaks of the inscrutable malice which reigns in their hearts. And her hands are as bands for binding; for when they place their hands on a creature to bewitch it, then with the help of the devil they perform their design.

To conclude. All witchcraft comes from carnal lust, which is in women insatiable. See *Proverbs* xxx: There are three things that are never satisfied, yea, a fourth thing which says not, It is enough; that is, the mouth of the womb. Wherefore for the sake of fulfilling their lusts they consort even with devils. More such reasons could be brought forward, but to the understanding it is sufficiently clear that it is no matter for wonder that there are more women than men found infected with the heresy of witchcraft. And in consequence of this, it is better called the heresy of witches than of wizards, since the name is taken from the more powerful party. And blessed be the Highest Who has so far preserved the male sex from so great a crime: for since He was willing to be born and to suffer for us, therefore He has granted to men this privilege.

What sort of Women are found to be above all Others Superstitious and Witches.

As to our second inquiry, what sort of women more than others are found to be superstitious and infected with witchcraft; it must be said, as was shown in the preceding inquiry, that three general vices appear to have special dominion over wicked women, namely, infidelity, ambition, and lust. Therefore they are more than others inclined towards witchcraft, who more than others are given to these vices. Again, since of these three vices the last chiefly predominates, women being insatiable, etc., it follows that those among ambitious women are more deeply infected who are more hot to satisfy their filthy lusts; and such are adulteresses, fornicatresses, and the concubines of the Great.

Now there are, as it is said in the Papal Bull, seven methods by which they infect with witchcraft the venereal act and the conception of the womb: First by inclining the minds of men to inordinate passion; second, by obstructing their generative force; third, by removing the members accommodated to that act; fourth, by changing men into beasts by their magic art; fifth, by destroying the generative force in women; sixth, by procuring abortion; seventh, by offering children to devils, besides other animals and fruits of the earth with which they work much harm. And all these will be considered later; but for the present let us give our minds to the injuries towards men.

And first concerning those who are bewitched into an inordinate love or hatred, this is a matter of a sort that it is difficult to discuss before the general intelligence. Yet it must be granted that it is a fact. For S. Thomas (IV, 34), treating of obstructions caused by witches, shows that God allows the devil greater power against men's venereal acts than against their other actions; and gives this reason, that this is likely to be so, since those women are chiefly apt to be witches who are most disposed to such acts.

For he says that, since the first corruption of sin by which man became the slave of the devil came to us through the act of generation, therefore greater power is allowed by God to the devil in this act than in all others. Also the power of witches is more apparent in serpents, as it is said, than in other animals, because through the means of a serpent the devil tempted woman. For this reason also, as is shown afterwards, although matrimony is a work of God, as being instituted by Him, yet it is sometimes wrecked by the work of the devil: not indeed through main force, since then he might be thought stronger than God, but with the permission of God, by causing some temporary or permanent impediment in the conjugal act.

And touching this we may say what is known by experience; that these women satisfy their filthy lusts not only in themselves, but even in the mighty ones of the age, of whatever state and condition; causing by all sorts of witchcraft the death of their souls through the excessive infatuation of carnal love, in such a way that for no shame or persuasion can they desist from such acts. And through such men, since the witches will not permit any harm to come to them either from themselves or from others once they have them in their power, there arises the great danger of the time, namely, the extermination of the Faith. And in this way do witches every day increase.

And would that this were not true according to experience. But indeed such hatred is aroused by witchcraft between those joined in the sacrament of matrimony, and such freezing up of the generative forces, that men are unable to perform the necessary action for begetting offspring. But since love and hate exist in the soul, which even the devil cannot enter, lest these things should seem incredible to anyone, they must be inquired into; and by meeting argument with argument the matter will be made clear.

René Descartes

The full title that René Descartes (1596–1650) gave to the work from which the following selection is taken clearly reveals the nature of his interests. It is *Discourse on the Method of Rightly Conducting the Reason and Seeking Truth in the Sciences*. Like his older contemporary Francis Bacon, Descartes wanted to develop a method that could be used to yield scientific truth. But he did not place his hopes in the results to be obtained by simple induction. Rather, he recognized the need for a more sophisticated procedure, one that relied heavily on deductive argument and mathematics.

Besides being one of the greatest figures in the history of French philosophy, Descartes was one of the leaders in the scientific revolution of the seventeenth century. In mathematics he was the founder of analytic geometry, and in physics he developed an explanation of the universe, which for a century rivaled Newton's theory of universal gravitation.

During his lifetime Descartes became recognized as the most advanced thinker in Europe. His fame spread as far as Sweden, whose reigning queen, a self-styled intellectual, summoned him to her court to instruct her in philosophy. Descartes arrived in Sweden in the autumn of 1649 to discover to his dismay that the queen wished to be taught philosophy every morning at dawn. To a man accustomed to lie abed until noon, such a schedule, coupled with the rigors of the northern climate, proved too much. Descartes did not survive the winter, dying in February of 1650.

Consider the following questions as you study the text below.

1. Describe the basic components of Descartes's system of inquiry. Would you describe Descartes as a scientist or a philosopher?

2. What did Descartes mean when he said "I think, therefore, I am"? From his point of view, why was it essential to make this assumption?

Discourse on Method

Part I

Good sense is, of all things among men, the most equally distributed; for every one thinks himself so abundantly provided with it, that those even who are the most difficult to satisfy in everything else, do not usually desire

Trans. J. Veitch. Some minor modifications have been made in the translation.

a larger measure of this quality than they already possess. And in this it is not likely that all are mistaken. The conviction is rather to be held as testifying that the power of judging aright and of distinguishing truth from error, which is properly what is called good sense or reason, is by nature equal in all men; and that the diversity of our opinions, consequently, does not arise from some being endowed with a larger share of reason than others, but solely from this, that we conduct our thoughts along different ways, and do not fix our attention on the same objects. For to be possessed of a vigorous mind is not enough; the prime requisite is rightly to apply it. The greatest minds, as they are capable of the highest excellencies, are open likewise to the greatest aberrations; and those who travel very slowly may yet make far greater progress, provided they keep always to the straight road, than those who, while they run, forsake it.

For myself, I have never fancied my mind to be in any respect more perfect than those of the generality; on the contrary, I have often wished that I were equal to some others in promptitude of thought, or in clearness and distinctness of imagination, or in fullness and readiness of memory. And besides these, I know of no other qualities that contribute to the perfection of the mind; for as to the reason or sense, inasmuch as it is that alone which constitutes us men, and distinguishes us from the brutes, I am disposed to believe that it is to be found complete in each individual; and on this point to adopt the common opinion of philosophers, who say that the difference of greater and less holds only among the accidents, and not among the forms or natures of individuals of the same species.

I will not hesitate, however, to express my belief that it has been my singular good fortune to have very early in life fallen into certain tracks which have conducted me to considerations and maxims, of which I have formed a method that gives me the means, I think, of gradually augmenting my knowledge and of raising it little by little to the highest point which the mediocrity of my talents and the brief duration of my life will permit me to reach. For I have already reaped from it such fruits that, although I have been accustomed to think lowly enough of myself, and although when I look with the eye of a philosopher on the varied courses and pursuits of mankind at large, I find scarcely one which does not appear vain and useless, I nevertheless derive the highest satisfaction from the progress I conceive myself to have already made in the search after truth, and I cannot help entertaining such expectations of the future as to believe that if, among the occupations of men as men, there is any one really excellent and important, it is that which I have chosen.

However, it is possible I may be mistaken and it is but a little copper and glass, perhaps, that I take for gold and diamonds. I know how very liable we are to delusion in what relates to ourselves, and also how much the judgments of our friends are to be suspected when given in our favor. But I shall endeavor in this Discourse to describe the paths I have followed, and to delineate my life as in a picture, in order that each one may be able to judge of them for himself, and that in the general opinion entertained of them, as gathered from current report, I myself may have a new help towards instruction to be added to those I have been in the habit of employing.

My present design, then, is not to teach the method which each ought to follow for the right conduct of his reason, but solely to describe the way in which I have endeavored to conduct my own. They who set themselves to give precepts must of course regard themselves as possessed of greater skill than those to whom they prescribe; and if they err in the slightest particular they subject themselves to censure. But as this tract is put forth merely as a history or, if you will, as a tale, in which, amid some examples worthy of imitation, there will be found, perhaps, as many more which it were advisable not to follow, I hope it will prove useful to some without being hurtful to any and that my openness will find some favor with all.

From my childhood I have been familiar with letters; and as I was given to believe that by their help a clear and certain knowledge of all that is useful in life might be acquired, I was ardently desirous of instruction. But as soon as I had finished the entire course of study, at the close of which it is customary to be admitted into the order of the learned, I completely changed my opinion. For I found myself involved in so many doubts and errors that I was convinced I had advanced no farther in all my attempts at learning than the discovery at every turn of my own ignorance. And yet I was studying in one of the most celebrated schools in Europe,[1] in which I thought there must be learned men, if such were anywhere to be found. I had been taught all that others learned there; and not contented with the sciences actually taught us, I had, in addition, read all the books that had fallen into my hands, treating of such branches as are esteemed the most curious and rare. I knew the judgment which others had formed of me and I did not find that I was considered inferior to my fellows, although there were among them some who were already marked out to fill the places of our instructors. And our age appeared to me as flourishing and as fertile in powerful minds as any preceding one. I was thus led to take the liberty of judging of all other men by myself, and of concluding that there was no science in existence that was of such a nature as I had previously been given to believe.

I still continued, however, to hold in esteem the studies of the schools. I was aware that the languages taught in them are necessary to the understanding of the writings of the ancients; that the grace of fable stirs the mind; that the memorable deeds of history elevate it and, if read with discretion, aid in forming the judgment; that the perusal of all excellent books is, as it were, an interview with the noblest men of past ages who have written them, and even a studied interview, in which are discovered to us only their choicest thoughts; that eloquence has incomparable force and beauty; that poesy

---

[1][The Jesuit College at La Flèche, France—*Ed.*]

has its ravishing graces and delights; that in mathematics there are many re-fined discoveries eminently suited to gratify the inquisitive, as well as fur-ther all the arts and lessen the labour of man; that numerous highly useful precepts and exhortations are contained in treatises on morals; that theology points out the path to heaven; that philosophy affords the means of dis-coursing with an appearance of truth on all matters and commands the ad-miration of the more simple; that jurisprudence, medicine, and the other sciences secure for their cultivators honors and riches; and, altogether, that it is useful to bestow some attention upon all, even upon those abounding the most in superstition and error, that we may be in a position to determine their real value and guard against being deceived.

But I believed that I had already given sufficient time to languages and likewise to the reading of the writings of the ancients, to their histories and fables. For to hold converse with those of other ages and to travel are almost the same thing. It is useful to know something of the manners of different na-tions, that we may be able to form a more correct judgment regarding our own and be prevented from thinking that everything contrary to our cus-toms is ridiculous and irrational—a conclusion usually come to by those whose experience has been limited to their own country. On the other hand, when too much time is occupied in travelling we become strangers to our native country; and the over-curious in the customs of the past are generally ignorant of those of the present. Besides, fictitious narratives lead us to imag-ine the possibility of many events that are impossible and even the most faithful histories, if they do not wholly misrepresent matters, or exaggerate their importance to render the account of them more worthy of perusal, omit, at least, almost always the meanest and least striking of the attendant circumstances; hence it happens that the remainder does not represent the truth and that such as regulate their conduct by examples drawn from this source are apt to fall into the extravagances of the knights-errant of romance, and to entertain projects that exceed their powers.

I esteemed eloquence highly and was in raptures with poesy but I thought that both were gifts of nature rather than fruits of study. Those in whom the faculty of reason is predominant, and who most skilfully dispose their thoughts with a view to render them clear and intelligible, are always the best able to persuade others of the truth of what they lay down, though they should speak only in the language of Lower Brittany, and be wholly ignorant of rules of rhetoric; and those whose minds are stored with the most agreeable fancies, and who can give expression to them with the greatest embellishment and harmony, are still the best poets, though unacquainted with the art of poetry.

I was especially delighted with mathematics on account of the certi-tude and evidence of its reasonings, but I had not as yet a precise knowledge of its true use; and thinking that it but contributed to the advancement of the mechanical arts, I was astonished that foundations so strong and solid should have had no loftier superstructure reared on them. On the other hand, I compared the disquisitions of the ancient moralists to very towering and magnificent palaces with no better foundation than sand and mud. They laud the virtues very highly and exhibit them as estimable far above anything on earth but they give us no adequate criterion of virtue, and frequently that which they designate with so fine a name is but apathy, or pride, or despair, or parricide.

I revered our theology and aspired as much as anyone to reach heaven, but being given assuredly to understand that the way is not less open to the most ignorant than to the most learned, and that the revealed truths which lead to heaven are above our comprehension, I did not presume to subject them to the impotency of my reason; and I thought that in order competently to undertake their examination there was need of some special help from heaven and of being more than man.

Of philosophy I will say nothing, except that when I saw that it had been cultivated for many ages by the most distinguished men and that yet there is not a single matter within its sphere which is not still in dispute and nothing, therefore, which is above doubt, I did not presume to anticipate that my success would be greater in it than that of others; and further, when I considered the number of conflicting opinions about a single matter that may be upheld by learned men, while there can be but one that is true, I reckoned as well-nigh false all that was only probable.

As to the other sciences, inasmuch as these borrow their principles from philosophy, I judged that no solid superstructures could be reared on foundations so infirm and neither the honor nor the gain held out by them was sufficient to determine me to their cultivation, for I was not, thank heaven, in a condition which compelled me to make merchandise of science for the bettering of my fortune; and though I might not profess to scorn glory as a cynic, I yet made very slight account of that honor which I hoped to acquire only through fictitious titles. Of false sciences I thought I knew the worth sufficiently to escape being deceived by the professions of an alchemist, the predictions of an astrologer, the impostures of a magician, or by the artifices and boasting of any of those who profess to know things of which they are ignorant.

For these reasons, as soon as my age permitted me to pass from under the control of my instructors, I entirely abandoned the study of letters and resolved no longer to seek any other science than the knowledge of myself, or of the great book of the world. I spent the remainder of my youth in travelling, in visiting courts and armies, in holding intercourse with men of different dispositions and ranks, in collecting varied experience, in proving myself in the different situations into which fortune threw me, and, above all, in making such reflections on the matter of my experience as to secure my improvement. For it occurred to me that I should find much more truth in the reasonings of each individual with reference to the affairs in which he is personally interested and the issue of which must presently punish him if he has judged amiss than in those connected by a man of letters in his study, regarding speculative matters that are of no practical moment, and followed by no consequences to himself, farther, perhaps, than that they foster the vanity the better the more remote they are from common sense, requiring, as they must in this case, the exercise of greater ingenuity and art to render them probable. In addition, I had always a most earnest desire to know how to distinguish the true from the false, in order that I might be able clearly to discriminate the right path in life and proceed in it with confidence.

It is true that, while busied only in considering the manners of other men, I found here, too, scarce any ground for settled conviction and re-marked hardly less contradiction among them than in the opinions of the philosophers. So the greatest advantage I derived from the study consisted in this, that, observing many things which, however extravagant and ridiculous to our appprehension, are yet by common consent received and approved by other great nations, I learned not to believe too firmly what I had learned only from example and wisdom, and thus I gradually extricated myself from many errors powerful enough to darken our natural intelligence and inca-pacitate us in great measure from listening to reason. But after I had been oc-cupied several years in thus studying the book of the world, and in essaying to gather some experience, I at length resolved to make myself an object of study and to employ all the powers of my mind in choosing the path I ought to follow, an undertaking which was accompanied with greater success than it would have been had I never quitted my country or my books.

Part II

I was then in Germany, attracted thither by the wars in that country[2] which have not yet been brought to a termination; and as I was returning to the army from the coronation of the Emperor, the setting in of winter stopped me in a locality where, as I found no society to interest me, and was besides fortunately undisturbed by any cares or passions, I remained the whole day in seclusion, with full opportunity to occupy my attention with my own thoughts. Of these one of the very first that occurred to me was that there is seldom so much perfection in works composed of many separate parts, upon which different hands have been employed, as in those complet-ed by a single master. Thus it is observable that the buildings which a single architect has planned and executed are generally more elegant and com-modious than those which several have attempted to improve, by making old walls serve for purposes for which they were not originally built. Thus also those ancient cities which, from being at first only villages, have be-come, in course of time, large towns, are usually but ill laid out compared with the regularly constructed towns which a professional architect has freely planned on an open plain; so that although several buildings of the

[2][The Thirty Years' War—*Ed.*]

former may often equal or surpass in beauty those of the latter, yet when one observes their indiscriminate juxtaposition, there a large one and here a small, and the consequent crookedness and irregularity of the streets one is disposed to conclude that chance rather than any human will guided by reason must have led to such an arrangement. And if we consider that nevertheless there have been at all times certain officers whose duty it was to see that private buildings contributed to public ornament the difficulty of reaching high perfection with but the materials of others to operate on will be readily acknowledged. In the same way I fancied that those nations which, starting from a semi-barbarous state and advancing to civilization by slow degrees, have had their laws successively determined and, as it were, forced upon them simply by experience of the hurtfulness of particular crimes and disputes, would by this process come to be possessed of less perfect institutions than those which, from the commencement of their association as communities, have followed the appointments of some wise legislator. It is thus quite certain that the constitution of the true religion, the ordinances of which are derived from God, must be incomparably superior to that of every other. And, to speak of human affairs, I believe that the past pre-eminence of Sparta was due not to the goodness of each of its laws in particular, for many of these were very strange and even opposed to good morals, but to the circumstance that, originated by a single individual, they all tended to a single end. In the same way I thought that the sciences contained in books (such of them at least as are made up of probable reasonings, without demonstrations) composed as they are of the opinions of many different individuals massed together, are farther removed from truth than the simple inferences which a man of good sense using his natural and unprejudiced judgment draws respecting the matters of his experience. And because we have all to pass through a state of infancy to manhood and have been of necessity, for a length of time, governed by our desires and preceptors (whose dictates were frequently conflicting, while neither perhaps always counselled us for the best) I further concluded that it is almost impossible that our judgments can be so correct or solid as they would have been, had our reason been mature from the moment of our birth and had we always been guided by it alone.

It is true, however, that it is not customary to pull down all the houses of a town with the single design of rebuilding them differently and thereby rendering the streets more handsome; but it often happens that a private individual takes down his own with the view of erecting it anew, and that people are even sometimes constrained to do this when their houses are in danger of falling from age, or when the foundations are insecure. With this before me by way of example, I was persuaded that it would indeed be preposterous for a private individual to think of reforming a state by fundamentally changing it throughout and overturning it in order to set it up amended; and the same I thought was true of any similar project for reforming the body of the sciences or the order of teaching them established in the schools. But as for the opinions which up to that time I had embraced, I thought that I could not do better than resolve at once to sweep them wholly away, that I might afterwards be in a position to admit either others more correct, or even perhaps the same when they had undergone the scrutiny of reason. I firmly believed that in this way I should much better succeed in the conduct of my life than if I built only upon old foundations and leant upon principles which, in my youth, I had taken upon trust. For although I recognized various difficulties in this undertaking, these were not, however, without remedy, nor once to be compared with such as attend the slightest reformation in public affairs. Large bodies, if once overthrown, are with great difficulty set up again, or even kept erect when once seriously shaken, and the fall of such is always disastrous. Then if there are any imperfections in the constitutions of states (and that many such exist the diversity of constitutions is alone sufficient to assure us) custom has without doubt materially smoothed their inconveniences and has even managed to steer altogether clear of or insensibly corrected a number which sagacity could not have provided against with equal effect; and, in sum, the defects are almost always more tolerable than the change necessary for their removal, in the same manner that highways which wind among mountains, by being much frequented, become gradually so smooth and commodious that it is much better to follow them than to seek a straighter path by climbing over the tops of rocks and descending to the bottoms of precipices.

Hence it is that I cannot in any degree approve of those restless and busy meddlers who, called neither by birth nor fortune to take part in the management of public affairs, are yet always projecting reforms; and if I thought that this tract contained anything which might justify the suspicion that I was a victim of such folly I would by no means permit its publication. I have never contemplated anything higher than the reformation of my own opinions, and basing them on a foundation wholly my own. And although my own satisfaction with my work has led me to present here a draft of it, I do not by any means therefore recommend to everyone else to make a similar attempt. Those whom God has endowed with a larger measure of genius will entertain, perhaps, designs still more exalted but for the many I am much afraid lest even the present undertaking be more than they can safely venture to imitate. The single design to strip one's self of all past beliefs is one that ought not to be taken by everyone. The majority of men is composed of two classes, for neither of which would this be at all a befitting resolution—in the first place, of those who with more than a due confidence in their own powers are precipitate in their judgments and lack the patience needed for orderly and circumspect thinking; whence it happens, that if men of this class once take the liberty to doubt of their accustomed opinions, and quit the beaten highway, they will never be able to thread the byway that would lead them by a shorter course and will lose themselves and continue to wander for life and, in the second place, of those who, possessed of sufficient sense or modesty to determine that there are others who excel them in the power of discriminating between truth and error, and by whom they may be instructed, ought rather to content themselves with the opinions of these than search for better ones themselves.

For my own part, I should doubtless have belonged to the latter class, had I received instruction from but one master, or had I never known the diversities of opinion that from time immemorial have prevailed among men of the greatest learning. But I had become aware, even so early as during my college life, that no opinion, however absurd and incredible, can be imagined, which has not been maintained by some one of the philosophers; and afterwards in the course of my travels I remarked that all those whose opinions are decidedly repugnant to ours are not on that account barbarians and savages but on the contrary that many of these nations make an equally good, if not a better, use of their reason than we do. I took into account also the very different character which a person brought up from infancy in France or Germany exhibits from that which, with the same mind originally, this individual would have possessed had he lived always among the Chinese or with savages, and the circumstance that in dress itself the fashion which pleased us ten years ago, and which may again, perhaps, be received into favour before ten years have gone, appears to us at this moment extravagant and ridiculous. I was thus led to infer that the ground of our opinions is far more custom and example than any certain knowledge. And, finally, although such be the ground of our opinions, I remarked that a plurality of beliefs is no guarantee of truth where it is at all of difficult discovery, as in such cases it is much more likely that it will be found by one than by many. I could, however, select from the crowd no one whose opinions seemed worthy of preference and thus I found myself constrained to use my own reason in the conduct of my life.

But like one walking alone and in the dark I resolved to proceed so slowly and with such circumspection that if I did not advance far I would at least guard against falling. I did not even choose to dismiss summarily any of the opinions that had crept into my belief without having been introduced by reason, but first of all took sufficient time carefully to satisfy myself of the general nature of the task I was setting myself and ascertain the true method by which to arrive at the knowledge of whatever lay within my powers.

Among the branches of philosophy I had, at an earlier period, given some attention to logic, and among those of mathematics to geometrical analysis and algebra—three arts or sciences which ought, I thought, to contribute something to my design. But, on examination, I found that, as for logic, its syllogisms and the majority of its precepts are of avail rather in the communication of what we already know, or even as the art of Lully,[3] in speaking without judgment of things of which we are ignorant, than in the investigation of the unknown; and although this science contains a number of correct and very excellent precepts, there are, nevertheless, so many

---

[3][Italian-French composer of the seventeenth century—*Ed.*]

others that are either injurious or superfluous mingled with the former, that it is almost quite as difficult to effect a severance of the true from the false as it is to extract a Diana or a Minerva from a rough block of marble. Then as to the analysis of the ancients and the algebra of the moderns, besides that they embrace only matters highly abstract and, to appearance, of no use, the former is so exclusively restricted to the consideration of figures, that it can exercise the understanding only on condition of greatly fatiguing the imagination and, in the latter, there is so complete a subjection to certain rules and formulas that there results an art full of confusion and obscurity calculated to embarrass, instead of a science fitted to cultivate the mind. By these considerations I was induced to seek some other method which would comprise the advantages of the three and be exempt from their defects. And as a multitude of laws often only hampers justice, so that a state is best governed when, with few laws, these are rigidly administered, in like manner, I believed that instead of the great number of precepts of which logic is composed, the four following would prove perfectly sufficient for me, provided I took the firm and unwavering resolution never in a single instance to fail in observing them.

The first was never to accept anything for true which I did not clearly know to be such; that is to say, carefully to avoid precipitancy and prejudice, and to comprise nothing more in my judgment than what was presented to my mind so clearly and distinctly as to exclude all ground of doubt.

The second, to divide each of the difficulties under examination into as many parts as possible and as might be necessary for its adequate solution.

The third, to conduct my thoughts in such order that, by commencing with objects the simplest and easiest to know, I might ascend little by little, and step by step, to the knowledge of the more complex, assigning in thought a certain order even to those subjects which in their own nature do not stand in a relation of antecedence and sequence.

And the last, in every case to make enumerations so complete, and reviews so general, that I might be assured that nothing was omitted.

· · ·

Part IV

· · ·

I had long before remarked that, in relation to practice, it is sometimes necessary to adopt, as if above doubt, opinions which we discern to be highly uncertain, as has been already said; but as I then desired to give my attention solely to the search after truth, I thought that a procedure exactly the opposite was called for and that I ought to reject as absolutely false all opinions in regard to which I could suppose the least ground for doubt, in order to ascertain whether after that there remained anything in my belief that was wholly indubitable. Accordingly, seeing that our senses sometimes deceive us, I was willing to suppose that there existed nothing really such as they presented to us and because some men err in reasoning, and fall into paralogisms, even on the simplest matters of geometry, I, convinced that I was as open to error as any other, rejected as false all the reasonings I had hitherto taken for demonstrations; and finally, when I considered that the very same presentations which we experience when awake may also be experienced when we are asleep, while there is at that time not one of them true, I supposed that all the presentations that had ever entered into my mind when awake had in them no more truth than the illusions of my dreams. But immediately upon this I observed that, while I thus wished to think that all was false, it was absolutely necessary that I, who thus thought, should be somewhat; and as I observed that this truth, *I think, therefore I am*, was so certain and of such evidence that no ground of doubt, however extravagant, could be alleged by the sceptics capable of shaking it, I concluded that I might accept it as the first principle of the philosophy of which I was in search.

In the next place, I attentively examined what I was, and as I observed that I could suppose that I had no body and that there was no world nor any place in which I might be, but that I could not therefore suppose that I was not and that, on the contrary, from the very circumstances that I thought to doubt the truth of other things, it most clearly and certainly followed that I was; while, on the other hand, if I had only ceased to think, although all the other objects which I had ever imagined had been in reality existent, I would have had no reason to believe that I existed; I thence concluded that I was a substance whose whole essence or nature consists only in thinking, and which, that it may exist, has need of no place, nor is dependent on any material thing so that "I," that is to say, the mind by which I am what I am, is wholly distinct from the body, and is even more easily known than the latter and is such, that although the latter were not, it would still continue to be all that it is.

After this I inquired in general into what is essential to the truth and certainty of a proposition; for since I had discovered one which I knew to be true, I thought that I must likewise be able to discover the ground of this certainty. And as I observed that in the words *I think, therefore I am*, there is nothing at all which gives me assurance of their truth beyond this, that I see very clearly that in order to think it is necessary to exist, I concluded that I might take, as a general rule, the principle that all the things which we very clearly and distinctly conceive are true, only observing, however, that there is some difficulty in rightly determining the objects which we distinctly conceive.

In the next place, from reflecting on the circumstance that I doubted, and that consequently my being was not wholly perfect (for I clearly saw that it was a greater perfection to know than to doubt), I was led to inquire whence I had learned to think of something more perfect than myself and I clearly recognized that I must hold this notion from some Nature which in reality was more perfect. As for thoughts of many other objects external to me, as of the sky, the earth, light, heat, and a thousand more, I was less at a loss to know whence these came; for since I remarked in them nothing which seemed to render them superior to myself, I could believe that, if these were true, they were dependencies on my own nature, in so far as it possessed a certain perfection, and, if they were false, that I held them from nothing, that is to say, that they were in me because of a certain imperfection of my nature. But this could not be the case with the idea of a Nature more perfect than myself; for to receive it from nothing was a thing manifestly impossible and, because it is not less repugnant that the more perfect should be an effect of, and dependent on, the less perfect than that something should proceed from nothing, it was equally impossible that I could hold it from myself. Accordingly, it must follow that it had been placed in me by a Nature which was in reality more perfect than mine, and which even possessed within itself all the perfections of which I could form any idea—that is to say God.

Galileo Galilei

On June 22, 1633, kneeling in criminal's garb, an aged Galileo (1564–1642) suffered condemnation for his heretical views about the universe by a panel of judges composed of cardinals of the Catholic church. Following the pronouncement of his sentence, Galileo was forced to recite a formal abjuration of his scientific beliefs. The crucial passages of this recital read: "I, Galileo Galilei, son of the late Vincenzio Galilei of Florence, aged seventy years ... swear that I have always believed, and, with the help of God, will in the future believe, every article which the Holy Catholic and Apostolic Church of Rome holds, teaches, and preaches. But because I have been enjoined, by this Holy Office, altogether to abandon the false opinion which maintains that the sun is the center and immovable, and forbidden to hold, defend, or teach the said false doctrine in any manner; and because, after it had been signified to me that the said doctrine is repugnant to the Holy Scripture, I have written and printed a book in which I treat of the same condemned doctrine, and adduce reasons with great force in support of the same, without giving any solution, and therefore have been judged grievously suspected of heresy; that is to say, that I held and believed that the sun is the center of the world and immovable, and that the earth is not the center and movable, I am willing to remove from the minds of your Eminences, and of every Catholic Christian, this vehement suspicion rightly entertained towards me, therefore with a sincere heart and unfeigned faith, I abjure, curse, and detest the said errors and heresies, and generally every other error and sect contrary to the said Holy Church; and I swear that I will never more in the future say, or assert anything, verbally or in writing, which may give rise to a similar suspicion of me." (The widespread story that Galileo rose at the end of his abjuration and muttered, "Still, it moves," is almost surely apocryphal.)

The train of events that culminated in Galileo's condemnation had begun more than twenty years earlier. Following the publication of his *Letters on Sunspots* in the spring of 1613, in which he openly adopted the heliocentric theory of Copernicus, Galileo and his supporters increasingly abandoned their reticence about supporting the new view in public. This led in turn to increased opposition, not only among members of the clergy, but also among important laymen under their influence. Prominent among the latter was the Grand Duchess Christina, mother of Cosimo II, grand duke of Tuscany (where Galileo lived). In a long letter to the grand duchess in 1615, Galileo defended the scientific discoveries made by both Copernicus and himself. Although he took great pains in his letter to make the point that these discoveries were in no way inconsistent with the Scriptures—never suggesting that the Scriptures themselves might be in error—it is clear from the events of 1633 that he was unsuccessful in this effort.

Consider the following questions as you study the text below.

1. Describe Galileo's approach to the Bible. Did he believe that the Bible and human reason could contradict one another?

2. According to Galileo, why does the Bible contain "false statements"? What should the reader assume when he or she encounters a passage that is contradicted by reason, experience, or another passage in the Bible?

Letter to the Grand Duchess Christina

GALILEO GALILEI TO THE MOST SERENE GRAND DUCHESS MOTHER:

Some years ago, as Your Serene Highness well knows, I discovered in the heavens many things that had not been seen before our own age. The novelty of these things, as well as some consequences which followed from them in contradiction to the physical notions commonly held among academic philosophers, stirred up against me no small number of professors—as if I had placed these things in the sky with my own hands in order to upset nature and overturn the sciences. They seemed to forget that the increase of known truths stimulates the investigation, establishment, and growth of the arts; not their diminution or destruction.

Showing a greater fondness for their own opinions than for truth, they sought to deny and disprove the new things which, if they had cared to look for themselves, their own senses would have demonstrated to them. To this end they hurled various charges and published numerous writings filled with vain arguments, and they made the grave mistake of sprinkling these with passages taken from places in the Bible which they had failed to understand properly, and which were ill suited to their purposes.

These men would perhaps not have fallen into such error had they but paid attention to a most useful doctrine of St. Augustine's, relative to our making positive statements about things which are obscure and hard to understand by means of reason alone. Speaking of a certain physical conclusion about the heavenly bodies, he wrote: "Now keeping always our respect for moderation in grave piety, we ought not to believe anything inadvisedly on a dubious point, lest in favor to our error we conceive a prejudice against something that truth hereafter may reveal to be not contrary in any way to the sacred books of either the Old or the New Testament."

Well, the passage of time has revealed to everyone the truths that I previously set forth; and, together with the truth of the facts, there has come to light the great difference in attitude between those who simply and dispassionately refused to admit the discoveries to be true, and those who combined with their incredulity some reckless passion of their own. Men who were well grounded in astronomical and physical science were persuaded as soon as they received my first message. There were others who denied them or remained in doubt only because of their novel and unexpected character, and because they had not yet had the opportunity to see for themselves. These men have by degrees come to be satisfied. But some, besides allegiance to their original error, possess I know not what fanciful interest in remaining hostile not so much toward the things in question as toward their discoverer. No longer being able to deny them, these men now take refuge in obstinate silence, but being more than ever exasperated by that which has pacified and quieted other men, they divert their thoughts to other fancies and seek new ways to damage me.

I should pay no more attention to them than to those who previously contradicted me—at whom I always laugh, being assured of the eventual outcome—were it not that in their new calumnies and persecutions I perceive that they do not stop at proving themselves more learned than I am (a claim which I scarcely contest), but go so far as to cast against me the imputations of crimes which must be, and are, more abhorrent to me than death itself. I cannot remain satisfied merely to know that the injustice of this is recognized by those who are acquainted with these men and with me, as perhaps it is not known to others.

Persisting in their original resolve to destroy me and everything mine by any means they can think of, these men are aware of my views in astronomy and philosophy. They know that as to the arrangement of the parts of the universe, I hold the sun to be situated motionless in the center of the revolution of the celestial orbs while the earth revolves about the sun. They know also that I support this position not only by refuting the arguments of Ptolemy and Aristotle, but by producing many counterarguments; in particular, some which relate to physical effects whose causes can perhaps be assigned in no other way. In addition there are astronomical arguments derived from many things in my new celestial discoveries that plainly confute the Ptolemaic system while admirably agreeing with and confirming the contrary hypothesis. Possibly because they are disturbed by the known truth of other propositions of mine which differ from those commonly held, and therefore mistrusting their defense so long as they confine themselves to the field of philosophy, these men have resolved to fabricate a shield for their fallacies out of the mantle of pretended religion and the authority of the Bible. These they apply, with little judgment, to the refutation of arguments that they do not understand and have not even listened to.

First they have endeavored to spread the opinion that such propositions in general are contrary to the Bible and are consequently damnable and heretical. They know that it is human nature to take up causes whereby a man may oppress his neighbor, no matter how unjustly, rather than those from which a man may receive some just encouragement. Hence they have had no trouble in finding men who would preach the damnability and heresy of the new doctrine from their very pulpits with unwonted confidence, thus doing impious and inconsiderate injury not only to that doctrine and its followers but to all mathematics and mathematicians in general. Next, becoming bolder, and hoping (though vainly) that this seed which first took root in their hypocritical minds would send out branches and ascend to heaven, they began scattering rumors among the people that before long this doctrine would be condemned by the supreme authority. They know, too, that official condemnation would not only suppress the two propositions which I have mentioned, but would render damnable all other astronomical and physical statements and observations that have any necessary relation or connection with these.

In order to facilitate their designs, they seek so far as possible (at least among the common people) to make this opinion seem new and to belong to me alone. They pretend not to know that its author, or rather its restorer and confirmer, was Nicholas Copernicus; and that he was not only a Catholic, but a priest and a canon. He was in fact so esteemed by the church that when the Lateran Council under Leo X took up the correction of the church calendar, Copernicus was called to Rome from the most remote parts of Germany to undertake its reform. At that time the calendar was defective because the true measures of the year and the lunar month were not exactly known. The Bishop of Culm, then superintendent of this matter, assigned Copernicus to seek more light and greater certainty concerning the celestial motions by means of constant study and labor. With Herculean toil he set his admirable mind to this task, and he made such great progress in this science and brought our knowledge of the heavenly motions to such precision that he became celebrated as an astronomer. Since that time not only has the calendar been regulated by his teachings, but tables of all the motions of the planets have been calculated as well.

Having reduced his system into six books, he published these at the instance of the Cardinal of Capua and the Bishop of Culm. And since he had assumed his laborious enterprise by order of the supreme pontiff, he dedicated this book *On the celestial revolutions* to Pope Paul III. When printed, the book was accepted by the holy Church, and it has been read and studied by everyone without the faintest hint of any objection ever being conceived against its doctrines. Yet now that manifest experiences and necessary proofs have shown them to be well grounded, persons exist who would strip the author of his reward without so much as looking at his book, and add the shame of having him pronounced a heretic. All this they would do merely to satisfy their personal displeasure conceived without any cause against another man, who has no interest in Copernicus beyond approving his teachings.

Now as to the false aspersions which they so unjustly seek to cast upon me, I have thought it necessary to justify myself in the eyes of all men, whose judgment in matters of religion and of reputation I must hold in great esteem. I shall therefore discourse of the particulars which these men produce to make this opinion detested and to have it condemned not merely as false but as heretical. To this end they make a shield of their hypocritical zeal for religion. They go about invoking the Bible, which they would have minister to their deceitful purposes. Contrary to the sense of the Bible and the intention of the holy Fathers, if I am not mistaken, they would extend such authorities until even in purely physical matters—where faith is not involved—they would have us altogether abandon reason and the evidence of our senses in favor of some biblical passage, though under the surface meaning of its words this passage may contain a different sense.

I hope to show that I proceed with much greater piety than they do, when I argue not against condemning this book, but against condemning it in the way they suggest—that is, without understanding it, weighing it, or so much as reading it. For Copernicus never discusses matters of religion or faith, nor does he use arguments that depend in any way upon the authority of sacred writings which he might have interpreted erroneously. He stands always upon physical conclusions pertaining to the celestial motions, and deals with them by astronomical and geometrical demonstrations, founded primarily upon sense experiences and very exact observations. He did not ignore the Bible, but he knew very well that if his doctrine were proved, then it could not contradict the Scriptures when they were rightly understood. And thus at the end of his letter of dedication, addressing the pope, he said:

"If there should chance to be any exegetes ignorant of mathematics who pretend to skill in that discipline, and dare to condemn and censure this hypothesis of mine upon the authority of some scriptural passage twisted to their purpose, I value them not, but disdain their unconsidered judgment. For it is known that Lactantius—a poor mathematician though in other respects a worthy author—writes very childishly about the shape of the earth when he scoffs at those who affirm it to be a globe. Hence it should not seem strange to the ingenious if people of that sort should in turn deride me. But mathematics is written for mathematicians, by whom, if I am not deceived, these labors of mine will be recognized as contributing something to their domain, as also to that of the Church over which Your Holiness now reigns."

Such are the people who labor to persuade us that an author like Copernicus may be condemned without being read, and who produce various authorities from the Bible, from theologians, and from Church Councils to make us believe that this is not only lawful but commendable. Since I hold these to be of supreme authority, I consider it rank temerity for anyone to contradict them—when employed according to the usage of the holy Church. Yet I do not believe it is wrong to speak out when there is reason to suspect that other men wish, for some personal motive, to produce and employ such authorities for purposes quite different from the sacred intention of the holy Church.

Therefore I declare (and my sincerity will make itself manifest) not only that I mean to submit myself freely and renounce any errors into which I may fall in this discourse through ignorance of matters pertaining to religion, but that I do not desire in these matters to engage in disputes with anyone, even on points that are disputable. My goal is this alone; that if, among errors that may abound in these considerations of a subject remote from my profession, there is anything that may be serviceable to the holy Church in making a decision concerning the Copernican system, it may be taken and utilized as seems best to the superiors. And if not, let my book be torn and burnt, as I neither intend nor pretend to gain from it any fruit that is not pious and Catholic. And though many of the things I shall reprove have been heard by my own ears, I shall freely grant to those who have spoken them that they never said them, if that is what they wish, and I shall confess myself to have been mistaken. Hence let whatever I reply be addressed not to them, but to whoever may have held such opinions.

The reason produced for condemning the opinion that the earth moves and the sun stands still is that in many places in the Bible one may read that the sun moves and the earth stands still. Since the Bible cannot err, it follows as a necessary consequence that anyone takes a erroneous and heretical position who maintains that the sun is inherently motionless and the earth movable.

With regard to this argument, I think in the first place that it is very pious to say and prudent to affirm that the holy Bible can never speak untruth—whenever its true meaning is understood. But I believe nobody will deny that it is often very abstruse, and may say things which are quite different from what its bare words signify. Hence in expounding the Bible if one were always to confine oneself to the unadorned grammatical meaning, one might fall into error. Not only contradictions and propositions far from true might thus be made to appear in the Bible, but even grave heresies and follies. Thus it would be necessary to assign to God feet, hands, and eyes, as well as corporeal and human affections, such as anger, repentance, hatred, and sometimes even the forgetting of things past and ignorance of those to come. These propositions uttered by the Holy Ghost were set down in that manner by the sacred scribes in order to accommodate them to the capacities of the common people, who are rude and unlearned. For the sake of those who deserve to be separated from the herd, it is necessary that wise expositors should produce the true senses of such passages, together with the special reasons for which they were set down in these words. This doctrine is so widespread and so definite with all theologians that it would be superfluous to adduce evidence for it.

Hence I think that I may reasonably conclude that whenever the Bible has occasion to speak of any physical conclusion (especially those which are very abstruse and hard to understand), the rule has been observed of avoiding confusion in the minds of the common people which would render them contumacious toward the higher mysteries. Now the Bible, merely to condescend to popular capacity, has not hesitated to obscure some very important pronouncements, attributing to God himself some qualities extremely remote from (and even contrary to) His essence. Who, then, would positively declare that this principle has been set aside, and the Bible has confined itself rigorously to the bare and restricted sense of its words, when speaking but casually of the earth, of water, of the sun, or of any other created thing? Especially in view of the fact that these things in no way concern the primary purpose of the sacred writings, which is the service of God and the salvation of souls—matters infinitely beyond the comprehension of the common people.

This being granted, I think that in discussions of physical problems we ought to begin not from the authority of scriptural passages, but from sense-experiences and necessary demonstrations; for the holy Bible and the phenomena of nature proceed alike from the divine Word, the former as the dictate of the Holy Ghost and the latter as the observant executrix of God's commands. It is necessary for the Bible, in order to be accommodated to the understanding of every man, to speak many things which appear to differ from the absolute truth so far as the bare meaning of the words is concerned. But Nature, on the other hand, is inexorable and immutable; she never transgresses the laws imposed upon her, or cares a whit whether her abstruse reasons and methods of operation are understandable to men. For that reason it appears that nothing physical which sense-experience sets before our eyes, or which necessary demonstrations prove to us, ought to be called in question (much less condemned) upon the testimony of biblical passages which may have some different meaning beneath their words. For the Bible is not chained in every expression to conditions as strict as those which govern all physical effects; nor is God any less excellently revealed in Nature's actions than in the sacred statements of the Bible. Perhaps this is what Tertullian meant by these words:

"We conclude that God is known first through Nature, and then again, more particularly, by doctrine, by Nature in His works, and by doctrine in His revealed word."

From this I do not mean to infer that we need not have an extraordinary esteem for the passages of holy Scripture. On the contrary, having arrived at any certainties in physics, we ought to utilize these as the most appropriate aids in the true exposition of the Bible and in the investigation of those meanings which are necessarily contained therein, for these must be concordant with demonstrated truths. I should judge that the authority of the Bible was designed to persuade men of those articles and propositions which, surpassing all human reasoning, could not be made credible by science, or by any other means than through the very mouth of the Holy Spirit.

Yet even in those propositions which are not matters of faith, this authority ought to be preferred over that of all human writings which are supported only by bare assertions or probable arguments, and not set forth in a demonstrative way. This I hold to be necessary and proper to the same extent that divine wisdom surpasses all human judgment and conjecture.

But I do not feel obliged to believe that the same God who has endowed us with senses, reason, and intellect has intended to forego their use and by some other means to give us knowledge which we can attain by them. He would not require us to deny sense and reason in physical matters which are set before our eyes and minds by direct experience or necessary demonstrations. This must be especially true in those sciences of which but the faintest trace (and that consisting of conclusions) is to be found in the Bible. Of astronomy, for instance, so little is found that none of the planets except Venus are so much as mentioned, and this only once or twice under the name of "Lucifer." If the sacred scribes had had any intention of teaching people certain arrangements and motions of the heavenly bodies, or had they wished us to derive such knowledge from the Bible, then in my opinion they would not have spoken of these matters so sparingly in comparison with the infinite number of admirable conclusions which are demonstrated in that science. Far from pretending to teach us the constitution and motions of the heavens and the stars, with their shapes, magnitudes, and distances, the authors of the Bible intentionally forbore to speak of these things, though all were quite well known to them. Such is the opinion of the holiest and most learned Fathers, and in St. Augustine we find the following words:

"It is likewise commonly asked what we may believe about the form and shape of the heavens according to the Scriptures, for many contend much about these matters. But with superior prudence our authors have forborne to speak of this, as in no way furthering the student with respect to a blessed life—and, more important still, as taking up much of that time which should be spent in holy exercises. What is it to me whether heaven, like a sphere, surrounds the earth on all sides as a mass balanced in the center of the universe, or whether like a dish it merely covers and overcasts the earth? Belief in Scripture is urged rather for the reason we have often mentioned; that is, in order that no one, through ignorance of divine passages, finding anything in our Bibles or hearing anything cited from them of such a nature as may seem to oppose manifest conclusions, should be induced to suspect their truth when they teach, relate, and deliver more profitable matters. Hence let it be said briefly, touching the form of heaven, that our authors knew the truth but the Holy Spirit did not desire that men should learn things that are useful to no one for salvation."

The same disregard of these sacred authors toward beliefs about the phenomena of the celestial bodies is repeated to us by St. Augustine in his next chapter. On the question whether we are to believe that the heaven moves or stands still, he writes thus:

"Some of the brethren raise a question concerning the motion of heaven, whether it is fixed or moved. If it is moved, they say, how is it a firmament? If it stands still, how do these stars which are held fixed in it go round from east to west, the more northerly performing shorter circuits near the pole, so that the heaven (if there is another pole unknown to us) may seem to revolve upon some axis, or (if there is no other pole) may be thought to move as a discus? To these men I reply that it would require many subtle and profound reasonings to find out which of these things is actually so; but to undertake this and discuss it is consistent neither with my leisure nor with the duty of those whom I desire to instruct in essential matters more directly conducing to their salvation and to the benefit of the holy Church."

From these things it follows as a necessary consequence that, since the Holy Ghost did not intend to teach us whether heaven moves or stands still, whether its shape is spherical or like a discus or extended in a plane, nor whether the earth is located at its center or off to one side, then so much the less was it intended to settle for us any other conclusion of the same kind. And the motion or rest of the earth and the sun is so closely linked with the things just named, that without a determination of the one, neither side can be taken in the other matters. Now if the Holy Spirit has purposely neglected to teach us propositions of this sort as irrelevant to the highest goal (that is, to our salvation), how can anyone affirm that it is obligatory to take sides on them, that one belief is required by faith, while the other side is erroneous? Can an opinion be heretical and yet have no concern with the salvation of souls? Can the Holy Ghost be asserted not to have intended teaching us something that does concern our salvation? I would say here something that was heard from an ecclesiastic of the most eminent degree: "That the intention of the Holy Ghost is to teach us how one goes to heaven, not how heaven goes."

But let us again consider the degree to which necessary demonstrations and sense experiences ought to be respected in physical conclusions, and the authority they have enjoyed at the hands of holy and learned theologians. From among a hundred attestations I have selected the following:

"We must also take heed, in handling the doctrine of Moses, that we altogether avoid saying positively and confidently anything which contradicts manifest experiences and the reasoning of philosophy or the other sciences. For since every truth is in agreement with all other truth, the truth of Holy Writ cannot be contrary to the solid reasons and experiences of human knowledge."

And in St. Augustine we read: "If anyone shall set the authority of Holy Writ against clear and manifest reason, he who does this knows not what he has undertaken; for he opposes to the truth not the meaning of the Bible, which is beyond his comprehension, but rather his own interpretation, not what is in the Bible, but what he has found in himself and imagines to be there."

This granted, and it being true that two truths cannot contradict one another, it is the function of wise expositors to seek out the true senses of scriptural texts. These will unquestionably accord with the physical conclusions which manifest sense and necessary demonstrations have previously made certain to us. Now the Bible, as has been remarked, admits in many places expositions that are remote from the signification of the words for reasons we have already given. Moreover, we are unable to affirm that all interpreters of the Bible speak by divine inspiration, for if that were so there would exist no differences between them about the sense of a given passage. Hence I should think it would be the part of prudence not to permit anyone to usurp scriptural texts and force them in some way to maintain any physical conclusion to be true, when at some future time the senses and demonstrative or necessary reasons may show the contrary. Who indeed will set bounds to human ingenuity? Who will assert that everything in the universe capable of being perceived is already discovered and known? Let us rather confess quite truly that "Those truths which we know are very few in comparison with those which we do not know."

We have it from the very mouth of the Holy Ghost that God delivered up the world to disputations, *so that man cannot find out the work that God hath done from the beginning even to the end.* In my opinion no one, in contradiction to that dictum, should close the road to free philosophizing about mundane and physical things, as if everything had already been discovered and revealed with certainty. Nor should it be considered rash not to be satisfied with those opinions which have become common. No one should be scorned in physical disputes for not holding to the opinions which happen to please other people best, especially concerning problems which have been debated among the greatest philosophers for thousands of years. One of these is the stability of the sun and mobility of the earth, a doctrine believed by Pythagoras and all his followers, by Heracleides of Pontus (who was one of them), by Philolaus the teacher of Plato, and by Plato himself according to Aristotle. Plutarch writes in his *Life of Numa* that Plato, when he had grown old, said it was most absurd to believe otherwise. The same doctrine was held by Aristarchus of Samos, as Archimedes tells us; by Seleucus the mathematician, by Nicetas the philosopher (on the testimony of Cicero), and by many others. Finally this opinion has been amplified and confirmed with many observations and demonstrations by Nicholas Copernicus. And Seneca, a most eminent philosopher, advises us in his book on comets that we should more diligently seek to ascertain whether it is in the sky or in the earth that the diurnal rotation resides.

Hence it would probably be wise and useful counsel if, beyond articles which concern salvation and the establishment of our Faith, against the stability of which there is no danger whatever that any valid and effective doctrine can ever arise, men would not aggregate further articles unnecessarily. And it would certainly be preposterous to introduce them at the request of persons who, besides not being known to speak by inspiration of divine grace, are clearly seen to lack that understanding which is necessary in order to comprehend, let alone discuss, the demonstrations by which such conclusions are supported in the subtler sciences. If I may speak my opinion freely, I should say further that it would perhaps fit in better with the decorum and majesty of the sacred writings to take measures for preventing every shallow and vulgar writer from giving to his compositions (often grounded upon foolish fancies) an air of authority by inserting in them passages from the Bible, interpreted (or rather distorted) into senses as far from the right meaning of Scripture as those authors are near to absurdity who thus ostentatiously adorn their writings. Of such abuses many examples might be produced, but for the present I shall confine myself to two which are germane to these astronomical matters. The first concerns those writings which were published against the existence of the Medicean planets recently discovered by me, in which many passages of holy Scripture were cited. Now that everyone has seen these planets, I should like to know what new interpretations those same antagonists employ in expounding the Scripture and excusing their own simplicity. My other example is that of a man who has lately published, in defiance of astronomers and philosophers, the opinion that the moon does not receive its light from the sun but is brilliant by its own nature. He supports this fancy (or rather thinks he does) by sundry texts of Scripture which he believes cannot be explained unless his theory is true; yet that the moon is inherently dark is surely as plain as daylight.

It is obvious that such authors, not having penetrated the true senses of Scripture, would impose upon others an obligation to subscribe to conclusions that are repugnant to manifest reason and sense, if they had any authority to do so. God forbid that this sort of abuse should gain countenance and authority, for then in a short time it would be necessary to proscribe all the contemplative sciences. People who are unable to understand perfectly both the Bible and the sciences far outnumber those who do understand them. The former, glancing superficially through the Bible, would arrogate to themselves the authority to decree upon every question of physics on the strength of some word which they have misunderstood, and which was employed by the sacred authors for some different purpose. And the smaller number of understanding men could not dam up the furious torrent of such people, who would gain the majority of followers simply because it is much more pleasant to gain a reputation for wisdom without effort or study than to consume oneself tirelessly in the most laborious disciplines. Let us therefore render thanks to Almighty God, who in His beneficence protects us from this danger by depriving such persons of all authority, reposing the power of consultation, decision, and decree on such important matters in the high wisdom and benevolence of most prudent Fathers, and in the supreme authority of those who cannot fail to order matters properly under the guidance of the Holy Ghost. Hence we need not concern ourselves with the shallowness of those men whom grave and holy authors rightly reproach, and of whom in particular St. Jerome said, in reference to the Bible:

"This is ventured upon, lacerated, and taught by the garrulous old woman, the doting old man, and the prattling sophist before they have learned it. Others, led on by pride, weigh heavy words and philosophize amongst women concerning holy Scripture. Others—oh, shame!—learn from women what they teach to men, and (as if that were not enough) glibly expound to others that which they themselves do not understand. I forebear to speak of those of my own profession who, attaining a knowledge of the holy Scriptures after mundane learning, tickle the ears of the people with affected and studied expressions, and declare that everything they say is to be taken as the law of God. Not bothering to learn what the prophets and the apostles have maintained, they wrest incongruous testimonies into their own senses—as if distorting passages and twisting the Bible to their individual and contradictory whims were the genuine way of teaching, and not a corrupt one."

I do not wish to place in the number of such lay writers some theologians whom I consider men of profound learning and devout behavior, and who are therefore held by me in great esteem and veneration. Yet I cannot deny that I feel some discomfort which I should like to have removed, when I hear them pretend to the power of constraining others by scriptural authority to follow in a physical dispute that opinion which they think best agrees with the Bible, and then believe themselves not bound to answer the opposing reasons and experiences. In explanation and support of this opinion they say that since theology is queen of all the sciences, she need not bend in any way to accommodate herself to the teachings of less worthy sciences which are subordinate to her; these others must rather be referred to her as their supreme empress, changing and altering their conclusions according to her statutes and decrees. They add further that if in the inferior sciences any conclusion should be taken as certain in virtue of demonstrations or experiences, while in the Bible another conclusion is found repugnant to this, then the professors of that science should themselves undertake to undo their proofs and discover the fallacies in their own experiences, without bothering the theologians and exegetes. For, they say, it does not become the dignity of theology to stoop to the investigation of fallacies in the subordinate sciences; it is sufficient for her merely to determine the truth of a given conclusion with absolute authority, secure in her inability to err.

Now the physical conclusions in which they say we ought to be satisfied by Scripture, without glossing or expounding it in senses different from the literal, are those concerning which the Bible always speaks in the same manner and which the holy Fathers all receive and expound in the same way. But with regard to these judgments I have had occasion to consider several things, and I shall set them forth in order that I may be corrected by those who understand more than I do in these matters—for to their decisions I submit at all times.

First, I question whether there is not some equivocation in failing to specify the virtues which entitle sacred theology to the title of "queen." It might deserve that name by reason of including everything that is included from all the other sciences and establishing everything by better methods and with profounder learning. It is thus, for example, that the rules for measuring fields and keeping accounts are much more excellently contained in arithmetic and in the geometry of Euclid than in the practices of surveyors and accountants. Or theology might be queen because of being occupied with a subject which excels in dignity all the subjects which compose the other sciences, and because her teachings are divulged in more sublime ways.

That the title and authority of queen belongs to theology in the first sense, I think, will not be affirmed by theologians who have any skill in the other sciences. None of these, I think, will say that geometry, astronomy, music, and medicine are much more excellently contained in the Bible than they are in the books of Archimedes, Ptolemy, Boethius, and Galen. Hence it seems likely that regal pre-eminence is given to theology in the second sense; that is, by reason of its subject and the miraculous communication of divine revelation of conclusions which could not be conceived by men in any other way, concerning chiefly the attainment of eternal blessedness.

Let us grant then that theology is conversant with the loftiest divine contemplation, and occupies the regal throne among sciences by dignity. But acquiring the highest authority in this way, if she does not descend to the lower and humbler speculations of the subordinate sciences and has no regard for them because they are not concerned with blessedness, then her professors should not arrogate to themselves the authority to decide on controversies in professions which they have neither studied nor practiced. Why, this would be as if an absolute despot, being neither a physician nor an architect but knowing himself free to command, should undertake to administer medicines and erect buildings according to his whim—at grave peril of his poor patients' lives, and the speedy collapse of his edifices.

Again, to command that the very professors of astronomy themselves see to the refutation of their own observations and proofs as mere fallacies and sophisms is to enjoin something that lies beyond any possibility of accomplishment. For this would amount to commanding that they must not see what they see and must not understand what they know, and that in searching they must find the opposite of what they actually encounter. Before this could be done they would have to be taught how to make one mental faculty command another, and the inferior powers the superior, so that the imagination and the will might be forced to believe the opposite of what the intellect understands. I am referring at all times to merely physical propositions, and not to supernatural things which are matters of faith.

I entreat those wise and prudent Fathers to consider with great care the difference that exists between doctrines subject to proof and those subject to opinion. Considering the force exerted by logical deductions, they may ascertain that it is not in the power of the professors of demonstrative sciences to change their opinions at will and apply themselves first to one side and then to the other. There is a great difference between commanding a mathematician or a philosopher and influencing a lawyer or a merchant, for demonstrated conclusions about things in nature or in the heavens cannot be changed with the same facility as opinions about what is or is not lawful in a contract, bargain, or bill of exchange. This difference was well understood by the learned and holy Fathers, as proven by their having taken great pains in refuting philosophical fallacies. This may be found expressly in some of them; in particular, we find the following words of St. Augustine: "It is to be held as an unquestionable truth that whatever the sages of this world have demonstrated concerning physical matters is in no way contrary to our Bibles, hence whatever the sages teach in their books that is contrary to the holy Scriptures may be concluded without any hesitation to be quite false. And according to our ability let us make this evident, and let us keep the faith of our Lord, in whom are hidden all the treasures of wisdom, so that we neither become seduced by the verbiage of false philosophy nor frightened by the superstition of counterfeit religion."

From the above words I conceive that I may deduce this doctrine: That in the books of the sages of this world there are contained some physical truths which are soundly demonstrated, and others that are merely stated; as to the former, it is the office of wise divines to show that they do not contradict the holy Scriptures. And as to the propositions which are stated but not rigorously demonstrated, anything contrary to the Bible involved by them must be held undoubtedly false and should be proved so by every possible means.

Now if truly demonstrated physical conclusions need not be subordinated to biblical passages, but the latter must rather be shown not to interfere with the former, then before a physical proposition is condemned it must be shown to be not rigorously demonstrated—and this is to be done not by those who hold the proposition to be true, but by those who judge it to be false. This seems very reasonable and natural, for those who believe an argument to be false may much more easily find the fallacies in it than men who consider it to be true and conclusive. Indeed, in the latter case it will happen that the more the adherents of an opinion turn over their pages, examine the arguments, repeat the observations, and compare the experiences, the more they will be confirmed in that belief. And Your Highness knows what happened to the late mathematician of the University of Pisa who undertook in his old age to look into the Copernican doctrine in the hope of shaking its foundations and refuting it, since he considered it false only because he had never studied it. As it fell out, no sooner had he understood its grounds, procedures, and demonstrations than he found himself persuaded, and from an opponent he became a very staunch defender of it. I might also name other mathematicians who, moved by my latest discoveries, have confessed it necessary to alter the previously accepted system of the world, as this is simply unable to subsist any longer.

If in order to banish the opinion in question from the world it were sufficient to stop the mouth of a single man—as perhaps those men persuade themselves who, measuring the minds of others by their own, think it impossible that this doctrine should be able to continue to find adherents—then that would be very easily done. But things stand otherwise. To carry out such a decision it would be necessary not only to prohibit the book of Copernicus and the writings of other authors who follow the same opinion, but to ban the whole science of astronomy. Furthermore, it would be necessary to forbid men to look at the heavens, in order that they might not see Mars and Venus sometimes quite near the earth and sometimes very distant, the variation being so great that Venus is forty times and Mars sixty times as large at one time as another. And it would be necessary to prevent Venus being seen round at one time and forked at another, with very thin horns; as well as many other sensory observations which can never be reconciled with the Ptolemaic system in any way, but are very strong arguments for the Copernican. And to ban Copernicus now that his doctrine is daily reinforced by many new observations and by the learned applying themselves to the reading of his book, after this opinion has been allowed and tolerated for these many years during which it was less followed and less confirmed, would seem in my judgment to be a contravention of truth, and an attempt to hide and suppress her the more as she revealed herself the more clearly and plainly. Not to abolish and censure his whole book, but only to condemn as erroneous this particular proposition, would (if I am not mistaken) be a still greater detriment to the minds of men, since it would afford them occasion to see a proposition proved that it was heresy to believe. And to prohibit the whole science would be but to censure a hundred passages of holy Scripture which teach us that the glory and greatness of Almighty God are marvelously discerned in all his works and divinely read in the open book of heaven. For let no one believe that reading the lofty concepts written in that book leads to nothing further than the mere seeing of the splendor of the sun and the stars and their rising and setting, which is as far as the eyes of brutes and of the vulgar can penetrate. Within its pages are couched mysteries so profound and concepts so sublime that the vigils, labors, and studies of hundreds upon hundreds of the most acute minds have still not pierced them, even after the continual investigations for thousands of years. The eyes of an idiot perceive little by beholding the external appearance of a human body, as compared with the wonderful contrivances which a careful and practiced anatomist or philosopher discovers in that same body when he seeks out the use of all those muscles, tendons, nerves, and bones; or when examining the functions of the heart and the other principal organs, he seeks the seat of

the vital faculties, notes and observes the admirable structure of the sense organs, and (without ever ceasing in his amazement and delight) contemplates
the receptacles of the imagination, the memory, and the understanding.
Likewise, that which presents itself to mere sight is as nothing in comparison
with the high marvels that the ingenuity of learned men discovers in the
heavens by long and accurate observation. ...

Your Highness may thus see how irregularly those persons proceed
who in physical disputes arrange scriptural passages (and often those ill-
understood by them) in the front rank of their arguments. If these men really
believe themselves to have the true sense of a given passage, it necessarily
follows that they believe they have in hand the absolute truth of the conclusion they intend to debate. Hence they must know that they enjoy a great advantage over their opponents, whose lot it is to defend the false position; and
he who maintains the truth will have many sense-experiences and rigorous
proofs on his side, whereas his antagonist cannot make use of anything but
illusory appearances, quibbles, and fallacies. Now if these men know they
have such advantages over the enemy even when they stay within proper
bounds and produce no weapons other than those proper to philosophy,
why do they, in the thick of the battle, betake themselves to a dreadful
weapon which cannot be turned aside, and seek to vanquish the opponent
by merely exhibiting it? If I may speak frankly, I believe they have themselves been vanquished, and, feeling unable to stand up against the assaults
of the adversary, they seek ways of holding him off. To that end they would
forbid him the use of reason, divine gift of Providence, and would abuse the
just authority of holy Scripture—which, in the general opinion of theologians, can never oppose manifest experiences and necessary demonstrations
when rightly understood and applied. If I am correct, it will stand them in no
stead to go running to the Bible to cover up their inability to understand (let
alone resolve) their opponents' arguments, for the opinion which they fight
has never been condemned by the holy Church. If they wish to proceed in
sincerity, they should by silence confess themselves unable to deal with such
matters. Let them freely admit that although they may argue that a position
is false, it is not in their power to censure a position as erroneous—or in the
power of anyone except the Supreme Pontiff, or the Church Councils. Reflecting upon this, and knowing that a proposition cannot be both true and
heretical, let them employ themselves in the business which is proper to
them; namely, demonstrating its falsity. And when that is revealed, either
there will no longer be any necessity to prohibit it (since it will have no followers), or else it may safely be prohibited without the risk of any scandal.

Therefore let these men begin to apply themselves to an examination of
the arguments of Copernicus and others, leaving condemnation of the doctrine as erroneous and heretical to the proper authorities. Among the circumspect and most wise Fathers, and in the absolute wisdom of one who
cannot err, they may never hope to find the rash decisions into which they

allow themselves to be hurried by some particular passion or personal interest. With regard to this opinion, and others which are not directly matters of faith, certainly no one doubts that the Supreme Pontiff has always an absolute power to approve or condemn; but it is not in the power of any created being to make things true or false, for this belongs to their own nature and to the fact. Therefore in my judgment one should first be assured of the necessary and immutable truth of the fact, over which no man has power. This is wiser counsel than to condemn either side in the absence of such certainty, thus depriving oneself of continued authority and ability to choose by determining things which are now undetermined and open and still lodged in the will of supreme authority. And in brief, if it is impossible for a conclusion to be declared heretical while we remain in doubt as to its truth, then these men are wasting their time clamoring for condemnation of the motion of the earth and stability of the sun, which they have not yet demonstrated to be impossible or false.

Bishop Bossuet

Early modern Europe witnessed the rise of the nation-state, as increasingly large territories were consolidated into single political units. Concurrently, it witnessed the rise of absolute monarchy as the form of political rule for these states. During the sixteenth and seventeenth centuries the notion of royal absolutism was espoused by leading rulers in Western Europe, such as Philip II of Spain, James I of England, and, preeminently, Louis XIV of France, the "Sun King." Although the ascendency of royal rulers was accomplished in large measure by force and diplomacy, it also had a theoretical rationale, called "the divine right of kings." As its name implies, this is a simple theory, which asserts that kings receive their right to rule directly from God and from God alone.

One of the leading proponents of the divine-right theory was Bishop Jacques Bossuet (1627–1704), an eminent historian as well as theologian. Bossuet was a close spiritual and political advisor to Louis XIV and was given the position of tutor to the Dauphin, the heir to the French throne. For him he wrote *Politics Drawn from the Very Words of Holy Scripture*, a title that is amply justified by the frequent and diverse references to the Bible that the author introduces to support his conclusions. Although Bossuet does not hesitate to assert the royal prerogatives, it should also be recognized that he laid on the king the divine obligation to rule wisely and for the welfare of his people.

Consider the following questions as you study the text below.

1. What did Bossuet mean by the absolute authority of kings? How did absolute authority differ from arbitrary authority?

2. In Bossuet's view, why were kings necessary to good social order? What connections did he make between order in the family and order in the state?

Politics Drawn from the Very Words of Holy Scripture

Third Book

IN WHICH WE BEGIN TO EXPLAIN
THE NATURE AND PROPERTIES OF ROYAL AUTHORITY

Article I. Essential characteristics are noted.

SINGLE PROPOSITION: *There are four characteristics or qualities essential to royal authority*: Firstly, royal authority is sacred; Secondly, it is paternal; Thirdly, it is absolute; Fourthly, it is subject to reason. This is what must be established systematically in the following articles.

Article II. Royal authority is sacred.

FIRST PROPOSITION: *God establishes kings as his ministers and reigns through them over the peoples of the world.*—We have already seen that all power comes from God.

"The ruler," adds St. Paul, "is God's minister for good. But if you do evil, be afraid, for he does not wield the sword in vain. He is a minister of God, an avenger of evil deeds."

Rulers thus act as God's ministers and as His lieutenants on earth. It is through them that He exercises His dominion. "Do you believe yourselves capable of resisting the kingdom of the Lord, that He possesses through the children of David?"

It is for this reason that we have seen that the royal throne is not the throne of a man, but the throne of God himself. "God has chosen my son Solomon in order to place him on the throne where the Lord reigns over Israel." And furthermore: "Solomon sits on the throne of the Lord."

And in order that we should not believe that to have kings established by God is characteristic only of the Israelites, here is what Ecclesiastes says: "God gives to each people their governor; and Israel is manifestly reserved for Himself."

He thus governs all peoples, and gives to all of them their kings. However He governs Israel in a more particular and more direct fashion.

SECOND PROPOSITION: *The person of the king is sacred.*—It follows from the above that the person of the king is sacred, and any attempt upon the lives of kings is a sacrilege.

God has had them anointed by His prophets with a sacred ointment, as He has had His pontiffs and His altars anointed.

Trans. Owen Ulph.

But even without the application of this ointment to their bodies, they are sacred by virtue of their charge, as the representatives of the divine majesty, delegated by His providence to the execution of His designs. It is thus that God, Himself, calls Cyrus His anointed. "Here is what the Lord said to Cyrus, my anointed, whom I have taken by the hand to subject all peoples to him."

The title of christ is given to kings, and everywhere they are seen to be called christs, or the anointed of the Lord.

Under this venerable name, even the prophets revere them, and regard them as associated with the sovereign power of God, whose authority they exercise over the people. "Speak of me boldly before the Lord, and before His christ. Speak out if I have taken someone's bull or someone's ass, if I have taken bribes from someone, if I have oppressed someone. And they replied: Never. And Samuel said: the Lord and His christ are thus witnesses that you have no complaint against me."

It is thus that Samuel, after having judged the people for God with absolute power for twenty-one years, gives an account of his conduct before God and before Saul, to whom he appeals as witnesses to the testimony establishing his innocence.

Kings must be protected as sacred objects; and whoever neglects to protect them is worthy of death. "Long live the Lord," said David to Saul's captains, "all of you who do not safeguard your master, the anointed of the Lord, are the children of death."

. . .

THIRD PROPOSITION: *The ruler must be obeyed out of the principle of religion and conscience.*—St. Paul, after having stated that the ruler is the minister of God, concluded as follows: "It is thus necessary that you subject yourself to him not only through fear of his wrath, but through the obligation of your conscience."

This is why "it is necessary to serve him not merely in a way to meet the eye as if to please men, but with pure intent, with fear, with respect, and with a heart as sincere as that of Jesus Christ."

And furthermore: "Servants, obey your temporal masters in all things, never serving only in a way to meet the eye as if to please men, but in simplicity of heart and in the fear of God. Do all that you do with a good heart as though serving God and not men, assured of receiving from God Himself the reward for your services. Look upon Jesus Christ as your master."

If the apostle speaks thus of servitude, a state contrary to nature, what ought we to think of legitimate subjection to rulers and magistrates, protectors of public liberty!

That is why St. Peter said: "For the love of God, be thus subjected to the order which is established among men. Be subjected to the king as to God, possessor of the supreme power. Be subjected to those to whom He gives His authority and who are sent by Him to praise good deeds and punish evil ones."

Even though they may not acquit themselves of this duty, their charge and their ministry must be respected. "Obey your masters, not only those who are good and moderate, but even those who are vexatious and unjust."

There is thus something religious in the respect one renders to the ruler. Service to God and respect for kings are one, and St. Peter links these two duties together: "Fear God, honor the king."

Thus has God put into rulers something divine. "I have said: You are gods, and you are all children of the Almighty." It is God Himself whom David causes to speak thus.

From this it ensues that the servants of God swear by the safety and life of the king, as by a divine and sacred thing. Uriah speaking to David: "By your safety and by the conservation of your life, I will never do that thing."

Even though the king should prove unfaithful, according to the view we must hold of the order of God: "By the safety of Pharaoh, I will not let you leave here."

It is necessary to listen to the first Christians, and to Tertullian who speaks for all of them as follows: "We swear not by the ghosts of the Caesars; but by their life and safety, which is more august than all their ghosts. Don't you know that spirits are demons? But we, who see in the emperors the choice and judgment of God who has given them command over all peoples, respect in them what God has placed there and we hold these things at great oath."

He adds: "What more shall I say for our religion and our piety towards the emperor than that we should respect the one whom our God has chosen. In a manner I can say that Caesar is more ours than yours because it is our God who has established him."

It is therefore the spirit of Christianity to cause kings to be respected religiously. So much so that the same Tertullian appropriately calls our faith, "the religion of the second majesty."

The second majesty is but a derivative of the first, that is to say, of the divine being, Who, for the good of human things, has wished to cause some portion of His splendor to shine forth upon kings.

FOURTH PROPOSITION: *Kings must respect their own power and use it only for the public good.*—Since their power, as it has thus been said, comes from on high, they must not believe that they are the masters to use it as they please. They must use it with fear and moderation as a thing which comes to them from God, and for which God will demand an accounting. "Listen, O kings, and understand! Learn, judges of the earth! Lend an ear, O you who hold the peoples under your power, and be pleased to see the multitudes that surround you. It is God who has given you the power. Your strength comes from the Almighty who will examine your work and sound the depths of your thoughts. Because, being ministers of His kingdom, you have not judged well and you have not proceeded according to His will, He will soon appear to you in a terrible manner. Because to those who command is reserved the most harsh punishment, the small and the weak will be pitied but the powerful will be severely tormented. God fears the power of no one, because He has made both the great and the small and He is equally concerned for one and the other. And the strongest will be tormented most strongly. I speak unto you, O kings! so that you may be wise, and so that you fall not from grace."

Kings must, therefore, tremble as they use the power that God gives them, and reflect how horrible is the sacrilege of using a power that comes from God for evil.

We have seen the kings seated on the throne of the Lord, holding the sword that He has placed in their hands. How profane and audacious are those unjust kings who sit on the throne of God and use the sword, which He puts into their hands, to commit violent deeds, and to cut the throats of His children!

Thus they respect their power because it is not their power, but the power of God which it is necessary to employ in a holy and religious manner. St. Gregory of Nazianzus speaks thus to the emperors: "Respect your purple. Recognize within your persons the mystery of God. He governs celestial things alone, He shares those of the earth with you. Be thus gods to your subjects." That is to say, govern them as God governs, in a noble, impartial, beneficial, and, in a word, in a manner divine.

Article III.   Royal authority is paternal, and its fundamental quality is benevolence. After what has been said, this truth needs no further proofs.

We have seen that kings hold rank from God, who is the true father of the human race. We have also seen that the first concept of power that existed among men is that of paternal power and that kings have been molded in the image of fathers. Also, everyone is in agreement that the obedience which is due to public power is found in the *Decalogue* only in the precept that obliges us to honor our fathers. From all this it seems that the appellation *king* is synonymous with the appellation *father*, and that benevolence is the most natural characteristic of kings.

.   .   .

Fourth Book

CONTINUATION OF THE CHARACTERISTICS OF ROYALTY

Article I.   Royal authority is absolute.

In order to render this term odious and insufferable, many persons attempt to confuse absolute government with arbitrary government. But there are no terms more distinguished by their difference as we shall see when we speak of justice.

FIRST PROPOSITION: *The prince need render account to no one for what he orders.*—"Observe the commandments that come from the mouth of the king, and keep the oath that you have made to him. Do not seek to escape his view, and do not indulge in evil undertakings, because he will do what he wishes. The word of the king is powerful. And no one can say to him: Why do you act thus? He who obeys will come to no harm."

Without this absolute authority he can neither do good nor suppress evil. His power must be such that no one may hope to escape from it. And finally, the only defense of individuals against public power must be their innocence.

This doctrine conforms to the words of St. Paul: "If you do not want to fear power, do good."

SECOND PROPOSITION: *Once the prince has judged there is no other judgment.*—Sovereign judgments are attributed to God Himself. When Joseph established the judges to judge the people, he said: "It is not in the name of men that you judge, but in the name of God."

That is what causes Ecclesiastes to say: "Do not judge against the judge." This is even more important when the sovereign judge is the king. And the reason that supports this, "is that he is judging according to justice." It is not that he is always so judging, but that he is assumed to be so judging and no one has the right to judge or to review after him.

It is thus necessary to obey rulers as though they were identical with justice, without which there is neither order nor justice in affairs.

They are gods, and in a manner they share divine independence. "I have said: You are gods and you are all children of the Almighty."

Only God is able to judge their judgments and their persons. "God has taken His seat in the assembly of the gods and, seated in the center, He judges the gods."

It is for that reason that St. Gregory, bishop of Tours, said to King Chilperic in a council: "We speak to you, but you listen to us only if you want to. If you don't want to, who will condemn you other than He who has said that He was justice itself?"

It follows that he who does not want to obey the ruler is not referred to another tribunal, but is condemned irremissably to death as an enemy of the public peace and of human society. "Whoever will be proud and will not obey the command of the pontiff and the ordinance of the judge will die and you will thus eradicate the evil from among you." And furthermore: "Whoever shall refuse to obey all your orders, may he die." It is the people who speak thus to Joshua.

The ruler can correct himself when he knows that he has done badly, but against his authority there can be no remedy except his authority.

That is why he must certainly be careful what he orders. "Be careful of what you order. All that you judge will fall back upon you. Fear God. Do everything with great care."

It is thus that Joseph instructed the judges to whom he was entrusting his authority. How much of this he recollected when he himself had to judge.

THIRD PROPOSITION: *There is no co-active force against the ruler.*—A co-active force is a power to constrain and to execute what is legitimately ordained. Legitimate power belongs to the ruler alone. To him alone belongs the co-active force.

It is for that reason also that St. Paul gives the sword to him alone. "If you do not do well, be afraid, because it is not in vain that he wields the sword."

In the state only the ruler should be armed, otherwise everything is in confusion and the state falls back into anarchy.

He who creates a sovereign ruler puts everything together into his hands, all the sovereign authority to judge and all the forces of the state. "Our king will judge and he will march before us and he will conduct our wars." This is what the Jewish people said when they asked for a king. Samuel declares to them upon this basis that the power of their ruler will be absolute, incapable of being restrained by any other power. Here is the right of the king who will reign over you, sayeth the Lord: "He will take your children and place them into his service. He will seize some of your lands and the best of that which you have in order to give it to his servants," and so forth.

Will they have the right to do all that legally? God forbid! Because God does not grant such powers. But they will have the right to do it with impunity and without regard for human justice. That is why David said: "I have sinned against you alone. O Lord, have pity on me!" Commenting on this passage, St. Jerome said: "Because he was king, he had only God to fear."

.   .   .

To the ruler alone belongs the general care of the people. That is the first article and the foundation of all others. To him the public works; to him the squares and arms; to him the decrees and ordinances; to him the marks of distinction; no power but that which is dependent on his; no assembly except by his authority.

It is thus that for the good of a state all the power is united in one. To put the power somewhere else is to divide the state. It is to destroy the public peace. It is to create two masters against which the oracle of the Scriptures states: "No man can serve two masters."

The ruler is by his charge the father of the people. He is by his grandeur above petty interests. Even more, all his grandeur and all his natural interest is that the people be conserved, since lacking the people he is no longer ruler. There is nothing better than to leave all the power of the state to the one who has the greatest interest in the conservation and the glory of the state itself.

.   .   .

Fifth Book

FOURTH AND FINAL CHARACTERISTIC
OF ROYAL AUTHORITY

Article I.   Royal authority is subject to reason.

FIRST PROPOSITION: *Government is a work of reason and intelligence.—* "Now, listen, O kings, and be instructed, judges of the earth."

All men are created capable of understanding. But principally you upon whom reposes an entire nation, you who should be the soul and intelligence of a State, in whom must be found the first reason for all its movements, the less it is necessary for you to justify yourself to others, the more you must have justification and intelligence within yourself.

The contrary of acting out of reason is to act out of passion or anger. To act out of anger as Saul acted against David, driven by his jealousy or possessed by his black melancholy, entails all kinds of irregularities, inconsistencies, inequalities, anomalies, injustices, and confusion in one's conduct.

Though one has only a horse to lead and a flock to guide, one cannot do it without reason. How much more is needed for the leadership of men and a rational flock!

"The Lord took David from the care of his sheep to have him conduct Jacob, his servant, and Israel, his inheritance. And he led them in the innocence of his heart with an able and intelligent hand."

Everything among men is accomplished through intelligence and through counsel. "Houses are built out of wisdom and become solid through prudence. Ability fills the granaries and amasses riches. The wise man is courageous. The able man is robust and strong because war is waged by strategy and by industry, and salvation is found where there is much counsel."

Wisdom herself says: "It is through me that kings rule and through me legislators prescribe what is just."

She is so born to command that she gives the empire even to those born in servitude. "The wise servant will command the children of the house who lack wisdom, and he will apportion their lots." And furthermore: "Free people will subject themselves to a judicious servant."

God, upon installing Joshua, orders him to study the law of Moses which was the law of the kingdom, "in order," He says, "that you should understand all that you do." And furthermore: "And then you will carry out your designs and you will understand what you do."

David said as much to Solomon in the last instructions he gave to him upon dying. "Take care to observe the laws of God so that you may understand all that you do and to which side you are to turn."

"So that you may not be turned, turn yourself knowingly. Let reason direct all your movements. Know what you do and why you are doing it."

.   .   .

Article IV.   Consequences of the Preceding Doctrine of Majesty and Its Attendant Features.

FIRST PROPOSITION: *What majesty is.*—I do not call majesty that pomp which surrounds kings, or that external brilliance which dazzles the vulgar. That is the reflection of majesty and not majesty itself.

Majesty is the image of the grandeur of God in the ruler.

God is infinite. God is all. The ruler in his capacity as ruler is not looked upon as a private individual. He is a public figure. The entire state is in him. The will of all the people is contained in his. As all perfection and all virtue is united in God, thus all the power of individuals is reunited in the person of the ruler. What grandeur that a single man should contain so much of it!

The power of God makes itself felt in an instant from one end of the world to the other. Royal power acts simultaneously throughout the entire kingdom. It holds the whole kingdom in a state of polity as God holds the whole world.

Should God withdraw His hand, the world will fall back into nothingness. Should authority cease in the kingdom, all will be in confusion.

Consider the ruler in his cabinet. From there all orders emanate which make the magistrates and the captains, the citizens and the soldiers, the provinces and the armies on land and sea, act in concert. It is the image of God who seated on His throne in the highest part of the heavens directs all of nature.

"What movement is caused," said St. Augustine, "simply by the command of the emperor! He only moves his lips—there is no slighter movement—and the whole empire moves. It is the image of God who does all by His word. He has spoken and things have been done. He has commanded and they have been created."

We admire His works. Nature is a matter to expound upon for the curious. "God gives them the world to meditate upon, but they will never discover the secret of His work from the beginning to the end." We see some portion of it, but the depth is impenetrable. Thus is the secret of the ruler.

The designs of the ruler are only known through their execution. Thus are the counsels of God likewise manifested, and no one shares them save those whom God admits.

If the power of God extends everywhere, magnificence accompanies it. There is no corner of the universe where shining examples of His goodness do not appear. Behold the order, behold the justice, behold the tranquility in all the kingdom! It is the natural effect of the authority of the ruler.

There is nothing more majestic than kindness widely displayed, and there is no greater vilification of majesty than the misery of the people caused by the ruler.

The evil hide in vain. God's light follows them everywhere. His arm reaches them from the highest heavens to the depths of the abyss. "Where shall I go before your spirit and where shall I flee before your face? If I climb to heaven you are there. If I throw myself into the depths of hell, I find you there. If I rise in the morning and retreat to the most distant seas it is your hand that leads me there and your right hand holds me there. And I have said that perhaps the shadows will cover me, but night has been as day around me. Before you, darkness is not dark. The night is lighted as the day. Darkness and light are one and the same." The evil find God everywhere, high and low, night and day. Whatever morning they get up, He warns them. However far they should travel, His hand is on them.

Thus God gives the ruler the power of discovering the most secret conspiracies. He has eyes and hands everywhere. We have seen that the birds of the sky report to him what is going on. He has even received from God through practiced experience a certain insight which makes one suspect him of powers of divination. Once he has penetrated intrigue, his long arms reach out to seize his enemies from the extremities of the world. He ferrets them out from the depths of the abyss. There is no asylum secure against such power.

Finally, let yourself gather before your eyes those things so great and so august that we have said concerning royal authority. Behold an immense people united in a single person. Behold the sacred power, paternal and absolute. Behold the secret reason which governs the entire body of the state enclosed in a single head. See the image of God in the king and you have the concept of royal majesty.

God is holiness itself, goodness itself, power itself, reason itself. In these things resides the majesty of God. In the image of these things is the majesty of the ruler.

This majesty is so great that it cannot be the same in the ruler as it is in the source. It is borrowed from God who gives it to him for the good of the people for whom it is good to be constrained by a superior force.

I do not know what divine attribute attaches itself to the ruler and inspires fear in the people. May the king not forget himself for that reason. "I have said that it is God who speaks. I have said: You are gods and you are all children of the Almighty but you will die like men and you will fall like the great." I have said, you are gods. That is to say, you have authority in you. You carry on your forehead a divine character. You are the children of the Almighty. It is He who has established your power for the welfare of mankind. But, O gods of flesh and blood, O gods of mud and dust, you will die like men, you will fall like the great. Greatness separates men for a time. A common fall at the end makes them all equal.

O kings, exercise your power thus boldly because it is divine and beneficial to mankind! But exercise it with humility. It is applied to you from without. In the end it leaves you feeble, it leaves you mortal, it leaves you sinners and makes you all the more responsible before God.

Thomas Hobbes

The revolutions in seventeenth-century England produced two major political philosophers, Thomas Hobbes (1588–1679) and John Locke (1632–1704). Their writings, which coincided respectively with the English Civil War and the Glorious Revolution, reflect the ways in which these political upheavals differed from each other.

Hobbes's *Leviathan*, published in 1651, is filled with overtones of the insecurity, fear, and violence of the civil war just finished. Hobbes himself, because of his associations with the English aristocracy, had been forced to flee during the revolution to France, where he tutored the future King Charles II, also a refugee, in mathematics. However, the *Leviathan* is much more than a mirror of its troubled times, being a carefully argued defense of the theory of political absolutism. Hobbes found a philosophical justification for absolutism in the ancient theory of materialism, which had been revived during the seventeenth century in the scientific works of writers such as Galileo and Descartes. Applying the assumptions of these scientists to human nature, Hobbes then deduced his absolutistic position in politics from them.

Hobbes's theory of absolutism is sometimes confused with the theory of the divine right of kings, which was defended by some of his contemporaries, like Bishop Bossuet. Although both theories supported political absolutism, they did so in very different ways. For divine-right theorists the sovereign is justified in his rule by reason of his hereditary right of succession to the throne, but for Hobbes the "right" to rule reduced simply to the sovereign's ability to stay in power and keep the peace.

Consider the following questions as you study the text below.

1. Why did Hobbes believe that before the rise of governments a state of war existed, with "every man" pitted "against every man"? According to Hobbes, were ideas like justice and injustice absolute truths that had always existed or were they invented by human beings at a particular point in time?

2. Compare the arguments in support of the absolute power of kings put forth by Thomas Hobbes and Bishop Bossuet. Aside from their ultimate conclusions, on what, if anything, did they agree?

Leviathan

The Introduction

Nature, the art whereby God hath made and governs the world, is by the *art* of man, as in many other things, so in this also imitated, that it can make an artificial animal. For seeing life is but a motion of limbs, the beginning whereof is in some principal part within; why may we not say, that all *automata* (engines that move themselves by springs and wheels as doth a watch) have an artificial life? For what is the *heart*, but a *spring*; and the *nerves*, but so many *strings*; and the *joints*, but so many *wheels*, giving motion to the whole body, such as was intended by the artificer? *Art* goes yet further, imitating that rational and most excellent work of nature, *man*. For by art is created that great LEVIATHAN called a COMMONWEALTH, or STATE, in Latin CIVITAS, which is but an artificial man; though of greater stature and strength than the natural, for whose protection and defence it was intended; and in which the *sovereignty* is an artificial *soul*, as giving life and motion to the whole body; the *magistrates*, and other *officers* of judicature and execution, artificial *joints*; *reward* and *punishment*, by which fastened to the seat of the sovereignty every joint and member is moved to perform his duty, are the *nerves*, that do the same in the body natural; the *wealth* and *riches* of all the particular members, are the *strength*; *salus populi*, the *people's safety*, its *business*; *counsellors*, by whom all things needful for it to know are suggested unto it, are the *memory*; *equity*, and *laws*, an artificial *reason* and *will*; *concord*, *health*; *sedition*, *sickness*; and *civil war*, *death*. Lastly, the *pacts* and *covenants*, by which the parts of this body politic were at first made, set together, and united, resemble that *fiat*, or the *let us make man*, pronounced by God in creation.

. . .

Chapter XIII

OF THE NATURAL CONDITION OF MANKIND AS CONCERNING THEIR FELICITY, AND MISERY

Nature hath made men so equal, in the faculties of the body, and mind; as that though there be found one man sometimes manifestly stronger in body, or of quicker mind than another; yet when all is reckoned together, the difference between man, and man, is not so considerable, as that one man

The English Works of Thomas Hobbes, Vol. III, ed. W. Molesworth.

can thereupon claim to himself any benefit, to which another may not pretend, as well as he. For as to the strength of body, the weakest has strength enough to kill the strongest, either by secret machination, or by confederacy with others, that are in the same danger with himself.

And as to the faculties of the mind, setting aside the arts grounded upon words, and especially that skill of proceeding upon general, and infallible rules, called science; which very few have, and but in few things; as being not a native faculty, born with us; nor attained, as prudence, while we look after somewhat else, I find yet a greater equality amongst men, than that of strength. For prudence, is but experience; which equal time, equally bestows on all men, in those things they equally apply themselves unto. That which may perhaps make such equality incredible, is but a vain conceit of one's own wisdom, which almost all men think they have in a greater degree, than the vulgar; that is, than all men but themselves, and a few others, whom by fame, or for concurring with themselves, they approve. For such is the nature of men, and howsoever they may acknowledge many others to be more witty, or more eloquent, or more learned; yet they will hardly believe there be many so wise as themselves; for they see their own wit at hand, and other men's at a distance. But this proveth rather that men are in that point equal, than unequal. For there is not ordinarily a greater sign of the equal distribution of any thing, than that every man is contented with his share.

From this equality of ability, ariseth equality of hope in the attaining of our ends. And therefore if any two men desire the same thing, which nevertheless they cannot both enjoy, they become enemies; and in the way to their end, which is principally their own conservation, and sometimes their delectation only, endeavour to destroy, or subdue one another. And from hence it comes to pass, that where an invader hath no more to fear; than another man's single power; if one plant, sow, build, and possess a convenient seat, others may probably be expected to come prepared with forces united, to dispossess, and deprive him, not only of the fruit of his labour, but also of his life, or liberty. And the invader again is in the like danger of another.

And from this diffidence of one another, there is no way for any man to secure himself, so reasonable, as anticipation; that is, by force, or wiles, to master the persons of all men he can, so long, till he see no other power great enough to endanger him; and this is no more than his own conservation requireth, and is generally allowed. Also because there be some, that taking pleasure in contemplating their own power in the acts of conquest, which they pursue farther than their security requires; if others, that otherwise would be glad to be at ease within modest bounds, should not by invasion increase their power, they would not be able, long time, by standing only on their defence, to subsist. And by consequence, such augmentation of dominion over men being necessary to a man's conservation, it ought to be allowed him.

Again, men have no pleasure, but on the contrary a great deal of grief, in keeping company, where there is no power able to over-awe them all. For every man looketh that his companion should value him, at the same rate he sets upon himself: and upon all signs of contempt, or undervaluing, naturally endeavours, as far as he dares (which amongst them that have no common power to keep them in quiet, is far enough to make them destroy each other), to extort a greater value from his contemners, by damage; and from others, by the example.

So that in the nature of man, we find three principal causes of quarrel. First, competition; secondly, diffidence; thirdly, glory.

The first, maketh men invade for gain; the second, for safety; and the third, for reputation. The first use violence, to make themselves masters of other men's persons, wives, children, and cattle; the second, to defend them; the third, for trifles, as a word, a smile, a different opinion, and any other sign of undervalue, either direct in their persons, or by reflection in their kindred, their friends, their nation, their profession, or their name.

Hereby, it is manifest, that during the time men live without a common power to keep them all in awe, they are in that condition which is called war; and such a war, as is of every man, against every man. For WAR, consisteth not in battle only, or the act of fighting; but in a tract of time, wherein the will to contend by battle is sufficiently known; and therefore the notion of *time*, is to be considered in the nature of war; as it is in the nature of weather. For as the nature of foul weather, lieth not in a shower or two of rain; but in an inclination thereto of many days together; so the nature of war, consisteth not in actual fighting; but in the known disposition thereto, during all the time there is no assurance to the contrary. All other time is PEACE.

Whatsoever therefore is consequent to a time of war, where every man is enemy to every man; the same is consequent to the time, wherein men live without other security, than what their own strength, and their own invention shall furnish them withal. In such condition, there is no place for industry; because the fruit thereof is uncertain; and consequently no culture of the earth; no navigation, nor use of the commodities that may be imported by sea; no commodious building; no instruments of moving, and removing, such things as require much force; no knowledge of the face of the earth; no account of time; no arts; no letters; no society; and which is worst of all, continual fear, and danger of violent death; and the life of man, solitary, poor, nasty, brutish, and short.

It may seem strange to some man, that has not well weighed these things; that nature should thus dissociate, and render men apt to invade, and destroy one another; and he may therefore, not trusting to this inference, made from the passions, desire perhaps to have the same confirmed by experience. Let him therefore consider with himself, when taking a journey, he arms himself, and seeks to go well accompanied; when going to sleep, he locks his doors; when even in his house he locks his chests; and this when he knows there will be laws, and public officers, armed, to revenge all injuries shall be done him; what opinion he has of his fellow-subjects, when he rides armed; of his fellow-citizens, when he locks his doors; and of his children, and servants, when he locks his chests. Does he not there as much accuse mankind by his actions, as I do by my words? But neither of us accuse man's nature in it. The desires, and other passions of man, are in themselves no sin. No more are the actions, that proceed from those passions, till they know a law that forbids them: which till laws be made they cannot know: nor can any law be made, till they have agreed upon the person that shall make it.

It may peradventure be thought, there was never such a time, nor condition of war as this, and I believe it was never generally so, over all the world: but there are many places, where they live so now. For the savage people in many places of America, except the government of small families, the concord whereof dependeth on natural lust, have no government at all; and live at this day in that brutish manner, as I said before. Howsoever, it may be perceived what manner of life there would be, where there were no common power to fear, by the manner of life, which men that have formerly lived under a peaceful government, use to degenerate into, in a civil war.

But there had never been any time, wherein particular men were in a condition of war one against another; yet in all times, kings, and persons of sovereign authority, because of their independency, are in continual jealousies, and in the state and posture of gladiators; having their weapons pointing, and their eyes fixed on one another; that is, their forts, garrisons, and guns upon the frontiers of their kingdoms; and continual spies upon their neighbours; which is a posture of war. But because they uphold thereby, the industry of their subjects; there does not follow from it, that misery, which accompanies the liberty of particular men.

To this war of every man, against every man, this is also consequent; that nothing can be unjust. The notions of right and wrong, justice and injustice have there no place. Where there is no common power, there is no law: where no law, no injustice. Force, and fraud, are in war the two cardinal virtues. Justice, and injustice are none of the faculties neither of the body, or mind. If they were, they might be in a man that were alone in the world, as well as his senses, and passions. They are qualities, that relate to men in society, not in solitude. It is consequent also to the same condition, that there be no propriety, no dominion, no *mine* and *thine* distinct; but only that to be every man's, that he can get; and for so long, as he can keep it. And thus much for the ill condition, which man by mere nature is actually placed in; though with a possibility to come out of it, consisting partly in the passions, partly in his reason.

The passions that incline men to peace, are fear of death; desire of such things as are necessary to commodious living; and a hope by their industry to obtain them. And reason suggesteth convenient articles of peace, upon which men may be drawn to agreement. These articles, are they, which otherwise are called the Laws of Nature, whereof I shall speak more particularly, in the two following chapters.

Chapter XIV

OF THE FIRST AND SECOND NATURAL LAWS, AND OF CONTRACTS

The RIGHT OF NATURE, which writers commonly call *jus naturale*, is the liberty each man hath, to use his own power, as he will himself, for the preservation of his own nature; that is to say, of his own life; and consequently, of doing any thing, which in his own judgment, and reason, he shall conceive to be the aptest means thereunto.

By LIBERTY, is understood, according to the proper signification of the word, the absence of external impediments; which impediments, may oft take away part of man's power to do what he would; but cannot hinder him from using the power left him, according as his judgment, and reason shall dictate to him.

A LAW OF NATURE, *lex naturalis*, is a precept or general rule, found out by reason, by which a man is forbidden to do that, which is destructive of his life, or taketh away the means of preserving the same; and to omit that, by which he thinketh it may be best preserved. For though they that speak of this subject, use to confound *jus*, and *lex*, *right* and *law*; yet they ought to be distinguished; because RIGHT, consisteth in liberty to do, or to forbear; whereas LAW, determineth, and bindeth to one of them: so that law, and right, differ as much, as obligation and liberty; which in one and the same matter are inconsistent.

And because the condition of man, as hath been declared in the precedent chapter, is a condition of war of every one against every one: in which case every one is governed by his own reason; and there is nothing he can make use of, that may not be a help unto him, in preserving his life against his enemies; it followeth, that in such a condition, every man has a right to every thing; even to another's body. And therefore, as long as this natural right of every man to every thing endureth, there can be no security to any man, how strong or wise soever he be, of living out the time, which nature ordinarily alloweth men to live. And consequently it is a precept, or general rule of reason, *that every man, ought to endeavor peace, as far as he has hope of obtaining it; and when he cannot obtain it, that he may seek, and use, all helps, and advantages of war*. The first branch of which rule, containeth the first and fundamental law of nature; which is, *to seek peace and follow it*. The second, the sum of the right of nature; which is, *by all means we can, to defend ourselves*.

From this fundamental law of nature, by which men are commanded to endeavour peace, is derived this second law; *that a man be willing, when others are so too, as far-forth, as for peace, and defence of himself he shall think it necessary, to lay down this right to all things; and be contented with so much liberty against other men, as he would allow other men against himself*. For as long as every man holdeth this right, of doing any thing he liketh, so long are all men in the conditions of war. But if other men will not lay down their right, as well as he; then there is no reason for any one, to divest himself of his: for that were to expose himself to prey, which no man is bound to, rather than to dispose himself to peace. This is that law of the Gospel: *whatsoever you require that others should do to you, that do ye to them.* And that law of all men, *quod tibi fieri non vis, alteri ne feceris.*

To *lay down* a man's *right* to any thing, is to *divest* himself of the *liberty,* of hindering another of the benefit of his own right to the same. For he that renounceth, or passeth away his right, giveth not to any other man a right which he had not before; because there is nothing to which every man had not right by nature: but only standeth out of his way, that he may enjoy his own original right, without hindrance from him; not without hindrance from another. So that the effect which redoundeth to one man, by another man's defect of right, is but so much diminution of impediments to the use of his own right original.

Right is laid aside, either by simply renouncing it, or by transferring it to another. By *simply* RENOUNCING; when he cares not to whom the benefit thereof redoundeth. By TRANSFERRING; when he intendeth the benefit thereof to some certain person, or persons. And when a man has in either manner abandoned, or granted away his right, then he is said to be OBLIGED, or BOUND, not to hinder those, to whom such right is granted, or abandoned, from the benefit of it: and that he *ought,* and it is his DUTY, not to make void that voluntary act of his own: and that such hindrance is INJUSTICE, and INJURY, as being *sine jure;* the right being before renounced, or transferred. So that *injury,* or *injustice,* in the controversies of the world, is somewhat like to that, which in the disputations of scholars is called *absurdity.* For as it is there called an absurdity, to contradict what one maintained in the beginning: so in the world, it is called injustice, and injury, voluntarily to undo that, which from the beginning he had voluntarily done. The way by which a man either simply renounceth, or transferreth his right, is a declaration, or signification, by some voluntary and sufficient sign, or signs, that he doth so renounce, or transfer; or hath so renounced, or transferred the same, to him that accepteth it. And these signs are either words only, or actions only; or, as it happeneth most often, both words, and actions. And the same are the BONDS, by which men are bound, and obliged: bonds, that have their strength, not from their own nature, for nothing is more easily broken than a man's word, but from fear of some evil consequence upon the rupture.

Whensoever a man transferreth his right, or renounceth it; it is either in consideration of some right reciprocally transferred to himself; or for some other good he hopeth for thereby. For it is a voluntary act: and of the voluntary acts of every man the object is some *good to himself.* And therefore there be some rights, which no man can be understood by any words, or other signs, to have abandoned, or transferred. At first a man cannot lay down the right of resisting them, that assault him by force, to take away his life;

because he cannot be understood to aim thereby, at any good to himself. The same may be said of wounds, and chains, and imprisonment; both because there is no benefit consequent to such patience; as there is to the patience of suffering another to be wounded, or imprisoned: as also because a man cannot tell, when he seeth men proceed against him by violence, whether they intend his death or not. And lastly the motive, and end for which this renouncing, and transferring of right is introduced, is nothing else but the security of a man's person, in his life, and in the means of so preserving life, as not to be weary of it. And therefore if a man by words, or other signs, seem to despoil himself of the end, for which those signs were intended; he is not to be understood as if he meant it, or that it was his will; but that he was ignorant of how such words and actions were to be interpreted.

The mutual transferring of right, is that which men call CONTRACT.

· · ·

If a covenant be made, wherein neither of the parties perform presently, but trust one another; in the condition of mere nature, which is a condition of war of every man against every man, upon any reasonable suspicion, it is void: but if there be a common power set over them both, with right and force sufficient to compel performance, it is not void. For he that performeth first, has no assurance that the other will perform after; because the bonds of words are too weak to bridle men's ambition, avarice, anger, and other passions, without the fear of some coercive power; which in the condition of mere nature, where all men are equal, and judges of the justness of their own fears, cannot possibly be supposed. And therefore he which performeth first, does but betray himself to his enemy; contrary to the right, he can never abandon, of defending his life, and means of living.

But in a civil estate, where there is a power set up to constrain those that would otherwise violate their faith, that fear is no more reasonable; and for that cause, he which by the covenant is to perform first, is obliged so to do.

· · ·

The force of words, being, as I have formerly noted, too weak to hold men to the performance of their covenants; there are in man's nature, but two imaginable helps to strengthen it. And those are either a fear of the consequences of breaking their word; or a glory, or pride in appearing not to need to break it. This latter is a generosity too rarely found to be presumed on, especially in the pursuers of wealth, command, or sensual pleasure; which are the greatest part of mankind. The passion to be reckoned upon, is fear.

· · ·

Chapter XV

OF OTHER LAWS OF NATURE

From that law of nature, by which we are obliged to transfer to another, such rights, as being retained, hinder the peace of mankind, there followeth a third; which is this, *that men perform their covenants made*: without which, covenants are in vain, and but empty words; and the right of all men to all things remaining, we are still in the condition of war.

And in this law of nature consisteth the fountain and original of JUSTICE. For where no covenant hath preceded, there hath no right been transferred, and every man has right to every thing; and consequently, no action can be unjust. But when a covenant is made, then to break it is *unjust*; and the definition of INJUSTICE, is no other than *the not performance of covenant*. And whosoever is not unjust, is *just*.

But because covenants of mutual trust, where there is a fear of not performance on either part, as hath been said in the former chapter, are invalid; though the original of justice be the making of covenants; yet injustice actually there can be none, till the cause of such fear be taken away; which while men are in the natural condition of war, cannot be done. Therefore before the names of just, and unjust can have place, there must be some coercive power, to compel men equally to the performance of their covenants, by the terror of some punishment, greater than the benefit they expect by the breach of their covenant; and to make good that propriety, which by mutual contract men acquire, in recompense of the universal right they abandon: and such power there is none before the erection of a commonwealth. And this is also to be gathered out of the ordinary definition of justice in the Schools: for they say, that *justice is the constant will of giving to every man his own*. And therefore where there is no *own*, that is no propriety, there is no injustice; and where there is no coercive power erected, that is, where there is no commonwealth, there is no propriety; all men having right to all things: therefore where there is no commonwealth, there nothing is unjust. So that the nature of justice, consisteth in keeping of valid covenants: but the validity of covenants begins not but with the constitution of a civil power, sufficient to compel men to keep them: and then it is also that propriety begins.

· · ·

Chapter XVII

OF THE CAUSES, GENERATION, AND DEFINITION OF A COMMONWEALTH

The final cause, end, or design of men, who naturally love liberty, and dominion over others, in the introduction of that restraint upon themselves, in which we see them live in commonwealths, is the foresight of their own preservation, and of a more contented life thereby; that is to say, of getting themselves out from that miserable condition of war, which is necessarily consequent, as hath been shown in Chapter XIII, to the natural passions of men, when there is no visible power to keep them in awe, and tie them by fear of punishment to the performance of their covenants, and observation of those laws of nature set down in the fourteenth and fifteenth chapters.

For the laws of nature, *as justice, equity, modesty, mercy,* and, in sum, *doing to others, as we would be done to,* of themselves, without the terror of some power, to cause them to be observed, are contrary to our natural passions that carry us to partiality, pride, revenge, and the like. And covenants, without the sword, are but words, and of no strength to secure a man at all. Therefore notwithstanding the laws of nature, which every one hath then kept, when he has the will to keep them, when he can do it safely, if there be no power erected, or not great enough for our security; every man will, and may lawfully rely on his own strength and art, for caution against all other men. And in all places, where men have lived by small families, to rob and spoil one another, has been a trade, and so far from being reputed against the law of nature, that the greater spoils they gained, the greater was their honour; and men observed no other laws therein, but the laws of honour; that is, to abstain from cruelty, leaving to men their lives, and instruments of husbandry. And as small families did then; so now do cities and kingdoms which are but greater families, for their own security, enlarge their dominions, upon all pretences of danger, and fear of invasion, or assistance that may be given to invaders, and endeavour as much as they can, to subdue, or weaken their neighbours, by open force, and secret arts, for want of other caution, justly; and are remembered for it in after ages with honour.

Nor is the joining together of a small number of men, that gives them this security; because in small numbers, small actions on the one side or the other, make the advantage of strength so great, as is sufficient to carry the victory; and therefore gives encouragement to an invasion. The multitude sufficient to confide in for our security, is not determined by any certain number, but by comparison with the enemy we fear; and is then sufficient, when the odds of the enemy is not of so visible and conspicuous moment, to determine the event of war, as to move him to attempt.

And be there never so great a multitude; yet if their actions be directed according to their particular judgments, and particular appetites, they can expect thereby no defence, nor protection, neither against a common enemy, nor against the injuries of one another. For being distracted in opinions concerning the best use and application of their strength, they do not help but hinder one another; and reduce their strength by mutual opposition to nothing: whereby they are easily, not only subdued by a very few that agree together; but also when there is no common enemy, they make war upon each other, for their particular interests. For if we could suppose a great multitude of men to consent in the observation of justice, and other laws of nature, without a common power to keep them all in awe; we might as well suppose all mankind to do the same; and then there neither would be, nor need to be any civil government, or commonwealth at all; because there would be peace without subjection.

Nor is it enough for the security, which men desire should last all the time of their life, that they be governed, and directed by one judgment, for a limited time; as in one battle, or one war. For though they obtain a victory by their unanimous endeavor against a foreign enemy; yet afterwards, when either they have no common enemy, or he that by one part is held for an enemy, is by another part held for a friend, they must needs by the difference of their interest dissolve, and fall again into a war amongst themselves.

It is true, that certain living creatures, as bees, and ants, live sociably one with another, which are therefore by Aristotle numbered amongst political creatures; and yet have no other direction, than their particular judgments and appetites; nor speech, whereby one of them can signify to another, what he thinks expedient for the common benefit: and therefore some man may perhaps desire to know, why mankind cannot do the same. To which I answer.

First, that men are continually in competition for honor and dignity, which these creatures are not; and consequently amongst men there ariseth on that ground, envy, and hatred, and finally war; but amongst these not so.

Secondly, that amongst these creatures, the common good differeth not from the private; and being by nature inclined to their private, they procure thereby the common benefit. But man, whose joy consisteth in comparing himself with other men, can relish nothing but what is eminent.

Thirdly, that these creatures, having not, as man, the use of their reason, do not see, nor think they see any fault, in the administration of their common business; whereas amongst men, there are very many, that think themselves wiser, and abler to govern the public, better than the rest; and these strive to perform and innovate, one this way, another that way, and thereby bring it into distraction and civil war.

Fourthly, that these creatures, though they have some use of voice, in making known to one another their desires, and other affections; yet they want that art of words, by which some men can represent to others, that which is good, in the likeness of evil; and evil, in the likeness of good; and augment, or diminish the apparent greatness of good and evil; discontenting men, and troubling their peace at their pleasure.

Fifthly, irrational creatures can not distinguish between *injury*, and *damage*; and therefore as long as they be at ease, they are not offended with their fellows; whereas man is then most troublesome, when he is most at ease: for then it is that he loves to shew his wisdom, and control the actions of them that govern the commonwealth.

Lastly, the agreement of these creatures is natural; that of men, is by covenant only, which is artificial: and therefore it is no wonder if there be somewhat else required, besides covenant, to make their agreement constant and lasting; which is a common power, to keep them in awe, and to direct their actions to the common benefit.

The only way to erect such a common power, as may be able to defend them from the invasion of foreigners, and the injuries of one another, and thereby to secure them in such sort, as that by their own industry, and by the fruits of the earth, they may nourish themselves and live contentedly; is, to confer all their power and strength upon one man, or upon one assembly of men, that may reduce all their wills, by plurality of voices, unto one will: which is as much as to say, to appoint one man, or assembly of men, to bear their person; and every one to own, and acknowledge himself to be author of whatsoever he that so beareth their person, shall act, or cause to be acted, in those things which concern the common peace and safety; and therein to submit their wills, every one to his will, and their judgments, to his judgment. This is more than consent, or concord; it is a real unity of them all, in one and the same person, made by covenant of every man with every man, in such manner, as if every man should say to every man, *I authorise and give up my right of governing myself, to this man, or to this assembly of men, on this condition, that thou give up thy right to him, and authorise all his actions in like manner*. This done, the multitude so united in one person, is called a COMMONWEALTH, in Latin CIVITAS. This is the generation of that great LEVIATHAN, or rather, to speak more reverently, of that *mortal god*, to which we owe under the *immortal God*, our peace and defence. For by this authority, given him by every particular man in the commonwealth, he hath the use of so much power and strength conferred on him, that by terror thereof, he is enabled to perform the wills of them all, to peace at home, and mutual aid against their enemies abroad. And in him consisteth the essence of the commonwealth; which, to define it, is *one person of whose acts a great multitude, by mutual covenants one with another, have made themselves every one the author, to the end he may use the strength and means of them all, as he shall think expedient, for their peace and common defence*.

And he that carrieth this person, is called SOVEREIGN, and said to have *sovereign power*; and every one besides, his SUBJECT.

John Locke

Just as the political philosophy of Thomas Hobbes was in part a reaction against the anarchy of the 1640s in England, so that of John Locke (1632–1704) represented a response to the Glorious Revolution of 1688. As Locke stated in the preface of his *Of Civil Government,* he hoped "to establish the throne of our present King William; to make good his title, in the consent of the people … and to justify to the world the people of England, whose love of their just and natural rights, with their resolution to preserve them, saved the nation when it was on the very birth of slavery and ruin."

Locke was himself involved in the crises that led to the revolution. As physician and secretary to the earl of Shaftesbury, a prominent Whig politician and leader of the opposition to Charles II, he shared the political fortunes of his employer. When Shaftesbury, implicated in a plot to prevent the accession of James II, fled to Holland in 1683, Locke was forced to follow him. During his exile in Holland Locke wrote *Of Civil Government,* which is divided into two treatises. The first is a refutation of the theory of the divine right of kings, and the second (from which the following selection is taken) is a statement of his own political theory. Although Locke's second treatise, like Hobbes's *Leviathan,* grew out of the author's reaction to a particular political situation, both in its content and in its influence it far transcended the local scene. It was the first philosophical statement of the modern position known as liberalism, a position to be reformulated by Jeremy Bentham in the eighteenth century, John Stuart Mill in the nineteenth, and John Dewey in the twentieth. The second treatise had its greatest practical effects during the eighteenth century, when the leaders of the American and French revolutions found in it an intellectual justification for their cause. Many of the passages in the Declaration of Independence, for example, paraphrase the language of the second treatise.

It is interesting to compare and contrast Locke's view of human nature and the justification of legitimate power of government with that of Hobbes.

Consider the following questions as you study the text below.

1. Compare Locke's and Hobbes's visions of the "state of nature." How did their ideas about the state of nature shape their ideas about government?

2. According to Locke, what was the purpose of government? Under what conditions could a people dissolve their current government and form a new one?

Of Civil Government

Book II, Chapter 1

. . .

I think it may not be amiss to set down what I take to be political power; that the power of a magistrate over a subject may be distinguished from that of a father over his children, a master over his servants, a husband over his wife, and a lord over his slave. All which distinct powers happening sometimes together in the same man, if he be considered under these different relations, it may help us to distinguish these powers one from another, and show the difference betwixt a ruler of a commonwealth, a father of a family, and a captain of a galley.

Political power, then, I take to be a right of making laws with penalties of death, and consequently all less penalties, for the regulating and preserving of property, and of employing the force of the community, in the execution of such laws, and in the defence of the commonwealth from foreign injury; and all this only for the public good.

Chapter II

OF THE STATE OF NATURE

To understand political power right, and derive it from its original, we must consider what state all men are naturally in, and that is, a state of perfect freedom to order their actions and dispose of their possessions and persons, as they think fit, within the bounds of the law of nature; without asking leave, or depending upon the will of any other man.

A state also of equality, wherein all the power and jurisdiction is reciprocal, no one having more than another; there being nothing more evident, than that creatures of the same species and rank, promiscuously born to all the same advantages of nature, and the use of the same faculties, should also be equal one amongst another without subordination or subjection; unless the lord and master of them all should, by any manifest declaration of his will, set one above another, and confer on him, by an evident and clear appointment, an undoubted right to dominion and sovereignty. ...

"Of Civil Government," in *The Works of John Locke*, 12th ed., Vol. IV.

But though this be a state of liberty, yet it is not a state of license: though man in that state have an uncontrollable liberty to dispose of his person or possessions, yet he has not liberty to destroy himself, or so much as any creature in his possession, but where some nobler use than its bare preservation calls for it. The state of nature has a law of nature to govern it, which obliges every one: and reason, which is that law, teaches all mankind, who will but consult it, that being all equal and independent, no one ought to harm another in his life, health, liberty, or possessions: for men being all the workmanship of one omnipotent and infinitely wise Maker; all the servants of one sovereign master, sent into the world by his order, and about his business; they are his property, whose workmanship they are, made to last during his, not another's pleasure: and being furnished with like faculties, sharing all in one community of nature, there cannot be supposed any such subordination among us, that may authorize us to destroy another, as if we were made for one another's uses, as the inferior ranks of creatures are for ours. Every one, as he is bound to preserve himself, and not to quit his station wilfully, so by the like reason, when his own preservation comes not in competition, ought he, as much as he can, to preserve the rest of mankind, and may not, unless it be to do justice to an offender, take away or impair the life, or what tends to the preservation of life, the liberty, health, limb, or goods of another.

And that all men may be restrained from invading others' rights, and from doing hurt to one another, and the law of nature be observed, which willeth the peace and preservation of all mankind, the execution of the law of nature is, in that state, put into every man's hands, whereby every one has a right to punish the transgressors of that law to such a degree as may hinder its violation: for the law of nature would, as all other laws that concern men in this world, be in vain, if there were nobody that in the state of nature had a power to execute the law, and thereby preserve the innocent and restrain offenders. And if any one in the state of nature may punish another for any evil he has done, every one may do so: for in that state of perfect equality, where naturally there is no superiority or jurisdiction of one over another, what any may do in prosecution of that law, every one must needs have a right to do.

And thus, in the state of nature, "one man comes by a power over another"; but yet no absolute or arbitrary power, to use a criminal, when he has got him in his hands, according to the passionate heats, or boundless extravagancy of his own will; but only to retribute to him, so far as calm reason and conscience dictate, what is proportionate to his transgression; which is so much as may serve for reparation and restraint: for these two are the only reasons, why one man may lawfully do harm to another, which is that we call punishment. In transgressing the law of nature, the offender declares himself to live by another rule than that of reason and common equity, which is that measure God has set to the actions of men, for their mutual security;

and so he becomes dangerous to mankind, the tie, which is to secure them from injury and violence, being slighted and broken by him. Which being a trespass against the whole species, and the peace and safety of it, provided for by the law of nature; every man upon this score, by the right he hath to preserve mankind in general, may restrain, or, where it is necessary, destroy things noxious to them, and so may bring such evil on any one, who hath transgressed that law, as may make him repent the doing of it, and thereby deter him, and by his example others, from doing the like mischief. And in this case, and upon this ground, "every man hath a right to punish the offender, and be executioner of the law of nature."

. . .

Chapter III

OF THE STATE OF WAR

The state of war is a state of enmity and destruction: and therefore declaring by word or action, not a passionate and hasty, but a sedate settled design upon another man's life, puts him in a state of war with him against whom he has declared such an intention, and so has exposed his life to the other's power to be taken away by him, or any one that joins with him in his defence, and espouses his quarrel; it being reasonable and just, I should have a right to destroy that which threatens me with destruction; for, by the fundamental law of nature, man being to be preserved as much as possible, when all cannot be preserved, the safety of the innocent is to be preferred: and one may destroy a man who makes war upon him, or has discovered an enmity to his being, for the same reason that he may kill a wolf or a lion; because such men are not under the ties of the common law of reason, have no other rule, than that of force and violence, and so may be treated as beasts of prey, those dangerous and noxious creatures, that will be sure to destroy him whenever he falls into their power.

And hence it is, that he who attempts to get another man in to his absolute power, does thereby put himself into a state of war with him; it being to be understood as a declaration of a design upon his life: for I have reason to conclude, that he who would get me into his power without my consent, would use me as he pleased when he got me there, and destroy me too when he had a fancy to it; for nobody can desire to have me in his absolute power, unless it be to compel me by force to that which is against the right of my freedom, *i.e.*, make me a slave. To be free from such force is the only security of my preservation; and reason bids me look on him, as an enemy to my preservation, who would take away that freedom which is the fence to it; so that he who makes an attempt to enslave me, thereby puts himself into a state of war with me. He that, in the state of nature, would take away the freedom that belongs to any one in that state, must necessarily be supposed to have a design to take away everything else, that freedom being the foundation of all the rest; as he that, in the state of society, would take away the freedom belonging to those of that society or commonwealth, must be supposed to design to take away from them every thing else, and so be looked on as in a state of war.

This makes it lawful for a man to kill a thief, who has not in the least hurt him, nor declared any design upon his life, any farther than, by the use of force, so to get him in his power, as to take away his money, or what he pleases, from him; because using force, where he has no right, to get me into his power, let his pretence be what it will, I have no reason to suppose, that he, who would take away my liberty, would not, when he had me in his power, take away every thing else. And therefore it is lawful for me to treat him as one who has put himself into a state of war with me, *i.e.*, kill him if I can; for to that hazard does he justly expose himself, whoever introduces a state of war, and is aggressor in it.

And here we have the plain "difference between the state of nature and the state of war," which however some men have confounded, are as far distant as a state of peace, goodwill, mutual assistance and preservation, and a state of enmity, malice, violence and mutual destruction, are one from another. Men living together according to reason, without a common superior on earth, with authority to judge between them, is properly the state of nature. But force, or a declared design of force, upon the person of another where there is no common superior on earth to appeal to for relief, is the state of war: and it is the want of such an appeal gives a man the right of war even against an aggressor, though he be in society and a fellow-subject.

. . .

Chapter IV

OF SLAVERY

The natural liberty of man is to be free from any superior power on earth, and not to be under the will or legislative authority of man, but to have only the law of nature for his rule. The liberty of man, in society, is to be under no other legislative power, but that established, by consent, in the commonwealth; nor under the dominion of any will, or restraint of any law, but what that legislative shall enact, according to the trust put in it. Freedom then is not what Sir Robert Filmer[1] tells us, "a liberty for every one to do what he lists, to

---

[1][English political theorist and a defender of the divine right of kings (c. 1598–1653)—*Ed.*]

live as he pleases, and not be tied by any laws": but freedom of men under government is, to have a standing rule to live by, common to every one of that society, and made by the legislative power erected in it; a liberty to follow my own will in all things, where the rule prescribes not; and not to be subject to the inconstant, uncertain, unknown, arbitrary will of another man: as freedom of nature is, to be under no other restraint but the law of nature.

This freedom from absolute, arbitrary power, is so necessary to, and closely joined with a man's preservation, that he cannot part with it, but by what forfeits his preservation and life together.

.   .   .

Chapter V

OF PROPERTY

God, who hath given the world to men in common, hath also given them reason to make use of it to the best advantage of life, and convenience. The earth, and all that is therein, is given to men for the support and comfort of their being. And though all the fruits it naturally produces, and beasts it feeds, belong to mankind in common, as they are produced by the spontaneous hand of nature; and nobody has originally a private dominion, exclusive of the rest of mankind, in any of them, as they are thus in their natural state; yet being given for the use of men, there must of necessity be a means to appropriate them some way or other, before they can be of any use, or at all beneficial to any particular man. The fruit, or venison, which nourishes the wild Indian, who knows no enclosure, and is still a tenant in common, must be his, and so his, *i.e.*, a part of him, that another can no longer have any right to it, before it can do him any good for the support of his life.

Though the earth, and all inferior creatures, be common to all men, yet every man has a property in his own person: this nobody has any right to but himself. The labour of his body, and the work of his hands, we may say, are properly his. Whatsoever then he removes out of the state that nature hath provided, and left it in, he hath mixed his labour with, and joined it to something that is his own, and thereby makes it his property. It being by him removed from the common state nature hath placed it in, it hath by his labour something annexed to it, that excludes the common right of other men. For this labour being the unquestionable property of the labourer, no man but he can have a right to what that is once joined to, at least where there is enough, and as good, left in common for others.

He that is nourished by the acorns he picked up under an oak, or the apples he gathered by the trees in the wood, has certainly appropriated them to himself. Nobody can deny but the nourishment is his. I ask then, when did they begin to be his? when he digested? or when he eat? or when he boiled? or when he brought them home? or when he picked them up? and it is plain, if the first gathering made them not his, nothing else could. That labour put a distinction between them and common: that added something to them more than nature, the common mother of all, had done and so they became his private right. And will any one say he had no right to those acorns or apples he thus appropriated, because he had not the consent of all mankind to make them his? was it a robbery thus to assume to himself what belonged to all in common? If such a consent as that was necessary, man had starved, notwithstanding the plenty God had given him. We see in commons, which remain so by compact, that it is the taking any part of what is common, and removing it out of the state nature leaves it in, which begins the property; without which the common is of no use. And the taking of this or that part does not depend on the express consent of all the commoners. Thus the grass my horse has bit; the turfs my servant has cut; and the ore I have digged in any place, where I have a right to them in common with others, become my property, without the assignation or consent of any body. The labour that was mine, removing them out of that common state they were in, hath fixed my property in them.

. . .

It will perhaps be objected to this, that "if gathering the acorns, or other fruits of the earth, &c. makes a right to them, then any one may engross as much as he will." To which I answer. Not so. The same law of nature, that does by this means give us property, does also bound this property too. "God has given us all things richly" I Tim. vi. 17, is the voice of reason confirmed by inspiration. But how far has he given it us? To enjoy. As much as any one can make use of to any advantage of life before it spoils, so much he may by his labor fix a property in: whatever is beyond this is more than his share, and belongs to others. Nothing was made by God for man to spoil or destroy. And thus, considering the plenty of natural provisions there was a long time in the world, and the few spenders; and to how small a part of that provision the industry of one man could extend itself; and engross it to the prejudice of others; especially keeping within the bounds, set by reason, of what might serve for his use; there could be then little room for quarrels or contentions about property so established.

But the chief matter of property being now not the fruits of the earth, and the beasts that subsist on it, but the earth itself; as that which takes in, and carries with it all the rest; I think it is plain, that property in that too is acquired as the former. As much land as a man tills, plants, improves, cultivates, and can use the product of, so much is his property. He by his labour does, as it were, enclose it from the common. Nor will it invalidate his right,

to say every body else has an equal title to it, and therefore he cannot appropriate, he cannot enclose, without the consent of all his fellow commoners, all
mankind. God, when he gave the world in common to all mankind, commanded man also to labour, and the penury of his condition required it of
him. God and his reason commanded him to subdue the earth, *i.e.*, improve it
for the benefit of life, and therein lay out something upon it that was his own,
his labour. He that, in obedience to this command of God, subdued, tilled,
and sowed any part of it, thereby annexed to it something that was his property, which another had no title to, nor could without injury take from him.

.   .   .

Nor is it so strange, as perhaps before consideration it may appear, that
the property of labour should be able to over-balance the community of
land; for it is labour indeed that put the difference of value on every thing;
and let any one consider what the difference is between an acre of land
planted with tobacco or sugar, sown with wheat or barley, and an acre of the
same land lying in common, without any husbandry upon it, and he will
find, that the improvement of labour makes the far greater part of the value.
I think it will be but a very modest computation to say, that of the products
of the earth useful to the life of man, nine-tenths are the effects of labour; nay,
if we will rightly estimate things as they come to our use, and cast up the
several expenses about them, what in them is purely owing to nature, and
what to labour, we shall find, that in most of them ninety-nine hundredths
are wholly to be put on the account of labour.

.   .   .

Chapter VII

OF POLITICAL OR CIVIL SOCIETY

Whenever … any number of men are so united into one society, as to
quit everyone his executive power of the law of nature, and to resign it to the
public, there and there only is a political, or civil society. And this is done,
wherever any number of men, in the state of nature, enter into society to
make one people, one body politic, under one supreme government; or else
when any one joins himself to, and incorporates with any government already made: for hereby he authorizes the society, or, which is all one, the legislative thereof, to make laws for him, as the public good of the society shall
require; to the execution whereof, his own assistance (as to his own degrees)
is due. And this puts men out of a state of nature into that of a commonwealth, by setting up a judge on earth, with authority to determine all the

controversies, and redress the injuries that may happen to any member of the commonwealth: which judge is the legislative, or magistrate appointed by it. And wherever there are any number of men, however associated, that have no such decisive power to appeal to, there they are still in the state of nature.

Hence it is evident, that absolute monarchy, which by some men is counted the only government in the world, is indeed inconsistent with civil society, and so can be no form of civil government at all; for the end of civil society being to avoid and remedy these inconveniences of the state of nature, which necessarily follow from every man being judge in his own case, by setting up a known authority, to which every one of that society may appeal upon any injury received, or controversy that may arise, and which every one of the society ought to obey; wherever any persons are, who have not such an authority to appeal to for the decision of any difference between them, there those persons are still in the state of nature and so is every absolute prince, in respect of those who are under his dominion.

For he being supposed to have all, both legislative and executive power in himself alone, there is no judge to be found, no appeal lies open to any one, who may fairly and indifferently, and with authority decide, and from whose decision relief and redress may be expected of any injury or inconveniency that may be suffered from the prince, or by his order: so that such a man, however intitled, czar, or grand seignior, or how you please, is as much in the state of nature, with all under his dominion, as he is with the rest of mankind: for wherever any two men are, who have no standing rule, and common judge of appeal to on earth, for the determination of controversies of right betwixt them, there they are still in the state of nature, and under all the inconveniences of it, with only this woeful difference to the subject, or rather slave of an absolute prince; that whereas in the ordinary state of nature he has a liberty to judge of his right, and, according to the best of his power, to maintain it; now whenever his property is invaded by the will and order of his monarch, he has not only no appeal, as those in society ought to have, but, as if he were degraded from the common state of rational creatures, is denied a liberty to judge of, or to defend his right; and so is exposed to all the misery and inconveniences, that a man can fear from one, who being in the unrestrained state of nature, is yet corrupted with flattery, and armed with power.

For he that thinks absolute power purifies men's blood, and corrects the baseness of human nature, need read but the history of this or any other age, to be convinced of the contrary.

.   .   .

Chapter VIII

OF THE BEGINNING OF POLITICAL SOCIETIES

Men being, as has been said, by nature, all free, equal, and independent, no one can be put out of this estate, and subjected to the political power of another, without his own consent. The only way, whereby any one divests himself of his natural liberty, and puts on the bonds of civil society, is by agreeing with other men to join and unite into a community, for their comfortable, safe, and peaceable living one amongst another, in a secure enjoyment of their properties, and a greater security against any, that are not of it. This any number of men may do, because it injures not the freedom of the rest; they are left as they were in the liberty of the state of nature. When any number of men have so consented to make one community or government, they are thereby presently incorporated, and make one body politic, wherein the majority have a right to act and conclude the rest.

For when any number of men have, by the consent of every individual, made a community, they have thereby made that community one body, with a power to act as one body, which is only by the will and determination of the majority: for that which acts any community, being only the consent of the individuals of it, and it being necessary to that which is one body to move one way; it is necessary the body should move that way whither the greater force carries it, which is the consent of the majority: or else it is impossible it should act or continue one body, one community, which the consent of every individual that united into it, agreed that it should; and so every one is bound by that consent to be concluded by the majority. And therefore we see, that in assemblies, impowered to act by positive laws, where no number is set by that positive law which impowers them, the act of the majority passes for the act of the whole, and of course determines; as having, by the law of nature and reason, the power of the whole.

And thus every man, by consenting with others to make one body politic under one government, puts himself under an obligation, to every one of that society, to submit to the determination of the majority, and to be concluded by it; or else this original compact, whereby he with others incorporate into one society, would signify nothing, and be no compact, if he be left free, and under no other ties than he was in before in the state of nature.

.   .   .

Chapter IX

OF THE ENDS OF POLITICAL SOCIETY AND GOVERNMENT

If man in the state of nature be so free, as has been said; if he be absolute lord of his own person and possessions, equal to the greatest, and subject to nobody, why will he part with his freedom? why will he give up his empire, and subject himself to the dominion and control of any other power? To which it is obvious to answer, that though in the state of nature he hath such a right, yet the enjoyment of it is very uncertain, and constantly exposed to the invasion of others; for all being kings as much as he, every man his equal, and the greater part no strict observers of equity and justice, the enjoyment of the property he has in this state is very unsafe, very unsecure. This makes him willing to quit a condition, which however free, is full of fears and continual dangers: and it is not without reason, that he seeks out, and is willing to join in society with others, who are already united, or have a mind to unite, for the mutual preservation of their lives, liberties, and estates, which I call by the general name, property.

The great and chief end, therefore, of men's uniting into commonwealths, and putting themselves under government, is the preservation of their property. To which in the state of nature there are many things wanting.

First, There wants an established, settled, known law, received and allowed by common consent to be the standard of right and wrong, and the common measure to decide all controversies between them; for though the law of nature be plain and intelligible to all rational creatures; yet men being biassed by their interest, as well as ignorant for want of studying it, are not apt to allow of it as a law binding to them in the application of it to their particular cases.

Secondly, In the state of nature there wants a known and indifferent judge, with authority to determine all differences according to the established law: for every one in that state being both judge and executioner of the law of nature, men being partial to themselves, passion and revenge is very apt to carry them too far, and with too much heat, in their own cases; as well as negligence and unconcernedness, to make them too remiss in other men's.

Thirdly, In the state of nature, there often wants power to back and support the sentence when right, and to give it due execution. They who by any injustice offend, will seldom fail, where they are able, by force to make good their injustice; such resistance many times makes the punishment dangerous, and frequently destructive, to those who attempt it.

Thus mankind, notwithstanding all the privileges of the state of nature, being but in an ill condition, while they remain in it, are quickly driven into society. Hence it comes to pass that we seldom find any number of men live any time together in this state. The inconveniences that they are therein exposed to, by the irregular and uncertain exercise of the power every man has of punishing the transgressions of others, make them take sanctuary under the established laws of government, and therein seek the preservation of their property. It is this makes them so willingly give up every one his single power of punishing, to be exercised by such alone, as shall be appointed to it amongst them; and by such rules as the community, or those authorized by them to that purpose, shall agree on. And in this we have the original right of both the legislative and executive power, as well as of the governments and societies themselves.

.   .   .

But though men, when they enter into society, give up the equality, liberty, and executive power they had in the state of nature, into the hands of the society, to be so far disposed of by the legislature, as the good of the society shall require; yet it being only with an intention in every one the better to preserve himself, his liberty and property; (for no rational creature can be supposed to change his condition with an intention to be worse) the power of the society, or legislative constituted by them, can never be supposed to extend farther, than the common good; but is obliged to secure every one's property, by providing against those three defects above mentioned, that made the state of nature so unsafe and uneasy. And so whoever has the legislative or supreme power of any commonwealth, is bound to govern by established standing laws, promulgated and known to the people, and not by extemporary decrees; by indifferent and upright judges, who are to decide controversies by those laws; and to employ the force of the community at home, only in the execution of such laws; or abroad to prevent or redress foreign injuries, and secure the community from inroads and invasion. And all this to be directed to no other end, but the peace, safety, and public good of the people.

.   .   .

Chapter XIII

OF THE SUBORDINATION OF THE POWERS OF THE COMMONWEALTH

Though in a constituted commonwealth, standing upon its own basis, and acting according to its own nature, that is, acting for the preservation of the community, there can be but one supreme power, which is the legislative, to which all the rest are and must be subordinate; yet the legislative being only a fiduciary power to act for certain ends, there remains still "in the people a supreme power to remove or alter the legislative," when they find the legislative act contrary to the trust reposed in them: for all power given with trust for the attaining an end, being limited by that end; whenever that end is manifestly neglected or opposed, the trust must necessarily be forfeited, and the power devolve into the hands of those that gave it, who may place it anew where they shall think best for their safety and security. And thus the community perpetually retains a supreme power of saving themselves from the attempts and designs of any body, even of their legislators, whenever they shall be so foolish, or so wicked, as to try and carry on designs against the liberties and properties of the subject: for no man, or society of men, having a power to deliver up their preservation, or consequently the means of it, to the absolute will and arbitrary dominion of another; whenever any one shall go about to bring them into such a slavish condition, they will always have a right to preserve what they have not a power to part with; and to rid themselves of those who invade this fundamental, sacred, and unalterable law of self-preservation, for which they entered into society. And thus the community may be said in this respect to be always the supreme power.

. . .

Chapter XIX

OF THE DISSOLUTION OF GOVERNMENT

The reason why men enter into society, is the preservation of their property; and the end why they choose and authorize a legislative is, that there may be laws made, and rules set, as guards and fences to the properties of all the members of the society: to limit the power, and moderate the dominion, of every part and member of the society: for since it can never be supposed to be the will of the society, that the legislature should have a power to destroy that which every one designs to secure by entering into society, and for which the people submitted themselves to legislators of their own making; whenever the legislators endeavor to take away and destroy the property of the people, or to reduce them to slavery under arbitrary power, they put themselves into a state of war with the people, who are thereupon absolved from any farther obedience, and are left to the common refuge, which God hath provided for all men, against force and violence. Whensoever therefore the legislative shall transgress this fundamental rule of society; and either by ambition, fear, folly or corruption, endeavour to grasp themselves or put into the hands of any other, an absolute power over the lives, liberties, and estates of the people, by this breach of trust they forfeit the power the people had put into their hands for quite contrary ends, and it devolves to the people, who have a right to resume their original liberty, and, by the establishment of a new legislative, (such as they shall think fit) provide for their own safety and security, which is the end for which they are in society. What I have said here, concerning the legislative in general holds true also concerning the supreme executor, who having a double trust put in him, both to have a part in the legislative, and the supreme execution of the law, acts against both, when he goes about to set up his own arbitrary will as the law of the society. He acts also contrary to his trust, when he either employs the force, treasure, and offices of the society to corrupt the representatives, and gain them to his purposes; or openly pre-engages the electors, and prescribes to their choice, such, whom he has, by solicitations, threats, promises, or otherwise, won to his designs: and employs them to bring in such, who have promised beforehand what to vote, and what to enact. Thus to regulate candidates and electors, and new-model the ways of election, what is it but to cut up the government by the roots, and poison the very fountain of public security?

. . .

But it will be said, this hypothesis lays a ferment for frequent rebellion. To which I answer,

First, no more than any other hypothesis: for when the people are made miserable, and find themselves exposed to the ill-usage of arbitrary power, cry up their governors as much as you will, for sons of Jupiter; let them be sacred or divine, descended, or authorized from heaven; give them out for whom or what you please, the same will happen. The people generally ill-treated, and contrary to right, will be ready upon any occasion to ease themselves of a burden that sits heavy upon them. They will wish, and seek for the opportunity, which in the change, weakness, and accidents of human affairs, seldom delays long to offer itself. He must have lived but a little while in the world, who has not seen examples of this in his time; and he must have read very little, who cannot produce examples of it in all sorts of governments in the world.

Secondly, I answer, such revolutions happen not upon every little mismanagement in public affairs. Great mistakes in the ruling part, many wrong and inconvenient laws, and all the slips of human frailty, will be borne by the people without mutiny or murmur. But if a long train of abuses, prevarications, and artifices, all tending the same way, make the design visible to the people, and they cannot but feel what they lie under, and see whither they are going; it is not to be wondered, that they should then rouse themselves, and endeavor to put the rule into such hands which may secure to them the ends for which government was at first erected.

. . .

Whosoever uses force without right, as every one does in society, who does it without law, puts himself into a state of war with those against whom he so used it; and in that state all former ties are cancelled, all other rights cease, and every one has a right to defend himself, and to resist the aggressor.

Adam Smith

European economic practices before Adam Smith were guided by the theory of mercantilism. Often described as the doctrine that a nation's wealth consists in the amount of money, in the form of precious metals, it possesses, it follows from mercantile theory that the nation should adopt the policy of maximizing its exports (particularly in the form of valuable manufactured goods) and minimizing its imports, thus increasing its intake of bullion. But this is only a superficial account of a much more complex theory. To understand mercantilism one must view it in its historical context—that of the emerging nation-states of Europe. So understood, mercantilism, like warfare, can be seen as one of the methods employed by these burgeoning nations to increase their power, particularly in relation to that of their neighbors. Although one of the means to this end was to achieve a favorable balance of trade, others included the encouragement of manufacturing industries, the increase of an urban over a rural population, the acquisition of colonies (particularly in the Western hemisphere), and others. But most important was the idea that economics was an organ of national power and that, therefore, the state should exercise tight control over every facet of its economy.

Although the mercantilist system was by no means a failure in serving the needs of the times, it began to come under attack during the eighteenth century. Perhaps the sharpest, and certainly the most influential, of its critics was the Scotsman Adam Smith (1723–1790). By profession Smith was not an economist but a philosopher, being for several years a professor of moral philosophy at the University of Glasgow. His great work, whose full title is *An Inquiry into the Nature and Causes of the Wealth of Nations*, was published in 1776.

Smith focused his attack on mercantilism on its central tenet—that the economic life of a nation should be under the strict control of the government. Rather than encouraging economic activity, he argued, such a policy increasingly stifles it. In his mind the best way to maximize the wealth of a nation is to allow each individual to pursue his own interests with a minimum of restraints. Thus he advocated the economics that has come to be known as the free enterprise system, and his book, *The Wealth of Nations*, laid the theoretical foundations on which modern capitalism was to develop.

Consider the following questions as you study the text below.

1. With what assumptions of mercantilist theory did Smith disagree? Did Smith believe there was a finite amount of wealth in the world? Why or why not?

2. Why did Smith oppose taxes and tariffs? Did he believe that free trade would ever be established in England? Why or why not?

An Inquiry into the Nature and Causes of the Wealth of Nations

Book IV, Chapter II

OF RESTRAINTS UPON THE IMPORTATION FROM FOREIGN COUNTRIES OF SUCH GOODS AS CAN BE PRODUCED AT HOME

By restraining, either by high duties, or by absolute prohibitions, the importation of such goods from foreign countries as can be produced at home, the monopoly of the home-market is more or less secured to the domestic industry employed in producing them. Thus the prohibition of importing either live cattle or salt provisions from foreign countries secures to the graziers of Great Britain the monopoly of the home-market for butchers'-meat. The high duties upon the importation of corn, which in times of moderate plenty amount to a prohibition, give a like advantage to the growers of that commodity. The prohibition of the importation of foreign woollens is equally favourable to the woollen manufactures. The silk manufacture, though altogether employed upon foreign materials, has lately obtained the same advantage. The linen manufacture has not yet obtained it, but is making great strides towards it. Many other sorts of manufactures have, in the same manner, obtained in Great Britain, either altogether, or very nearly a monopoly against their countrymen. The variety of goods of which the importation into Great Britain is prohibited, either absolutely, or under certain circumstances, greatly exceeds what can easily be suspected by those who are not well acquainted with the laws of the customs.

That this monopoly of the home-market frequently gives great encouragement to that particular species of industry which enjoys it, and frequently turns toward that employment a greater share of both the labour and stock of the society than would otherwise have gone to it, cannot be doubted. But whether it tends either to increase the general industry of the society, or to give it the most advantageous direction, is not, perhaps, altogether so evident.

Adam Smith, *An Inquiry into the Nature and Causes of the Wealth of Nations*, 8th ed.

The general industry of the society never can exceed what the capital of the society can employ. As the number of workmen that can be kept in employment by any particular person must bear a certain proportion to his capital, so the number of those that can be continually employed by all the members of a great society, must bear a certain proportion to the whole capital of that society, and never can exceed that proportion. No regulation of commerce can increase the quantity of industry in any society beyond what its capital can maintain. It can only divert a part of it into a direction into which it might not otherwise have gone; and it is by no means certain that this artificial direction is likely to be more advantageous to the society than that into which it would have gone of its own accord.

Every individual is continually exerting himself to find out the most advantageous employment for whatever capital he can command. It is his own advantage, indeed, and not that of the society, which he has in view. But the study of his own advantage naturally, or rather necessarily leads him to prefer that employment which is most advantageous to the society.

First, every individual endeavours to employ his capital as near home as he can, and consequently as much as he can in the support of domestic industry; provided always that he can thereby obtain the ordinary, or not a great deal less than the ordinary profits of stock.

Thus, upon equal or nearly equal profits, every wholesale merchant naturally prefers the home-trade to the foreign trade of consumption, and the foreign trade of consumption to the carrying trade. In the home-trade his capital is never so long out of his sight as it frequently is in the foreign trade of consumption. He can know better the character and situation of the persons whom he trusts, and if he should happen to be deceived, he knows better the laws of the country from which he must seek redress. ... Upon equal, or only nearly equal profits, therefore, every individual naturally inclines to employ his capital in the manner in which it is likely to afford the greater support to domestic industry, and to give revenue and employment to the greatest number of people of his own country.

Secondly, every individual who employs his capital in the support of domestic industry, necessarily endeavours so to direct that industry, that its produce may be of the greatest possible value.

The produce of industry is what it adds to the subject or materials upon which it is employed. In proportion as the value of this produce is great or small, so will likewise be the profits of the employer. But it is only for the sake of profit that any man employs a capital in the support of industry; and he will always, therefore, endeavour to employ it in the support of that industry of which the produce is likely to be of the greatest value, or to exchange for the greatest quantity either of money or of other goods.

But the annual revenue of every society is always precisely equal to the exchangeable value of the whole annual produce of its industry, or rather is precisely the same thing with that exchangeable value. As every individual, endeavours as much as he can both to employ his capital in the support of domestic industry, and so to direct that industry that its produce may be of the greatest value; every individual necessarily labours to render the annual revenue of the society as great as he can. He generally, indeed, neither intends to promote the public interest, nor knows how much he is promoting it. By preferring the support of domestic to that of foreign industry, he intends only his own security; and by directing that industry in such a manner as its produce may be of the greatest value, he intends only his own gain, and he is in this, as in many other cases, led by an invisible hand to promote an end which was no part of his intention. Nor is it always the worse for the society that it was no part of it. By pursuing his own interest he frequently promotes that of the society more effectually than when he really intends to promote it. I have never known much good done by those who affected to trade for the public good. It is an affectation, indeed, not very common among merchants, and very few words need be employed in dissuading them from it.

What is the species of domestic industry which his capital can employ, and of which the produce is likely to be of the greatest value, every individual, it is evident, can, in his local situation, judge much better than any statesman or lawgiver can do for him. The statesman, who should attempt to direct private people in what manner they ought to employ their capitals, would not only load himself with a most unnecessary attention, but assume an authority which could safely be trusted, not only to no single person, but to no council or senate whatever, and which would nowhere be so dangerous as in the hands of a man who had folly and presumption enough to fancy himself fit to exercise it.

To give the monopoly of the home-market to the produce of domestic industry, in any particular art or manufacture, is in some measure to direct private people in what manner they ought to employ their capitals, and must, in almost all cases, be either a useless or a hurtful regulation. If the produce of domestic can be brought there as cheap as that of foreign industry, the regulation is evidently useless. If it cannot, it must generally be hurtful. It is the maxim of every prudent master of a family, never to attempt to make at home what it will cost him more to make than to buy. The taylor does not attempt to make his own shoes, but buys them of the shoemaker. The shoemaker does not attempt to make his own clothes, but employs a taylor. The farmer attempts to make neither the one nor the other, but employs those different artificers. All of them find it for their interest to employ their whole industry in a way in which they have some advantage over their neighbours, and to purchase with a part of its produce, or what is the same thing, with the price of a part of it, whatever else they have occasion for.

What is prudence in the conduct of every family, can scarce be folly in that of a great kingdom. If a foreign country can supply us with a commodity cheaper than we ourselves can make it, better buy it of them with some part of the produce of our own industry, employed in a way in which we have some advantage. The general industry of the country, being always in proportion to the capital which employs it, will not thereby be diminished, no more than that of the above-mentioned artificers; but only left to find out the way in which it can be employed with the greatest advantage. It is certainly not employed to the greatest advantage, when it is thus directed towards an object which it can buy cheaper than it can make. The value of its annual produce is certainly more or less diminished, when it is thus turned away from producing commodities evidently of more value than the commodity which it is directed to produce. According to the supposition, that commodity could be purchased from foreign countries cheaper than it can be made at home. It could, therefore, have been purchased with a part only of the commodities, or, what is the same thing, with a part only of the price of the commodities, which the industry employed by an equal capital would have produced at home, had it been left to follow its natural course. The industry of the country, therefore, is thus turned away from a more to a less advantageous employment, and the exchangeable value of its annual produce, instead of being increased, according to the intention of the lawgiver, must necessarily be diminished by every such regulation.

By means of such regulations, indeed, a particular manufacture may sometimes be acquired sooner than it could have been otherwise, and after a certain time may be made at home as cheap or cheaper than in the foreign country. But though the industry of the society may be thus carried with advantage into a particular channel sooner than it could have been otherwise, it will by no means follow that the sum total, either of its industry, or of its revenue, can ever be augmented by any such regulation. The industry of the society can augment only in proportion as its capital augments, and its capital can augment only in proportion to what can be gradually saved out of its revenue. But the immediate effect of every such regulation is to diminish its revenue, and what diminishes its revenue is certainly not very likely to augment its capital faster than it would have augmented of its own accord, had both capital and industry been left to find out their natural employments.

Though for want of such regulations the society should never acquire the proposed manufacture, it would not, upon that account, necessarily be the poorer in any one period of its duration. In every period of its duration its whole capital and industry might still have been employed, though upon different objects, in the manner that was most advantageous at the time. In every period its revenue might have been the greatest which its capital could afford, and both capital and revenue might have been augmented with the greatest possible rapidity.

The natural advantages which one country has over another in producing particular commodities are sometimes so great, that it is acknowledged by all the world to be in vain to struggle with them. By means of glasses, hotbeds, and hotwalls, very good grapes can be raised in Scotland, and very good wine too can be made of them at about thirty times the expense for which at least equally good can be brought from foreign countries. Would it be a reasonable law to prohibit the importation of all foreign wines, merely to encourage the making of claret and burgundy in Scotland? But if there would be a manifest absurdity in turning towards any employment thirty times more of the capital and industry of the country, than would be necessary to purchase from foreign countries an equal quantity of the commodities wanted, there must be an absurdity, though not altogether so glaring, yet exactly of the same kind, in turning towards any such employment a thirtieth, or even a three hundredth part more of either. Whether the advantages which one country has over another be natural or acquired, is in this respect of no consequence. As long as the one country has those advantages, and the other wants them, it will always be more advantageous for the latter, rather to buy of the former than to make. It is an acquired advantage only, which one artificer has over his neighbour, who exercises another trade; and yet they both find it more advantageous to buy of one another, than to make what does not belong to their particular trades.

Merchants and manufacturers are the people who derive the greatest advantage from this monopoly of the home-market. The prohibition of the importation of foreign cattle, and of salt provisions, together with the high duties upon foreign corn, which in times of moderate plenty amount to a prohibition, are not near so advantageous to the graziers and farmers of Great Britain, as other regulations of the same kind are to its merchants and manufacturers. Manufactures, those of the finer kind especially, are more easily transported from one country to another than corn or cattle. It is in the fetching and carrying manufactures, accordingly, that foreign trade is chiefly employed. In manufactures, a very small advantage will enable foreigners to undersell our own workmen, even in the home-market. It will require a very great one to enable them to do so in the rude produce of the soil. If the free importation of foreign manufactures were permitted, several of the home manufactures would probably suffer, and some of them, perhaps, go to ruin altogether, and a considerable part of the stock and industry at present employed in them would be forced to find out some other employment. But the freest importation of the rude produce of the soil could have no such effect upon the agriculture of the country.

. . .

Even the free importation of foreign corn could very little affect the interest of the farmers of Great Britain. Corn is a much more bulky commodity than butchers'-meat. A pound of wheat at a penny is as dear as a pound of butchers'-meat at fourpence. The small quantity of foreign corn imported even in times of the greatest scarcity, may satisfy our farmers that they can have nothing to fear from the freest importation. The average quantity imported one year with another, amounts only, according to the very well-informed author of the tracts upon the corn trade, to twenty-three thousand seven hundred and twenty-eight quarters of all sorts of grain, and does not exceed the five hundredth and seventy-one part of the annual consumption. But as the bounty upon corn occasions a greater exportation in years of plenty, so it must of consequence occasion a greater importation in years of scarcity, than in the actual state of tillage would otherwise take place. By means of it, the plenty of one year does not compensate the scarcity of another, and as the average quantity exported is necessarily augmented by it, so much likewise, in the actual state of tillage, the average quantity imported. If there were no bounty, as less corn would be exported, so it is probable that, one year with another, less would be imported than at present. The corn merchant, the fetchers and carriers of corn between Great Britain and foreign countries, would have much less employment, and might suffer considerably; but the country gentlemen and farmers could suffer very little. It is in the corn merchants accordingly, rather than in the country gentlemen and farmers, that I have observed the greatest anxiety for the renewal and continuation of the bounty.

Country gentlemen and farmers are, to their great honour, of all people, the least subject to the wretched spirit of monopoly. The undertaker of a great manufactory is sometimes alarmed if another work of the same kind is established within twenty miles of him. The Dutch undertaker of all the woollen manufacture at Abbeville stipulated, that no work of the same kind should be established within thirty leagues of that city. Farmers and country gentlemen, on the contrary, are generally disposed rather to promote than to obstruct the cultivation and improvement of their neighbours' farms and estates. They have no secrets, such as those of the greater part of manufacturers, but are generally rather fond of communicating to their neighbours, and of extending as far as possible any new practice which they have found to be advantageous. ... Country gentlemen and farmers, dispersed in different parts of the country, cannot so easily combine as merchants and manufacturers, who being collected into towns, and accustomed to that exclusive corporation spirit which prevails in them, naturally endeavour to obtain against all their countrymen, the same exclusive privilege which they generally possess against the inhabitants of their respective towns. They accordingly seem to have been the original inventors of those restraints upon the importation of foreign goods, which secure to them the monopoly of the home-market. It was probably in imitation of them, and to put themselves upon a level with those who, they found, were disposed to oppress them, that the country gentlemen and farmers of Great Britain so far forgot the generosity which is natural to their station, as to demand the exclusive privilege of supplying their countrymen with corn and butchers'-meat. They did not perhaps take time to consider, how much less their interest could be affected by the freedom of trade than that of the people whose example they followed.

To prohibit by a perpetual law the importation of foreign corn and cattle, is in reality to enact, that the population and industry of the country shall at no time exceed what the rude produce of its own soil can maintain.

There seem, however, to be two cases in which it will generally be advantageous to lay some burden upon foreign, for the encouragement of domestic industry.

The first is, when some particular sort of industry is necessary for the defense of the country. The defense of Great Britain, for example, depends very much upon the number of its sailors and shipping. The act of navigation, therefore, very properly endeavours to give the sailors and shipping of Great Britain the monopoly of the trade of their own country, in some cases, by absolute prohibitions, and in others by heavy burdens upon the shipping of foreign countries. The following are the principal dispositions of this act.

First, all ships, of which the owners, masters, and three-fourths of the mariners are not British subjects, are prohibited, upon pain of forfeiting ship and cargo, from trading to the British settlements and plantations, or from being employed in the coasting trade of Great Britain.

Secondly, a great variety of the most bulky articles of importation can be brought into Great Britain only, either in such ships as are above described, or in ships of the country where those goods are produced, and of which the owners, masters, and three-fourths of the mariners, are of that particular country; and when imported even in ships of this latter kind, they are subject to double aliens duty. If imported in ships of any other country, the penalty is forfeiture of ship and goods. When this act was made, the Dutch were, what they still are, the great carriers of Europe, and by this regulation they were entirely excluded from being carriers to Great Britain, or from importing to us the goods of any other European country.

Thirdly, a great variety of the most bulky articles of importation are prohibited from being imported, even in British ships, from any country but that in which they are produced; under pain of forfeiting ship and cargo. This regulation too was probably intended against the Dutch. Holland was then, as now, the great emporium for all European goods, and by this regulation, British ships were hindered from loading in Holland the goods of any other European country.

Fourthly, salt fish of all kinds, whale fins, whale-bone, oil, and blubber, not caught by and cured on board British vessels, when imported into Great Britain, are subjected to double aliens duty. The Dutch, as they are still the principal, were then the only fishers in Europe that attempted to supply foreign nations with fish. By this regulation, a very heavy burden was laid upon their supplying Great Britain.

When the act of navigation was made, though England and Holland were not actually at war, the most violent animosity subsisted between the two nations. It had begun during the government of the long parliament, which first framed this act, and it broke out soon after in the Dutch wars during that of the Protector and of Charles the second. It is not impossible, therefore, that some of the regulations of this famous act may have proceeded from national animosity. They are as wise, however, as if they had all been dictated by the most deliberate wisdom. National animosity at that particular time aimed at the very same object which the most deliberate wisdom would have recommended, the diminution of the naval power of Holland, the only naval power which could endanger the security of England.

The act of navigation is not favourable to foreign commerce or to the growth of that opulence which can arise from it. The interest of a nation in its commercial relations to foreign nations is, like that of a merchant with regard to the different people with whom he deals, to buy as cheap and to sell as dear as possible. But it will be most likely to buy cheap, when by the most perfect freedom of trade it encourages all nations to bring to it the goods which it has occasion to purchase; and, for the same reason, it will be most likely to sell dear, when its markets are thus filled with the greatest number of buyers. The act of navigation, it is true, lays no burden upon foreign ships that come to export the produce of British industry. Even the ancient aliens duty, which used to be paid upon all goods exported as well as imported, has, by several subsequent acts, been taken off from the greater part of the articles of exportation. But if foreigners, either by prohibitions or high duties, are hindered from coming to sell, they cannot always afford to come to buy; because coming without a cargo, they must lose the freight from their own country to Great Britain. By diminishing the number of sellers, therefore, we necessarily diminish that of buyers, and are thus likely not only to buy foreign goods dearer, but to sell our own cheaper, than if there was a more perfect freedom of trade. As defense, however, is of much more importance than opulence, the act of navigation is, perhaps, the wisest of all the commercial regulations of England.

The second case, in which it will generally be advantageous to lay some burden upon foreign for the encouragement of domestic industry, is when some tax is imposed at home upon the produce of the latter. In this case, it seems reasonable that an equal tax should be imposed upon the like produce of the former. This would not give the monopoly of the home-market to domestic industry, not turn towards a particular employment a greater share of the stock and labour of the country, than what would naturally go to it. It would only hinder any part of what would naturally go to it from being turned away by the tax, into a less natural direction, and would leave the competition between foreign and domestic industry, after the tax, as nearly as possible upon the same footing as before it. In Great Britain, when any such tax is laid upon the produce of domestic industry, it is usual at the same time, in order to stop the clamorous complaints of our merchants and manufacturers, that they will be undersold at home, to lay a much heavier duty upon the importation of all foreign goods of the same kind.

This second limitation of the freedom of trade according to some people should, upon some occasions, be extended much farther than to the precise foreign commodities which could come into competition with those which had been taxed at home. When the necessaries of life have been taxed in any country, it becomes proper, they pretend, to tax not only the like necessaries of life imported from other countries, but all sorts of foreign goods which can come into competition with any thing that is the produce of domestic industry. Subsistence, they say, becomes necessarily dearer in consequence of such taxes; and the price of labour must always rise with the price of the labourers' subsistence. Every commodity, therefore, which is the produce of domestic industry, though not immediately taxed itself, becomes dearer in consequence of such taxes, because the labour which produces it becomes so. Such taxes, therefore, are really equivalent, they say, to a tax upon every particular commodity produced at home. In order to put domestic upon the same footing with foreign industry, therefore, it becomes necessary, they think, to lay some duty upon every foreign commodity, equal to this enhancement of the price of the home commodities with which it can come into competition.

Whether taxes upon the necessaries of life, such as those in Great Britain upon soap, salt, leather, candles, &c. necessarily raise the price of labour, and consequently that of all other commodities, I shall consider hereafter, when I come to treat of taxes. Supposing, however, in the mean time, that they have this effect, and they have it undoubtedly, this general enhancement of the price of all commodities, in consequence of that of labour, is a case which differs in the two following respects from that of a particular commodity, of which the price was enhanced by a particular tax immediately imposed upon it.

First, it might always be known with great exactness how far the price of such a commodity could be enhanced by such a tax: but how far the general enhancement of the price of labour might affect that of every different commodity about which labour was employed, could never be known with any tolerable exactness. It would be impossible, therefore, to proportion with any tolerable exactness the tax upon every foreign, to this enhancement of the price of every home commodity.

Secondly, taxes upon the necessaries of life have nearly the same effect upon the circumstances of the people as a poor soil and a bad climate. Provisions are thereby rendered dearer in the same manner as if it required extraordinary labour and expense to raise them. As in the natural scarcity arising from soil and climate, it would be absurd to direct the people in what manner they ought to employ their capitals and industry, so is it likewise in the artificial scarcity arising from such taxes. To be left to accommodate, as well as they could, their industry to their situation, and to find out those employments in which, notwithstanding their unfavourable circumstances, they might have some advantage either in the home or in the foreign market, is what in both cases would evidently be most for their advantage. To lay a new tax upon them, because they are already overburdened with taxes, and because they already pay too dear for the necessaries of life, to make them likewise pay too dear for the greater part of other commodities, is certainly a most absurd way of making amends.

Such taxes, when they have grown up to a certain height, are a curse equal to the barrenness of the earth and the inclemency of the heavens; and yet it is in the richest and most industrious countries that they have been most generally imposed. No other countries could support so great a disorder. As the strongest bodies only can live and enjoy health, under an unwholesome regimen; so the nations only, that in every sort of industry have the greatest natural and acquired advantages, can subsist and prosper under such taxes. Holland is the country in Europe in which they abound most, and which from peculiar circumstances continues to prosper, not by means of them, as has been most absurdly supposed, but in spite of them.

· · ·

To expect, indeed, that the freedom of trade should ever be entirely restored in Great Britain, is as absurd as to expect that an Oceana or Utopia should ever be established in it. Not only the prejudices of the public, but what is much more unconquerable, the private interests of many individuals, irresistibly oppose it. Were the officers of the army to oppose with the same zeal and unanimity any reduction in the number of forces, with which master manufacturers set themselves against every law that is likely to increase the number of their rivals in the home-market; were the former to animate their soldiers, in the same manner as the latter inflame their workmen, to attack with violence and outrage the proposers of any such regulation; to attempt to reduce the army would be as dangerous as it has now become to attempt to diminish in any respect the monopoly which our manufacturers have obtained against us. This monopoly has so much increased the number of some particular tribes of them, that, like an overgrown standing army, they have become formidable to the government, and upon many occasions intimidate the legislature. The member of parliament who supports every proposal for strengthening this monopoly is sure to acquire not only the reputation of understanding trade, but great popularity and influence with the order of men whose numbers and wealth render them of great importance. If he opposes them, on the contrary, and still more if he has authority enough to be able to thwart them, neither the most acknowledged probity, nor the highest rank, nor the greatest public services, can protect him from the most infamous abuse and detraction, from personal insults, nor sometimes from real danger, arising from the insolent outrage of furious and disappointed monopolists.

Olaudah Equiano

The early European explorers of the Western hemisphere were soon followed by colonists, who quickly came to recognize the vast wealth of these untapped lands. Not only gold, silver, and precious stones could be found in them but the land itself produced highly desired crops, such as sugar, tobacco, tea, and coffee. In increasing waves, settlers came, to clear the land, stake out farms, and plant crops. Since most of the farming was labor-intensive and since the local populations were often decimated by diseases brought in from Europe, it became necessary to search elsewhere for farm laborers. The problem was resolved by the slave trade.

Most of the slaves were Africans, brought across the Atlantic in a trade that began in the sixteenth century and did not end until the middle of the nineteenth century. They came mainly from West Africa, the majority of them being prisoners captured in wars among various local tribes. Some, however, were simply kidnapped from their villages by professional thieves and then sold to slave-traders. The major European powers established trading posts along the Atlantic coast, where they purchased the slaves brought to them from the interior and then transported them for sale across the ocean. It is impossible to say what the total number of slaves imported into the Americas during these centuries was but the best estimates place the figure in excess of ten million. And, approximately three times this number never completed the sea voyage across the Atlantic but perished en route to their destinations. Although the slaves were consigned to areas throughout the Western hemisphere, only a small portion of them, perhaps 5 percent, came to the United States. The vast bulk ended in the Caribbean islands and on the mainland of Latin America, particularly in Brazil.

One of the millions of victims of the slave trade was Olaudah Equiano. But he was more fortunate than most of the others. Born in a part of west-central Africa near the lower Niger River in 1745, he was kidnapped at the age of eleven and eventually sold to British slavers who transported him to Barbados in the West Indies. Soon afterward he was moved to Virginia where he was bought by a British naval officer who took him to England. He served in the British navy during the Seven Years' War and at its end was returned to the West Indies where he was bought by a Quaker merchant-trader from Philadelphia, who employed him on one of his ships. There he was able to earn enough money to buy his freedom in 1766. After that he migrated to London but spent a number of years as a sailor, visiting many parts of the world. Later in life he became an active participant in the British antislavery movement. His autobiography, which he wrote at the request of friends, was published in 1789. Equiano's curious alternative name, with its royal connotations, was given him by the British naval officer who purchased him in Virginia.

The following selection is taken from the first two chapters of Equiano's memoirs. Its importance lies not only in its vivid description of the conditions under which he, and those like him, were shipped across the ocean and sold at auction in the slave market but also, in contrast, of its account of his early life and experiences in his homeland before his abduction.

Consider the following questions as you study the text below.

1. According to Equiano, what were the most important differences between European and African society? Which did he prefer and why?

2. Who was most likely to read Equiano's work? How might eighteenth-century readers have responded to his autobiography?

The Life of Gustavus Vassa*

. . .

The part of Africa known by the name of Guinea, to which the trade for slaves is carried on, extends along the coast above 3,400 miles, from Senegal to Angola, and includes a variety of kingdoms. Of these the most considerable is the kingdom of Benin, both as to extent and wealth, the richness and cultivation of the soil, the power of its king, and the number and warlike disposition of the inhabitants. It is situated nearly under the line, and extends along the coast above 170 miles, but runs back into the interior part of Africa, to a distance hitherto, I believe, unexplored by any traveller and seems only terminated at length by the empire of Abyssinia, near 1,500 miles from its beginning. This kingdom is divided into many provinces or districts, in one of the most remote and fertile of which I was born, in the year 1745, situated in a charming fruitful vale named Essaka. The distance of this province from the capital of Benin and the sea coast must be very considerable for I had never heard of white men or Europeans, nor of the sea; and our subjection to the king of Benin was little more than nominal for every transaction of the government, as far as my slender observation extended, was conducted by

---

* [A substitute name for Olaudah Equiano—*Ed.*]

Published in London in 1789. Minor changes have been made in spelling and punctuation.

the chiefs or elders of the place. The manners and government of a people who have little commerce with other countries are generally very simple and the history of what passes in one family or village may serve as a specimen of the whole nation. My father was one of those elders or chiefs I have spoken of and was styled Embrenche, a term, as I remember, importing the highest distinction, and signifying in our language a mark of grandeur. This mark is conferred on the person entitled to it by cutting the skin across at the top of the forehead and drawing it down to the eye-brows and while it is in this situation applying a warm hand and rubbing it until it shrinks up into a thick weal across the lower part of the forehead. Most of the judges and senators were thus marked; my father had long borne it; I had seen it conferred on one of my brothers and I also was destined to receive it by my parents. Those Embrenche, or chief men, decided disputes and punished crimes, for which purpose they always assembled together. The proceedings were generally short and in most cases the law of retaliation prevailed. I remember a man was brought before my father and the other judges for kidnapping a boy and, although he was the son of a chief or senator, he was condemned to make recompense by a man and woman slave. Adultery, however, was sometimes punished with slavery or death, a punishment which I believe is inflicted on it throughout most of the nations of Africa, so sacred among them is the honour of the marriage bed and so jealous are they of the fidelity of their wives.

. . .

We are almost a nation of dancers, musicians, and poets. Thus every great event, such as a triumphant return from battle, or other cause of public rejoicing, is celebrated in public dances, which are accompanied with songs and music suited to the occasion. The assembly is separated into four divisions, which dance either apart or in succession, and each with a character peculiar to itself. The first division contains the married men, who in their dances frequently exhibit feats of arms and the representation of a battle. To these succeed the married women, who dance in the second division. The young men occupy the third and the maidens the fourth. Each represents some interesting scene of real life, such as a great achievement, domestic employment, a pathetic story, or some rural sport and, as the subject is generally founded on some recent event, it is therefore ever new. This gives our dances a spirit and variety which I have scarcely seen elsewhere. We have many musical instruments, particularly drums of different kinds, a piece of music which resembles a guitar, and another much like a stickado. These last are chiefly used by betrothed virgins, who play on them on all grand festivals.

As our manners are simple, our luxuries are few. The dress of both sexes are nearly the same. It generally consists of a long piece of calico, or muslin, wrapped loosely round the body, somewhat in the form of a Highland plaid. This is usually dyed blue, which is our favourite colour. It is extracted from a berry and is brighter and richer than any I have seen in Europe. Besides this, our women of distinction wear golden ornaments, which they dispose with some profusion on their arms and legs. When our women are not employed with the men in tillage their usual occupation is spinning and weaving cotton, which they afterwards dye and make into garments. They also manufacture earthen vessels, of which we have many kinds. Among the rest tobacco pipes, made after the same fashion and used in the same manner, as those in Turkey.

Our manner of living is entirely plain, for as yet the natives are unacquainted with those refinements in cookery which debauch the taste—bullocks, goats, and poultry supply the greatest part of their food. These constitute likewise the principal wealth of the country and the chief articles of its commerce. The flesh is usually stewed in a pan. To make it savory we sometimes use also pepper and other spices and we have salt made of wood ashes. Our vegetables are mostly plantains, cadas, yams, beans, and Indian corn. The head of the family usually eats alone, his wives and slaves have also their separate tables. Before we taste food we always wash our hands; indeed our cleanliness on all occasions is extreme, but on this it is an indispensible ceremony. After washing libation is made by pouring out a small portion of the drink on the floor, and tossing a small quantity of the food in a certain place, for the spirits of departed relations, which the natives suppose to preside over their conduct and guard them from evil. They are totally unacquainted with strong or spiritous liquors and their principal beverage is palm wine. This is got from a tree of that name, by tapping it at the top and fastening a large gourd to it, and sometimes one tree will yield three or four gallons in a night. When just drawn it is of a most delicious sweetness but in a few days it acquires a tartish and most spiritous flavour, though I never saw anyone intoxicated by it. The same tree also produces nuts and oil. Our principal luxury is in perfumes; one sort of these is an odoriferous wood of delicious fragrance, the other a kind of earth, a small portion of which thrown into the fire diffuses a most powerful odour. We beat this wood into powder and mix it with palm oil, with which both men and women perfume themselves.

In our buildings we study convenience rather than ornament. Each master of a family has a large square piece of ground, surrounded with a moat or fence or inclosed with a wall made of red earth tempered, which, when dry, is as hard as brick. Within this are his houses to accommodate his family and slaves, which, if numerous, frequently present the appearance of a village. In the middle stands the principal building, appropriated to the sole use of the master, and consisting of two apartments, in one of which he sits in the day with his family; the other is left apart for the reception of his friends. He has besides these a distinct apartment in which he sleeps, together with his male children. On each side are the apartments of his wives, who have also their separate day and night houses. The habitations of the slaves and their families are distributed throughout the rest of the inclosure. These houses never exceed one story in height; they are always built of wood, or stakes driven into the ground, crossed with wattles and neatly plastered within and without. The roof is thatched with reeds. Our day houses are left open at the sides but those in which we sleep are always covered and plastered in the inside with a composition mixed with cow-dung, to keep off the different insects which annoy us during the night. The walls and floors also of these are generally covered with mats. Our beds consist of a platform, raised three or four feet from the ground, on which are laid skins and different parts of a spungy tree called plantain. Our covering is calico, or muslin, the same as our dress. The usual seats are a few logs of wood but we have benches, which are generally perfumed, to accommodate strangers; these compose the greater part of our household furniture. Houses so constructed and furnished require but little skill to erect them. Every man is a sufficient architect for the purpose. The whole neighbourhood afford their unanimous assistance in building them and, in return, receive and expect no other recompense than a feast.

As we live in a country where nature is prodigal of her favors our wants are few, and easily supplied; of course we have few manufactures. They consist for the most part of calicoes, earthen ware, ornaments, and instruments of war and husbandry. But these make no part of our commerce, the principal articles of which, as I have observed, are provisions. In such a state money is of little use; however we have some small pieces of coin, if I may call them such. They are made something like an anchor but I do not remember either their value or denomination. We have also markets, at which I have been frequently with my mother. These are sometimes visited by stout, mahogany-colored men from the southwest of us; we call them *Oye-Eboe*, which term signifies red men living at a distance. They generally bring us fire-arms, gun-powder, hats, beads, and dried fish. The last we esteemed a great rarity, as our waters were only brooks and springs. These articles they barter with us for odoriferous woods and earth, and our salt of wood-ashes. They always carry slaves through our land but the strictest account is exacted of their manner of procuring them before they are suffered to pass. Sometimes indeed we sold slaves to them but they were only prisoners of war, or such among us as had been convicted of kidnapping, or adultery, and some other crimes which we esteemed heinous. This practice of kidnapping induces me to think that, notwithstanding all our strictness, their principal business among us was to trepan our people. I remember too they carried great sacks along with them which, not long after, I had an opportunity of fatally seeing applied to that infamous purpose.

Our land is uncommonly rich and fruitful and produces all kinds of vegetables in great abundance. We have plenty of Indian corn, and vast quantities of cotton and tobacco. Our pine apples grow without culture; they are about the size of the largest sugar-loaf, and finely flavoured. We have also spices of different kinds, particularly of pepper, and a variety of delicious fruits which I have never seen in Europe, together with gums of various kinds and honey in abundance. All our industry is exerted to improve those blessings of nature. Agriculture is our chief employment and every one, even the children and women, are engaged in it. Thus we are all habituated to labour from our earliest years. Every one contributes something to the common stock and, as we are unacquainted with idleness, we have no beggars. The benefits of such a mode of living are obvious. The West India planters prefer the slaves of Benin or Eboe to those of any other part of Guinea, for their hardiness, intelligence, integrity, and zeal. Those benefits are felt by us in the general healthiness of the people and in their vigor and activity; I might add too in their comeliness. Deformity is indeed unknown among us, I mean that of shape. Numbers of the natives of Eboe, now in London, might be brought in support of this assertion for, in regard to complexion, ideas of beauty are wholly relative. I remember while in Africa to have seen three negro children who were tawny, and another quite white, who were universally regarded by myself and the natives in general, as far as related to their complexions, as deformed. Our women too were, in my eyes at least, uncommonly graceful, alert, and modest to a degree of bashfulness; nor do I remember to have ever heard of an instance of incontinence among them before marriage. They are also remarkably cheerful. Indeed cheerfulness and affability are two of the leading characteristics of our nation.

Our tillage is exercised in a large plain or common, some hours walk from our dwellings, and all the neighbours resort thither in a body. They use no beasts of husbandry and their only instruments are hoes, axes, shovels, and beaks, or pointed iron, to dig with. Sometimes we are visited by locusts which come in large clouds so as to darken the air and destroy our harvest. This however happens rarely, but when it does a famine is produced by it. I remember an instance or two wherein this happened. This common is oftimes the theater of war and therefore when our people go out to till their land they not only go in a body but generally take their arms with them for fear of a surprise, and when they apprehend an invasion they guard the avenues to their dwellings by driving sticks into the ground which are so sharp at one end as to pierce the foot and are generally dipt in poison. From what I can recollect of these battles, they appear to have been irruptions of one little state or district on the other, to obtain prisoners or booty. Perhaps they were incited to this by those traders who brought the European goods I mentioned among us. Such a mode of obtaining slaves in Africa is common and I believe more are procured this way, and by kidnapping, than any other. When a trader wants slaves he applies to a chief for them and tempts him with his wares. It is not extraordinary if on this occasion he yields to the temptation with as little firmness, and accepts the price of his fellow creatures' liberty with as little reluctance, as the enlightened merchant. Accordingly, he falls on his neighbours and a desperate battle ensues. If he prevails and takes prisoners he gratifies his avarice by selling them but if his party be vanquished and he falls into the hands of the enemy he is put to death; for, as he has been known to foment their quarrels, it is thought dangerous to let him survive and no ransom can save him, though all other prisoners may be redeemed.

.   .   .

As to religion, the natives believe that there is one Creator of all things, and that he lives in the sun and is girded round with a belt; that he may never eat or drink, but according to some he smokes a pipe, which is our own favourite luxury. They believe he governs events, especially our deaths or captivity but, as for the doctrine of eternity, I do not remember to have ever heard of it; some however believe in the transmigration of souls to a certain degree. Those spirits which are not transmigrated, such as their dear friends or relations, they believe always attend them and guard them from the bad spirits of their foes. For this reason they always, before eating, as I have observed, put some small portion of the meat, and pour some of their drink, on the ground for them, and they often make oblations of the blood of beasts or fowls at their graves.

.   .   .

My father, besides many slaves, had a numerous family, of which seven lived to grow up, including myself and a sister, who was the only daughter. As I was the youngest of the sons, I became, of course, the greatest favourite with my mother, and was always with her, and she used to take particular pains to form my mind. I was trained up from my earliest years in the arts of agriculture and war; my daily exercise was shooting and throwing javelins and my mother adorned me with emblems, after the manner of our greatest warriors. In this way I grew up till I was turned the age of eleven, when an end was put to my happiness in the following manner: Generally, when the grown people in the neighbourhood were gone far in the fields to labour, the children assembled together in some of the neighbours premises to play, and commonly some of us used to get up a tree to look out for any assailant or kidnapper that might come upon us, for they sometimes took these opportunities of our parents' absence to attack and carry off as many as they could seize. One day, as I was watching at the top of a tree in our yard, I saw one of those people come into the yard of our next neighbour but one, to kidnap, there being many stout young people in it. Immediately on this I gave the alarm of the rogue and he was surrounded by the stoutest of them, who entangled him with cords, so that he could not escape till some of the grown people came and secured him. But, alas! ere long it was my fate to be thus attacked, and to be carried off, when none of the grown people were nigh. One day, when all our people were gone out to their works as usual, and only I and my dear sister were left to mind the house, two men and a woman got over our walls and in a moment seized us both and, without giving us time to cry out, or make resistance, they stopped our mouths, tied our hands, and ran off with us into the nearest wood, and continued to carry us as far as they could, till night came on, when we reached a small house, where the robbers halted for refreshment and spent the night. We were then unbound but were unable to take any food and being quite overpowered by fatigue and grief our only relief was some slumber, which allayed our misfortune for a short time. The next morning we left the house and continued travelling all the day. For a long time we had kept the woods but at last we came into a road which I believed I knew. I had now some hopes of being delivered for we had advanced but a little way before I discovered some people at a distance, on which I began to cry out for their assistance; but my cries had no other effect than to make them tie me faster and stop my mouth, and then they put me into a large sack. They also stopped my sister's mouth and tied her hands and in this manner we proceeded till we were out of the sight of these people.

When we went to rest the following night they offered us some victuals but we refused them, and the only comfort we had was in being in one another's arms all that night and bathing each other with our tears. But, alas! we were soon deprived of even the smallest comfort of weeping together. The next day proved a day of greater sorrow than I had yet experienced for my sister and I were then separated, while we lay clasped in each other's arms. It was in vain that we besought them not to part us; she was torn from me and immediately carried away while I was left in a state of distraction not to be described.

. . .

Thus I continued to travel, sometimes by land, sometimes by water, through different countries, and various nations till, at the end of six or seven months after I had been kidnapped, I arrived at the sea coast. It would be tedious and uninteresting to relate all the incidents which befell me during this journey, and which I have not yet forgotten, of the various lands I passed through, and the manners and customs of all the different people among whom I lived. I shall therefore only observe that, in all the places where I was the soil was exceedingly rich, the pomkins, eadas, plantains, yams, Ec. Ec. were in great abundance, and of incredible size. There were also large quantities of different gums, though not used for any purpose, and every where a great deal of tobacco. The cotton even grew quite wild and there was plenty of red wood. I saw no mechanics whatever in all the way, except such as I have mentioned. The chief employment in all these countries was agriculture and both the males and females, as with us, were brought up to it, and trained in the arts of war.

The first object which saluted my eyes when I arrived on the coast was the sea, and a slave-ship, which was then riding at anchor and waiting for its cargo. These filled me with astonishment, which was soon converted into terror, which I am yet at a loss to describe, nor the then feelings of my mind. When I was carried on board I was immediately handled, and tossed up, to see if I were sound, by some of the crew, and I was now persuaded that I had got into a world of bad spirits and that they were going to kill me. Their complexions too differing so much from ours, their long hair, and the language they spoke, which was very different from any I had ever heard, united to confirm me in this belief. Indeed, such were the horrors of my views and fears at the moment that, if ten thousand worlds had been my own, I would have freely parted with them all to have exchanged my condition with that of the meanest slave in my own country. When I looked round the ship too and saw a large furnace or copper boiling, and a multitude of black people of every description chained together, every one of their countenances expressing dejection and sorrow, I no longer doubted of my fate and, quite overpowered with horror and anguish, I fell motionless on the deck and fainted. When I recovered a little I found some black people about me, who I believed were some of those who brought me on board and had been receiving their pay; they talked to me in order to cheer me, but all in vain. I asked them if we were not to be eaten by those white men with horrible looks, red faces, and long hair. They told me I was not, and one of the crew brought me a small portion of spiritous liquor in a wine glass but, being afraid of him, I would not take it out of his hand. One of the blacks therefore took it from him and gave it to me and I took a little down my palate which, instead of reviving me, as they thought it would, threw me into the greatest consternation at the strange feeling it produced, having never tasted any such liquor before. Soon after this the blacks who brought me on board went off and left me abandoned to despair. I now saw myself deprived of all chance of returning to my native country, or even the least glimpse of hope of gaining the shore, which I now considered as friendly, and even wished for my former slavery, in preference to my present situation, which was filled with horrors of every kind, still heightened by my ignorance of what I was to undergo. I was not long suffered to indulge my grief; I was soon put down under the decks and there I received such a salutation in my nostrils as I had never experienced in my life, so that with the loathsomeness of the stench, and crying together, I became so sick and low that I was not able to eat, nor had I the least desire to taste any thing. I now wished for the last friend, Death, to relieve me, but soon, to my grief, two of the white men offered me eatables and, on my refusing to eat, one of them held me fast by the hands and laid me across, I think, the windlass and tied my feet, while the other flogged me severely. I had never experienced any thing of this kind before and although not being used to the water I naturally feared that element the first time I saw it, yet, nevertheless, could I have got over the nettings, I would have jumped over the side, but I could not and, besides, the crew used to watch us very closely who were not chained down to the decks, lest we should leap into the water, and I have seen some of these poor African prisoners most severely cut for attempting to do so and hourly whipped for not eating. This indeed was often the case with myself. In a little time after, amongst the poor chained men, I found some of my own nation, which in a small degree gave ease to my mind. I inquired of them what was to be done with us. They gave me to understand we were to be carried to these white people's country to work for them. I then was a little revived and thought, if it were no worse than working, my situation was not so desperate, but still I feared I should be put to death. The white people looked and acted, as I thought, in so savage a manner, for I had never seen among any people such instances of brutal cruelty, and this not only shewn towards us blacks, but also to some of the whites themselves. One white man in particular I saw, when we were permitted to be on deck, flogged so unmercifully with a large rope near the foremast that he died in consequence of it, and they tossed him over the side as they would have done a brute. This made me fear these people the more and I expected nothing less than to be treated in the same manner. I could not help expressing my fears and apprehensions to some of my countrymen. I asked them if these people had no country but lived in this hollow place the ship. They told me they did not but came from a distant one. "Then," said I, "how comes it in all our country we never heard of them?" They told me, because they lived so very far off. I then asked, Where were their women? Had they any like themselves? I was told they had. "And why," said I, "do we not see them?" They answered, because they were left behind. I asked how the vessel could go. They told me they could not tell but that there were cloth put upon the masts by the help of the ropes I saw and then the vessel went on, and the white men had some spell or magic they put in the water when they liked in order to stop the vessel. I was exceedingly amazed at this account and really thought they were spirits. I therefore wished much to be from amongst them for I expected they would sacrifice me, but my wishes were vain for we were so quartered that it was impossible for any of us to make our escape. While we staid on the coast I was mostly on deck and one day, to my great astonishment, I saw one of these vessels coming in with the sails up. As soon as the whites saw it they gave a great shout, at which we were amazed, and the more so as the vessel appeared larger by approaching nearer. At last she came to an anchor in my sight and when the anchor was let go I and my countrymen who saw it were lost in astonishment to observe the vessel stop and were now convinced it was done by magic. Soon after the other ship got her boats out and they came on board of us and the people of both ships seemed very glad to see each other. Several of the strangers also shook hands with us black people and made motions with their hands signifying, I suppose, we were to go to their country, but we did not understand them. At last, when the ship we were in had got in all her cargo, they made ready with many fearful noises, and we were all put under deck so that we could not see how they managed the vessel. But this disappointment was the least of my sorrow. The stench of the hold while we were on the coast was so intolerably loathsome that it was too dangerous to remain there for any time and some of us had been permitted to stay on the deck for the fresh air, but now that the whole ship's cargo were confined together it became absolutely pestilential. The closeness of the place and the heat of the climate, added to the number in the ship, which was so crowded that each had scarcely room to turn himself, almost suffocated us. This produced copious perspiration so that the air soon became unfit for respiration, from a variety of loathsome smells, and brought on a sickness amongst the slaves of which many died, thus falling victims to the improvident avarice, as I may call it, of their purchasers. This wretched situation was again aggravated by the galling of the chains, now become insupportable, and the filth of the necessary tubs, into which the children often fell and were almost suffocated. The shrieks of the women and the groans of the dying rendered the whole a scene of horror almost inconceivable. Happily perhaps for myself I was soon reduced so low here that it was thought necessary to keep me almost always on deck, and from my extreme youth I was not put in fetters. In this situation I expected every hour to share the fate of my companions, some of whom were almost daily brought upon deck at the point of death, which I began to hope would soon put an end to my miseries. Often did I think many of the inhabitants of the deep much more happy than myself. I envied them the freedom they enjoyed and as often wished I could change my condition for theirs. Every circumstance I met with served only to render my state more painful and heighten my apprehensions and my opinion of the cruelty of the whites. One day they had taken a number of fishes and when they had killed and satisfied themselves with as many as they thought fit, to our astonishment who were on the deck, rather than give any of them to us to eat, as we expected, they tossed the remaining fish into the sea again, although we begged and prayed for some as well as we could, but in vain, and some of my countrymen, being pressed by hunger, took an opportunity, when they thought no one saw them, of trying to get a little privately but they were discovered and the attempt procured them some very severe floggings.

One day, when we had a smooth sea and moderate wind, two of my wearied countrymen, who were chained together (I was near them at the time), preferring death to such a life of misery, somehow made through the nettings and jumped into the sea. Immediately another quite dejected fellow who, on account of his illness, was suffered to be out of irons also followed their example and I believe many more would very soon have done the same, if they had not been prevented by the ship's crew, who were instantly alarmed. Those of us that were the most active were, in a moment, put down under the deck and there was such a noise and confusion amongst the people of the ship as I never heard before, to stop her, and get the boat out to go after the slaves. However, two of the wretches were drowned but they got the other and afterwards flogged him unmercifully, for thus attempting to prefer death to slavery. In this manner we continued to undergo more hardships than I can now relate, hardships which are inseparable from this accursed trade. Many a time we were near suffocation, from the want of fresh air, which we were often without for whole days together. This, and the stench of the necessary tubs, carried off many. During our passage I first saw flying fishes, which surprised me very much. They used frequently to fly across the ship and many of them fell on the deck. I also now first saw the use of the quadrant. I had often with astonishment seen the mariners make observations with it and I could not think what it meant. They at last took notice of my surprise and one of them, willing to increase it as well as to gratify my curiosity, made me one day look through it. The clouds appeared to me to be land, which disappeared as they passed along. This heightened my wonder and I was now more persuaded than ever that I was in another world and that every thing about me was magic. At last, we came in sight of the island of Barbadoes, at which the whites on board gave a great shout and made many signs of joy to us. We did not know what to think of this but, as the vessel drew nearer, we plainly saw the harbour, and other ships of different kinds and sizes, and we soon anchored amongst them off Bridge Town. Many merchants and planters now came on board, though it was in the evening. They put us in separate parcels and examined us attentively. They also made us jump, and pointed to the land, signifying we were to go there. We thought by this we should be eaten by these ugly men, as they appeared to us, and when, soon after we were all put down under the deck again, there was much dread and trembling among us, and nothing but bitter cries to be heard all the night from these apprehensions, insomuch that at last the white people got some old slaves from the land to pacify us. They told us we were not to be eaten, but to work, and were soon to go on land, where we should see many of our country people. This report eased us much and sure enough, soon after we landed, there came to us Africans of all languages. We were conducted immediately to the merchant's yard, where we were all pent up together like so many sheep in a fold, without regard to sex or age. As every object was new to me, every thing I saw filled me with surprise. What struck me first was that the houses were built with bricks, in stories, and in every other respect different from those I have seen in Africa, but I was still more astonished on seeing people on horseback. I did not know what this could mean and indeed I thought these people were full of nothing but magical arts. While I was in this astonishment one of my fellow prisoners spoke to a countryman of his about the horses who said they were the same kind they had in their country. I understood them, though they were from a distant part of Africa, and I thought it odd I had not seen any horses there but afterwards, when I came to converse with different Africans I found they had many horses amongst them, and much larger than those I then saw. We were not many days in the merchant's custody before we were sold after their usual manner, which is this: On a signal given (as the beat of a drum), the buyers rush at once into the yard where the slaves are confined and make choice of that parcel they like best. The noise and clamour with which this is attended, and the eagerness visible in the countenances of the buyers, serve not a little to increase the apprehension of the terrified Africans, who may well be supposed to consider them as the ministers of that destruction to which they think themselves devoted. In this manner, without scruple, are relations and friends separated, most of them never to see each other again.

Antoine-Nicolas de Condorcet

Born into a noble family, Antoine-Nicholas de Condorcet (1743–1794) embraced the rationalistic intellectual and social ideas that were championed most forcefully in France by Voltaire and the *philosophes* under the leadership of Denis Diderot, editor of the *Encyclopedie*. Imbued by these ideals, Condorcet joined in a campaign of agitation for social reforms that culminated in the French Revolution, in which he played an important role. However, as the level of violence rose, he drew back, only to be denounced by his more zealous revolutionary compatriots, tried in absentia, and sentenced to death. He went into hiding for nine months, then attempted to escape from Paris, was captured, and died in his cell under mysterious circumstances, a victim of the revolution he had helped to inspire.

The essay from which the following selection is taken exhibits many of the leading ideas of the Enlightenment, in particular the conviction that history reveals a record of human progress achieved through the application of reason to the natural and social problems facing humankind. After describing nine stages of this progress through history, Condorcet turns at the end of his essay to the future progress of the human mind. The essay was never published by Condorcet; rather he left it at his death in the form of a sketch, written while he was hiding from the revolutionary authorities. Something of his state of mind at that time—both his faith in reason and his disillusionment with the course of the Revolution—is revealed in the final paragraph.

Consider the following questions as you study the text below.

1. What relationship did Condorcet see between historical progress and the progress of the human mind? What did he predict would be the culmination of historical and human development?

2. What was Condorcet's attitude toward the colonization of the non-European world? What did he hope would result from such efforts?

The Progress of the Human Mind

Introduction

Man is born with the capacity to receive sensations. In those he receives, he is able to perceive and to distinguish the simple sensations of which they are composed. He can retain, recognize, and combine them. He can preserve or recall them to his memory; he can compare their different combinations; he can ascertain what they have in common and how they differ; lastly, he can attach signs to all these objects to recognize them more easily and to form new combinations from them.

This faculty is developed in him by the action of external objects, that is, by the action of certain complex sensations the constancy of which, even through change, is independent of himself. It is also exercised by communication with other individuals and by all the artificial means which, from the first development of this faculty, men have succeeded in inventing.

Sensations are accompanied by pleasure or pain and man has the further faculty of converting these momentary impressions into lasting feelings of a corresponding nature and of experiencing these feelings either at the sight or recollection of the pleasure or pain of beings like himself. From this faculty, united with that of forming and combining ideas, arise, between him and his fellow creatures, the ties of interest and duty, to which nature has attached the most precious part of our happiness and the most poignant of our sufferings.

If we were to confine our observations to an inquiry into the general facts and laws which the development of these faculties presents to us, in what is common to the different individuals of the human species, our inquiry would be called metaphysics.

But if we consider this development in relation to the individuals who live at the same time in any given place and follow it through from generation to generation, it then exhibits a picture of the progress of the human mind. This progress is subject to the same general laws, observable in the development of our individual faculties, and is the result of that development considered at once in a great number of individuals united in society. The result which every moment presents depends upon that of the preceding moments and has an influence on what the future will bring.

This picture, therefore, is historical; subject to constant change, it is the result of the successive observation of human societies during different stages through which they have passed. It will therefore record the order in which the changes have taken place, explain the influence of every past period upon that which follows it, and thus show, by the changes which the human species has experienced as it ceaselessly renews itself through the immensity of the ages, the course which it has pursued, and the steps which it has taken towards knowledge and happiness. From these observations on what man has been in the past and what he is now we shall be able to find the means of securing and of accelerating the further progress that human nature allows him to hope for.

Such is the aim of the work I have undertaken, the result of which will be to show, from reasoning and from facts, that no bounds have been set to the improvement of the human faculties; that the perfectibility of man is absolutely indefinite; that the progress of this perfectibility, now beyond the control of any power that would stop it, has no other limit than the duration of the globe on which nature has placed us. The course of this progress may no doubt be more or less rapid, but it can never be reversed, at least as long as the earth retains its place in the system of the universe and the laws of this system shall neither produce a general cataclysm on the globe nor cause such changes as will prevent the human race from preserving and exercising its present faculties and finding the same resources.

. . .

The Tenth Stage

THE FUTURE PROGRESS OF THE HUMAN MIND

If man can predict, almost with certainty, those phenomena of which he knows the laws; if, even when he does not know the laws, experience of the past enables him to foresee, with considerable probability, future phenomena, why should we suppose it an impossible undertaking to sketch, with some degree of truth, the future destiny of mankind based on the results of its history? The only foundation of the natural sciences is the principle that the general laws, known or unknown, which regulate the phenomena of the universe are regular and constant and why should this principle, applicable to the other operations of nature, be less true when applied to the development of the intellectual and moral faculties of man? Since beliefs based on experience of similar conditions are the only guide by which the wisest of men govern their conduct, why should the philosopher be prohibited from supporting his conjectures in a similar way as long as he does not give them a greater certainty than is warranted by the number, the consistency, and the accuracy of his actual observations?

Our hopes regarding the future condition of the human species may be stated in three points: the abolition of inequality between nations, the progress of equality within each nation, and the true perfection of man.

Will not every nation one day reach the state of civilization attained by those people who are most enlightened, most free, most exempt from prejudices, as the French, for instance, and the Anglo-Americans? ... In a word, will not men be continually moving towards that state in which all will possess the knowledge needed to conduct themselves in the ordinary affairs of life by their own reason and to preserve that reason free of prejudice; to understand their rights and exercise them according to their beliefs and their conscience; to be able, by the development of their faculties, to secure the means of providing for their wants; lastly, to reach a state in which folly and wretchedness will be accidents, happening only now and then, and not the habitual lot of a considerable portion of society? ...

In examining these three questions we shall find the strongest reasons to believe, from past experience, from observation of the progress which the sciences and civilization have hitherto made, and from the analysis of the progress of the human mind and the development of its faculties, that nature has set no limits to the realization of our hopes.

If we survey the existing state of the world, we shall find, in the first place, that in Europe the principles of the French constitution are those of every enlightened mind. We shall see that they are too widely disseminated and too openly professed for tyrants and priests to prevent them from penetrating by degrees into the miserable abodes of their slaves, where they will soon awaken those remnants of good sense and arouse that suppressed indignation which suffering and terror have failed to extinguish completely in the minds of the oppressed.

If we next look at the different nations, we shall observe in each what special obstacles oppose this revolution and what dispositions favor it. We shall find some in which it will be effected, perhaps slowly, by the wisdom of their governments and others in which the governments rendered violent by their resistance, will themselves become involved in its swift and terrible convulsions.

Can we doubt that either the wisdom or the senseless feuds of European nations adding to the slow but certain effects of the progress of their colonies will not soon bring about the independence of the entire new world and that then the European population of these colonies will fail to civilize or remove, even without conquest, those savage nations still occupying these immense tracts of country?

Run through the history of our projects and settlements in Africa or in Asia and you will see how our monopolies, our treachery, our bloody contempt for men of a different color or creed and the proselyting ardor or the intrigues of our priests have destroyed any feelings of respect and goodwill which the superiority of our knowledge and the advantages of our commerce had at first obtained from the inhabitants. But the time is doubtless approaching when, no longer appearing to these people simply as corruptors or tyrants, we shall become to them instruments for their benefit and the generous champions of their freedom from bondage.

· · ·

Then the inhabitants of Europe, satisfied with an unrestricted commerce and too enlightened as to their own rights to deny those of others, will respect that independence which they have hitherto flagrantly violated. Then will their settlements—instead of being filled by power-hungry adventurers, who, using their place and privilege, hasten, by plunder and deceit, to amass wealth, in order to purchase, honors and titles on their return home— be peopled with industrious men, seeking in those happy climates the ease and comfort lacking in their native country. They will remain there because of their love of liberty, ambition having lost its allurements and those settlements of robbers will then become colonies of citizens, who will plant in Africa and Asia the principles and example of the freedom, reason, and illumination of Europe. Those monks too, who indoctrinate the natives of the countries in question in the most shameful superstitions and who arouse antagonism by menacing the people with a new tyranny, will be succeeded by men of integrity and benevolence, eager to spread among these people truths useful to their happiness and to inform them of their interests as well as their rights, for the love of truth is also a passion and when it shall have at home no gross prejudices to combat and no degrading errors to dissipate it will naturally extend itself to remote and foreign lands.

. . .

The progress of these people will be less slow and more sure than ours has been because they will borrow from us that illumination which we have had to discover and because for them to acquire the simple truths and infallible methods which we have obtained only after many errors they need only grasp our discoveries and developments as they appear in our writings. If the progress of the Greeks was lost to later nations, it was the result of a lack of communication between peoples; for this we have the tyrannical domination of the Romans to blame. But when mutual needs shall have drawn the ties of all mankind closer; when the most powerful nations shall have established the political principles of equality between societies as between individuals and respect for the independence of weaker states, as well as compassion for ignorance and misery; when the maxims which tend to crush human faculties shall be replaced by those which favor their action and energy will there still be reason to fear that the earth will contain lands devoid of knowledge or that the pride of despotism will be able to raise barriers to truth that cannot quickly be surmounted?

The moment will then arrive in which the sun will observe in its course free nations only, recognizing no other master than reason, in which tyrants and slaves, priests and their stupid or hypocritical instruments will exist only in works of history and on the stage; in which our only concern will be to pity their past victims and dupes, and by the memory of their horrid excesses to keep a vigilant watch so that we may be able instantly to recognize and effectually to stifle by the force of reason the seeds of superstition and tyranny, should they ever attempt to make their appearance upon the earth again.

In tracing the history of societies we have had occasion to remark that there frequently is a considerable difference between the rights which the law allows the citizens of a state and those which they really enjoy, between the equality established by political institutions and that which actually exists between individuals, and that this disproportion was a chief cause of the destruction of liberty in the ancient republics, of the storms which they had to encounter and the weakness that delivered them into the power of foreign tyrants.

These distinctions have three principal causes: inequality of wealth, inequality of condition between the individual whose means of subsistence are hereditary and one whose resources end with his life or rather that part of his life in which he is capable of labor, and lastly, inequality in education.

· · ·

Let us compare the actual population with the extent of territory in the enlightened nations of Europe; let us observe the way in which labor and the means of subsistence are distributed in agriculture and industry and we shall see that it will be impossible to maintain these means to the same degree, and therefore to maintain the same level of population if a large number of individuals cease to have their labor, and the small capital necessary to set it at work or to make its profit sufficient to supply their own wants and those of their family. But this labor and the small capital we have mentioned can exist only as long as each head of a family is alive and healthy. Their small fortune is at best an annuity but in reality more precarious than an annuity; as a result there is an important difference between this class of society and the class of men whose income depends either on landed wealth or the interest on capital, which depend little on personal labor and are therefore not subject to similar risks.

Here then is a necessary cause of inequality, of dependence, and even of misery, which ceaselessly threatens the most numerous and active class in our society.

This inequality may, however, be greatly reduced by providing support for anyone who becomes aged taken from his savings, but augmented by the savings of other persons, who, having made a similar addition to a common stock, do not survive so long; in procuring, in the same way, an equal income for women who may lose their husbands or children who may lose their father; lastly, in providing for young men when they reach an age at which they can begin to work for themselves and to start a new family, sufficient capital to allow them to work, derived from those who die before they reach that age. It is to the application of mathematics to the probabilities of life and the investment of money that we owe the idea of these methods, which are already being employed with some success, though they have not been carried far enough or employed widely enough to make them truly beneficial, not merely to a few families, but to the entire society, which would as a result be able to avoid the periodic ruin observable in a number of families, causing recurrent misery and suffering.

.   .   .

The equality in education we can hope to attain, and with which we ought to be satisfied, is that which excludes every kind of dependence, either forced or voluntary. An easy method by which this end may be attained can be found, given the actual state of human knowledge, even for those who can attend school for only a few years and in later life can devote only occasional hours of leisure to study. We might show that, by a careful choice of the subjects to be taught and of teaching methods, the entire population can be instructed in everything necessary for the management of their households, for the transaction of their business, for the free development of their labor and their faculties, for the knowledge, exercise and protection of their rights, for a recognition of their duties and the will to discharge them, for the capacity to judge both their own actions and those of others by their own understanding, for the acquisition of all the noble and delicate feelings that are an honor to humanity, for freeing themselves from a blind dependence on those to whom they may entrust the care of their interests and the security of their rights, for choosing and guarding themselves so as no longer to be the dupes of those popular errors that torment the life of man with superstitious fears and chimerical hopes, for defending themselves against prejudices by the strength of reason alone, and finally for escaping from the delusions of those who would spread snares for their fortune, their health, their freedom of thought and of conscience, under the pretext of enriching, healing, and saving them.

.   .   .

The different causes of equality we have enumerated do not act in isolation; rather they unite, combine, and support each other, and their combined influence leads to stronger, surer, and more constant action. Greater equality of education will lead to greater equality of industry, and hence of wealth, and equality of wealth necessarily contributes to equality of education. Finally, the equality of nations, like that between individuals, has a similar effect.

To sum up, a proper kind of education corrects the natural inequality of men's abilities, instead of strengthening it, just as good laws remedy the natural inequality of the means of subsistence or just as, in societies whose institutions have achieved this equality, liberty, though subject to law, will be more extensive and complete than in the total independence of savage life. Then the social art will have accomplished its end—that of securing and extending to all the enjoyment of the common rights that nature has given to them.

.   .   .

Men cannot become enlightened upon the nature and development of their moral feelings, upon the principles of morality, upon the reasons for conforming their conduct to those principles, and upon their interest, whether as individuals or as members of society, without at the same time improving their moral practice, an advance no less real than that of moral science itself. Is not a mistaken sense of interest the most frequent cause of actions contrary to the general welfare? Is not the violence of our passions the constant result either of habits we have developed through miscalculation or of ignorance about how to resist these passions or to divert, govern, and direct their action?

Is not the practice of reflecting on our conduct, of examining it through reason and conscience, of exercising those humane feelings that blend our happiness with that of others the necessary consequence of a well-conceived study of morality and of a greater equality in the provisions of the social compact? Will not the consciousness of his own dignity, in a man who is free, along with a system of education built on a more profound knowledge of our moral constitution, render common to almost every man those principles of strict and unsullied justice, those habits of an active and enlightened benevolence, of a delicate and generous sensibility, of which nature has planted the seeds in our hearts, whose flowering needs only the benign influence of knowledge and liberty? Just as the mathematical and physical sciences tend to improve the arts that we employ for our most simple wants, so is it not equally a part of the necessary order of nature that the moral and political sciences should have a similar influence on the motives that direct our feelings and actions?

What is the goal of the improvement of laws and public institutions, resulting from the progress of these sciences, but to reconcile, blend, and unite the interest of each individual with the common interest of all? What is the aim of the social art but to surmount the opposition between these two apparently conflicting interests? Will not the constitution and laws of a country be in closest accord with reason and nature whenever the practice of virtue becomes least difficult and the temptations to deviate from her path least numerous and least powerful?

What vicious habit, what practice contrary to good faith, what crime even, can we find that does not have its origin in the legislation, institutions, and prejudices of the country in which we observe this habit, this practice, or this crime to exist?

In short, will not the progress of the useful arts—a result of their being founded on sound theory as well as improved legislation derived from the truths of the political sciences—lead to a well-being and prosperity that will naturally dispose men to humanity, to benevolence, and to justice? Do not all the observations I have made and which I hope to develop further prove that the moral goodness of man, the necessary consequence of his constitution, is, like all his other faculties, capable of indefinite improvement and that nature has linked together in an unbreakable chain truth, happiness, and virtue?

Among the causes of human improvement that are of most importance to the general welfare there must be included the total elimination of the prejudices which have established an inequality of rights between sexes, fatal even to the sex that the inequality favors. We would search in vain to find reasons to justify this prejudice, whether we look to differences of physical organization, of intellect, or of moral sensibility. The inequality of the sexes had its origin solely in the abuse of strength and all attempts which have since been made to excuse it are nothing but vain sophisms.

Further, it can be shown that the elimination of the customs based on this prejudice and of the laws it has dictated would increase the happiness of family life by encouraging the practice of the domestic virtues, on which all the others depend. It would improve education by making it truly general, either because it would include both sexes with greater equality or because it cannot become general, even to men, without the support of the mothers of families. Would not this tribute, even though belated, to equity and good sense put an end to the too-fertile principles of injustice, cruelty, and crime, by overcoming the opposition between the natural inclination of self-interest, most strong and difficult to subdue though it may be, and the interests of mankind or one's duties to society? Would it not produce, what has until now been only a dream, national manners that are mild and pure and are formed, not by proud asceticism or hypocrisy or the fear of shame or religious terrors but by freely contracted habits that are inspired by nature and fortified by reason?

Once people become more enlightened and have recognized their right to dispose of their own life and wealth as they choose, they will gradually come to regard war as the most dreadful of all calamities, the most terrible of all crimes. The first wars that will disappear will be those into which the usurpers of power have in the past forced their subjects, in support of their pretended hereditary rights.

Nations will understand that they cannot become conquerors without losing their freedom, that permanent confederations are their only means of maintaining their independence, and that their goal should be security and not power. Gradually commercial prejudices will die away and a false sense of mercantile interest will lose the terrible power it has had of drenching the earth in blood and of ruining nations under the pretext of enriching them. As the people of different countries gradually are drawn together by the principles of politics and morality, as each, for its own welfare, permits foreigners to share the benefits it derives either from nature or its own industry, all the causes which produce, poison and perpetuate national animosities will disappear one by one, hence will no longer encourage or even arouse the insanity of war.

. . .

All the causes that contribute to the perfection of the human race, all the means we have listed that insure its progress, must, from their very nature, exercise a continuing, active influence that constantly increases its scope. We have provided the proofs of this and their further development in the work itself will serve only to strengthen them. So we may conclude then that the perfectibility of man is indefinite. Meanwhile we have to this point considered him as possessing only the same natural faculties and the same organization as he has at present. How much greater would be the certainty, how much wider the scope of our hopes, if we could prove that these natural faculties themselves, this very organization, are themselves improvable? This is the last question we shall examine.

The organic perfectibility or deterioration of the classes of vegetables or the species of the animal kingdom can be regarded as one of the general laws of nature. This law applies to the human race as well. It cannot be doubted that the progress of medicine, the availability of more wholesome food and better housing, plus a mode of life that will develop our physical powers by exercise without at the same time impairing them by excess, in general, that the elimination of the two most active causes of deterioration—poverty and misery on the one hand and enormous wealth on the other—will necessarily result in prolonging the length of life and giving people better health and stronger bodies. It is obvious that the practice of medicine will improve and become more efficacious through the progress of reason and the social order and must finally eliminate infectious or contagious diseases, as well as those general illnesses resulting from climate, food, and conditions of labor. Nor would it be difficult to prove that we can have the same hope about almost every other malady, whose causes and cure we can reasonably expect to discover. Would it be absurd then to assume that this improvement of the human species is susceptible of indefinite progress, to suppose that a time must one day come when death will be the effect either of extraordinary accidents or of the slow and gradual decay of the vital powers and that the duration of life—of the time between the birth of man and this decay—will itself have no assignable limit? Certainly man will not become immortal but may not the time between the moment in which he draws his first breath and the common term when, in the natural course of nature, without disease or accident, he draws his last, be necessarily increased?

. . .

But are not our physical faculties and the strength, dexterity, and acuteness of our senses included in the qualities whose perfection in the individual may be transmitted? Observation of the different breeds of domestic animals leads us to answer this question affirmatively, a conclusion that is confirmed by direct observation of the human species.

Finally, may we not say the same of the intellectual and moral faculties? May not our parents, who transmit to us the advantages or defects of their constitution and from whom we receive our features and shape, as well as our tendencies to certain physical affections, transmit to us also that part of their constitution on which intellect, intelligence, energy of soul, and moral sensibility depend as well? Is it not probable that education, by perfecting these qualities, will at the same time influence, modify, and perfect this organization itself? Analogy, investigation of the human faculties, and certain facts all appear to substantiate these conjectures and thus to enlarge the boundary of our hopes.

These are the questions with which we shall finish the final stage. How admirably does this view of the human race, emancipated from its chains, released from the dominion of chance, as well as from that of the enemies of progress, and advancing with a firm and sure step in the paths of truth, console the philosopher who laments the errors, the flagrant acts of injustice and the crimes with which the earth is still polluted. It is the contemplation of this prospect that rewards him for all his efforts to assist the progress of reason and the defense of liberty. He dares to regard these efforts as part of the eternal chain of human destiny and in this persuasion he finds the true delight of virtue and the pleasure of having performed a lasting service, which no stroke of fate calculated to restore the reign of prejudice and slavery can ever destroy. This contemplation is for him an asylum into which he retires, where the memory of his persecutors cannot follow him. He lives there in imagination, with man restored to his natural rights and dignity; he forgets human greed, fear or envy, which corrupt and torment. Here he truly lives with his peers in an elysium created by reason and embellished by the purest pleasures known to the lover of humanity.

Jean-Jacques Rousseau

Reason had its detractors, the most eloquent of whom was the Swiss-Frenchman Jean-Jacques Rousseau (1712–1778). Yet Rousseau's views were ambivalent. Closely associated with the *philosophes* for many years, he agreed with their criticisms of the decaying monarchies of Europe, especially that of France under Louis XV. In his most famous work, *The Social Contract*, he proposed a new kind of society, a form of direct democracy in which political power would reside not in the hands of a hereditary monarch but in the general will of the people.

On the value of reason Rousseau disagreed vehemently with most of his intellectual contemporaries. His most outspoken views on the subject appear in the short essay from which the following selection is taken. It was written in 1750 for a competition sponsored by the Academy of Dijon, on the question: Has the restoration of the arts and sciences had a purifying effect on morals? Rousseau answered with a resounding "No!"—and won the prize. One wonders what led the judges to their decision, for the argument of the essay, despite its passion, is clearly oversimple and overstated. But this essay, and Rousseau's attitude toward reason, is historically important. Through his denigration of human rational faculties and his championing of feeling and sentiment, Rousseau became the chief prophet of a new movement that would sweep Europe after his death—romanticism.

Consider the following questions as you study the text below.

1. Compare Rousseau's assumptions about human nature with those of Thomas Hobbes. What are the most important differences between the two men's ideas about human beings?

2. Why was Rousseau so critical of the arts and sciences? What did he hope would result from their abolition?

A Discourse on the Moral Effects of the Arts and Sciences

The question before me is: "Whether the Restoration of the arts and sciences has had the effect of purifying or corrupting morals." Which side am I

Jean-Jacques Rousseau, *The Social Contract and Discourses*, trans. G. D. H. Cole (London: J. M. Dent & Sons, Ltd., Everyman's Library Edition, 1913). Reprinted by permission of J. M. Dent & Sons, Ltd.

to take? That, gentlemen, which becomes an honest man, who is sensible of his own ignorance, and thinks himself none the worse for it.

I feel the difficulty of treating this subject fittingly, before the tribunal which is to judge of what I advance. How can I presume to belittle the sciences before one of the most learned assemblies in Europe, to commend ignorance in a famous Academy, and reconcile my contempt for study with the respect due to the truly learned?

I was aware of these inconsistencies, but not discouraged by them. It is not science, I said to myself, that I am attacking; it is virtue that I am defending, and that before virtuous men—and goodness is ever dearer to the good than learning to the learned.

What then have I to fear? The sagacity of the assembly before which I am pleading? That, I acknowledge, is to be feared; but rather on account of faults of construction than of the views I hold. Just sovereigns have never hesitated to decide against themselves in doubtful cases; and indeed the most advantageous situation in which a just claim can be, is that of being laid before a just and enlightened arbitrator, who is judge in his own case.

To this motive, which encouraged me, I may add another which finally decided me. And this is, that as I have upheld the cause of truth to the best of my natural abilities, whatever my apparent success, there is one reward which cannot fail me. That reward I shall find in the bottom of my heart.

The First Part

It is a noble and beautiful spectacle to see man raising himself, so to speak, from nothing by his own exertions; dissipating, by the light of reason, all the thick clouds in which he was by nature enveloped; mounting above himself; soaring in thought even to the celestial regions; like the sun, encompassing with giant strides the vast extent of the universe; and, what is still grander and more wonderful, going back into himself, there to study man and get to know his own nature, his duties and his end. All these miracles we have seen renewed within the last few generations.

Europe had relapsed into the barbarism of the earliest ages; the inhabitants of this part of the world, which is at present so highly enlightened, were plunged, some centuries ago, in a state still worse than ignorance. A scientific jargon, more despicable than mere ignorance, had usurped the name of knowledge, and opposed an almost invincible obstacle to its restoration.

Things had come to such a pass, that it required a complete revolution to bring men back to common sense. This came at last from the quarter from which it was least to be expected. It was the stupid Mussulman, the eternal scourge of letters, who was the immediate cause of their revival among us. The fall of the throne of Constantine brought to Italy the relics of ancient Greece; and with these precious spoils France in turn was enriched. The sciences soon followed literature, and the art of thinking joined that of writing: an order which may seem strange, but is perhaps only too natural. The world now began to perceive the principal advantage of an intercourse with the Muses, that of rendering mankind more sociable by inspiring them with the desire to please one another with performances worthy of their mutual approbation.

The mind, as well as the body, has its needs: those of the body are the basis of society, those of the mind its ornaments.

So long as government and law provide for the security and well-being of men in their common life, the arts, literature, and the sciences, less despotic though perhaps more powerful, fling garlands of flowers over the chains which weigh them down. They stifle in men's breasts that sense of original liberty, for which they seem to have been born; cause them to love their own slavery, and so make of them what is called a civilized people.

Necessity raised up thrones; the arts and sciences have made them strong. Powers of the earth, cherish all talents and protect those who cultivate them. Civilized peoples, cultivate such pursuits; to them, happy slaves, you owe that delicacy and exquisiteness of taste, which is so much your boast, that sweetness of disposition and urbanity of manners which make intercourse so easy and agreeable among you—in a word, the appearance of all the virtues, without being in possession of one of them.

It was for this sort of accomplishment, which is by so much the more captivating, as it seems less affected, that Athens and Rome were so much distinguished in the boasted times of their splendour and magnificence: and it is doubtless in the same respect that our own age and nation will excel all periods and peoples. An air of philosophy without pedantry; an address at once natural and engaging, distant equally from Teutonic clumsiness and Italian pantomime: these are the effects of a taste acquired by liberal studies and improved by conversation with the world. What happiness would it be for those who live among us, if our external appearance were always a true mirror of our hearts; if decorum were but virtue; if the maxims we professed were the rules of our conduct; and if real philosophy were inseparable from the title of a philosopher! But so many good qualities too seldom go together; virtue rarely appears in so much pomp and state.

Richness of apparel may proclaim the man of fortune, and elegance the man of taste; but true health and manliness are known by different signs. It is under the homespun of the laborer, and not beneath the gilt and tinsel of the courtier, that we should look for strength and vigour of body.

External ornaments are no less foreign to virtue, which is the strength and activity of the mind. The honest man is an athlete, who loves to wrestle stark naked; he scorns all those vile trappings, which prevent the exertion of his strength, and were, for the most part, invented only to conceal some deformity.

Before art had molded our behavior, and taught our passions to speak an artificial language, our morals were rude but natural; and the different ways in which we behaved proclaimed at the first glance the difference of our dispositions. Human nature was not at bottom better then than now; but men found their security in the ease with which they could see through one another, and this advantage, of which we no longer feel the value, prevented their having many vices.

In our day, now that more subtle study and a more refined taste have reduced the art of pleasing to a system, there prevails in modern manners a servile and deceptive conformity; so that one would think every mind had been cast in the same mold. Politeness requires this thing; decorum that; ceremony has its forms, and fashion its laws, and these we must always follow, never the promptings of our own nature.

We no longer dare seem what we really are, but lie under a perpetual restraint; in the meantime the herd of men, which we call society, all act under the same circumstances exactly alike, unless very particular and powerful motives prevent them. Thus we never know with whom we have to deal; and even to know our friends we must wait for some critical and pressing occasion; that is, till it is too late; for it is on those very occasions that such knowledge is of use to us.

What a train of vices must attend this uncertainty! Sincere friendship, real esteem, and perfect confidence are banished from among men. Jealousy, suspicion, fear, coldness, reserve, hate, and fraud lie constantly concealed under that uniform and deceitful veil of politeness; that boasted candour and urbanity, for which we are indebted to the light and leading of this age. We shall no longer take in vain by our oaths the name of our Creator; but we shall insult Him with our blasphemies, and our scrupulous ears will take no offence. We have grown too modest to brag of our own deserts; but we do not scruple to decry those of others. We do not grossly outrage even our enemies, but artfully calumniate them. Our hatred of other nations diminishes, but patriotism dies with it. Ignorance is held in contempt; but a dangerous scepticism has succeeded it. Some vices indeed are condemned and others grown dishonourable; but we have still many that are honoured with the names of virtues, and it has become necessary that we should either have, or at least pretend to have them. Let who will extol the moderation of our modern sages, I see nothing in it but a refinement of intemperance as unworthy of my commendation as their artificial simplicity.

Such is the purity to which our morals have attained; this is the virtue we have made our own. Let the arts and sciences claim the share they have had in this salutary work. I shall add but one reflection more; suppose an inhabitant of some distant country should endeavor to form an idea of European morals from the state of the sciences, the perfection of the arts, the propriety of our public entertainments, the politeness of our behavior, the affability of our conversation, our constant professions of benevolence, and from those tumultuous assemblies of people of all ranks, who seem, from morning till night, to have no other care than to oblige one another. Such a stranger, I maintain, would arrive at a totally false view of our morality.

Where there is no effect, it is idle to look for a cause: but here the effect is certain and the depravity actual; our minds have been corrupted in proportion as the arts and sciences have improved. Will it be said, that this is a misfortune peculiar to the present age? No, gentlemen, the evils resulting from our vain curiosity are as old as the world. The daily ebb and flow of the tides are not more regularly influenced by the moon than the morals of a people by the progress of the arts and sciences. As their light has risen above our horizon, virtue has taken flight, and the same phenomenon has been constantly observed in all times and places.

.   .   .

Thus it is that luxury, profligacy, and slavery have been, in all ages, the scourge of the efforts of our pride to emerge from that happy state of ignorance, in which the wisdom of providence had placed us. That thick veil with which it has covered all its operations seems to be a sufficient proof that it never designed us for such fruitless researches. But is there, indeed, one lesson it has taught us, by which we have rightly profited, or which we have neglected with impunity? Let men learn for once that nature would have preserved them from science, as a mother snatches a dangerous weapon from the hands of her child. Let them know that all the secrets she hides are so many evils from which she protects them, and that the very difficulty they find in acquiring knowledge is not the least of her bounty towards them. Men are perverse; but they would have been far worse, if they had had the misfortune to be born learned.

How humiliating are these reflections to humanity, and how mortified by them our pride should be! What! it will be asked, is uprightness the child of ignorance? Is virtue inconsistent with learning? What consequences might not be drawn from such suppositions? But to reconcile these apparent contradictions, we need only examine closely the emptiness and vanity of those pompous titles, which are so liberally bestowed on human knowledge, and which so blind our judgment. Let us consider, therefore, the arts and sciences in themselves. Let us see what must result from their advancement, and let us not hesitate to admit the truth of all those points on which our arguments coincide with the inductions we can make from history.

The Second Part

An ancient tradition passed out of Egypt into Greece, that some god, who was an enemy to the repose of mankind, was the inventor of the sciences. What must the Egyptians, among whom the sciences first arose, have thought of them? And they beheld, near at hand, the sources from which they sprang. In fact, whether we turn to the annals of the world, or eke out with philosophical investigations the uncertain chronicles of history, we shall not find for human knowledge an origin answering to the idea we are pleased to entertain of it at present. Astronomy was born of superstition, eloquence of ambition, hatred, falsehood, and flattery; geometry of avarice; physics of an idle curiosity; and even moral philosophy of human pride. Thus the arts and sciences owe their birth to our vices; we should be less doubtful of their advantages, if they had sprung from our virtues.

Their evil origin is, indeed, but too plainly reproduced in their objects. What would become of the arts, were they not cherished by luxury? If men were not unjust, of what use were jurisprudence? What would become of history, if there were no tyrants, wars, or conspiracies? In a word who would pass his life in barren speculations, if everybody, attentive only to the obligations of humanity and the necessities of nature, spent his whole life in serving his country, obliging his friends, and relieving the unhappy? Are we then made to live and die on the brink of that well at the bottom of which Truth lies hid? This reflection alone is, in my opinion, enough to discourage at first setting out every man who seriously endeavours to instruct himself by the study of philosophy.

What a variety of dangers surrounds us! What a number of wrong paths present themselves in the investigation of the sciences! Through how many errors, more perilous than truth itself is useful, must we not pass to arrive at it? The disadvantages we lie under are evident; for falsehood is capable of an infinite variety of combinations; but the truth has only one manner of being. Besides, where is the man who sincerely desires to find it? Or even admitting his good will, by what characteristic marks is he sure of knowing it? Amid the infinite diversity of opinions where is the criterion by which we may certainly judge of it? Again, what is still more difficult, should we even be fortunate enough to discover it, who among us will know how to make right use of it?

If our sciences are futile in the objects they propose, they are no less dangerous in the effects they produce. Being the effect of idleness, they generate idleness in their turn; and an irreparable loss of time is the first prejudice which they must necessarily cause to society. To live without doing some good is a great evil as well in the political as in the moral world; and hence every useless citizen should be regarded as a pernicious person. Tell me then, illustrious philosophers, of whom we learn the ratios in which attraction acts *in vacuo*; and in the revolution of the planets, the relations of spaces traversed in equal times; by whom we are taught what curves have conjugate points, points of inflexion, and cusps; how the soul and body correspond, like two clocks, without actual communication; what planets may be inhabited; and what insects reproduce in an extraordinary manner. Answer me, I say, you from whom we receive all this sublime information, whether we should have been less numerous, worse governed, less formidable, less flourishing, or more perverse, supposing you had taught us none of all these fine things.

Reconsider therefore the importance of your productions; and, since the labours of the most enlightened of our learned men and the best of our citizens are of so little utility, tell us what we ought to think of that numerous herd of obscure writers and useless *littérateurs*, who devour without any return the substance of the State.

Useless, do I say? Would God they were! Society would be more peaceful, and morals less corrupt. But these vain and futile declaimers go forth on all sides, armed with their fatal paradoxes, to sap the foundations of our faith, and nullify virtue. They smile contemptuously at such old names as patriotism and religion, and consecrate their talents and philosophy to the destruction and defamation of all that men hold sacred. Not that they bear any real hatred to virtue or dogma; they are the enemies of public opinion alone; to bring them to the foot of the altar, it would be enough to banish them to a land of atheists. What extravagancies will not the rage of singularity induce men to commit!

The waste of time is certainly a great evil; but still greater evils attend upon literature and the arts. One is luxury, produced like them by indolence and vanity. Luxury is seldom unattended by the arts and sciences; and they are always attended by luxury. I know that our philosophy, fertile in paradoxes, pretends, in contradiction to the experience of all ages, that luxury contributes to the splendour of States. But, without insisting on the necessity of sumptuary laws, can it be denied that rectitude of morals is essential to the duration of empires, and that luxury is diametrically opposed to such rectitude? Let it be admitted that luxury is a certain indication of wealth; that it even serves, if you will, to increase such wealth; what conclusion is to be drawn from this paradox, so worthy of the times? And what will become of virtue if riches are to be acquired at any cost? The politicians of the ancient world were always talking of morals and virtue; ours speak of nothing but commerce and money. One of them will tell you that in such a country a man is worth just as much as he will sell for at Algiers: another, pursuing the same mode of calculation, finds that in some countries a man is worth nothing, and in others still less than nothing; they value men as they do droves of oxen.

.   .   .

We cannot reflect on the morality of mankind without contemplating with pleasure the picture of the simplicity which prevailed in the earliest times. This image may be justly compared to a beautiful coast, adorned only by the hands of nature; towards which our eyes are constantly turned, and which we see receding with regret. While men were innocent and virtuous and loved to have the gods for witnesses of their actions, they dwelt together in the same huts; but when they became vicious, they grew tired of such inconvenient onlookers, and banished them to magnificent temples. Finally, they expelled their deities even from these, in order to dwell there themselves; or at least the temples of the gods were no longer more magnificent than the palaces of the citizens. This was the height of degeneracy; nor could vice ever be carried to greater lengths than when it was seen, supported, as it were, at the doors of the great, on columns of marble, and graven on Corinthian capitals.

As the conveniences of life increase, as the arts are brought to perfection, and luxury spreads, true courage flags, the virtues disappear; and all this is the effect of the sciences and of those acts which are exercised in the privacy of men's dwellings. When the Goths ravaged Greece, the libraries only escaped the flames owing to an opinion that was set on foot among them, that it was best to leave the enemy with a possession so calculated to divert their attention from military exercises, and keep them engaged in indolent and sedentary occupations.

Charles the Eighth found himself master of Tuscany and the kingdom of Naples, almost without drawing sword; and all his court attributed this unexpected success to the fact that the princes and nobles of Italy applied themselves with greater earnestness to the cultivation of their understandings than to active and martial pursuits. In fact, says the sensible person who records these characteristics, experience plainly tells us that in military matters and all that resemble them application to the sciences tends rather to make men effeminate and cowardly than resolute and vigorous.

The Romans confessed that military virtue was extinguished among them, in proportion as they became connoisseurs in the arts of the painter, the engraver, and the goldsmith, and began to cultivate the fine arts. Indeed, as if this famous country was to be for ever an example to other nations, the rise of the Medici and the revival of letters has once more destroyed, this time perhaps for ever, the martial reputation which Italy seemed a few centuries ago to have recovered.

The ancient republics of Greece, with that wisdom which was so conspicuous in most of their institutions, forbade their citizens to pursue all those inactive and sedentary occupations, which by enervating and corrupting the body diminish also the vigour of the mind. With what courage, in fact, can it be thought that hunger and thirst, fatigues, dangers, and death, can be faced by men whom the smallest want overwhelms and the slightest difficulty repels? With what resolution can soldiers support the excessive toils of war, when they are entirely unaccustomed to them? With what spirits can they make forced marches under officers who have not even the strength to travel on horseback? It is no answer to cite the reputed valour of all the modern warriors who are so scientifically trained. I hear much of their bravery in a day's battle; but I am told nothing of how they support excessive fatigue, how they stand the severity of the seasons and the inclemency of the weather. A little sunshine or snow, or the want of a few superfluities, is enough to cripple and destroy one of our finest armies in a few days. Intrepid warriors! permit me for once to tell you the truth, which you seldom hear. Of your bravery I am fully satisfied. I have no doubt that you would have triumphed with Hannibal at Cannae, and at Trasimene: that you would have passed the Rubicon with Caesar, and enabled him to enslave his country; but you never would have been able to cross the Alps with the former, or with the latter to subdue your own ancestors, the Gauls.

A war does not always depend on the events of battle: there is in generalship an art superior to that of gaining victories. A man may behave with great intrepidity under fire, and yet be a very bad officer. Even in the common soldier, a little more strength and vigor would perhaps be more useful than so much courage, which after all is no protection from death. And what does it matter to the State whether its troops perish by cold and fever, or by the sword of the enemy?

If the cultivation of the sciences is prejudicial to military qualities, it is still more so to moral qualities. Even from our infancy an absurd system of education serves to adorn our wit and corrupt our judgment. We see, on every side, huge institutions, where our youth are educated at great expense, and instructed in everything but their duty. Your children will be ignorant of their own language, when they can talk others which are not spoken anywhere. They will be able to compose verses which they can hardly understand; and, without being capable of distinguishing truth from error, they will possess the art of making them unrecognizable by specious arguments. But magnanimity, equity, temperance, humanity, and courage will be words of which they know not the meaning. The dear name of country will never strike on their ears; and if they ever hear speak of God, it will be less to fear than to be frightened of Him. I would as soon, said a wise man, that my pupil had spent his time in the tennis court as in this manner; for there his body at least would have got exercise.

I well know that children ought to be kept employed, and that idleness is for them the danger most to be feared. But what should they be taught? This is undoubtedly an important question. Let them be taught what they are to practise when they come to be men; not what they ought to forget.

Our gardens are adorned with statues and our galleries with pictures. What would you imagine these masterpieces of art, thus exhibited to public admiration, represent? The great men who have defended their country, or the still greater men who have enriched it by their virtues? Far from it. They are the images of every perversion of heart and mind, carefully selected from ancient mythology, and presented to the early curiosity of our children, doubtless that they may have before their eyes the representations of vicious actions, even before they are able to read.

Whence arise all those abuses, unless it be from that fatal inequality introduced among men by the difference of talents and the cheapening of virtue? This is the most evident effect of all our studies, and the most dangerous of all their consequences. The question is no longer whether a man is honest, but whether he is clever. We do not ask whether a book is useful, but whether it is well written. Rewards are lavished on wit and ingenuity, while virtue is left unhonoured. There are a thousand prizes for fine discourses, and none for good actions. I should be glad, however, to know whether the honour attaching to the best discourse that ever wins the prize in this Academy is comparable with the merit of having founded the prize.

A wise man does not go in chase of fortune; but he is by no means insensible to glory, and when he sees it so ill distributed, his virtue, which might have been animated by a little emulation, and turned to the advantage of society, droops and dies away in obscurity and indigence. It is for this reason that the agreeable arts must in time everywhere be preferred to the useful; and this truth has been but too much confirmed since the revival of the arts and sciences. We have physicists, geometricians, chemists, astronomers, poets, musicians, and painters in plenty; but we have no longer a citizen among us; or if there be found a few scattered over our abandoned countryside, they are left to perish there unnoticed and neglected. Such is the condition to which we are reduced, and such are our feelings towards those who give us our daily bread, and our children milk.

I confess, however, that the evil is not so great as it might have become. The eternal providence, in placing salutary simples beside noxious plants, and making poisonous animals contain their own antidote, has taught the sovereigns of the earth, who are its ministers, to imitate its wisdom. It is by following this example that the truly great monarch, to whose glory every age will add new lustre, drew from the very fountains of a thousand lapses from rectitude, those famous societies, which, while they are depositories of the dangerous trust of human knowledge, are yet the sacred guardians of morals, by the attention they pay to their maintenance among themselves in all their purity, and by the demands which they make on every member whom they admit.

These wise institutions, confirmed by his august successor and imitated by all the kings of Europe, will serve at least to restrain men of letters, who, all aspiring to the honour of being admitted into these Academies, will keep watch over themselves, and endeavour to make themselves worthy of such honour by useful performances and irreproachable morals. Those Academies, also, which, in proposing prizes for literary merit, make choice of such subjects as are calculated to arouse the love of virtue in the hearts of citizens, prove that it prevails in themselves, and must give men the rare and real pleasure of finding learned societies devoting themselves to the enlightenment of mankind, not only by agreeable exercises of the intellect, but also by useful instructions.

An objection which may be made is, in fact, only an additional proof of my argument. So much precaution proves but too evidently the need for it. We never seek remedies for evils that do not exist. Why, indeed, must these bear all the marks of ordinary remedies, on account of their inefficacy? The numerous establishments in favour of the learned are only adapted to make

men mistake the objects of the sciences, and turn men's attention to the cultivation of them. One would be inclined to think, from the precautions everywhere taken, that we are overstocked with husbandmen, and are afraid of a
shortage of philosophers. I will not venture here to enter into a comparison
between agriculture and philosophy, as they would not bear it. I shall only
ask: What is philosophy? What is contained in the writings of the most celebrated philosophers? What are the lessons of these friends of wisdom? To
hear them, should we not take them for so many mountebanks, exhibiting
themselves in public, and crying out, *Here, Here, come to me, I am the only true
doctor*? One of them teaches that there is no such thing as matter, but that
everything exists only in representation. Another declares that there is no
other substance than matter, and no other God than the world itself. A third
tells you that there are no such things as virtue and vice, and that moral good
and evil are chimeras; while a fourth informs you that men are only beasts of
prey, and may conscientiously devour one another. Why, my great philosophers, do you not reserve these wise and profitable lessons for your friends
and children? You would soon reap the benefit of them, nor should we be
under the apprehension of our own becoming your disciples.

Such are the wonderful men, whom their contemporaries held in the
highest esteem during their lives, and to whom immortality has been attributed since their decease. Such are the wise maxims we have received from
them, and which are transmitted, from age to age, to our descendants. Pa-
ganism, though given over to all the extravagances of human reason, has left
nothing to compare with the shameful monuments which have been prepared by the art of printing, during the reign of the gospel. The impious
writings of Leucippus and Diagoras[1] perished with their authors. The world,
in their days, was ignorant of the art of immortalizing the errors and extravagances of the human mind. But thanks to the art of printing and the use we
make of it, the pernicious reflections of Hobbes and Spinoza[2] will last for
ever. Go, famous writings, of which the ignorance and rusticity of our forefathers would have been incapable. Go to our descendants, along with those
still more pernicious works which reek of the corrupted manners of the present age! Let them together convey to posterity a faithful history of the
progress and advantages of our arts and sciences. If they are read, they will
leave not a doubt about the question we are now discussing, and unless
mankind should then be still more foolish than we, they will lift up their
hands to Heaven and exclaim in bitterness of heart: "Almighty God! Thou
who holdest in Thy hand the minds of men, deliver us from the fatal arts and
sciences of our forefathers; give us back ignorance, innocence, and poverty,
which alone can make us happy and are precious in Thy sight."

---

[1][ancient Greek thinkers—*Ed.*]
[2][Dutch philosopher (1632–1677)—*Ed.*]

Liberty, Equality, and Fraternity

Olympe de Gouges (1745–1793) was the daughter of a butcher. Married to an older man at age sixteen, she was a widow most of her adult life. After her husband's death, she vowed never to remarry and sought to support herself as a writer. De Gouges was the author of numerous plays and political pamphlets. When the Revolution came, de Gouges was a tireless advocate of the notion that the freedom the Revolution promised should be extended to all people, regardless of race or gender. These positions, combined with her public opposition to the violent excesses of the Terror, led to her arrest and execution as a traitor in 1793.

Her "Declaration of the Rights of Women" was a direct response to the "Declaration of the Rights of Man and Citizen" approved by the National Assembly in August 1789. Her contention was that the rights and freedoms described in that document were not being applied to women and, until this was remedied, the nation could never achieve the goals of the Revolution. As you read the Declaration, pay particular attention to de Gouges's ideas about the character of the nation. On what is the nation founded? What must be done for a nation to achieve its most perfect form?

Consider the following questions as you study the text below.

1. Compare the "Declaration of the Rights of Man and Citizen" with the "Declaration of the Rights of Women." How do they differ? According to de Gouges, how were the ambitions embodied in the "Declaration of the Rights of Man and Citizen" undermined by the National Assembly's failure to address the rights of women?

2. How would you explain de Gouges's emphasis on marriage and property rights? Why might these issues have been so important to her? What connection did de Gouges make between the rights of women and the rights of slaves?

Declaration of the Rights of Man and Citizen

The representatives of the French people, organized in National Assembly, considering that ignorance, forgetfulness, or contempt of the rights of man are the sole causes of public misfortunes and of the corruption of governments, have resolved to set forth in a solemn declaration the natural, inalienable, and sacred rights of man, in order that such declaration, continually before all members of the social body, may be a perpetual reminder of their rights and duties; in order that the acts of the legislative power and those of the executive power may constantly be compared with the aim of every political institution and may accordingly be more respected; in order that the demands of the citizens, founded henceforth upon simple and incontestable principles, may always be directed towards the maintenance of the Constitution and the welfare of all.

Accordingly, the National Assembly recognizes and proclaims, in the presence and under the auspices of the Supreme Being, the following rights of man and citizen.

1.   Men are born and remain free and equal in rights; social distinctions may be based only upon general usefulness.

2.   The aim of every political association is the preservation of the natural and inalienable rights of man; these rights are liberty, property, security, and resistance to oppression.

3.   The source of all sovereignty resides essentially in the nation; no group, no individual may exercise authority not emanating expressly therefrom.

4.   Liberty consists of the power to do whatever is not injurious to others; thus the enjoyment of the natural rights of every man has for its limits only those that assure other members of society the enjoyment of those same rights; such limits may be determined only by law.

5.   The law has the right to forbid only actions which are injurious to society. Whatever is not forbidden by law may not be prevented, and no one may be constrained to do what it does not prescribe.

6.   Law is the expression of the general will; all citizens have the right to concur personally, or through their representatives, in its formation; it must be the same for all, whether it protects or punishes. All citizens, being equal before it, are equally admissible to all public offices, positions, and employments, according to their capacity, and without other distinction than that of virtues and talents.

7.   No man may be accused, arrested, or detained except in the cases determined by law, and according to the forms prescribed thereby. Whoever solicit, expedite, or execute arbitrary orders, or have them executed, must be punished; but every citizen summoned or apprehended in pursuance of the law must obey immediately; he renders himself culpable by resistance.

8.   The law is to establish only penalties that are absolutely and obviously necessary; and no one may be punished except by virtue of a law established and promulgated prior to the offence and legally applied.

9.   Since every man is presumed innocent until declared guilty, if arrest be deemed indispensable, all unnecessary severity for securing the person of the accused must be severely repressed by law.

10. No one is to be disquieted because of his opinions, even religious, provided their manifestation does not disturb the public order established by law.

11. Free communication of ideas and opinions is one of the most precious of the rights of man. Consequently, every citizen may speak, write, and print freely, subject to responsibility for the abuse of such liberty in the cases determined by law.

12. The guarantee of the rights of man and citizen necessitates a public force; such a force, therefore, is instituted for the advantage of all and not for the particular benefit of those to whom it is entrusted.

13. For the maintenance of the public force and for the expenses of administration a common tax is indispensable; it must be assessed equally on all citizens in proportion to their means.

14. Citizens have the right to ascertain, by themselves or through their representatives, the necessity of the public tax, to consent to it freely, to supervise its use, and to determine its quota, assessment, payment, and duration.

15. Society has the right to require of every public agent an accounting of his administration.

16. Every society in which the guarantee of rights is not assured or the separation of powers not determined has no constitution at all.

17. Since property is a sacred and inviolate right, no one may be deprived thereof unless a legally established public necessity obviously requires it, and upon condition of a just and previous indemnity.

Declaration of the Rights of Women

Man, are you capable of being just? It is a woman who poses the question; you will not deprive her of that right at least. Tell me, what gives you sovereign empire to oppress my sex? Your strength? Your talents? Observe the Creator in his wisdom; survey in all her grandeur that nature with whom you seem to want to be in harmony, and give me, if you dare, an example of this tyrannical empire. Go back to animals, consult the elements, study plants, finally glance at all the modifications of organic matter, and surrender to the evidence when I offer you the means; search, probe, and distinguish, if you can, the sexes in the administration of nature. Everywhere you will find them mingled; everywhere they cooperate in harmonious togetherness in this immortal masterpiece.

Olympe de Gouges, "Declaration of the Rights of Women," in *Women in Revolutionary Paris: 1789–1795*, trans. Darline Gay Levy, Harriet Branson Applewhite, and Mary Durham Johnson (Urbana: University of Illinois Press, 1979), pp. 89–96. Reprinted by permission of the University of Illinois Press.

Man alone has raised his exceptional circumstances to a principle. Bizarre, blind, bloated with science and degenerated—in a century of enlightenment and wisdom—into the crassest ignorance, he wants to command as a despot a sex which is in full possession of its intellectual faculties; he pretends to enjoy the Revolution and to claim his rights to equality in order to say nothing more about it.

DECLARATION OF THE RIGHTS OF WOMAN AND THE FEMALE CITIZEN

For the National Assembly to decree in its last sessions, or in those of the next legislature:

PREAMBLE

Mothers, daughters, sisters [and] representatives of the nation demand to be constituted into a national assembly. Believing that ignorance, omission, or scorn for the rights of woman are the only causes of public misfortunes and of the corruption of governments, [the women] have resolved to set forth in a solemn declaration the natural, inalienable, and sacred rights of woman in order that this declaration, constantly exposed before all the members of the society, will ceaselessly remind them of their rights and duties; in order that the authoritative acts of women and the authoritative acts of men may be at any moment compared with and respectful of the purpose of all political institutions; and in order that citizens' demands, henceforth based on simple and incontestable principles, will always support the constitution, good morals, and the happiness of all.

Consequently, the sex that is as superior in beauty as it is in courage during the sufferings of maternity recognizes and declares in the presence and under the auspices of the Supreme Being, the following Rights of Woman and of Female Citizens.

Article I. Woman is born free and lives equal to man in her rights. Social distinctions can be based only on the common utility.

Article II. The purpose of any political association is the conservation of the natural and imprescriptible rights of woman and man; these rights are liberty, property, security, and especially resistance to oppression.

Article III. The principle of all sovereignty rests essentially with the nation, which is nothing but the union of woman and man; no body and no individual can exercise any authority which does not come expressly from it [the nation].

Article IV. Liberty and justice consist of restoring all that belongs to others; thus, the only limits on the exercise of the natural rights of woman are perpetual male tyranny; these limits are to be reformed by the laws of nature and reason.

Article V.   Laws of nature and reason proscribe all acts harmful to society; everything which is not prohibited by these wise and divine laws cannot be prevented, and no one can be constrained to do what they do not command.

Article VI.   The law must be the expression of the general will; all female and male citizens must contribute either personally or through their representatives to its formation; it must be the same for all: male and female citizens, being equal in the eyes of the law, must be equally admitted to all honors, positions, and public employment according to their capacity and without other distinctions besides those of their virtues and talents.

Article VII.   No woman is an exception; she is accused, arrested, and detained in cases determined by law. Women, like men, obey this rigorous law.

Article VIII.   The law must establish only those penalties that are strictly and obviously necessary, and no one can be punished except by virtue of a law established and promulgated prior to the crime and legally applicable to women.

Article IX.   Once any woman is declared guilty, complete rigor is [to be] exercised by the law.

Article X.   No one is to be disquieted for his very basic opinions; woman has the right to mount the scaffold; she must equally have the right to mount the rostrum, provided that her demonstrations do not disturb the legally established public order.

Article XI.   The free communication of thoughts and opinions is one of the most precious rights of woman, since that liberty assures the recognition of children by their fathers. Any female citizen thus may say freely, I am the mother of a child which belongs to you, without being forced by a barbarous prejudice to hide the truth; [an exception may be made] to respond to the abuse of this liberty in cases determined by the law.

Article XII.   The guarantee of the rights of woman and the female citizen implies a major benefit; this guarantee must be instituted for the advantage of all, and not for the particular benefit of those to whom it is entrusted.

Article XIII.   For the support of the public force and the expenses of administration, the contributions of woman and man are equal; she shares all the duties [*corvées*] and all the painful tasks; therefore, she must have the same share in the distribution of positions, employment, offices, honors, and jobs [*industrie*].

Article XIV.   Female and male citizens have the right to verify, either by themselves or through their representatives, the necessity of the public contribution. This can only apply to women if they are granted an equal share, not only of wealth, but also of public administration, and in the determination of the proportion, the base, the collection, and the duration of the tax.

Article XV.   The collectivity of women, joined for tax purposes to the aggregate of men, has the right to demand an accounting of his administration from any public agent.

Article XVI.   No society has a constitution without the guarantee of rights and the separation of powers; the constitution is null if the majority of individuals comprising the nation have not cooperated in drafting it.

Article XVII.   Property belongs to both sexes whether united or separate; for each it is an inviolable and sacred right; no one can be deprived of it, since it is the true patrimony of nature, unless the legally determined public need obviously dictates it, and then only with a just and prior indemnity.

POSTSCRIPT

Woman, *wake up*; the tocsin of reason is being heard throughout the whole universe; discover your rights. The powerful empire of nature is no longer surrounded by prejudice, fanaticism, superstition, and lies. The flame of truth has dispersed all the clouds of folly and usurpation. Enslaved man has multiplied his strength and needs recourse to yours to break his chains. Having become free, he has become unjust to his companion. Oh, women, women! When will you cease to be blind? What advantage have you received from the Revolution? A more pronounced scorn, a more marked disdain. In the centuries of corruption you ruled only over the weakness of men. The reclamation of your patrimony, based on the wise decrees of nature—what have you to dread from such a fine undertaking? The *bon mot* of the legislator of the marriage of Cana? Do you fear that our French legislators, correctors of that morality, long ensnared by political practices now out of date, will only say again to you: women, what is there in common between you and us? Everything, you will have to answer. If they persist in their weakness in putting this non sequitur in contradiction to their principles, courageously oppose the force of reason to the empty pretentions of superiority; unite yourselves beneath the standards of philosophy; deploy all the energy of your character, and you will soon see these haughty men, not groveling at your feet as servile adorers, but proud to share with you the treasures of the Supreme Being. Regardless of what barriers confront you, it is in your power to free yourselves; you have only to want to. Let us pass now to the shocking tableau of what you have been in society; and since national education is in question at this moment, let us see whether our wise legislators will think judiciously about the education of women.

Women have done more harm than good. Constraint and dissimulation have been their lot. What force had robbed them of, ruse returned to them; they had recourse to all the resources of their charms, and the most irreproachable person did not resist them. Poison and the sword were both subject to them; they commanded in crime as in fortune. The French government, especially, depended throughout the centuries on the nocturnal administration of women; the cabinet kept no secret from their indiscretion; ambassadorial post, command, ministry, presidency, pontificate, college of cardinals; finally, anything which characterizes the folly of men, profane and sacred, all have been subject to the cupidity and ambition of this sex, formerly contemptible and respected, and since the revolution, respectable and scorned.

In this sort of contradictory situation, what remarks could I nor make! I have but a moment to make them, but this moment will fix the attention of the remotest posterity. Under the Old Regime, all was vicious, all was guilty; but could not the amelioration of conditions be perceived even in the substance of vices? A woman only had to be beautiful or amiable; when she possessed these two advantages, she saw a hundred fortunes at her feet. If she did not profit from them, she had a bizarre character or a rare philosophy which made her scorn wealth; then she was deemed to be like a crazy woman; the most indecent made herself respected with gold; commerce in women was a kind of industry in the first class [of society], which, henceforth, will have no more credit. If it still had it, the revolution would be lost, and under the new relationships we would always be corrupted; however, reason can always be deceived [into believing] that any other road to fortune is closed to the woman whom a man buys, like the slave on the African coasts. The difference is great; that is known. The slave is commanded by the master; but if the master gives her liberty without recompense, and at an age when the slave has lost all her charms, what will become of this unfortunate woman? The victim of scorn, even the doors of charity are closed to her; she is poor and old, they say; why did she not know how to make her fortune? Reason finds other examples that are even more touching. A young, inexperienced woman, seduced by a man whom she loves, will abandon her parents to follow him; the ingrate will leave her after a few years, and the older she has become with him, the more inhuman is his inconstancy; if she has children, he will likewise abandon them. If he is rich, he will consider himself excused from sharing his fortune with his noble victims. If some involvement binds him to his duties, he will deny them, trusting that the laws will support him. If he is married, any other obligation loses its rights. Then what laws remain to extirpate vice all the way to its root? The law of dividing wealth and public administration between men and women. It can easily be seen that one who is born into a rich family gains very much from such equal sharing. But the one born into a poor family with merit and virtue— what is her lot? Poverty and opprobrium. If she does not precisely excel in music or painting, she cannot be admitted to any public function when she has all the capacity for it. I do not want to give only a sketch of things; I will go more deeply into this in the new edition of all my political writings, with notes, which I propose to give to the public in a few days.

I take up my text again on the subject of morals. Marriage is the tomb of trust and love. The married woman can with impunity give bastards to her husband, and also give them the wealth which does not belong to them. The woman who is unmarried has only one feeble right; ancient and inhuman laws refuse to her for her children the right to the name and the wealth of their father; no new laws have been made in this matter. If it is considered a paradox and an impossibility on my part to try to give my sex an honorable and just consistency, I leave it to men to attain glory for dealing with this matter; but while we wait, the way can be prepared through national education, the restoration of morals, and conjugal conventions.

FORM FOR A SOCIAL CONTRACT BETWEEN MAN AND WOMAN

We, _____ and _____, moved by our own will, unite ourselves for the duration of our lives, and for the duration of our mutual inclinations, under the following conditions: We intend and wish to make our wealth communal, meanwhile reserving to ourselves the right to divide it in favor of our children and of those toward whom we might have a particular inclination, mutually recognizing that our property belongs directly to our children, from whatever bed they come, and that all of them without distinction have the right to bear the name of the fathers and mothers who have acknowledged them, and we are charged to subscribe to the law which punishes the renunciation of one's own blood. We likewise obligate ourselves, in case of separation, to divide our wealth and to set aside in advance the portion the law indicates for our children, and in the event of a perfect union, the one who dies will divest himself of half his property in his children's favor, and if one dies childless, the survivor will inherit by right, unless the dying person has disposed of half the common property in favor of one whom he judged deserving.

That is approximately the formula for the marriage act I propose for execution. Upon reading this strange document, I see rising up against me the hypocrites, the prudes, the clergy, and the whole infernal sequence. But how it [my proposal] offers to the wise the moral means of achieving the perfection of a happy government! I am going to give in a few words the physical proof of it. The rich, childless Epicurean finds it very good to go to his poor neighbor to augment his family. When there is a law authorizing a poor man's wife to have a rich one adopt their children, the bonds of society will be strengthened and morals will be purer. This law will perhaps save the community's wealth and hold back the disorder which drives so many victims to the almshouses of shame, to a low station, and into degenerate human principles where nature has groaned for so long. May the detractors of wise philosophy then cease to cry out against primitive morals, or may they lose their point in the source of their citations.

Moreover, I would like a law which would assist widows and young girls deceived by the false promises of a man to whom they were attached;

I would like, I say, this law to force an inconstant man to hold to his obligations or at least [to pay] an indemnity equal to his wealth. Again, I would like this law to be rigorous against women, at least those who have the effrontery to have recourse to a law which they themselves had violated by their misconduct, if proof of that were given. At the same time, as I showed in *Le Bonheur primitif de l'homme*, in 1788, that prostitutes should be placed in designated quarters. It is not prostitutes who contribute the most to the depravity of morals, it is the women of society. In regenerating the latter, the former are changed. This link of fraternal union will first bring disorder, but in consequence it will produce at the end a perfect harmony.

I offer a foolproof way to elevate the soul of women; it is to join them to all the activities of man; if man persists in finding this way impractical, let him share his fortune with woman, not at his caprice, but by the wisdom of laws. Prejudice falls, morals are purified, and nature regains all her rights. Add to this the marriage of priests and the strengthening of the king on his throne, and the French government cannot fail.

It would be very necessary to say a few words on the troubles which are said to be caused by the decree in favor of colored men in our islands. There is where nature shudders with horror; there is where reason and humanity have still not touched callous souls; there, especially, is where division and discord stir up their inhabitants. It is not difficult to divine the instigators of these incendiary fermentations; they are even in the midst of the National Assembly; they ignite the fire in Europe which must inflame America. Colonists make a claim to reign as despots over the men whose fathers and brothers they are; and, disowning the rights of nature, they trace the source of [their rule] to the scantiest tint of their blood. These inhuman colonists say: our blood flows in their veins, but we will shed it all if necessary to glut our greed or our blind ambition. It is in these places nearest to nature where the father scorns the son; deaf to the cries of blood, they stifle all its attraction; what can be hoped from the resistance opposed to them? To constrain [blood] violently is to render it terrible; to leave [blood] still enchained is to direct all calamities towards America. A divine hand seems to spread liberty abroad throughout the realms of man; only the law has the right to curb this liberty if it degenerates into license, but it must be equal for all; liberty must hold the National Assembly to its decree dictated by prudence and justice. May it act the same way for the state of France and render her as attentive to new abuses as she was to the ancient ones which each day become more dreadful. My opinion would be to reconcile the executive and legislative power, for it seems to me that the one is everything and the other is nothing—whence comes, unfortunately perhaps, the loss of the French Empire. I think that these two powers, like man and woman, should be united but equal in force and virtue to make a good household. ...

During the nineteenth century, child labor was common throughout the industrializing world. In this photograph, young miners pose outside of a mine in Kingston, Pennsylvania.

THE NINETEENTH
CENTURY

The history of the nineteenth century was molded in great part by two very different but related events, the French Revolution and the Industrial Revolution. We can speak without ambiguity of the French Revolution as an event, for it can be dated with precision, from the spring of 1789 to the Battle of Waterloo in 1815. But the Industrial Revolution had neither a precise beginning nor an ending. The best we can say is that it was under way, certainly in England, by the last quarter of the eighteenth century, that it transformed Europe's economy and society during the nineteenth, and that it continued into the twentieth.

Although one of these revolutions was primarily political and the other economic, they were not without influence on each other. It is now generally agreed, as Karl Marx first clearly pointed out, that the French Revolution was a bourgeois, or middle-class, upheaval. The rising capitalist class in France led the revolution, profited most from it, and then assumed the initiative in the industrial expansion that followed. In England, too, the French Revolution had important economic consequences. For the difficulties caused by the Napoleonic Wars, including the effects on England of the Continental System and the necessity for a vast increase in military and naval power to defeat the French, led to a rapid expansion of English industrial production.

The nineteenth-century reaction to these two great revolutions can best be seen in the host of doctrines and movements that began to dominate the European scene, particularly in the years following 1815. Although some of these had earlier beginnings, they proliferated widely during the century. Whatever their individual differences, which were many, they shared one feature in common—the suffix "*ism*". That most of the major nineteenth-century *isms*, particularly those that were primarily political or economic in emphasis, were responses to the revolutions can be seen by an examination of some of them. Both conservatism and nationalism, for example, were directly inspired by the events of the French Revolution and the Napoleonic era.

Conservatism rejected the French Revolution, not only for its effects but also for its methods. Revolution, conservatives such as the Englishman Edmund Burke argued, necessarily destroys its ideals in its very attempt to achieve them. Social and political progress cannot be brought about through violence and destruction; it is achieved only through the conservation and enrichment of the traditions of the past.

Perhaps more influential in the long term was nationalism. This doctrine, first espoused by the French during the Revolution, later spread across Europe in reaction to the Napoleonic empire. Across the Continent, peoples who had been conquered by the armies of Napoleon came to equate French culture with French imperialism. To assert their cultural independence from France, they searched their history and traditions for the foundations of a national culture that would equal or even surpass that of France. This cultural nationalism almost always had political implications. And political nationalism expressed itself in a variety of ways. With the German philosopher G. W. F. Hegel, it led to a worship of the state; with the Italian patriot Giuseppe Mazzini, it became the basis for a humanitarian crusade against political oppression. In practical politics, nationalism led to movements for independence in many areas of Europe, resulting, for example, in the liberation of Greece from the Turks and of Belgium from the Dutch. Perhaps the most important result of nineteenth-century nationalism was the unification of Italy and of Germany.

Three other nineteenth-century *isms*, all of them both political and economic, merit attention. The first of these was liberalism. Although liberalism eventually spread over most of Europe, its homeland was England and its greatest spokesman was John Stuart Mill. The liberals tried to adapt the ideals of the Enlightenment to the era of industrialism. Believing firmly in human rationality, they held that each individual must be given a maximum of freedom to develop his or her potential to the highest. The liberals were defenders of constitutional government and of lawful rather than violent political change. They believed, also, that government interference in the activities of citizens should be held to a minimum. In economics, this meant that they generally advocated laissez-faire. The history of liberalism in the past hundred years has centered in a growing conflict between the humanitarian ideals of the liberals, on the one hand, and their belief in government noninterference, on the other.

A second movement, more radical than liberalism, was republicanism. The republicans considered themselves the heirs of the French Revolution and the Republic of 1793. Republicanism, which spread from France over the entire Continent, was suppressed by the police of reactionary governments everywhere. But the republicans fought back by forming secret societies and by agitating for the revival of the revolutionary spirit in Europe. They were leaders in the many revolutions that rocked Europe during the century, particularly in 1848.

Most radical of the major *isms* was socialism, particularly as developed by Karl Marx. The socialists differed from the liberals and the republicans in one important respect. Both the liberals and the republicans rejected the prerevolutionary social structure of Europe, but they accepted the new bourgeois society that grew out of industrialism. The socialists, however, rejected bourgeois society as well and championed the cause of a new class, the industrial proletariat, also a product of the Industrial Revolution. Although Marx was the most important of the socialists, he had been preceded by several other socialistic writers, mainly in France, and he was followed by a variety of socialistic groups that showed his influence. Often called *revisionists*, these groups included, most prominently, the Social Democratic party in Germany and the Labour party in Great Britain. They differed from Marx mainly in their belief that the social goals of the laboring class could be attained through constitutional means without recourse either to class warfare or to the elimination of the bourgeoisie.

Perhaps the most pervasive *ism* of nineteenth-century society was optimism. With few exceptions the intellectual leaders of the period were firm believers in progress. For Hegel, progress was a metaphysical necessity; for Marx, it was a historical necessity; and even Charles Darwin seemed to accept it as a biological necessity. The general optimism of nineteenth-century thought found a firm basis in the undeniable fact that progress was actually being made. For it was clear, even to the casual observer, that through industrialization people were rapidly conquering nature and bending her to serve their material needs. The prophets of progress looked forward to an era in which the economic, political, and social advances achieved by Europeans might be shared by all the world.

Such hopes plus, unfortunately, others less lofty led to still another characteristic nineteenth-century *ism*: imperialism.

Another source for the optimism of the nineteenth-century lay in the freedom from general warfare that lasted for an entire century, from Waterloo to 1914. No such era of peace had been known in the West since the *Pax Romana*. This is not to imply, however, that the period was without violence. For in addition to several limited wars, the century witnessed a series of revolutions that were symptomatic of the underlying flaws in European society. The most serious flaw was the failure of society to keep pace with the rapid progress being made in politics and economics. The political developments leading to democracy and the economic developments leading to industrial urbanization combined to produce the modern "mass man," who could not be assimilated into the pattern of traditional European civilization. With the tremendous growth of population that almost all countries have experienced since the Industrial Revolution, this new type of person has become an increasingly influential force in society. The consequences of the appearance of this new social force in the European scene, though partially revealed in certain of the *isms* as well as in the revolutions of the nineteenth century, did not become fully apparent until our own century, on whose turbulent history they have had a profound effect.

LOOKING AHEAD

As you learn about nineteenth-century Europe, consider the following questions.

1. What connections do you see between economic and political change in nineteenth-century Europe? What was the relationship between industrialization and the expansion of political suffrage in the nineteenth century?

2. Describe nineteenth-century nationalism. How did it differ from the forms of nationalism that preceded it?

3. What arguments did nineteenth-century Europeans make for and against the idea of historical progress? Why were so many Europeans convinced that their civilization was superior to all others?

Edmund Burke

The French Revolution was greeted with enthusiasm by many of the intellectual leaders of Europe, but not by all. Perhaps the most influential of its critics was the British writer and politician, Edmund Burke, whose *Reflections on the Revolution in France* was an impassioned condemnation of the revolutionaries for overthrowing the established order.

Along with other conservatives, Burke deplored the Revolution for its destruction of the *ancien regime* and its "cashiering" of the king, as well as for its violence and bloodshed. But his opposition had much deeper roots, in a rejection of the philosophical principles of the Enlightenment that underlay the Revolution. Two of these, in particular, he found repugnant. First was the belief in natural rights, such as Jefferson's "unalienable rights" to "life, liberty and the pursuit of happiness," which were embedded in the Declaration of Independence. For Burke, individuals do not possess rights by nature; rather they have rights (and obligations) conferred on them by long-standing custom and tradition. Second, Burke took issue with the *philosophes'* appeal to reason as a basis for the ordering of society. Instead of turning to rational principles, he put his trust in the past, in the way that society had been ordered from time immemorial. It is clear from the language he uses in *Reflections* that Burke's reverence for the past was essentially a form of religious faith. To most readers today, Burke's essay, despite its lofty rhetoric, undoubtedly appears out of touch with reality. The reason is apparent: The social order he was defending was even then on the wane and in the process of gradually being replaced by modern liberal democracies whose heralds were the American and French revolutions. Nevertheless, for a considerable time during the early nineteenth century, Burke's views wielded a powerful influence on political thought and action in Europe.

Edmund Burke (1729–1793) was Irish by birth and education. But he moved to London in 1750 where he lived for the remainder of his life. After briefly practicing law, which he detested, he was for a short time a political writer. He then became a member of Parliament, remaining in that position for the rest of his career and becoming a spokesman for a wing of the Whig party. His *Reflections* was written in the form of a letter to a French friend. In fact, however, it was a reply to a speech that had been delivered before the English Revolution Society by Dr. Richard Price, in which the speaker had praised the French Revolution. Although it was originally published in 1790, *Reflections* has been placed here because of its influence on European political thought in the nineteenth century.

Consider the following questions as you study the text below.

1. Why did Burke reject the notion that citizens had a right to rebel? How might John Locke have responded to Burke's argument?

2. According to Burke, what were the biggest mistakes made by the French revolutionaries? Why was he not surprised that the Revolution unfolded the way that it did?

Reflections on the Revolution in France

. . .

Kings, in one sense, are undoubtedly the servants of the people, because their power has no other rational end than that of the general advantage; but it is not true that they are, in the ordinary sense, (by our constitution at least), anything like servants, the essence of whose situation is to obey the commands of some other, and to be removable at pleasure. But the king of Great Britain obeys no other person; all other persons are individually, and collectively too, under him, and owe to him a legal obedience. The law, which knows neither to flatter nor to insult, calls this high magistrate, not our servant, as this humble divine calls him, but *"our sovereign Lord the king"*; and we, on our parts, have learned to speak only the primitive language of the law, and not the confused jargon of their Babylonian pulpits.

As he is not to obey us, but as we are to obey the law in him, our constitution has made no sort of provision towards rendering him, as a servant, in any degree responsible. Our constitution knows nothing of a magistrate like the *Justicia* of Arragon; nor of any court legally appointed, nor of any process legally settled, for submitting the king to the responsibility belonging to all servants. In this he is not distinguished from the Commons and the Lords; who, in their several public capacities, can never be called to an account of their conduct; although the Revolution Society chooses to assert in direct opposition to one of the wisest and most beautiful parts of our constitution, that "a king is no more than the first servant of the public, created by it, *and responsible to it."*

Ill would our ancestors at the Revolution [*of 1688—Ed.*] have deserved their fame for wisdom, if they had found no security for their freedom, but in rendering their government feeble in its operations and precarious in its tenure; if they had been able to contrive no better remedy against arbitrary power than civil confusion. Let these gentlemen state who that *representative* public is to whom they will affirm the king, as a servant, to be responsible.

It will be then time enough for me to produce to them the positive statute law which affirms that he is not.

The ceremony of cashiering kings, of which these gentlemen talk so much at their ease, can rarely, if ever, be performed without force. It then becomes a case of war, and not of constitution. Laws are commanded to hold their tongues amongst arms; and tribunals fall to the ground with the peace they are no longer able to uphold. The Revolution of 1688 was obtained by a just war, in the only case in which any war, and much more a civil war, can be just. "Justa bella quibus *necessaria*."[1] The question of dethroning, or, if these gentlemen like the phrase better "cashiering kings," will always be, as it has always been, an extraordinary question of state, and wholly out of the law; a question (like all other questions of state) of dispositions, and of means, and of probable consequences, rather than of positive rights. As it was not made for common abuses, so it is not to be agitated by common minds. The speculative line of demarcation, where obedience ought to end, and resistance must begin, is faint, obscure, and not easily definable. It is not a single act, or a single event, which determines it. Governments must be abused and deranged indeed, before it can be thought of; and the prospect of the future must be as bad as the experience of the past. When things are in that lamentable condition, the nature of the disease is to indicate the remedy to those whom nature has qualified to administer in extremities this critical, ambiguous, bitter potion to a distempered state. Times, and occasions, and provocations, will teach their own lessons. The wise will determine from the gravity of the case; the irritable, from sensibility to oppression; the high-minded, from disdain and indignation at abusive power in unworthy hands; the brave and bold, from the love of honourable danger in a generous cause; but, with or without right, a revolution will be the very last resource of the thinking and the good.

The third head of right, asserted by the pulpit of the Old Jewry, namely, the "right to form a government for ourselves," has, at least, as little countenance from anything done at the Revolution [*of 1688—Ed.*], either in precedent or principle, as the two first of their claims. The Revolution was made to preserve our *ancient*, indisputable laws and liberties, and that *ancient* constitution of government which is our only security for law and liberty. If you are desirous of knowing the spirit of our constitution, and the policy which predominated in that great period which has secured it to this hour, pray look for both in our histories, in our records, in our acts of parliament, and journals of parliament, and not in the sermons of the Old Jewry, and the after-dinner toasts of the Revolution Society. In the former you will find other ideas and another language. Such a claim is as ill-suited to our temper and wishes as it is unsupported by an appearance of authority. The very idea

---

[1]["Wars are just to those to whom they are necessary."—*Ed.*]

of the fabrication of a new government is enough to fill us with disgust and horror. We wished at the period of the Revolution, and do now wish, to derive all we possess as *an inheritance from our forefathers*. Upon that body and stock of inheritance we have taken care not to inoculate any scion alien to the nature of the original plant. All the reformations we have hitherto made have proceeded upon the principle of reverence to antiquity: and I hope, nay I am persuaded, that all those which possibly may be made hereafter, will be carefully formed upon analogical precedent, authority, and example.

Our oldest reformation is that of Magna Charta. You will see that Sir Edward Coke, that great oracle of our law, and indeed all the great men who follow him, to Blackstone, are industrious to prove the pedigree of our liberties. They endeavour to prove, that the ancient charter, the Magna Charta of King John, was connected with another positive charter from Henry I, and that both the one and the other were nothing more than a reaffirmance of the still more ancient standing law of the kingdom. In the matter of fact, for the greater part, these authors appear to be in the right; perhaps not always; but if the lawyers mistake in some particulars, it proves my position still the more strongly; because it demonstrates the powerful prepossession towards antiquity, with which the minds of all our lawyers and legislators, and of all the people whom they wish to influence, have been always filled; and the stationary policy of this kingdom in considering their most sacred rights and franchises as an *inheritance*.

In the famous law of the 3rd of Charles I, called the *Petition of Right*, the parliament says to the king, "Your subjects have *inherited* this freedom," claiming their franchises not on abstract principles "as the rights of men," but as the rights of Englishmen, and as a patrimony derived from their forefathers. Selden, and the other profoundly learned men, who drew this Petition of Right, were as well acquainted, at least, with all the general theories concerning the "rights of men," as any of the discourses in our pulpits, or on your tribune; full as well as Dr. Price, or as the Abbé Siéyès. But, for reasons worthy of that practical wisdom which superseded their theoretic science, they preferred this positive, recorded, *hereditary* title to all which can be dear to the man and the citizen, to that vague speculative right, which exposed their sure inheritance to be scrambled for and torn to pieces by every wild, litigious spirit.

The same policy pervades all the laws which have since been made for the preservation of our liberties. In the 1st of William and Mary, in the famous statute, called the Declaration of Right, the two Houses utter not a syllable of "a right to frame a government for themselves." You will see, that their whole care was to secure the religion, laws, and liberties that had been long possessed, and had been lately endangered. "Taking into their most serious consideration the *best* means for making such an establishment, that their religion, laws, and liberties might not be in danger of being again subverted," they auspicate all their proceedings, by stating as some of those *best* means, "in the *first place*" to do "as their *ancestors in like cases have usually* done for vindicating their *ancient* rights and liberties, to *declare*";—and then they pray the king and queen, "that it may be *declared* and enacted, that *all and singular* the rights and *liberties asserted and declared*, are the true *ancient* and indubitable rights and liberties of the people of this kingdom."

You will observe that from Magna Charta to the Declaration of Right, it has been the uniform policy of our constitution to claim and assert our liberties, as an *entailed inheritance* derived to us from our forefathers, and to be transmitted to our posterity; as an estate specially belonging to the people of this kingdom, without any reference whatever to any other more general or prior right. By this means our constitution preserves a unity in so great a diversity of its parts. We have an inheritable crown; an inheritable peerage; and a House of Commons and a people inheriting privileges, franchises, and liberties, from a long line of ancestors.

This policy appears to me to be the result of profound reflection; or rather the happy effect of following nature, which is wisdom without reflection, and above it. A spirit of innovation is generally the result of a selfish temper, and confined views. People will not look forward to posterity, who never look backward to their ancestors. Besides, the people of England well know, that the idea of inheritance furnishes a sure principle of conservation, and a sure principle of transmission; without at all excluding a principle of improvement. It leaves acquisition free; but it secures what it acquires. Whatever advantages are obtained by a state proceeding on these maxims, are locked fast as in a sort of family settlement; grasped as in a kind of mortmain for ever. By a constitutional policy, working after the pattern of nature, we receive, we hold, we transmit our government and our privileges, in the same manner in which we enjoy and transmit our property and our lives. The institutions of policy, the goods of fortune, the gifts of providence, are handed down to us, and from us, in the same course and order. Our political system is placed in a just correspondence and symmetry with the order of the world, and with the mode of existence decreed to a permanent body composed of transitory parts; wherein, by the disposition of a stupendous wisdom, moulding together the great mysterious incorporation of the human race, the whole, at one time, is never old, or middle-aged, or young, but, in a condition of unchangeable constancy, moves on through the varied tenor of perpetual decay, fall, renovation, and progression. Thus, by preserving the method of nature in the conduct of the state, in what we improve, we are never wholly new; in what we retain, we are never wholly obsolete. By adhering in this manner and on those principles to our forefathers, we are guided not by the superstition of antiquarians, but by the spirit of philosophic analogy. In this choice of inheritance we have given to our frame of polity the image of a relation in blood; binding up the constitution of our country with our dearest domestic ties; adopting our fundamental laws into the bosom of our family affections; keeping inseparable, and cherishing with the warmth of all their combined and mutually reflected charities, our state, our hearts, our sepulchres, and our altars.

Through the same plan of a conformity to nature in our artificial institutions, and by calling in the aid of her unerring and powerful instincts to fortify the fallible and feeble contrivances of our reason, we have derived several others, and those no small benefits, from considering our liberties in the light of an inheritance. Always acting as if in the presence of canonized forefathers, the spirit of freedom, leading in itself to misrule and excess, is tempered with an awful gravity. This idea of a liberal descent inspires us with a sense of habitual native dignity, which prevents that upstart insolence almost inevitably adhering to and disgracing those who are the first acquirers of any distinction. By this means our liberty becomes a noble freedom. It carries an imposing and majestic aspect. It has a pedigree and illustrating ancestors. It has its bearings and its ensigns armorial. It has its gallery of portraits; its monumental inscriptions; its records, evidences, and titles. We procure reverence to our civil institutions on the principle upon which nature teaches us to revere individual men; on account of their age, and on account of those from whom they are descended. All your sophisters cannot produce anything better adapted to preserve a rational and manly freedom than the course that we have pursued, who have chosen our nature, rather than our speculations, our breasts rather than our inventions, for the great conservatories and magazines of our rights and privileges.

You [*in France—Ed.*] might, if you pleased, have profited of our example, and have given to your recovered freedom a correspondent dignity. Your privileges, though discontinued, were not lost to memory. Your constitution, it is true, whilst you were out of possession, suffered waste and dilapidation; but you possessed in some parts the walls, and, in all, the foundations, of a noble and venerable castle. You might have repaired those walls; you might have built on those old foundations. Your constitution was suspended before it was perfected; but you had the elements of a constitution very nearly as good as could be wished. In your old states you possessed that variety of parts corresponding with the various descriptions of which your community was happily composed; you had all that combination, and all that opposition of interests, you had that action and counteraction, which, in the natural and in the political world, from the reciprocal struggle of discordant powers, draws out the harmony of the universe. These opposed and conflicting interests, which you considered as so great a blemish in your old and in our present constitution, interpose a salutary check to all precipitate resolutions. They render deliberation a matter not of choice, but of necessity; they make all change a subject of *compromise*, which naturally begets moderation; they produce *temperaments* preventing the sore evil of harsh, crude, unqualified reformations; and rendering all the headlong exertions of arbitrary power, in the few or in the many, for ever impracticable. Through that diversity of members and interests, general liberty had as many securities as there were separate views in the several orders;

whilst by pressing down the whole by the weight of a real monarchy, the separate parts would have been prevented from warping, and starting from their allotted places.

You had all these advantages in your ancient states; but you chose to act as if you had never been moulded into civil society, and had everything to begin anew. You began ill, because you began by despising everything that belonged to you. You set up your trade without a capital. If the last generations of your country appeared without much lustre in your eyes, you might have passed them by, and derived your claims from a more early race of ancestors. Under a pious predilection for those ancestors, your imaginations would have realized in them a standard of virtue and wisdom, beyond the vulgar practice of the hour: and you would have risen with the example to whose imitation you aspired. Respecting your forefathers, you would have been taught to respect yourselves. You would not have chosen to consider the French as a people of yesterday, as a nation of low-born servile wretches until the emancipating year of 1789. In order to furnish, at the expense of your honour, an excuse to your apologists here for several enormities of yours, you would not have been content to be represented as a gang of Maroon slaves, suddenly broke loose from the house of bondage, and therefore to be pardoned for your abuse of the liberty to which you were not accustomed, and ill fitted. Would it not, my worthy friend, have been wiser to have you thought, what I, for one, always thought you, a generous and gallant nation, long misled to your disadvantage by your high and romantic sentiments of fidelity, honour, and loyalty; that events had been unfavourable to you, but that you were not enslaved through any illiberal or servile disposition; in your most devoted submission, you were actuated by a principle of public spirit, and that it was your country you worshipped, in the person of your king? Had you made it to be understood, that in the delusion of this amiable error you had gone further than your wise ancestors; that you were resolved to resume your ancient privileges, whilst you preserved the spirit of your ancient and your recent loyalty and honour; or if, diffident of yourselves, and not clearly discerning the almost obliterated constitution of your ancestors, you had looked to your neighbours in this land, who had kept alive the ancient principles and models of the old common law of Europe meliorated and adapted to its present state—by following wise examples you would have given new examples of wisdom to the world. You would have rendered the cause of liberty venerable in the eyes of every worthy mind in every nation. You would have shamed despotism from the earth, by showing that freedom was not only reconcilable, but, as when well disciplined it is, auxiliary to law. You would have an unoppressive but a productive revenue. You would have had a flourishing commerce to feed it. You would have had a free constitution; a potent monarchy; a disciplined army; a reformed and venerated clergy; a mitigated but spirited nobility, to lead your virtue, not to overlay it; you would have had a liberal order of commons, to emulate and to recruit that nobility; you would have had a protected, satisfied, laborious, and obedient people, taught to seek and to recognise the happiness that is to be found by virtue in all conditions; in which consists the true moral equality of mankind, and not in that monstrous fiction, which, by inspiring false ideas and vain expectations into men destined to travel in the obscure walk of laborious life, serves only to aggravate and embitter that real inequality, which it never can remove; and which the order of civil life establishes as much for the benefit of those whom it must leave in an humble state, as those whom it is able to exalt to a condition more splendid, but not more happy. You had a smooth and easy career of felicity and glory laid open to you, beyond anything recorded in the history of the world; but you have shown that difficulty is good for men.

Compute your gains: see what is got by those extravagant and presumptuous speculations which have taught your leaders to despise all their predecessors, and all their contemporaries, and even to despise themselves, until the moment in which they became truly despicable. By following those false lights, France has bought undisguised calamities at a higher price than any nation has purchased the most unequivocal blessings! France has bought poverty by crime! France has not sacrificed her virtue to her interest, but she has abandoned her interest, that she might prostitute her virtue. All other nations have begun the fabric of a new government, or the reformation of an old, by establishing originally, or by enforcing with greater exactness, some rites or other of religion. All other people have laid the foundations of civil freedom in severer manners, and a system of a more austere and masculine morality. France, when she let loose the reins of regal authority, doubled the license of a ferocious dissoluteness in manners, and of an insolent irreligion in opinions and practices; and has extended through all ranks of life, as if she were communicating some privilege, or laying open some secluded benefit, all the unhappy corruptions that usually were the disease of wealth and power. This is one of the new principles of equality in France.

France, by the perfidy of her leaders has utterly disgraced the tone of lenient council in the cabinets of princes, and disarmed it of its most potent topics. She has sanctified the dark, suspicious maxims of tyrannous distrust; and taught kings to tremble at (what will hereafter be called) the delusive plausibilities of moral politicians. Sovereigns will consider those, who advise them to place an unlimited confidence in their people, as subverters of their throne; as traitors who aim at their destruction, by leading their easy good-nature, under specious pretences, to admit combinations of bold and faithless men into a participation of their power. This alone (if there were nothing else) is an irreparable calamity to you and to mankind. Remember that your parliament of Paris told your king, that, in calling the states together, he had nothing to fear but the prodigal excess of their zeal in providing for the support of the throne. It is right that these men should hide their heads. It is right that they should bear their part in the ruin which their counsel has brought on their sovereign and their country. Such sanguine declarations tend to lull authority asleep; to encourage it rashly to engage in perilous adventures of untried policy; to neglect those provisions, preparations, and precautions, which distinguish benevolence from imbecility; and without which no man can answer for the salutary effect of any abstract plan of government or of freedom. For want of these, they have seen the medicine of the state corrupted into its poison. They have seen the French rebel against a mild and lawful monarch, with more fury, outrage, and insult, than ever any people has been known to rise against the most illegal usurper, or the most sanguinary tyrant. Their resistance was made to concession; their revolt was from protection; their blow was aimed at a hand holding out graces, favours, and immunities.

This was unnatural. The rest is in order. They have found their punishment in their success. Laws overturned; tribunals subverted; industry without vigor; commerce expiring, the revenue unpaid, yet the people impoverished; a church pillaged, and a state not relieved; civil and military anarchy made the constitution of the kingdom; everything human and divine sacrificed to the idol of public credit, and national bankruptcy the consequence; and, to crown all, the paper securities of new, precarious, tottering power, the discredited paper securities of impoverished fraud and beggared rapine, held out as a currency for the support of an empire, in lieu of the two great recognised species that represent the lasting, conventional credit of mankind, which disappeared and hid themselves in the earth from whence they came, when the principle of property, whose creatures and representatives they are, was systematically subverted.

Were all those dreadful things necessary? Were they the inevitable results of the desperate struggle of determined patriots, compelled to wade through blood and tumult, to the quiet shore of a tranquil and prosperous liberty? No! nothing like it. The fresh ruins of France, which shock our feelings wherever we can turn our eyes, are not the devastation of civil war; they are the sad but instructive monuments of rash and ignorant counsel in time of profound peace. They are the display of inconsiderate and presumptuous, because unresisted and irresistible, authority. The persons who have thus squandered away the precious treasure of their crimes, the persons who have made this prodigal and wild waste of public evils, (the last stage reserved for the ultimate ransom of the state), have met in their progress with little, or rather with no opposition at all. Their whole march was more like a triumphal procession, than the progress of war. Their pioneers have gone before them, and demolished and laid everything level at their feet. Not one drop of *their* blood have they shed in the cause of the country they have ruined. They have made no sacrifices to their projects of greater consequence than their shoe-buckles, whilst they were imprisoning their king, murdering their fellow-citizens, and bathing in tears, and plunging in poverty and distress, thousands of worthy men and worthy families. Their cruelty has not even been the base result of fear. It has been the effect of their sense of perfect safety, in authorizing treasons, robberies, rapes, assassinations, slaughters, and burnings, throughout their harassed land. But the cause of all was plain from the beginning.

This unforced choice, this fond election of evil, would appear perfectly unaccountable, if we did not consider the composition of the National Assembly: I do not mean its formal constitution, which, as it now stands, is exceptional enough, but the materials of which, in a great measure, it is composed, which is of ten thousand times greater consequence than all the formalities in the world. If we were to know nothing of this assembly but by its title and function, no colours could paint to the imagination anything more venerable. In that light the mind of an inquirer, subdued by such an awful image as that of the virtue and wisdom of a whole people collected into a focus, would pause and hesitate in condemning things even of the very worst aspect. Instead of blameable, they would appear only mysterious. But no name, no power, no function, no artificial institution whatsoever, can make the men of whom any system of authority is composed, any other than God, and nature, and education, and their habits of life have made them. Capacities beyond these the people have not to give. Virtue and wisdom may be the objects of their choice; but their choice confers neither the one nor the other on those upon whom they lay their ordaining hands. They have not the engagement of nature, they have not the promise of revelation, for any such powers.

After I have read over the list of the persons and descriptions elected into the *Tiers Etat*, nothing which they afterwards did could appear astonishing. Among them, indeed, I saw some of known rank; some of shining talents; but of any practical experience in the state, not one man was to be found. The best were only men of theory. But whatever the distinguished few may have been, it is the substance, the mass of the body which constitutes its character, and must finally determine its direction. In all bodies, those who will lead, must also, in a considerable degree, follow. They must conform their propositions to the taste, talent, and disposition, of those whom they wish to conduct: therefore, if an assembly is viciously or feebly composed in a very great part of it, nothing but such a supreme degree of virtue as very rarely appears in the world, and for that reason cannot enter into calculation, will prevent the men of talent disseminated through it from becoming only the expert instruments of absurd projects! If, what is the more likely event, instead of that unusual degree of virtue, they should be actuated by sinister ambition, and a lust of meretricious glory, then the feeble part of the assembly, to whom at first they conform, becomes in its turn the dupe and instrument of their designs. In this political traffic, the leaders will be obliged to bow to the ignorance of their followers, and the followers to become subservient to the worst designs of their leaders.

To secure any degree of sobriety in the propositions made by the leaders in any public assembly, they ought to respect, in some degree perhaps to fear, those whom they conduct. To be led any otherwise than blindly, the followers must be qualified, if not for actors, at least for judges; they must also be judges of natural weight and authority. Nothing can secure a steady and moderate conduct in such assemblies, but that the body of them should be respectably composed, in point of condition in life, of permanent property, of education, and of such habits as enlarge and liberalize the understanding.

In the calling of the Estates-General of France, the first thing that struck me, was a great departure from the ancient course. I found the representation for the third estate composed of six hundred persons. They were equal in number to the representatives of both the other orders. If the orders were to act separately, the number would not, beyond the consideration of the expense, be of much moment. But when it became apparent that the three orders were to be melted down into one, the policy and necessary effect of this numerous representation became obvious. A very small desertion from either of the other two orders must throw the power of both into the hands of the third. In fact, the whole power of the state was soon resolved into that body. Its due composition became therefore of infinitely the greater importance.

Judge, Sir, of my surprise, when I found that a very great proportion of the assembly (a majority, I believe, of the members who attended) was composed of practitioners in the law. It was composed, not of distinguished magistrates, who had given pledges to their country of their science, prudence, and integrity; not of leading advocates, the glory of the bar; not of renowned professors in universities—but for the far greater part, as it must in such a number, of the inferior, unlearned, mechanical, merely instrumental members of the profession. There were distinguished exceptions; but the general composition was of obscure provincial advocates, of stewards of petty local jurisdictions, country attorneys, notaries, and the whole train of the ministers of municipal litigation, the fomenters and conductors of the petty war of village vexation. From the moment I read the list, I saw distinctly, and very nearly as it has happened, all that was to follow.

The degree of estimation in which any profession is held becomes the standard of the estimation in which the professors hold themselves. Whatever the personal merits of many individual lawyers might have been, and in many it was undoubtedly very considerable, in that military kingdom no part of the profession had been much regarded, except the highest of all, who often united to their professional offices great family splendour, and were invested with great power and authority. These certainly were highly respected, and even with no small degree of awe. The next rank was not much esteemed; the mechanical part was in a very low degree of repute.

Whenever the supreme authority is vested in a body so composed, it must evidently produce the consequences of supreme authority placed in the hands of men not taught habitually to respect themselves; who had no previous fortune in character at stake; who could not be expected to bear with moderation, or to conduct with discretion, a power, which they themselves, more than any others, must be surprised to find in their hands. Who could flatter himself that these men, suddenly, and, as it were, by enchantment, snatched from the humblest rank of subordination, would not be intoxicated with their unprepared greatness? Who could conceive that men, who are habitually meddling, daring, subtle, active, of litigious dispositions and unquiet minds would easily fall back into their old condition of obscure contention, and laborious, low, and unprofitable chicane? Who could doubt but that, at any expense to the state, of which they understood nothing, they must pursue their private interests which they understood but too well? It was not an event depending on chance, or contingency. It was inevitable; it was necessary; it was planted in the nature of things. They must *join* (if their capacity did not permit them to *lead*) in any project which could procure them those innumerable lucrative jobs, which follow in the train of all great convulsions and revolutions in the state, and particularly in all great and violent permutations of property. Was it to be expected that they would attend to the stability of property, whose existence had always depended upon whatever rendered property questionable, ambiguous, and insecure? Their objects would be enlarged with their elevation, but their disposition and habits, and mode of accomplishing their designs, must remain the same.

Well! but these men were to be tempered and restrained by other descriptions, of more sober and more enlarged understandings. Were they then to be awed by the supereminent authority and awful dignity of a handful of country clowns, who have seats in that assembly, some of whom are said not to be able to read and write? and by not a great number of traders, who, though somewhat more instructed, and more conspicuous in the order of society, had never known anything beyond their countinghouse. No! both these descriptions were more formed to be overborne and swayed by the intrigues and artifices of lawyers, than to become their counterpoise. With such a dangerous disproportion, the whole must needs be governed by them. To the faculty of law was joined a pretty considerable proportion of the faculty of medicine. This faculty had not, any more than that of the law, possessed in France its just estimation. Its professors, therefore, must have the qualities of men not habituated to sentiments of dignity. But supposing they had ranked as they ought to do, and as with us they do actually, the sides of sick beds are not the academies for forming statemen and legislators. Then came the dealers in stock and funds, who must be eager, at any expense, to change their ideal paper wealth for the more solid substance of land. To these were joined men of other descriptions, from whom as little knowledge of, or attention to, the interests of a great state was to be expected, and as little regard to the stability of any institution; men formed to be instruments, not controls. Such in general was the composition of the *Tiers Etat* in the National Assembly; in which was scarcely to be perceived the slightest traces of what we call the natural landed interest of the country.

We know that the British House of Commons, without shutting its doors to any merit in any class, is, by the sure operation of adequate causes, filled with everything illustrious in rank, in descent, in hereditary and in acquired opulence, in cultivated talents, in military, civil, naval, and political distinction, that the country can afford. But supposing, what hardly can be supposed, as a case, that the House of Commons should be composed in the same manner with the *Tiers Etat* in France, would this dominion of chicane be borne with patience, or even conceived without horror? God forbid I should insinuate anything derogatory to that profession, which is another priesthood, administering the rights of sacred justice. But whilst I revere men in the functions which belong to them, and would do as much as one man can do to prevent their exclusion from any, I cannot, to flatter them, give the lie to nature. They are good and useful in the composition; they must be mischievous if they preponderate so as virtually to become the whole. Their very excellence in their peculiar functions may be far from a qualification for others. It cannot escape observation, that when men are too much confined to professional and faculty habits, and as it were inveterate in the recurrent employment of that narrow circle, they are rather disabled than qualified for whatever depends on the knowledge of mankind, on experience in mixed affairs, on a comprehensive, connected view of the various complicated, external and internal interests, which go to the formation of that multifarious thing called a state.

Romanticism

It is sometimes said that romanticism was a reaction against the rationalism of the Enlightenment, but this interpretation does not provide a complete explanation of the movement. Romanticism was more than an anti-intellectual outburst; it was a general rebellion against the whole civilization of late-eighteenth-century Europe. Some romantics, such as novelists Victor Hugo and Sir Walter Scott, immersed themselves in the medieval past; some, such as philosopher G. W. F. Hegel, identified themselves with a supernatural reality transcending the vicissitudes of time and space; some, such as political theorist Joseph de Maistre, found refuge in the traditions and authority of the Church; some, such as poet William Wordsworth, sought communion with an idyllic nature, itself soon to be despoiled by the mills and factories of the Industrial Revolution.

The first selection, by the French politician and writer François Chateaubriand (1768–1848), is taken from his popular book *The Genius of Christianity*, published in 1802. It is an outstanding example of the romantics' feeling for the remote past and the mysteries of religion.

The two poems that conclude the section illustrate respectively two major romantic themes: the rebellion of the individual against the gods and the worship of nature. The first, "Prometheus" (1774), is by the German writer Johann Wolfgang von Goethe (1749–1832). Goethe was too broad in his interests and attitudes to be classified as a romantic; indeed, he has been called the last *uomo universale* in Western civilization. The second poem, "Tintern Abbey" (1798), is by the English poet William Wordsworth (1770–1850).

Consider the following questions as you study the text below.

1. What did Chateaubriand admire most about Gothic churches? Why did he believe that it was impossible for modern churches to provide as satisfying a spiritual environment?

2. Compare Goethe and Wordsworth's approach to religion in the poems included below. According to each poet, what was the proper object of human worship?

Gothic Churches

Although "Everything ought to be put in its place" is a trivial truth which carries force by its constant repetition, nevertheless without accepting it one cannot, after all, have anything perfect. The Greeks would not have appreciated an Egyptian temple at Athens any more than the Egyptians would a Greek temple at Memphis. The two buildings in exchanging place would have lost their main beauty, that is to say their relationship with the institutions and practices of the people. We can apply the same reflection to old Christian edifices. It is pertinent to remark that, even in this century of unbelief, poets and novelists, by a natural return to the customs of our ancestors, like to introduce dungeons, ghosts, castles, and Gothic temples into their fictions; so great is the charm of memories linked with religion and the history of our country. Nations do not discard their ancient customs as people do their old clothes. Some part of them may be abandoned but remnants will remain, forming a shocking combination with their new manners.

In vain would you build Gothic temples ever so elegant and well lighted, for the purpose of assembling the good people of St. Louis and making them adore a metaphysical God; they would always miss Notre Dame of Rheims and of Paris, moss-covered cathedrals filled with generations of the dead and the spirits of their forefathers; they would always miss the tombs of the house of Montmorency on which they found comfort in kneeling during mass, to say nothing of the sacred fonts to which they were carried at birth. The reason is that all of these things are inextricably interwoven with our customs; that a monument is not venerable unless a long history of the past is so to speak inscribed beneath its vaulted ceilings, all black with age. For this reason also there is nothing marvelous in a temple we have watched being built, whose echoes and domes were formed before our eyes. God is the eternal law; his origin and everything that is concerned with his worship ought to remain hidden in the night of time.

One cannot enter a Gothic church without experiencing a kind of awe and a vague perception of the Divinity. All at once one finds himself carried back to the time when monks, after having meditated in the woods of their monasteries, met together to prostrate themselves at the altar and chant the praises of the Lord, in the calm and silence of the night. Ancient France seemed to be revived; one believed he saw its strange costumes, its people so different from those of today; one recalled the revolutions of its people, and its accomplishments, and its art. The more remote these times were, the more magical they appeared, the more they inspired thoughts, which always end with a reflection on the nothingness of man and the shortness of life.

The Gothic order, in spite of its barbarous proportions, nevertheless possesses a beauty that belongs to it alone.

F. R. Chateaubriand, *Génie du Christianisme* (1802), trans. Oliver A. Johnson.

The forests were the first temples of the Divinity, and men took from the forests their first idea of architecture. This art therefore should vary according to the climate. The Greeks have fashioned the elegant Corinthian column, with its capital of leaves modeled after the palm tree. The enormous pillars of ancient Egypt represent the sycamore, the oriental fig tree, the banana tree, and most of the gigantic trees of Africa and Asia.

The forests of Gaul in their turn have been translated into the temples of our forefathers, and our oak woods have thus maintained their sacred origin. Everything in a Gothic church—its ceilings carved with leaves, the posts supporting its walls and ending suddenly like broken tree trunks, the coolness of its vaults, the darkness of its sanctuary, its dim aisles, its secret passages, its low portals—reminds one of the labyrinths of a wood, everything excites a sense of religious awe, of mystery and of the Divinity. The two lofty towers erected at the entrance to the building rise above the elms and yews of the church-yard and produce a picturesque effect against the blue of the sky. Sometimes dawn illuminates their twin heads; at other times they appear to be crowned with a capital of clouds, or enlarged in an atmosphere of fog. The birds themselves seem to be confused by them, and take them for the trees of the forests; crows hover around their tops and perch on their balconies. But all at once a confused din escapes from the top of the towers and chases the frightened birds away. The Christian architect, not content with building forests, has wished to imitate their murmurs; and, by means of the organ and the bells, he has attached to the Gothic temple the very sound of the winds and the thunder that roar through the depths of the woods. Past epochs, evoked by these religious sounds, raise their venerable voices from the heart of the storms, and sigh through the vast cathedral. The sanctuary moans like the cavern of the ancient Sybil; and, while the bells swing loudly overhead, the vaults of death below remain profoundly silent.

Prometheus

Cover your heavens
In cloud-mists, Zeus,
And like a boy
Beheading thistles, go practice
On oaks and mountain tops!
Still you'll have to
Leave me my earth,
The hut you did not build,
And the hearth,
Whose fire
You envy me.
I know nothing under the sun

Johann Wolfgang von Goethe, *Prometheus*, trans. Milton Miller.

Less enviable than you gods!
Your majesty,
Wretchedly nourished
On exacted sacrifice
And breath of prayer,
Would famish were not
Children and beggars
Hopeful fools.
While yet a child,
Knowing no other way,
Lost, I turned my face
To the sun, as if up there
Some ear might hear my lamentation,
Some heart like mine
Pity my affliction.
Who helped me
Resist Titanic arrogance?
Who rescued me from death,
From slavery?
Didn't you accomplish it yourself,
High impassioned heart?
And yet, youthfully passionate and good
You gave deluded thanks for rescue
To the slumberer above.
Why should I honor you?
Did you ever soothe the pain
Of the oppressed?
Or still the tears
Of anguish, ever?
Wasn't I forged a man
By everlasting fate
And time omnipotent,
My lords and yours?
Did you suppose
I'd come to hate life,
Escape to deserts,
Because not all
Dreams blossomed?
Here I sit and create men
After my own image,
A race like myself,
To suffer, to weep,
To relish, to rejoice,
And to ignore you,
As do I!

Tintern Abbey

LINES COMPOSED A FEW MILES ABOVE TINTERN ABBEY, ON REVISITING THE BANKS OF THE WYE DURING A TOUR

July 13, 1798
Five years have past; five summers, with the length
Of five long winters! and again I hear
These waters, rolling from their mountain-springs
With a soft inland murmur.—Once again
Do I behold these steep and lofty cliffs,
That on a wild secluded scene impress
Thoughts of more deep seclusion; and connect
The landscape with the quiet of the sky.
The day is come when I again repose
Here, under this dark sycamore, and view
These plots of cottage-ground, these orchard-tufts,
Which at this season, with their unripe fruits,
Are clad in one green hue, and lose themselves
'Mid groves and copses. Once again I see
These hedge-rows, hardly hedge-rows, little lines
Of sportive wood run wild: these pastoral farms,
Green to the very door; and wreaths of smoke
Sent up, in silence, from among the trees!
With some uncertain notice, as might seem
Of vagrant dwellers in the houseless woods.
Or of some Hermit's cave, where by his fire
The Hermit sits alone.
        These beauteous forms,
Through a long absence, have not been to me
As is a landscape to a blind man's eye:
But oft, in lonely rooms, and 'mid the din
Of towns and cities, I have owed to them
In hours of weariness, sensations sweet,
Felt in the blood, and felt along the heart;
And passing even into my purer mind,
With tranquil restoration:—feelings too
Of unremembered pleasure: such, perhaps,
As have no slight or trivial influence
On that best portion of a good man's life

"Lines Composed a Few Miles above Tintern Abbey," in *The Poetical Works of Wordsworth* (London, 1889).

His little, nameless, unremembered, acts
Of kindness and of love. Nor less, I trust,
To them I may have owed another gift,
Of aspect more sublime; that blessed mood,
In which the burthen of the mystery,
In which the heavy and the weary weight
Of all this unintelligible world,
Is lightened:—that serene and blessed mood,
In which the affections gently lead us on,—
Until, the breath of this corporeal frame
And even the motion of our human blood
Almost suspended, we are laid asleep
In body, and become a living soul:
While with an eye made quiet by the power
Of harmony, and the deep power of joy,
We see into the life of things.
    If this
Be but a vain belief, yet, oh! how oft—
In darkness and amid the many shapes
Of joyless daylight; when the fretful stir
Unprofitable, and the fever of the world,
Have hung upon the beatings of my heart—
How oft, in spirit, have I turned to thee,
O sylvan Wye! thou wanderer thro' the woods,
How often has my spirit turned to thee!
And now, with gleams of half-extinguished thought,
With many recognitions dim and faint,
And somewhat of a sad perplexity,
The picture of the mind revives again:
While here I stand, not only with the sense
Of present pleasure, but with pleasing thoughts
That in this moment there is life and food
For future years. And so I dare to hope,
Though changed, no doubt, from what I was when first
I came among these hills; when like a roe
I bounded o'er the mountains, by the sides
Of the deep rivers, and the lonely streams,
Wherever nature led: more like a man
Flying from something that he dreads, than one
Who sought the thing he loved. For nature then
(The coarser pleasures of my boyish days,
And their glad animal movements all gone by)
To me was all in all.—I cannot paint
What then I was. The sounding cataract

Haunted me like a passion: the tall rock,
The mountain, and the deep and gloomy wood,
Their colours and their forms, were then to me
An appetite; a feeling and a love,
That had no need of a remoter charm,
By thought supplied, nor any interest
Unborrowed from the eye.—That time is past,
And all its aching joys are now no more,
And all its dizzy raptures. Not for this
Faint I, nor mourn nor murmur; other gifts
Have followed; for such loss, I would believe,
Abundant recompense. For I have learned
To look on nature, not as in the hour
Of thoughtless youth; but hearing oftentimes
The still, sad music of humanity,
Nor harsh nor grating, though of ample power
To chasten and subdue. And I have felt
A presence that disturbs me with the joy
Of elevated thoughts; a sense sublime
Of something far more deeply interfused,
Whose dwelling is the light of setting suns,
And the round ocean and the living air,
And the blue sky, and in the mind of man;
A motion and a spirit, that impels
All thinking things, all objects of all thought
And rolls through all things.
Therefore am I still
A lover of the meadows and the woods,
And mountains; and of all that we behold
From this green earth; of all the mighty world
Of eye, and ear,—both what they half create,
And what perceive; well pleased to recognise
In nature and the language of the sense,
The anchor of my purest thoughts, the nurse,
The guide, the guardian of my heart, and soul
Of all my moral being.
    Nor perchance,
If I were not thus taught, should I the more
Suffer my genial spirits to decay:
For thou art with me here upon the banks
Of this fair river; thou my dearest Friend,
My dear, dear Friend,[1] and in thy voice I catch

---

[1][Wordsworth is here addressing his sister Dorothy.—*Ed.*]

The language of my former heart, and read
My former pleasures in the shooting lights
Of thy wild eyes. Oh! yet a little while
May I behold in thee what I was once,
My dear, dear Sister! and this prayer I make,
Knowing that Nature never did betray
The heart that loved her; 'tis her privilege,
Through all the years of this our life, to lead
From joy to joy: for she can so inform
The mind that is within us, so impress
With quietness and beauty, and so feed
With lofty thoughts, that neither evil tongues,
Rash judgments, nor the sneers of selfish men,
Nor greetings where no kindness is, nor all
The dreary intercourse of daily life,
Shall e'er prevail against us, or disturb
Our cheerful faith, that all which we behold
Is full of blessings. Therefore let the moon
Shine on thee in thy solitary walk;
And let the misty mountain-winds be free
To blow against thee: and, in after years,
When these wild ecstasies shall be matured
Into a sober pleasure; when thy mind
Shall be a mansion for all lovely forms,
Thy memory be as a dwelling-place
For all sweet sounds and harmonies; oh! then,
If solitude, or fear, or pain, or grief,
Should be thy portion, with what healing thoughts
Of tender joy wilt thou remember me,
And these my exhortations! Nor, perchance—
If I should be where I no more can hear
Thy voice, nor catch from thy wild eyes these gleams
Of past existence—wilt thou then forget
That on the banks of this delightful stream
We stood together; and that I, so long
A worshipper of Nature, hither came
Unwearied in that service; rather say
With warmer love—oh! with far deeper zeal
Of holier love. Nor wilt thou then forget,
That after many wanderings, many years
Of absence, these steep woods and lofty cliffs,
And this green pastoral landscape, were to me
More dear, both for themselves and for thy sake!

Thomas Malthus

In 1798 Thomas Malthus advanced a revolutionary theory, which, after it had been elaborated, seems perfectly obvious: That human (and other organic) beings proliferate more rapidly than their food supply. The mathematical calculations to establish this conclusion are almost elementary; what is of significance are the human consequences that Malthus and others, particularly the classical economists and Charles Darwin, were to draw from them.

Malthus himself was essentially a pessimist. Although he suggests several ways in which the consequences of his demographical calculations might be temporarily ameliorated, it is clear that he believed that the overall disparity between population growth and food supply would lead inevitably to continuing and increasing human misery. As a result, his book came as a great shock to the learned world of his time, which had grown complacent from the sometimes easy optimism of the Enlightenment, and he was attacked for his unseemly pessimism. Often, however, the criticisms were misplaced. He was depicted as being callous, with no concern for the welfare of the poor, but a careful reading of his work reveals his compassion for them. Nevertheless, the fact that his predictions about the future failed to materialize indicates serious limitations in his theory. On the one side, the Industrial Revolution (which was only then just beginning) greatly changed the nature and enlarged the scope of production. On the other, the growth of population was not so rapid as he anticipated, mainly because of birth control—a procedure little practiced in his time and one of which he disapproved. Yet Malthus's dire vision of the future is one that is coming to be increasingly shared by demographers today.

The son of a prosperous family, Malthus (1766–1834) attended Cambridge University. After his graduation he became a clergyman but in 1805 accepted a professorial appointment at Haileybury College, an institution operated by the English East India Company. He devoted much of his life to the demographic researches that underlie the argument of his *Essay on the Principle of Population*. Altogether he published six editions of the book over a period of almost thirty years. The selection that follows is taken from the final edition, which was originally published in 1826.

Consider the following questions as you study the text below.

1. What biological "laws" did Malthus believe he had discovered? In his view, what consequences would result from the dynamics he described?

2. Did Malthus believe that reason could act as a check on population growth? In other words, did he believe that humans could foresee the demographic disaster he predicted and take effective steps to avoid it? Why or why not?

An Essay on the Principle of Population

Book I

OF THE CHECKS TO POPULATION IN THE LESS CIVILIZED PARTS OF THE WORLD AND IN PAST TIMES

Chapter I

STATEMENT OF THE SUBJECT. RATIOS OF THE INCREASE OF POPULATION AND FOOD

In an inquiry concerning the improvement of society, the mode of conducting the subject which naturally presents itself, is,

1. *To investigate the causes that have hitherto impeded the progress of mankind towards happiness; and,*

2. *To examine the probability of the total or partial removal of these causes in future.*

To enter fully into this question, and to enumerate all the causes that have hitherto influenced human improvement, would be much beyond the power of an individual. The principal object of the present essay is to examine the effects of the one great cause intimately united with the very nature of man; which, though it has been constantly and powerfully operating since the commencement of society, has been little noticed by the writers who have treated this subject. The facts which establish the existence of this cause have, indeed, been repeatedly stated and acknowledged; but its natural and necessary effects have been almost totally overlooked; though probably among these effects may be reckoned a very considerable portion of that vice and misery, and of that unequal distribution of the bounties of nature, which it has been the unceasing object of the enlightened philanthropist in all ages to correct.

The cause to which I allude, is the constant tendency in all animated life to increase beyond the nourishment prepared for it.

It is observed by Dr. Franklin that there is no bound to the prolific nature of plants or animals, but what is made by their crowding or interfering

Thomas Robert Malthus, *An Essay on the Principle of Population*.

with each other's means of subsistence. Were the face of the earth, he says, vacant of other plants, it might gradually be sowed and overspread with one kind only, as for instance with fennel: and were it empty of other inhabitants, it might in a few ages be replenished from one nation only, as for instance with Englishmen.

This is incontrovertibly true. Through the animal and vegetable kingdoms Nature has scattered the seeds of life abroad with the most profuse and liberal hand; but has been comparatively sparing in the room and the nourishment necessary to rear them. The germs of existence contained in this earth, if they could freely develop themselves, would fill millions of worlds in the course of a few thousand years. Necessity, that imperious, all pervading law of nature, restrains them within the prescribed bounds. The race of plants and the race of animals shrink under this great restrictive law; and man cannot by any efforts of reason escape from it.

In plants and irrational animals, the view of the subject is simple. They are all impelled by a powerful instinct to the increase of their species; and this instinct is interrupted by no doubts about providing for their offspring. Wherever, therefore, there is liberty, the power of increase is exerted; and the super-abundant effects are repressed afterwards by want of room and nourishment.

The effects of this check on man are more complicated. Impelled to the increase of his species by an equally powerful instinct, reason interrupts his career, and asks him whether he may not bring beings into the world, for whom he cannot provide the means of support. If he attend to this natural suggestion, the restriction too frequently produces vice. If he hear it not, the human race will be constantly endeavouring to increase beyond the means of subsistence. But as, by that law of our nature which makes food necessary to the life of man, population can never actually increase beyond the lowest nourishment capable of supporting it, a strong check on population, from the difficulty of acquiring food, must be constantly in operation. This difficulty must fall somewhere, and must necessarily be severely felt in some or other of the various forms of misery, or the fear of misery, by a large portion of mankind.

That population has this constant tendency to increase beyond the means of subsistence, and that it is kept to its necessary level by these causes, will sufficiently appear from a review of the different states of society in which man has existed. But, before we proceed to this review, the subject will, perhaps, be seen in a clearer light, if we endeavour to ascertain what would be the natural increase of population, if left to exert itself with perfect freedom, and what might be expected to be the rate of increase in the production of the earth, under the most favourable circumstances of human industry.

It will be allowed that no country has hitherto been known, where the manners were so pure and simple, and the means of subsistence so abundant, that no check whatever has existed to early marriages from the difficulty of providing for a family, and that no waste of the human species has been occasioned by vicious customs, by towns, by unhealthy occupations, or too severe labour. Consequently in no state that we have yet known, has the power of population been left to exert itself with perfect freedom.

Whether the law of marriage be instituted, or not, the dictate of nature and virtue seems to be an early attachment to one woman; and where there were no impediments of any kind in the way of a union to which such an attachment would lead, and no causes of depopulation afterwards, the increase of the human species would be evidently much greater than any increase which has been hitherto known.

In the northern states of America, where the means of subsistence have been more ample, the manners of the people more pure, and the checks to early marriages fewer, than in any of the modern states of Europe, the population has been found to double itself, for above a century and a half successively, in less than twenty-five years. Yet, even during these periods, in some of the towns, the deaths exceed the births, a circumstance which clearly proves that, in those parts of the country which supplied this deficiency, the increase must have been much more rapid than the general average.

In the back settlements, where the sole employment is agriculture, and vicious customs and unwholesome occupations are little known, the population has been found to double itself in fifteen years. Even this extraordinary rate of increase is probably short of the utmost power of population. Very severe labour is requisite to clear a fresh country; such situations are not in general considered as particularly healthy; and the inhabitants, probably, are occasionally subject to the incursions of the Indians, which may destroy some lives, or at any rate diminish the fruits of industry.

According to a table of Euler, calculated on a mortality of 1 in 36, if the births be to the deaths in the proportion of 3 to 1, the period of doubling will be only 12 years and 4/5ths. And this proportion is not only a possible supposition, but has actually occurred for short periods in more countries than one.

Sir William Petty supposes a doubling possible in so short a time as ten years.

But, to be perfectly sure that we are far within the truth, we will take the slowest of these rates of increase, a rate in which all concurring testimonies agree, and which has been repeatedly ascertained to be from procreation only.

It may safely be pronounced, therefore, that population, when unchecked, goes on doubling itself every twenty-five years, or increases in a geometrical ratio.

The rate according to which the productions of the earth may be supposed to increase, it will not be so easy to determine. Of this, however, we may be perfectly certain, that the ratio of their increase in a limited territory must be of a totally different nature from the ratio of the increase of population. A thousand millions are just as easily doubled every twenty-five years by the power of population as a thousand. But the food to support the increase from the greater number will by no means be obtained with the same facility. Man is necessarily confined in room. When acre has been added to acre till all the fertile land is occupied, the yearly increase of food must depend upon the melioration of the land already in possession. This is a fund, which, from the nature of all soils, instead of increasing, must be gradually diminishing. But population, could it be supplied with food, would go on with unexhausted vigour; and the increase of one period would furnish the power of a greater increase the next, and this without any limit.

From the accounts we have of China and Japan, it may be fairly doubted, whether the best-directed efforts of human industry could double the produce of these countries even once in any number of years. There are many parts of the globe, indeed, hitherto uncultivated, and almost unoccupied; but the right of exterminating, or driving into a corner where they must starve, even the inhabitants of these thinly-peopled regions, will be questioned in a moral view. The process of improving their minds and directing their industry would necessarily be slow; and during this time, as population would regularly keep pace with the increasing produce, it would rarely happen that a great degree of knowledge and industry would have to operate at once upon rich unappropriated soil. Even where this might take place, as it does sometimes in new colonies, a geometrical ratio increases with such extraordinary rapidity, that the advantage could not last long. If the United States of America continue increasing, which they certainly will do, though not with the same rapidity as formerly, the Indians will be driven further and further back into the country, till the whole race is ultimately exterminated, and the territory is incapable of further extension.

These observations are, in a degree, applicable to all parts of the earth, where the soil is imperfectly cultivated. To exterminate the inhabitants of the greatest part of Asia and Africa, is a thought that could not be admitted for a moment. To civilise and direct the industry of the various tribes of Tartars and Negroes, would certainly be a work of considerable time, and of variable and uncertain success.

Europe is by no means so fully peopled as it might be. In Europe there is the fairest chance that human industry may receive its best direction. The science of agriculture has been much studied in England and Scotland; and there is still a great portion of uncultivated land in these countries. Let us consider at what rate the produce of this island might be supposed to increase under circumstances the most favourable to improvement.

If it be allowed that by the best possible policy, and great encouragements to agriculture, the average produce of the island could be doubled in the first twenty-five years, it will be allowing, probably, a greater increase than could with reason be expected.

In the next twenty-five years, it is impossible to suppose that the produce could be quadrupled. It would be contrary to all our knowledge of the properties of land. The improvement of the barren parts would be a work of time and labour; and it must be evident to those who have the slightest acquaintance with agricultural subjects that in proportion as cultivation is extended, the additions that could yearly be made to the former average produce must be gradually and regularly diminishing. That we may be the better able to compare the increase of population and food, let us make a supposition, which, without pretending to accuracy, is clearly more favourable to the power of production in the earth, than any experience we have had of its qualities will warrant.

Let us suppose that the yearly additions which might be made to the former average produce, instead of decreasing, which they certainly would do, were to remain the same; and that the produce of this island might be increased every twenty-five years, by a quantity equal to what it at present produces. The most enthusiastic speculator cannot suppose a greater increase than this. In a few centuries it would make every acre of land in the island like a garden.

If this supposition be applied to the whole earth, and if it be allowed that the subsistence for man which the earth affords might be increased every twenty-five years by a quantity equal to what it at present produces, this will be supposing a rate of increase much greater than we can imagine that any possible exertions of mankind could make it.

It may be fairly pronounced, therefore, that, considering the present average state of the earth, the means of subsistence, under circumstances the most favourable to human industry, could not possibly be made to increase faster than in an arithmetical ratio.

The necessary effects of these two different rates of increase, when brought together, will be very striking. Let us call the population of this island eleven millions; and suppose the present produce equal to the easy support of such a number. In the first twenty-five years the population would be twenty-two millions, and the food also being doubled, the means of subsistence would be equal to this increase. In the next twenty-five years, the population would be forty-four millions, and the means of subsistence only equal to the support of thirty-three millions. In the next period the population would be eighty-eight millions, and the means of subsistence just equal to the support of half that number. And, at the conclusion of the first century, the population would be a hundred and seventy-six millions, and the means of subsistence only equal to the support of fifty-five millions, leaving a population of a hundred and twenty-one millions totally unprovided for.

Taking the whole earth, instead of this island, emigration would of course be excluded; and, supposing the present population equal to a thousand millions, the human species would increase as the numbers 1, 2, 4, 8, 16, 32, 64, 128, 256 and subsistence as 1, 2, 3, 4, 5, 6, 7, 8, 9. In two centuries the population would be to the means of subsistence as 256 to 9; in three centuries as 4096 to 13, and in two thousand years the difference would be almost incalculable.

In this supposition no limits whatever are placed to the produce of the earth. It may increase for ever and be greater than any assignable quantity; yet still the power of population being in every period so much superior, the increase of the human species can only be kept down to the level of the means of subsistence by the constant operation of the strong law of necessity, acting as a check upon the greater power.

Chapter II

OF THE GENERAL CHECKS TO POPULATION AND THE MODE OF THEIR OPERATION

The ultimate check to population appears then to be a want of food, arising necessarily from the different ratios according to which population and food increase. But this ultimate check is never the immediate check, except in cases of actual famine.

The immediate check may be stated to consist of all those customs, and all those diseases, which seem to be generated by a scarcity of the means of subsistence; and all those causes, independent of this scarcity, whether of a moral or physical nature, which tend prematurely to weaken and destroy the human frame.

These checks to population, which are constantly operating with more or less force in every society, and keep down the number to the level of the means of subsistence, may be classed under two general heads—the preventive, and the positive checks.

The preventive check, as far as it is voluntary, is peculiar to man, and arises from that distinctive superiority in his reasoning faculties, which enables him to calculate distant consequences. The checks to the indefinite increase of plants and irrational animals are all either positive, or, if preventive, involuntary. But man cannot look around him, and see the distress which frequently presses upon those who have large families; he cannot contemplate his present possessions or earnings, which he now nearly consumes himself, and calculate the amount of each share, when with very little addition they must be divided, perhaps, among seven or eight, without feeling a doubt whether, if he follow the bent of his inclinations, he may be able to support the offspring which he will probably bring into the world. In a state of equality, if such can exist, this would be the simple question. In the present state of society other considerations occur. Will he not lower his rank in life, and be obliged to give up in great measure his former habits? Does any mode of employment present itself by which he may reasonably hope to maintain a family? Will he not at any rate subject himself to greater difficulties, and more severe labour, than in his single state? Will he not be unable to transmit to his children the same advantages of education and improvement that he had himself possessed? Does he even feel secure that, should he have a large family, his utmost exertions can save them from rags and squalid poverty, and their consequent degradation from the community? And may he not be reduced to the grating necessity for forfeiting his independence, and of being obliged to the sparing hand of Charity for support?

These considerations are calculated to prevent, and certainly do prevent, a great number of persons in all civilised nations from pursuing the dictate of nature in an early attachment to one woman.

If this restraint does not produce vice, it is undoubtedly the least evil that can arise from the principle of population. Considered as a restraint on a strong natural inclination, it must be allowed to produce a certain degree of temporary unhappiness; but evidently slight, compared with the evils which result from any of the other checks to population; and merely of the same nature as many other sacrifices of temporary to permanent gratification, which it is the business of a moral agent continually to make.

When this restraint produces vice, the evils which follow are but too conspicuous. A promiscuous intercourse to such degree as to prevent the birth of children, seems to lower, in the most marked manner, the dignity of human nature. It cannot be without its effect on men, and nothing can be more obvious than its tendency to degrade the female character, and to destroy all its most amiable and distinguishing characteristics. Add to which, that among those unfortunate females, with which all great towns abound, more real distress and aggravated misery are, perhaps, to be found, than in any other department of human life.

When a general corruption of morals with regard to the sex, pervades all the classes of society, its effects must necessarily be, to poison the springs of domestic happiness, to weaken conjugal and parental affection, and to lessen the united exertion and ardour of parents in the care and education of their children:—effects which cannot take place without a decided diminution of the general happiness and virtue of the society; particularly as the necessity of art in the accomplishment and conduct of intrigues, and in the concealment of their consequences necessarily leads to many other vices.

The positive checks to population are extremely various, and include every cause, whether arising from vice or misery, which in any degree contributes to shorten the natural duration of human life. Under this head, therefore, may be enumerated all unwholesome occupations, severe labour and exposure to the seasons, extreme poverty, bad nursing of children, great towns, excesses of all kinds, the whole train of common diseases and epidemics, war, plagues, and famine.

On examining these obstacles to the increase of population which I have classed under the heads of preventive and positive checks, it will appear that they are all resolvable into moral restraint, vice, and misery.

Of the preventive checks, the restraint from marriage which is not followed by irregular gratifications may properly be termed moral restraint.[1]

Promiscuous intercourse, unnatural passions, violations of the marriage bed, and improper arts to conceal the consequences of irregular connexions, are preventive checks that clearly come under the head of vice.

Of the positive checks, those which appear to arise unavoidably from the laws of nature, may be called exclusively misery; and those which we obviously bring upon ourselves, such as wars, excesses, and many others which it would be in our power to avoid, are of a mixed nature. They are brought upon us by vice, and their consequences are misery.[2]

The sum of all these preventive and positive checks, taken together, forms the immediate check to population; and it is evident that, in every country where the whole of the procreative power cannot be called into action, the preventive and the positive checks must vary inversely as each other; that is, in countries either naturally unhealthy, or subject to a great mortality, from whatever cause it may arise, the preventive check will prevail very little. In those countries, on the contrary, which are naturally healthy, and where the preventive check is found to prevail with considerable force, the positive check will prevail very little, or the mortality be very small.

In every country some of these checks are, with more or less force, in constant operation; yet notwithstanding their general prevalence, there are few states in which there is not a constant effort in the population to increase beyond the means of subsistence. This constant effort as constantly tends to

---

[1]It will be observed, that I here use the term *moral* in its most confined sense. By moral restraint I would be understood to mean a restraint from marriage, from prudential motives, with a conduct strictly moral during the period of this restraint; and I have never intentionally deviated from this sense. When I have wished to consider the restraint from marriage connected with its consequences, I have either called it prudential restraint, or a part of the preventive check, of which indeed it forms the principal branch.

In my review of the different stages of society, I have been accused of not allowing sufficient weight in the prevention of population to moral restraint; but when the confined sense of the term, which I have here explained, is adverted to, I am fearful that I shall not be found to have erred much in this respect. I should be very glad to believe myself mistaken.

[2]As the general consequence of vice is misery, and as this consequence is the precise reason why an action is termed vicious, it may appear that the term misery alone would be here sufficient, and that it is superfluous to use both. But the rejection of the term vice would introduce a considerable confusion into our language and ideas. We want it particularly to distinguish those actions, the general tendency of which is to produce misery, and which are therefore prohibited by the commands of the Creator, and the precepts of the moralist, although, in their immediate or individual effects, they may produce perhaps exactly the contrary. The gratification of all our passions in its immediate effect is happiness, not misery; and, in individual instances, even the remote consequences (at least in this life) may possibly come under the same denomination. There may have been some irregular connexions with women, which have added to the happiness of both parties, and have injured no one. These individual actions, therefore, cannot come under the head of misery. But they are still evidently vicious, because an action is so denominated, which violates an express precept, founded upon its general tendency to produce misery, whatever may be its individual effect; and no person can doubt the general tendency of an illicit intercourse between the sexes, to injure the happiness of society.

subject the lower classes of society to distress, and to prevent any great permanent melioration of their condition.

These effects, in the present state of society, seem to be produced in the following manner. We will suppose the means of subsistence in any country just equal to the easy support of the inhabitants. The constant effort towards population, which is found to act even in the most vicious societies, increases the number of people before the means of subsistence are increased. The food, therefore, which before supported eleven millions, must now be divided among eleven millions and a half. The poor consequently must live much worse, and many of them be reduced to severe distress. The number of labourers also being above the proportion of work in the market, the price of labour must tend to fall, while the price of provisions would at the same time tend to rise. The labourer therefore must do more work, to earn the same as he did before. During this season of distress, the discouragements to marriage and the difficulty of rearing a family are so great, that the progress of population is retarded. In the mean time, the cheapness of labour, the plenty of labourers, and the necessity of an increased industry among them, encourage cultivators to employ more labour upon their land, to turn up fresh soil, and to manure and improve more completely what is already in tillage, till ultimately the means of subsistence may become in the same proportion to the population, as at the period from which we set out. The situation of the labourer being then again tolerably comfortable, the restraints to population are in some degree loosened; and, after a short period, the same retrograde and progressive movements, with respect to happiness, are repeated.

This sort of oscillation will not probably be obvious to common view; and it may be difficult even for the most attentive observer to calculate its periods. Yet that, in the generality of old states, some alternation of this kind does exist though in a much less marked, and in a much more irregular manner, than I have described it, no reflecting man, who considers the subject deeply, can well doubt.

One principal reason why this oscillation has been less remarked, and less decidedly confirmed by experience than might naturally be expected, is, that the histories of mankind which we possess are, in general, histories only of the higher classes. We have not many accounts that can be depended upon, of the manners and customs of that part of mankind, where these retrograde and progressive movements chiefly take place. A satisfactory history of this kind, of one people and of one period, would require the constant and minute attention of many observing minds in local and general remarks on the state of the lower classes of society, and the causes that influenced it; and to draw accurate inferences upon this subject, a succession of such historians for some centuries would be necessary. This branch of statistical knowledge has, of late years, been attended to in some countries, and we may promise ourselves a clearer insight into the internal structure of human society from the progress of these inquiries. But the science may be said yet to be in its infancy, and many of the objects, on which it would be desirable to have information, have been either omitted or not stated with sufficient accuracy. Among these, perhaps, may be reckoned the proportion of the number of adults to the number of marriages; the extent to which vicious customs have prevailed in consequence of the restraints upon matrimony; the comparative mortality among the children of the most distressed part of the community, and of those who live rather more at their ease; the variations in the real price of labour; the observable differences in the state of the lower classes of society, with respect to ease and happiness, at different times during a certain period; and very accurate registers of births, deaths, and marriages, which are of the utmost importance in this subject.

A faithful history, including such particulars, would tend greatly to elucidate the manner in which the constant check upon population acts; and would probably prove that existence of the retrograde and progressive movements that have been mentioned; though the times of their vibration must necessarily be rendered irregular from the operation of many interrupting causes; such as, the introduction or failure of certain manufactures; a greater or less prevalent spirit of agricultural enterprise; years of plenty, or years of scarcity; wars, sickly seasons, poor-laws, emigrations and other causes of a similar nature.

A circumstance which has, perhaps, more than any other, contributed to conceal this oscillation from common view, is the difference between the nominal and real price of labour. It very rarely happens that the nominal price of labour universally falls; but we well know that it frequently remains the same, while the nominal price of provisions has been gradually rising. This, indeed, will generally be the case, if the increase of manufacturers and commerce be sufficient to employ the new labourers that are thrown into the market, and to prevent the increased supply from lowering the money-price. But an increased number of labourers receiving the same money-wages will necessarily, by their competition, increase the money-price of corn. This is, in fact, a real fall in the price of labour; and, during this period, the condition of the lower classes of the community must be gradually growing worse. But the farmers and capitalists are growing rich from the real cheapness of labour. Their increasing capitals enable them to employ a greater number of men; and, as the population had probably suffered some check from the greater difficulty of supporting a family, the demand for labour, after a certain period, would be great in proportion to the supply, and its price would of course rise, if left to find its natural level; and thus the wages of labour, and consequently the condition of the lower classes of society, might have progressive and retrograde movements, though the price of labour might ever nominally fall.

In savage life, where there is no regular price of labour, it is little to be doubted that similar oscillations took place. When population has increased nearly to the utmost limits of the food, all the preventive and the positive checks will naturally operate with increased force. Vicious habits with respect to the sex will be more general, the exposing of children more frequent, and both the probability and fatality of wars and epidemics will be considerably greater; and these causes will probably continue their operation till the population is sunk below the level of the food; and then the return to comparative plenty will again produce an increase, and, after a certain period, its further progress will again be checked by the same causes.

But without attempting to establish these progressive and retrograde movements in different countries, which would evidently require more minute histories than we possess, and which the progress of civilisation naturally tends to counteract, the following propositions are intended to be proved:—

1. *Population is necessarily limited by the means of subsistence.*

2. *Population invariably increases when the means of subsistence increase, unless prevented by some powerful and obvious checks.*

3. *These checks, and the checks which repress the superior power of population, and keep its effects on a level with the means of subsistence, are all resolvable into moral restraint, vice, and misery.*

The first of these propositions scarcely needs illustration. The second and third will be sufficiently established by a review of the immediate checks to population in the past and present state of society.

Child Labor

By the early nineteenth century, the Industrial Revolution had spread from England and was beginning to transform Europe from a rural to an urban society. In England, this transformation often depressed the living standards of workers beneath even those of the cottage manufacturing system of an earlier era. In doing so, however, it paved the way for its own reform, for it bared to the public eye in an aggravated form conditions that had long existed but had passed relatively unnoticed. Poverty and misery could be overlooked as long as the workers remained scattered about the countryside, but once they were congregated in the hideous slums of the Midlands industrial centers, their plight became too obvious to remain unheeded. Consequently, social reform became the order of the day.

Among the most prominent of the English reformers was the seventh earl of Shaftesbury (1801–1885), who concentrated on working conditions in the factories. At Shaftesbury's instigation, another reformer, Michael Sadler, introduced a bill in Parliament in 1831 designed to regulate the working conditions of children in textile mills. The bill was referred to a committee, with Sadler as chairman. The selection that follows is an excerpt from the evidence presented before that committee. The committee's recommendations resulted in the Factory Act of 1833, which limited the working hours of children and set up a system of inspection to insure that its regulations would be carried out.

Consider the following questions as you study the text below.

1. In your opinion, what led to the abuses described in the Sadler Report? What groups in English society were most concerned by industrial work conditions and most interested in reform? How would you explain their interest?

2. On the whole, did the Industrial Revolution raise or lower the standard of living of the English working class? What is the basis of your assessment?

The Sadler Report

Veneris, 18° Die Maii, 1832

MICHAEL THOMAS SADLER, ESQUIRE, IN THE CHAIR

. . .

MR. MATTHEW CRABTREE, *called in; and Examined.*

What age are you?——Twenty-two.

What is your occupation?——A blanket manufacturer.

Have you ever been employed in a factory?——Yes.

At what age did you first go to work in one?——Eight.

How long did you continue in that occupation?——Four years.

Will you state the hours of labour at the period when you first went to the factory, in ordinary times?——From 6 in the morning to 8 at night.

Fourteen hours?——Yes.

With what intervals for refreshment and rest?——An hour at noon.

Then you had no resting time allowed in which to take your breakfast, or what is in Yorkshire called your "drinking"?——No.

When trade was brisk what were your hours?——From 5 in the morning to 9 in the evening.

Sixteen hours?——Yes.

With what intervals at dinner?——An hour.

How far did you live from the mill?——About two miles.

Was there any time allowed for you to get your breakfast in the mill?——No.

Did you take it before you left your home?——Generally.

During those long hours of labour could you be punctual; how did you awake?——I seldom did awake spontaneously; I was most generally awoke or lifted out of bed, sometimes asleep, by my parents.

Were you always in time?——No.

What was the consequence if you had been too late?——I was most commonly beaten.

Severely?——Very severely, I thought.

In whose factory was this?——Messrs. Hague & Cook's, of Dewsbury.

Will you state the effect that those long hours had upon the state of your health and feelings?——I was, when working those long hours, commonly very much fatigued at night, when I left my work; so much so that I sometimes should have slept as I walked if I had not stumbled and started awake again; and so sick often that I could not eat, and what I did eat I vomited.

The Sadler Report: Report from the Committee on the Bill to Regulate the Labour of Children in the Mills and Factories of the United Kingdom (London: House of Commons, 1832).

Did this labour destroy your appetite?———It did.

In what situation were you in that mill?———I was a piecener.

Will you state to this Committee whether piecening is a very laborious employment for children, or not?———It is a very laborious employment. Pieceners are continually running to and fro, and on their feet the whole day.

The duty of the piecener is to take the cardings from one part of the machinery, and to place them on another?———Yes.

So that the labour is not only continual, but it is unabated to the last?——— It is unabated to the last.

Do you not think, from your own experience, that the speed of the machinery is so calculated as to demand the utmost exertions of a child supposing the hours were moderate?———It is as much as they could do at the best; they are always upon the stretch, and it is commonly very difficult to keep up with their work.

State the condition of the children toward the latter part of the day, who have thus to keep up with the machinery.———It is as much as they do when they are not very much fatigued to keep up with their work, and toward the close of the day, when they come to be more fatigued, they cannot keep up with it very well, and the consequence is that they are beaten to spur them on.

Were you beaten under those circumstances?———Yes.

Frequently?———Very frequently.

And principally at the latter end of the day?———Yes.

And is it your belief that if you had not been so beaten, you should not have got through the work?———I should not if I had not been kept up to it by some means.

Does beating then principally occur at the latter end of the day, when the children are exceedingly fatigued?———It does at the latter end of the day, and in the morning sometimes, when they are very drowsy, and have not got rid of the fatigue of the day before.

What were you beaten with principally?———A strap.

Anything else?———Yes, a stick sometimes; and there is a kind of roller which runs on the top of the machine called a billy, perhaps two or three yards in length, and perhaps an inch and a half, or more in diameter; the circumference would be four or five inches; I cannot speak exactly.

Were you beaten with that instrument?———Yes.

Have you yourself been beaten, and have you seen other children struck severely with that roller?———I have been struck very severely with it myself, so much so as to knock me down, and I have seen other children have their heads broken with it.

You think that it is a general practice to beat the children with the roller?———It is.

You do not think then that you were worse treated than other children in the mill?———No, I was not, perhaps not so bad as some were.

In those mills is chastisement towards the latter part of the day going on perpetually?———Perpetually.

So that you can hardly be in a mill without hearing constant crying?—— Never an hour, I believe.

Do you think that if the overlooker were naturally a humane person it would be still found necessary for him to beat the children, in order to keep up their attention and vigilance at the termination of those extraordinary days of labour?——Yes, the machine turns off a regular quantity of cardings, and of course they must keep as regularly to their work the whole of the day; they must keep with the machine, and therefore however humane the slubber may be, as he must keep up with the machine or be found fault with, he spurs the children to keep up also by various means but that which he commonly resorts to is to strap them when they become drowsy.

At the time when you were beaten for not keeping up with your work, were you anxious to have done it if you possibly could?——Yes; the dread of being beaten if we could not keep up with our work was a sufficient impulse to keep us to it if we could.

When you got home at night after this labour, did you feel much fatigued?——Very much so.

Had you any time to be with your parents, and to receive instruction from them?——No.

What did you do?——All that we did when we got home was to get the little bit of supper that was provided for us and go to bed immediately. If the supper had not been ready directly, we should have gone to sleep while it was preparing.

Did you not, as a child, feel it a very grievous hardship to be roused so soon in the morning?——I did.

Were the rest of the children similarly circumstanced?——Yes, all of them; but they were not all of them so far from their work as I was.

And if you had been too late you were under the apprehension of being cruelly beaten?——I generally was beaten when I happened to be too late; and when I got up in the morning the apprehension of that was so great, that I used to run, and cry all the way as I went to the mill.

That was the way by which your punctual attendance was secured?——Yes.

And you do not think it could have been secured by any other means?——No.

Then it is your impression from what you have seen, and from your own experience, that those long hours of labour have the effect of rendering young persons who are subject to them exceedingly unhappy?——Yes.

You have already said it had a considerable effect upon your health?——Yes.

Do you conceive that it diminished your growth?——I did not pay much attention to that; but I have been examined by some persons who said they thought I was rather stunted, and that I should have been taller if I had not worked at the mill.

What were your wages at that time?——Three shillings.[1]

And how much a day had you for over-work when you were worked so exceedingly long?——A half-penny a day.

Did you frequently forfeit that if you were not always there to a moment?——Yes; I most frequently forfeited what was allowed for those long hours.

You took your food to the mill; was it in your mill, as is the case in cotton mills, much spoiled by being laid aside?——It was very frequently covered by flues from the wool; and in that case they had to be blown off with the mouth, and picked off with the fingers before it could be eaten.

So that not giving you a little leisure for eating your food, but obliging you to take it at the mill, spoiled your food when you did get it?——Yes, very commonly.

And that at the same time that this over-labour injured your appetite?——Yes.

Could you eat when you got home?——Not always.

What is the effect of this piecening upon the hands?——It makes them bleed; the skin is completely rubbed off, and in that case they bleed in perhaps a dozen parts.

The prominent parts of the hand?——Yes, all the prominent parts of the hand are rubbed down till they bleed; every day they are rubbed in that way.

All the time you continue at work?——All the time we are working. The hands never can be hardened in that work, for the grease keeps them soft in the first instance, and long and continual rubbing is always wearing them down, so that if they were hard they would be sure to bleed.

Is it attended with much pain?——Very much.

Do they allow you to make use of the back of the hand?——No; the work cannot be so well done with the back of the hand, or I should have made use of that.

Is the work done as well when you are so many hours engaged in it, as it would be if you were at it a less time?——I believe it is not done so well in those long hours; toward the latter end of the day the children become completely bewildered, and know not what they are doing, so that they spoil their work without knowing.

Then you do not think that the masters gain much by the continuance of the work to so great a length of time?——I believe not.

Were there girls as well as boys employed in this manner?——Yes.

Were they more tenderly treated by the overlookers, or were they worked and beaten in the same manner?——There was no difference in their treatment.

Were they beaten by the overlookers, or by the slubber?——By the slubber.

[1][per week—*Ed.*]

But the overlooker must have been perfectly aware of the treatment that the children endured at the mill?——Yes; and sometimes the overlooker beat them himself; but the man that they wrought under had generally the management of them.

Did he pay them their wages?——No; their wages were paid by the master.

But the overlooker of the mill was perfectly well aware that they could not have performed the duty exacted from them in the mill without being thus beaten?——I believe he was.

You seem to say that this beating is absolutely necessary, in order to keep the children up to their work; is it universal throughout all factories?——I have been in several other factories, and I have witnessed the same cruelty in them all.

Did you say that you were beaten for being too late?——Yes.

Is it not the custom in many of the factories to impose fines upon children for being too late, instead of beating them?——It was not in that factory.

What then were the fines by which you lost the money you gained by your long hours?——The spinner could not get on so fast with his work when we happened to be too late; he could not begin his work so soon, and therefore it was taken by him.

Did the slubber pay you your wages?——No, the master paid our wages.

And the slubber took your fines from you?——Yes.

Then you were fined as well as beaten?——There was nothing deducted from the ordinary scale of wages, but only from that received for over-hours, and I had only that taken when I was too late, so that the fine was not regular.

When you were not working over-hours, were you so often late as when you were working over-hours?——Yes.

You were not very often late whilst you were not working over-hours?——Yes, I was often late when I was not working over-hours; I had to go at 6 o'clock in the morning, and consequently had to get up at 5 to eat my breakfast and go to the mill, and if I failed to get up by 5 I was too late; and it was 9 o'clock before we could get home, and then we went to bed; in the best times I could not be much above eight hours at home, reckoning dressing and eating my meals, and everything.

Was it a blanket-mill in which you worked?——Yes.

Did you ever know that the beatings to which you allude inflicted a serious injury upon the children?——I do not recollect any very serious injury, more than that they had their heads broken, if that may be called a serious injury; that has often happened; I, myself, had no more serious injury than that.

You say that the girls as well as the boys were employed as you have described, and you observed no difference in their treatment?——No difference.

The girls were beat in this unmerciful manner?——They were.

They were subject, of course, to the same bad effects from this overworking?——Yes.

Could you attend an evening-school during the time you were employed in the mill?——No, that was completely impossible.

Did you attend the Sunday-school?——Not very frequently when I work at the mill.

How then were you engaged during the Sunday?——I very often slept till it was too late for school time or for divine worship, and the rest of the day I spent in walking out and taking a little fresh air.

Did your parents think that it was necessary for you to enjoy a little fresh air?——I believe they did; they never said anything against it; before I went to the mill I used to go to the Sunday-school.

Did you frequently sleep nearly the whole of the day on Sunday?——Very often.

At what age did you leave that employment?——I was about twelve years old.

Why did you leave that place?——I went very late one morning, about 7 o'clock, and I got severely beaten by the spinner, and he turned me out of the mill, and I went home, and never went any more.

Was your attendance as good as the other children?——Being at rather a greater distance than some of them, I was generally one of the latest.

Where was your next work?——I worked as bobbin-winder in another part of the works of the same firm.

How long were you a bobbin-winder?——About two years, I believe.

What did you become after that?——A weaver.

How long were you a weaver?——I was a weaver till March in last year.

A weaver of what?——A blanket-weaver.

With the same firm?——With the same firm.

Did you leave them?——No; I was dismissed from my work for a reason which I am willing and anxious to explain.

Have you had opportunities of observing the way in which the children are treated in factories up to a late period?——Yes.

You conceive that their treatment still remains as you first found it, and that the system is in great want of regulation?——It does.

Children you still observe to be very much fatigued and injured by the hours of labour?——Yes.

From your own experience, what is your opinion as to the utmost labour that a child in piecening could safely undergo?——If I were appealed to from my own feelings to fix a limit, I should fix it at ten hours, or less.

And you attribute to longer hours all the cruelties that you describe?——A good deal of them.

Are the children sleepy in mills?——Very.

Are they more liable to accidents in the latter part of the day than in the other part?——I believe they are; I believe a greater number of accidents happen in the latter part of the day than in any other. I have known them so sleepy that in the short interval while the others have been going out, some of them have fallen asleep, and have been left there.

Is it an uncommon case for children to fall asleep in the mill, and remain there all night?———Not to remain there all night; but I have known a case the other day, of a child whom the overlooker found when he went to lock the door, that had been left there.

So that you think there has been no change for the better in the treatment of those children; is it your opinion that there will be none, except Parliament interfere in their behalf?———It is my decided conviction.

Have you recently seen any cruelties in mills?———Yes; not long since I was in a mill and I saw a girl severely beaten; at a mill called Hicklane Mill, in Batley; I happened to be in at the other end of the room, talking; and I heard the blows, and I looked that way, and saw the spinner beating one of the girls severely with a large stick. Hearing the sound, led me to look round, and to ask what was the matter, and they said it was "Nothing but——— paying[2] 'his ligger-on.'"

What age was the girl?———About twelve years.

Was she very violently beaten?———She was.

Was this when she was overfatigued?———It was in the afternoon.

Can you speak as to the effect of this labour in the mills and factories on the morals of the children, as far as you have observed?———As far as I have observed with regard to morals in the mills, there is everything about them that is disgusting to every one conscious of correct morality.

Do you find that the children, the females especially, are very early demoralized in them?———They are.

Is their language indecent?———Very indecent; and both sexes take great familiarities with each other in the mills, without at all being ashamed of their conduct.

Do you connect their immorality of language and conduct with their excessive labour?———It may be somewhat connected with it, for it is to be observed that most of that goes on toward night, when they begin to be drowsy; it is a kind of stimulus which they use to keep them awake; they say some pert thing or other to keep themselves from drowsiness, and it generally happens to be some obscene language.

Have not a considerable number of the females employed in mills illegitimate children very early in life?———I believe there are; I have known some of them have illegitimate children when they were between sixteen and seventeen years of age.

How many grown-up females had you in the mill?———I cannot speak to the exact number that were grown up; perhaps there might be thirty-four or so that worked in the mill at that time.

[2][beating—*Ed.*]

How many of those had illegitimate children?——A great many of them; eighteen or nineteen of them, I think.

Did they generally marry the men by whom they had the children?——No; it sometimes happens that young women have children by married men, and I have known an instance, a few weeks since, where one of the young women had a child by a married man.

Is it your opinion that those who have the charge of mills very often avail themselves of the opportunity they have to debauch the young women?——No, not generally; most of the improper conduct takes place among the younger part of those that work in the mill.

Do you find that the children and young persons in those mills are moral in other respects, or does their want of education tend to encourage them in a breach of the law?——I believe it does, for there are very few of them that can know anything about it; few of them can either read or write.

Are criminal offences then very frequent?——Yes, theft is very common; it is practised a great deal in the mills, stealing their bits of dinner, or something of that sort. Some of them have not so much to eat as they ought to have, and if they can fall in with the dinner of some of their partners they steal it. The first day my brother and I went to the mill we had our dinner stolen, because we were not up to the tricks; we were more careful in future, but still we did not always escape.

Was there any correction going on at the mills for indecent language or improper conduct?——No, I never knew of any.

From what you have seen and known of those mills, would you prefer that the hours of labour should be so long with larger wages, or that they should be shortened with a diminution of wages?——If I were working at the mill now, I would rather have less labour and receive a trifle less, than so much labour and receive a trifle more.

Is that the general impression of individuals engaged in mills with whom you are acquainted?——I believe it is.

What is the impression in the country from which you come with respect to the effect of this Bill upon wages?——They do not anticipate that it will affect wages at all.

They think it will not lower wages?——They do.

Do you mean that it will not lower wages by the hour, or that you will receive the same wages per day?——They anticipate that it may perhaps lower their wages at a certain time of the year when they are working hard, but not at other times, so that they will have their wages more regular.

Does not their wish for this Bill mainly rest upon their anxiety to protect their children from the consequences of this excessive labour, and to have some opportunity of affording them a decent education?——Yes; such are the wishes of every humane father that I have heard speak about the thing.

Have they not some feeling of having the labour equalized?——That is the feeling of some that I have heard speak of it.

Did your parents work in the same factories?——No.

Were any of the slubbers' children working there?——Yes.

Under what slubber did you work in that mill?——Under a person of the name of Thomas Bennett, in the first place; and I was changed from him to another of the name of James Webster.

Did the treatment depend very much upon the slubber under whom you were?——No, it did not depend directly upon him, for he was obliged to do a certain quantity of work, and therefore to make us keep up with that.

Were the children of the slubbers strapped in the same way?——Yes, except that it is very natural for a father to spare his own child.

Did it depend upon the feelings of a slubber toward his children?——Very little.

Did the slubbers fine their own spinners?——I believe not.

You said that the piecening was very hard labour; what labour is there besides moving about; have you anything heavy to carry or to lift?——We have nothing heavy to carry, but we are kept upon our feet in brisk times from 5 o'clock in the morning to 9 at night.

How soon does the hand get sore in piecening?——How soon mine became sore I cannot speak to exactly; but they get a little hard on the Sunday, when we are not working, and they will get sore again very soon on the Monday.

Is it always the case in piecening that the hand bleeds, whether you work short or long hours?——They bleed more when we work more.

Do they always bleed when you are working?——Yes.

Do you think that the children would not be more competent to this task, and their hands far less hurt, if the hours were fewer every day, especially when their hands had become seasoned to the labour?——I believe it would have an effect for the longer they are worked the more their hands are worn, and the longer it takes to heal them, and they do not get hard enough after a day's rest to be long without bleeding again; if they were not so much worn down, they might heal sooner, and not bleed so often or so soon.

After a short day's work, have you found your hands hard the next morning?——They do not bleed much after we have ceased work; they then get hard; they will bleed soon in the morning when in regular work.

Do you think if the work of the children were confined to about ten hours a day, that they would not be able to perform this piecening without making their hands bleed?——I believe they would.

So that it is your opinion, from your experience, that if the hours were mitigated, their hands would not be so much worn, and would not bleed by the business of piecening?——Yes.

Do you mean to say that their hands would not bleed at all?——I cannot say exactly, for I always wrought long hours, and therefore my hands always did bleed.

Have you any experience of mills where they only work ten hours?——I have never wrought at such mills, and in most of the mills I have seen their hands bleed.

At a slack time, when you were working only a few hours, did your hands bleed?———No, they did not for three or four days, after we had been standing still for a week; the mill stood still sometimes for a week together, but when we did work we worked the common number of hours.

Were all the mills in the neighbourhood working the same number of hours in brisk times?———Yes.

So that if any parent found it necessary to send his children to the mill for the sake of being able to maintain them, and wished to take them from any mill where they were excessively worked, he could not have found any other place where they would have been less worked?———No, he could not; for myself, I had no desire to change, because I thought I was as well off as I could be at any other mill.

And if the parent, to save his child, had taken him from the mill, and had applied to the parish for relief, would the parish, knowing that he had withdrawn his child from its work, have relieved him?———No.

So that the long labour which you have described, or actual starvation, was, practically, the only alternative that was presented to the parent under such circumstances?———It was; they must either work at the mill they were at or some other, and there was no choice in the mills in that respect.

What, in your opinion, would be the effect of limiting the hours of labour upon the happiness, and the health, and the intelligence of the rising generation?———If the hours are shortened, the children may, perhaps, have a chance of attending some evening-school, and learning to read and write; and those that I know who have been to school and learned to read and write; have much more comfort than those who have not. For myself, I went to a school when I was six years old, and I learned to read and write a little then.

At a free-school?———Yes, at a free-school in Dewsbury; but I left school when I was six years old. The fact is, that my father was a small man-ufacturer, and in comfortable circumstances, and he got into debt with Mr. Cook for a wool bill, and as he had no other means of paying him, he came and agreed with my father, that my brother and I should go to work at his mill till that debt was paid; so that the whole of the time that we wrought at the mill we had no wages.

THOMAS BENNETT, *called in; and Examined.*

Where do you reside?———At Dewsbury.

What is your business?———A slubber.

What age are you?———About forty-eight.

Have you had much experience regarding the working of children in factories?———Yes, about twenty-seven years.

Have you a family?———Yes, eight children.

Have any of them gone to factories?———All.

At what age?———The first went at six years of age.

To whose mill?———To Mr. Halliley's, to piece for myself.

What hours did you work at that mill?——We have wrought from 4 to 9, from 4 to 10, and from 5 to 9, and from 5 to 10.

What sort of a mill was it?——It was a blanket-mill; we sometimes altered the time, according as the days increased and decreased.

What were your regular hours?——Our regular hours when we were not so throng, was from 6 to 7.

And when you were the throngest, what were your hours then?——From 5 to 9, and from 5 to 10, and from 4 to 9.

Seventeen hours?——Yes.

What intervals for meals had the children at that period?——Two hours; an hour for breakfast, and an hour for dinner.

Did they always allow two hours for meals at Mr. Halliley's?——Yes, it was allowed, but the children did not get it, for they had business to do at that time, such as fettling and cleaning the machinery.

But they did not stop in at that time, did they?——They all had their share of the cleaning and other work to do.

That is, they were cleaning the machinery?——Cleaning the machinery at the time of dinner.

How long a time together have you known those excessive hours to continue?——I have wrought so myself very nearly two years together.

Were your children working under you then?——Yes, two of them.

State the effect upon your children.——Of a morning when they have been so fast asleep that I have had to go up stairs and lift them out of bed, and have heard them crying with the feelings of a parent; I have been much affected by it.

Were not they much fatigued at the termination of such a day's labour as that?——Yes; many a time I have seen their hands moving while they have been nodding, almost asleep; they have been doing their business almost mechanically.

While they have been almost asleep, they have attempted to work?——Yes; and they have missed the carding and spoiled the thread, when we have had to beat them for it.

Could they have done their work towards the termination of such a long day's labour, if they had not been chastised to it?——No.

You do not think that they could have kept awake or up to their work till the seventeenth hour, without being chastised?——No.

Will you state what effect it had upon your children at the end of their day's work?——At the end of their day's work, when they have come home, instead of taking their victuals, they have dropped asleep with the victuals in their hands; and sometimes when we have sent them to bed with a little bread or something to eat in their hand, I have found it in their bed the next morning.

Had it affected their health?——I cannot say much of that; they were very hearty children.

Do you live at a distance from the mill?——Half a mile.

Did your children feel a difficulty in getting home?——Yes, I have had to carry the lesser child on my back, and it has been asleep when I got home.

Did these hours of labour fatigue you?——Yes, they fatigued me to that excess, that in divine worship I have not been able to stand according to order; I have sat to worship.

So that even during the Sunday you have felt fatigue from your labour in the week?——Yes, we felt it, and always took as much rest as we could.

Were you compelled to beat your own children, in order to make them keep up with the machine?——Yes, that was forced upon us, or we could not have done the work; I have struck them often, though I felt as a parent.

If the children had not been your own, you would have chastised them still more severely?——Yes.

What did you beat them with?——A strap sometimes; and when I have seen my work spoiled, with the roller.

Was the work always worse done at the end of the day?——That was the greatest danger.

Do you conceive it possible that the children could do their work well at the end of such a day's labour as that?——No.

Matthew Crabtree, the last Witness examined by this Committee, I think mentioned you as one of the slubbers under whom he worked?——Yes.

He states that he was chastised and beaten at the mill?——Yes, I have had to chastise him.

You can confirm then what he has stated as to the length of time he had to work as a child, and the cruel treatment that he received?——Yes, I have had to chastise him in the evening, and often in the morning for being too late; when I had one out of the three wanting I could not keep up with the machine, and I was getting behindhand compared with what another man was doing; and therefore I should have been called to account on Saturday night if the work was not done.

Was he worse than others?——No.

Was it the constant practice to chastise the children?——Yes.

It was necessary in order to keep up your work?——Yes.

And you would have lost your place if you had not done so?——Yes; when I was working at Mr. Wood's mill, at Dewsbury, which at present is burnt down, but where I slubbed for him until it was, while we were taking our meals he used to come up and put the machine agoing; and I used to say, "You do not give us time to eat"; he used to reply, "Chew it at your work"; and I often replied to him, "I have not yet become debased like a brute, I do not chew my cud." Often has that man done that, and then gone below to see if a strap were off, which would have shown if the machinery was not working, and then he would come up again.

Was this at the drinking time?——Yes, at breakfast and at drinking.

Was this where the children were working?——Yes, my own children and others.

Were your own children obliged to employ most of their time at breakfast and at the drinking in cleansing the machine, and in fettling the spindles?——I have seen at that mill, and I have experienced and mentioned it with grief, that the English children were enslaved worse than the Africans. Once when Mr. Wood was saying to the carrier who brought his work in and out, "How long has that horse of mine been at work?" and the carrier told him the time, and he said "Loose him directly, he has been in too long," I made this reply to him, "You have more mercy and pity for your horse than you have for your men."

Did not this beating go on principally at the latter part of the day?——Yes.

Was it not also dangerous for the children to move about those mills when they became so drowsy and fatigued?——Yes, especially by lamp-light.

Do the accidents principally occur at the latter end of those long days of labour?——Yes, I believe mostly so.

Do you know of any that have happened?——I know of one; it was at Mr. Wood's mill; part of the machinery caught a lass who had been drowsy and asleep, and the strap which ran close by her catched her at about her middle, and bore her to the ceiling, and down she came, and her neck appeared to be broken, and the slubber ran up to her and pulled her neck, and I carried her to the doctor myself.

Did she get well?——Yes, she came about again.

What time was that?——In the evening.

You say that you have eight children who have gone to the factories?——Yes.

There has been no opportunity for you to send them to a day-school?——No; one boy had about twelve months' schooling.

Have they gone to Sunday-schools?——Yes.

Can any of them write?——Not one.

They do not teach writing at Sunday-schools?——No; it is objected to, I believe.

So that none of your children can write?——No.

What would be the effect of a proper limitation of the hours of labour upon the conduct of the rising generation?——I believe it would have a very happy effect in regard to correcting their morals; for I believe there is a deal of evil that takes place in one or other in consequence of those long hours.

Is it your opinion that they would then have an opportunity of attending night-schools?——Yes; I have often regretted, while working those long hours, that I could not get my children there.

Is it your belief that if they were better instructed, they would be happier and better members of society?——Yes, I believe so.

Henry Mayhew

One of seventeen siblings, Henry Mayhew (1812–1887) was born into wealth and privilege. However, in defiance of his family, Mayhew chose the uncertain and poorly paying career of freelance journalist. In 1841 Mayhew, along with a group of close friends and writers, founded the now famous weekly journal of satire *Punch*. In 1849 he was commissioned by the *Morning Chronicle* newspaper to conduct a survey of the British lower classes. Perhaps because of Mayhew's unwillingness to soften the presentation of his sometimes shocking subject matter, his relationship with the *Morning Chronicle* was terminated in 1850. Nonetheless, he continued to write articles on Britain's poor, and in 1861 his articles were published in a four-volume collection entitled *London Labour and the London Poor*.

The selection included here is from Volume 4, "Those That Will Not Work," written by Mayhew, William Tuckniss, Bracebridge Hemyng, John Binny, and Andrew Halliday. Mayhew and his fellow contributors tried to break down their subject group into numerous divisions and types, defining each kind of person, their methods, and their habits. The volume also included county maps of England and Wales showing the concentration of criminal activity in each county, and correlating this data with other variables, such as the geographical concentration of illiteracy, illegitimacy, and teenage marriage. In the excerpt that follows, Mayhew explained the purpose and methodology of their investigation and laid out the basic taxonomy of "those who will not work." As you read the document, pay close attention to Mayhew's distinction between "mere matters of fact" and "the truth." Why was this distinction so important to him? How did it shape his approach to the study of the poor?

Consider the following questions as you study the text below.

1. Why did Mayhew believe that a thorough study of the poor was necessary? What did he hope to achieve?

2. What principles does he seem to have used in his division of the poor into distinct types? How "scientific" was Mayhew's classification of "those that will not work"?

London Labour and the London Poor

I enter upon this part of my subject with a deep sense of the misery, the vice, the ignorance, and the want that encompass us on every side—I enter upon it after much grave attention to the subject, observing closely, reflecting patiently, and generalizing cautiously upon the phenomena and causes of the vice and crime of this city—I enter upon it after a thoughtful study of the habits and character of the "outcast" class generally—I enter upon it, moreover, not only as forming an integral and most important part of the task I have imposed upon myself, but from a wish to divest the public mind of certain "idols" of the platform and conventicle—"idols" peculiar to our own time, and unknown to the great Father of the inductive philosophy—and "idols," too, that appear to me greatly to obstruct a proper understanding of the subject. Further, I am led to believe that I can contribute some new facts concerning the physics and economy of vice and crime generally, that will not only make the solution of the social problem more easy to us, but, setting more plainly before us some of its latent causes, make us look with more pity and less anger on those who want the fortitude to resist their influence; and induce us, or at least the more earnest among us, to apply ourselves steadfastly to the removal or alleviation of those social evils that appear to create so large a proportion of the vice and crime that we seek by punishment to prevent.

Such are the *ultimate* objects of my present labours: the result of them is given to the world with an earnest desire to better the condition of the wretched social outcasts of whom I have now to treat, and to contribute, if possible, my mite of good towards the common weal.

But though such be my ultimate object, let me here confess that my immediate aim is the elimination of the truth; without this, of course, all other principles must be sheer sentimentality—sentiments being, to my mind, opinions engendered by the feelings rather than the judgment. The attainment of the truth, then, will be my primary aim; but by the truth, I wish it to be understood, I mean something *more* than the bare facts. Facts, according to my ideas, are merely the elements of truths, and not the truths themselves; of all matters there are none so utterly useless by themselves as your mere matters of fact. A fact, so long as it remains an isolated fact, is a dull, dead, uninformed thing; no object nor event by itself can possibly give us any knowledge, we must compare it with some other, even to distinguish it; and it is the distinctive quality thus developed that constitutes the essence of a thing—that is to say, the point by which we cognize and recognise it when again presented to us. A fact must be assimilated with, or discriminated

Henry Mayhew, *London Labour and the London Poor*, Vol. 4 (London: Frank Cass and Company, 1967), pp. 1–2, 23–27. Reprinted by permission of Frank Cass and Company.

from, some other fact or facts, in order to be raised to the dignity of a truth, and made to convey the least knowledge to the mind. To say, for instance, that in the year 1850 there were 26,813 criminal offenders in England and Wales, is merely to oppress the brain with the record of a fact that, *per se*, is so much mental lumber. This is the very mummery of statistics; of what rational good can such information by itself be to any person? who can tell whether the number of offenders in that year be large or small, unless they compare it with the number of some other year, or in some other country? but to do this will require another fact, and even then this second fact can give us but little real knowledge. It may teach us, perhaps, that the past year was more or less criminal than some other year, or that the people of this country, in that year, were more or less disposed to the infraction of the laws than some other people abroad; still, what will all this avail us? If the year which we select to contrast criminally with that of 1850 be not itself compared with other years, how are we to know whether the number of criminals appertaining to it be above or below the average? or, in other words, how can the one be made a measure of the other?

To give the least mental value to facts, therefore, we must generalize them, that is to say, we must contemplate them in connection with other facts, and so discover their agreements and differences, their antecedents, concomitants, and consequences. It is true we may frame erroneous and defective theories in so doing; we may believe things which are similar in appearance to be similar in their powers and properties also; we may distinguish between things having no real difference; we may mistake concomitant events for consequences; we may generalize with too few particulars, and hastily infer that to be common to all which is but the special attribute of a limited number; nevertheless, if theory may occasionally teach us wrongly, facts without theory or generalization cannot possibly teach us at all. What the process of digestion is to food, that of generalizing is to fact; for as it is by the assimilation of the substances we eat with the elements of our bodies that our limbs are enlarged and our whole frames strengthened, so is it by associating perception with perception in our brains that our intellect becomes at once expanded and invigorated. Contrary to the vulgar notion, theory, that is to say, theory in its true Baconian sense, is not opposed to fact, but consists rather of a *large* collection of facts; it is not true of this or that thing alone, but of *all* things belonging to the same class—in a word, it consists not of *one* fact but an infinity. The theory of gravitation, for instance, expresses not only what occurs when a stone falls to the earth, but when every other body does the same thing; it expresses, moreover, what takes place in the revolution of the moon round our planet, and in the revolution of our planet and of all the other planets round our sun, and of all other suns round the centre of the universe; in fine, it is true not of one thing merely, but of every material object in the entire range of creation.

There are, of course, two methods of dealing philosophically with every subject—deductively and inductively. We may either proceed from principles to facts, or recede from facts to principles. The one explains, the other investigates; the former applies known general rules to the comprehension of particular phenomena, and the latter classifies the particular phenomena, so that we may ultimately come to comprehend their unknown general rules. The deductive method is the mode of *using* knowledge, and the inductive method the mode of *acquiring* it.

In a subject like the crime and vice of the metropolis, and the country in general, of which so little is known—of which there are so many facts, but so little comprehension—it is evident that we must seek by induction, that is to say, by a careful classification of the known phenomena, to render the matter more intelligible; in fine, we must, in order to arrive at a *comprehensive* knowledge of its antecedents, consequences, and concomitants, contemplate as large a number of facts as possible in as many different relations as the statistical records of the country will admit of our doing.

With this brief preamble I will proceed to treat generally of the class that will not work, and then particularly of that portion of them termed prostitutes. But first, who are those that *will* work, and who those that *will not* work? This is the primary point to be evolved.

Of the Workers and Non-Workers

The essential quality of an animal is that it seeks its own living, whereas a vegetable has its living brought to it. An animal cannot stick its feet in the ground and suck up the inorganic elements of its body from the soil, nor drink in the organic elements from the atmosphere. The leaves of plants are not only their lungs but their stomachs. As *they* breathe they acquire food and strength, but as animals breathe *they* gradually waste away. The carbon which is *secreted* by the process of respiration in the vegetable is excreted by the very same process in the animal. Hence a fresh supply of *carbonaceous* matter must be sought after and obtained at frequent intervals, in order to repair the continual waste of animal life.

Those who Will Not Work

VII. VAGRANTS OR TRAMPS

Under this head is included all that multifarious tribe of "sturdy rogues," who ramble across the country during the summer, sleeping at the "casual wards" of the workhouses, and who return to London in the winter to avail themselves of the gratuitous lodgings and food attainable at the several metropolitan refuges.

VIII. PROFESSIONAL BEGGARS AND THEIR DEPENDENTS

A. NAVAL AND MILITARY BEGGARS.
   1. Turnpike Sailors.
   2. Spanish Legion Men, &c.
   3. Veterans.

B. "DISTRESSED-OPERATIVE" BEGGARS.
   1. Pretended Starved-out Manufacturers, as the Nottingham "Driz" or Lace-Men.
   2. Pretended Unemployed Agriculturists.
   3. Pretended Frozen-out Gardeners.
   4. Pretended Hand-loom Weavers, and others deprived of their living by Machinery.

C. "RESPECTABLE" BEGGARS.
   1. Pretended Broken-down Tradesmen, or Decayed Gentlemen.
   2. Pretended Distressed Ushers, unable to take situation for want of clothes.
   3. "Clean-Family Beggars" with children in very white pinafores, their faces newly washed, and their hair carefully brushed.
   4. Ashamed Beggars, or those who "stand pad with a fakement" (remain stationary, holding a written placard), and pretend to hide their faces.

D. "DISASTER" BEGGARS.
   1. Shipwrecked Mariners.
   2. Blown-up Miners.
   3. Burnt-out Tradesmen.
   4. Lucifer Droppers.

E. BODILY AFFLICTED BEGGARS.
   1. Having real or pretended sores, vulgarly known as the "scaldrum dodge."
   2. Having swollen legs.
   3. Being crippled, deformed, maimed, or paralyzed.
   4. Being blind.
   5. Being subject to fits.
   6. Being in a decline, and appearing with bandages round the head.
   7. "Shallow coves," or those who exhibit themselves in the streets half clad, especially in cold weather.

F. FAMISHED BEGGARS.
   1. Those who chalk on the pavement, "I am starving."
   2. Those who "stand pad" with a small piece of paper similarly inscribed.

G. FOREIGN BEGGARS.
1. Frenchmen who stop passengers in the street and request to know if they can speak French, previous to presenting a written statement of their distress.
2. Pretended Destitute Poles.
3. Hindoos and Negroes, who stand shivering by the kerb.

H. PETTY TRADING BEGGARS.
1. Tract sellers.
2. Sellers of lucifers, boot-laces, cabbage-nets, tapes, and cottons.
₊ The several varieties of beggars admit of being sub-divided into—
   a. Patterers, or those who beg on the "blob," that is, by word of mouth.
   b. Screevers, or those who beg by *screeving*, that is, by written documents, setting forth imaginary cases of distress, such documents being either—
      i. "Slums" (letters).
      ii. "Fakements" (petitions).

I. THE DEPENDENTS OF BEGGARS.
1. Screevers Proper, or the writers of slums and fakements for those who beg by screeving.
2. Referees, or those who give characters to professional beggars when a reference is required.

IX. CHEATS AND THEIR DEPENDENTS

A. THOSE WHO CHEAT THE GOVERNMENT.
1. Smugglers defrauding the Customs.
2. "Jiggers" defrauding the Excise by working illicit stills, and the like.

B. THOSE WHO CHEAT THE PUBLIC.
1. Swindlers, defrauding those of whom they buy.
2. "Duffers" and "horse-chaunters," defrauding those to whom they sell.
3. "Charley-pitchers" and other low gamblers, defrauding those with whom they play.
4. "Bouncers and Besters" defrauding, by laying wagers, swaggering, or using threats.
5. "Flatcatchers," defrauding by pretending to find some valuable article—as Fawney or Ring-Droppers.
6. Bubble-Men, defrauding by instituting pretended companies —as Sham Next-of-Kin-Societies, Assurance and Annuity Offices, Benefit Clubs, and the like.

7. Douceur-Men, defrauding by offering for a certain sum to confer some boon upon a person as—
    a. To procure Government Situations for laymen, or benefices for clergymen.
    b. To provide Servants with Places.
    c. To teach some lucrative occupation.
    d. To put persons in possession of some information "to their advantage."
8. Deposit-Men, defrauding by obtaining a certain sum as security for future work or some promised place of trust.

C. The Dependents of Cheats are—
    1. "Jollies," and "Magsmen," or accomplices of the "Bouncers and Besters."
    2. "Bonnets," or accomplices of Gamblers.
    3. Referees, or those who give false characters to swindlers and others.

X. THIEVES AND THEIR DEPENDENTS

A. Those who Plunder with Violence.
    1. "Cracksmen"—as Housebreakers and Burglars.
    2. "Rampsmen," or Footpads.
    3. "Bludgers," or Stick-slingers, plundering in company with prostitutes.

B. Those who "Hocus," or Plunder their Victims when Stupified.
    1. "Drummers," or those who render people insensible.
        a. By handkerchiefs steeped in chloroform.
        b. By drugs poured into liquor.
    2. "Bug-hunters," or those who go round to the public-houses and plunder drunken men.

C. Those who Plunder by Manual Dexterity, by Stealth, or by Breach of Trust.
    1. "Mobsmen," or those who plunder by manual dexterity—as the "light-fingered gentry."
        a. "Buzzers," or those who abstract handkerchiefs and other articles from gentlemen's pockets.
            i. "Stook-Buzzers," those who steal handkerchiefs.
            ii. "Tail-Buzzers," those who dive into coat-pockets for sneezers (snuff-boxes,) skins and dummies (purses and pocket-books).
        b. "Wires," or those who pick ladies' pockets.
        c. "Prop-nailers," those who steal pins and brooches.

    d. "Thimble-screwers," those who wrench watches from their guards.

    e. "Shop-lifters," or those who purloin goods from shops while examining articles.

2. "Sneaksmen," or those who plunder by means of stealth.

    a. Those who purloin goods, provisions, money, clothes, old metal, &c.

       i. "Drag Sneaks," or those who steal goods or luggage from carts and coaches.

       ii. "Snoozers," or those who sleep at railway hotels, and decamp with some passenger's luggage or property in the morning.

       iii. "Star-glazers," or those who cut the panes out of shop-windows.

       iv. "Till Friskers," or those who empty tills of their contents during the absence of the shopmen.

       v. "Sawney-Hunters," or those who go purloining bacon from cheese-mongers' shop-doors.

       vi. "Noisy-racket Men," or those who steal china and glass from outside of china-shops.

       vii. "Area Sneaks," or those who steal from houses by going down the area steps.

       viii. "Dead Lurkers," or those who steal coats and umbrellas from passages at dusk, or on Sunday afternoons.

       ix. "Snow Gatherers," or those who steal clean clothes off the hedges.

       x. "Skinners," or those women who entice children and sailors to go with them and then strip them of their clothes.

       xi. "Bluey-Hunters," or those who purloin lead from the tops of house.

       xii. "Cat and Kitten Hunters," or those who purloin pewter quart and pint pots from the top of area railings.

       xiii. "Toshers," or those who purloin copper from the ships along shore.

       xiv. "Mudlarks," or those who steal pieces of rope and lumps of coal from among the vessels at the river-side.

    b. Those who steal animals.

       i. Horse Stealers.

       ii. Sheep, or "Woolly-bird," Stealers.

       iii. Deer Stealers.

       iv. Dog Stealers.

       v. Poachers, or Game Stealers.

       vi. "Lady and Gentlemen Racket Men," or those who steal cocks and hens.

        vii. Cat Stealers, or those who make away with cats for the sake of their skins and bones.

    c. Those who steal dead bodies—as the "Resurrectionists."

  3. Those who plunder by breach of trust.

    a. Embezzlers, or those who rob their employers.

        i. By receiving what is due to them, and never accounting for it.

        ii. By obtaining goods in their employer's name.

        iii. By purloining money from the till, or goods from the premises.

    b. Illegal Pawners.

        i. Those who pledge work given out to them by employers.

        ii. Those who pledge blankets, sheets, &c., from lodgings.

    c. Dishonest servants, those who make away with the property of their masters.

    d. Bill Stealers, or those who purloin bills of exchange entrusted to them, to get discounted.

    e. Letter Stealers.

D. "Shoful Men," or those who Plunder by Means of Counterfeits.

  1. Coiners or fabricators of counterfeit money.

  2. Forgers of bank notes.

  3. Forgers of checks and acceptances.

  4. Forgers of wills.

E. Dependents of Thieves.

  1. "Fences," or receivers of stolen goods.

  2. "Smashers," or utterers of base coin or forged notes.

XI. PROSTITUTES AND THEIR DEPENDENTS

A. Professional Prostitutes.

  1. Seclusives, or those who live in private houses or apartments.

    a. Kept Mistresses.

    b. "Prima Donnas," or those who belong to the "first class," and live in a superior style.

  2. Convives, or those who live in the same house with a number of others.

    a. Those who are independent of the mistress of the house.

    b. Those who are subject to the mistress of a brothel.

        i. "Board Lodgers," or those who give a portion of what they receive to the mistress of the brothel, in return for their board and lodging.

      ii. "Dress Lodgers," or those who give either a portion or the whole of what they get to the mistress of the brothel in return for their board, lodging, and clothes.
3. Those who live in low lodging-houses.
4. Sailors' and soldiers' women.
5. Park women, or those who frequent the parks at night, and other retired places.
6. Thieves' women, or those who entrap men into bye streets for the purpose of robbery.
7. The Dependents of Prostitutes:
   a. "Bawds," or Keepers of Brothels.
   b. Followers of Dress Lodgers.
   c. Keepers of Accommodation Houses.
   d. Procuresses, Pimps, and Panders.
   e. Fancy-Men.
   f. Magsmen and Bullies.

B. CLANDESTINE PROSTITUTES.
1. Female Operatives.
2. Maid Servants.
3. Ladies of Intrigue.
4. Keepers of Houses of Assignation.

C. COHABITANT PROSTITUTES.
1. Those whose paramours cannot afford to pay the marriage fees.
2. Those whose paramours do not believe in the sanctity of the ceremony.
3. Those who have married a relative forbidden by law.
4. Those whose paramours object to marry them for pecuniary or family reasons.
5. Those who would forfeit their income by marrying, as officers' widows in receipt of pensions, and those who hold property only while unmarried.

Karl Marx and Friedrich Engels

According to Lenin, Marxism was derived from three sources: German philosophy, English political economy, and French socialism. The German philosophy was the absolute idealism of G. W. F. Hegel, which Karl Marx had imbibed while a student at the University of Berlin. Central to this philosophy was the notion of *dialectic*, the theory that history is a series of struggles between opposing forces, with each successive struggle occurring on a higher level than the one that preceded it. Hegel viewed the struggles as taking place between opposing ideas embodied in distinct national cultures. But Marx shifted the struggles from the ideational plane to the economic or material plane, and transformed the antagonists from nations to classes. In other words, he replaced Hegel's dialectical idealism with his own dialectical materialism; or, as he put it, he turned the dialectic, which Hegel had stood on its head, back on its feet again.

The English political economy that Lenin referred to consisted of the writings of the classical economists, Adam Smith and David Ricardo, whose labor theory of value provided Marx with the basic assumption underlying his greatest work, *Capital*. But Marx reversed the argument of the classical economists: where they found in the labor theory of value a defense of capitalism, he found a weapon to attack it.

Finally, in his reference to French socialism Lenin had in mind the works of a group of writers, including Claude Saint-Simon, François Fourier, Pierre Proudhon, and Louis Blanc, whose views on the elimination of capitalism and the establishment of the ideal society greatly influenced Marx—though later he scornfully brushed their theories aside as "utopian" socialism, while claiming that his own were "scientific."

The *Communist Manifesto*, one of the greatest revolutionary documents in history, was the joint production of Marx (1818–1883) and his lifelong friend and collaborator Friedrich Engels (1820–1895). Composed in 1848 as a platform for the Communist League, a small organization of radical workmen, it contains in capsule form most of the major Marxist doctrines.

Consider the following questions as you study the text below.

1. According to Marx and Engels, why was the collapse of capitalist society inevitable? What signs did they see that such a collapse was imminent?

2. Describe Marx and Engels's vision of a classless society. In their view, would such a society eventually collapse, as all previous societies had? Why or why not?

Manifesto of the Communist Party

A specter is haunting Europe—the specter of Communism. All the powers of Old Europe have entered into a holy alliance to exorcise this specter; Pope and Czar, Metternich and Guizot, French Radicals and German police-spies.

Where is the party in opposition that has not been decried as communistic by its opponents in power? Where is the opposition that has not hurled back the branding reproach of Communism, against the more advanced opposition parties, as well as against its reactionary adversaries?

Two things result from this fact.

I. Communism is already acknowledged by all European powers to be in itself a power.

II. It is high time that Communists should openly, in the face of the whole world, publish their views, their aims, their tendencies, and meet this nursery tale of the specter of Communism with a Manifesto of the party itself.

To this end Communists of various nationalities have assembled in London, and sketched the following Manifesto to be published in the English, French, German, Italian, Flemish, and Danish languages.

I

BOURGEOIS AND PROLETARIANS[1]

The history of all hitherto existing society is the history of class struggles.

Freeman and slave, patrician and plebeian, lord and serf, guild-master and journey-man, in a word, oppressor and oppressed, stood in constant opposition to one another, carried on an uninterrupted, now hidden, now open fight, that each time ended, either in a revolutionary reconstitution of society at large, or in the common ruin of the contending classes.

In the earlier epochs of history we find almost everywhere a complicated arrangement of society into various orders, a manifold gradation of social rank. In ancient Rome we have patricians, knights, plebeians, slaves; in the Middle Ages, feudal lords, vassals, guild-masters, journey-men, apprentices, serfs; in almost all of these classes, again, subordinate gradations.

Karl Marx and Friedrich Engels, *Manifesto of the Communist Party*, trans. S. Moore.

---

[1] By bourgeoisie is meant the class of modern Capitalists, owners of the means of social production and employers of wage-labor. By proletariat the class of modern wage-laborers who, having no means of production of their own, are reduced to selling their labor-power in order to live.

The modern bourgeois society that has sprouted from the ruins of feudal society, has not done away with class antagonisms. It has but established new forms of struggle in place of the old ones.

Our epoch, the epoch of the bourgeoisie, possesses, however, this distinctive feature; it has simplified the class antagonisms. Society as a whole is more and more splitting up into two great hostile camps, into two great classes directly facing each other: Bourgeoisie and Proletariat.

From the serfs of the middle ages sprang the chartered burghers of the earliest towns. From these burgesses the first elements of the bourgeoisie were developed.

The discovery of America, the rounding of the Cape, opened up fresh ground for the rising bourgeoisie. The East-Indian and Chinese markets, the colonization of America, trade with the colonies, the increase in the means of exchange and in commodities generally, gave to commerce, to navigation, to industry, an impulse never before known, and thereby, to the revolutionary element in the tottering feudal society, a rapid development.

The feudal system of industry, under which industrial production was monopolized by closed guilds, now no longer sufficed for the growing wants of the new market. The manufacturing system took its place. The guild-masters were pushed on one side by the manufacturing middle class; division of labor between the different corporate guilds vanished in the face of division of labor in each single workshop.

Meantime the markets kept ever growing, the demand ever rising. Even manufacture no longer sufficed. Thereupon steam and machinery revolutionized industrial production. The place of manufacture was taken by the giant, Modern Industry, the place of the industrial middle class, by industrial millionaires, the leaders of whole industrial armies, the modern bourgeois.

Modern Industry has established the world's market, for which the discovery of America paved the way. This market has given an immense development to commerce, to navigation, to communication by land. This development has, in its turn, reacted on the extension of industry; and in proportion, as industry, commerce, navigation, railways extended, in the same proportion, the bourgeoisie developed, increased its capital, and pushed into the background every class handed down from the Middle Ages.

We see, therefore, how the modern bourgeoisie is itself the product of a long course of development, of a series of revolutions in the modes of production and of exchange.

Each step in the development of the bourgeoisie was accompanied by a corresponding political advance of that class. An oppressed class under the sway of the feudal nobility, an armed and self-governing association in the mediaeval commune, here independent urban republic (as in Italy and Germany), here taxable "third estate" of the monarchy (as in France), afterwards, in the period of manufacture proper, serving either the semifeudal or the absolute monarchy as a counterpoise against the nobility, and, in fact, cornerstone of the great monarchies in general, the bourgeoisie has at last, since the establishment of Modern Industry and of the world's market, conquered for itself, in the modern representative State, exclusive political sway. The executive of the modern State is but a committee for managing the common affairs of the whole bourgeoisie.

The bourgeoisie, historically, has played a most revolutionary part.

The bourgeoisie, wherever it has got the upper hand, has put an end to all feudal, patriarchal, idyllic relations. It has pitilessly torn asunder the motley feudal ties that bound man to his "natural superiors," and has left remaining no other nexus between man and man than naked self-interest, than callous "cash payment." It has drowned the most heavenly ecstasies of religious fervor, of chivalrous enthusiasm, of Philistine sentimentalism, in the icy water of egotistical calculation. It has resolved personal worth into exchange value, and in place of the numberless indefeasible chartered freedoms, has set up that single, unconscionable freedom—Free Trade. In one word, for exploitation, veiled by religious and political illusions, it has substituted naked, shameless, direct, brutal exploitation.

The bourgeoisie has stripped of its halo every occupation hitherto honored and looked up to with reverent awe. It has converted the physician, the lawyer, the priest, the poet, the man of science, into its paid wage-laborers.

The bourgeoisie has torn away from the family its sentimental veil, and has reduced the family relation to a mere money relation.

The bourgeoisie has disclosed how it came to pass that the brutal display of vigor in the Middle Ages, which reactionists so much admire, found its fitting complement in the most slothful indolence. It has been the first to show what man's activity can bring about. It has accomplished wonders far surpassing Egyptian pyramids, Roman aqueducts, and Gothic cathedrals; it has conducted expeditions that put in the shade all former Exoduses of nations and crusades.

The bourgeoisie cannot exist without constantly revolutionizing the instruments of production, and thereby the relations of production, and with them the whole relations of society. Conservation of the old modes of production in unaltered form, was, on the contrary, the first condition of existence for all earlier industrial classes. Constant revolutionizing of production, uninterrupted disturbance of all social conditions, everlasting uncertainty and agitation, distinguish the bourgeois epoch from all earlier ones. All fixed, fast-frozen relations, with their train of ancient and venerable prejudices and opinions, are swept away; all new-formed ones become antiquated before they can ossify. All that is solid melts into air, all that is holy is profaned, and man is at last compelled to face with sober senses his real conditions of life, and his relations with his kind.

The need of a constantly expanding market for its products chases the bourgeoisie over the whole surface of the globe. It must nestle everywhere, settle everywhere, establish connections everywhere.

The bourgeoisie has through its exploitation of the world's market given a cosmopolitan character to production and consumption in every country. To the great chagrin of reactionists, it has drawn from under the feet of industry the national ground on which it stood. All old established national industries have been destroyed or are daily being destroyed. They are dislodged by new industries, whose introduction becomes a life and death question for all civilized nations, by industries that no longer work up indigenous raw material, but raw material drawn from the remotest zones, industries whose products are consumed, not only at home, but in every quarter of the globe. In place of the old wants, satisfied by the productions of the country, we find new wants, requiring for their satisfaction the products of distant lands and climes. In place of the old local and national seclusion and self-sufficiency we have had intercourse in every direction, universal interdependence of nations. And as in material, so also in intellectual production. The intellectual creations of individual nations become common property. National onesidedness and narrow-mindedness become more and more impossible, and from the numerous national and local literatures, there arises a world-literature.

The bourgeoisie, by the rapid improvement of all instruments of production, by the immensely facilitated means of communication, draws all, even the most barbarian, nations into civilization. The cheap prices of its commodities are the heavy artillery with which it batters down all Chinese walls, with which it forces the barbarians' intensely obstinate hatred of foreigners to capitulate. It compels all nations, on pain of extinction, to adopt the bourgeois mode of production; it compels them to introduce what it calls civilization into their midst, *i.e.*, to become bourgeois themselves. In one word, it creates a world after its own image.

The bourgeoisie has subjected the country to the rule of the towns. It has created enormous cities, has greatly increased the urban population as compared with the rural, and has thus rescued a considerable part of the population from the idiocy of rural life. Just as it has made the country dependent on the towns, so it has made barbarian and semibarbarian countries dependent on the civilized ones, nations of peasants on nations of bourgeois, the East on the West.

The bourgeoisie keeps more and more doing away with the scattered state of the population, of the means of production, and of property. It has agglomerated population, centralized means of production, and has concentrated property in a few hands. The necessary consequence of this was political centralization. Independent, or but loosely connected provinces, with separate interests, laws, governments, and systems of taxation, became lumped together into one nation, with one government, one code of laws, one national class interest, one frontier, and one customs tariff.

The bourgeoisie, during its rule of scarce one hundred years, has created more massive and more colossal productive forces than have all preceding generations together. Subjection of Nature's forces to man, machinery, application of chemistry to industry and agriculture, steam-navigation, railways, electric telegraphs, clearing of whole continents for cultivation, canalization of rivers, whole populations conjured out of the ground—what earlier century had even a presentiment that such productive forces slumbered in the lap of social labor?

We see then: the means of production and of exchange on whose foundation the bourgeoisie built itself up, were generated in feudal society. At a certain stage in the development of these means of production and of exchange, the conditions under which feudal society produced and exchanged, the feudal organization of agriculture and manufacturing industry, in one word, the feudal relations of property, became no longer compatible with the already developed productive forces; they became so many fetters. They had to be burst asunder; they were burst asunder.

Into their places stepped free competition, accompanied by a social and political constitution adapted to it, and by the economical and political sway of the bourgeois class.

A similar movement is going on before our own eyes. Modern bourgeois society with its relations of production, of exchange, and of property, a society that has conjured up such gigantic means of production and of exchange, is like the sorcerer, who is no longer able to control the powers of the nether world whom he has called up by his spells. For many a decade past the history of industry and commerce is but the history of the revolt of modern productive forces against modern conditions of production, against the property relations that are the conditions for the existence of the bourgeoisie and of its rule. It is enough to mention the commercial crises that by their periodical return put on its trial, each time more threateningly, the existence of the bourgeois society. In these crises a great part not only of the existing products, but also of the previously created productive forces, is periodically destroyed. In these crises there breaks out an epidemic that, in all earlier epochs, would have seemed an absurdity—the epidemic of overproduction. Society suddenly finds itself put back into a state of momentary barbarism; it appears as if a famine, a universal war of devastation, had cut off the supply of every means of subsistence; industry and commerce seem to be destroyed; and why? because there is too much civilization, too much means of subsistence, too much industry, too much commerce. The productive forces at the disposal of society no longer tend to further the development of the conditions of bourgeois property; on the contrary, they have become too powerful for these conditions, by which they are fettered, and as soon as they overcome these fetters, they bring disorder into the whole of bourgeois society, endanger the existence of bourgeois property. The conditions of bourgeois society are too narrow to comprise the wealth created by them. And how does the bourgeoisie get over these crises? On the one hand by enforced destruction of a mass of productive forces; on the other, by the conquest of new markets, and by the more thorough exploitation of the old ones. That is to say, by paving the way for more extensive and more destructive crises, and by diminishing the means whereby crises are prevented.

The weapons with which the bourgeoisie felled feudalism to the ground are now turned against the bourgeoisie itself.

But not only has the bourgeoisie forged the weapons that bring death to itself; it has also called into existence the men who are to wield those weapons—the modern working class—the proletarians.

In proportion as the bourgeoisie, *i.e.*, capital, is developed, in the same proportion is the proletariat, the modern working class, developed; a class of laborers, who live only so long as they find work, and who find work only so long as their labor increases capital. These laborers, who must sell themselves piecemeal, are a commodity, like every other article of commerce, and are consequently exposed to all the vicissitudes of competition, to all the fluctuations of the market.

Owing to the extensive use of machinery and to division of labor, the work of the proletarians has lost all individual character, and consequently, all charm for the workman. He becomes an appendage of the machine, and it is only the most simple, most monotonous, and most easily acquired knack, that is required of him. Hence, the cost of production of a workman is restricted almost entirely to the means of subsistence that he requires for his maintenance, and for the propagation of his race. But the price of a commodity, and therefore also of labor, is equal to its cost of production. In proportion, therefore, as the repulsiveness of the work increases, the wage decreases. Nay, more, in proportion as the use of machinery and division of labor increases, in the same proportion the burden of toil also increases, whether by prolongation of the working hours, by increase of the work enacted in a given time, or by increased speed of the machinery, etc.

Modern industry has converted the little workshop of patriarchal master into the great factory of the industrial capitalist. Masses of laborers, crowded into factories, are organized like soldiers. As privates of the industrialized army they are placed under the command of a perfect hierarchy of officers and sergeants. Not only are they the slaves of the bourgeois class, and of the bourgeois State, they are daily and hourly enslaved by the machine, by the overlooker, and, above all, by the individual bourgeois manufacturer himself. The more openly this despotism proclaims gain to be its end and aim, the more petty, the more hateful and the more embittering it is.

The less skill and exertion of strength implied in manual labor, in other words, the more modern industry becomes developed, the more is the labor of men superseded by that of women. Differences of age and sex have no longer any distinctive social validity for the working class. All are instruments of labor, more or less expensive to use, according to age and sex.

No sooner is the exploitation of the laborer by the manufacturer, so far at an end, that he receives his wages in cash, than he is set upon by the other portions of the bourgeoisie, the landlord, the shopkeeper, and pawnbroker, etc.

The lower strata of the middle class—the small tradespeople, shop-keepers, and retired tradesmen generally, the handicraftsmen and peasant—all these sink gradually into the proletariat, partly because their diminutive capital does not suffice for the scale on which modern industry is carried on, and is swamped in the competition with the large capitalists, partly because their specialized skill is rendered worthless by new methods of production. Thus the proletariat is recruited from all classes of the population.

The proletariat goes through various stages of development. With its birth begins its struggle with the bourgeoisie. At first the contest is carried on by individual laborers, then by the workpeople of a factory, then by the op-eratives of one trade, in one locality, against the individual bourgeois who directly exploits them. They direct their attacks not against the bourgeois conditions of production, but against the instruments of production them-selves; they destroy imported wares that compete with their labor, they smash to pieces machinery, they set factories ablaze, they seek to restore by force the vanished status of the workman of the Middle Ages.

At this stage the laborers still form an incoherent mass scattered over the whole country, and broken up by their mutual competition. If anywhere they unite to form more compact bodies, this is not yet the consequence of their own active union, but of the union of the bourgeoisie, which class, in order to attain its own political ends, is compelled to set the whole proletari-at in motion, and is moreover yet, for a time, able to do so. At this stage therefore, the proletarians do not fight their enemies, but the enemies of their enemies, the remnants of absolute monarchy, the landowners, the non-industrial bourgeois, the petty bourgeoisie. Thus the whole historical move-ment is concentrated in the hands of the bourgeoisie; every victory so obtained is a victory for the bourgeoisie.

But with the development of industry the proletariat not only increases in number; it becomes concentrated in greater masses, its strength grows and it feels that strength more. The various interests and conditions of life within the ranks of the proletariat are more and more equalized, in proportion as machinery obliterates all distinctions of labor, and nearly everywhere re-duces wages to the same low level. The growing competition among the bourgeois, and the resulting commercial crises, make the wages of the work-ers even more fluctuating. The unceasing improvement of machinery, ever more rapidly developing, makes their livelihood more and more precarious; the collisions between individual workmen and individual bourgeois take more and more the character of collisions between two classes. Thereupon the workers begin to form combinations (Trades' Unions) against the bour-geois; they club together in order to keep up the rate of wages; they found permanent associations in order to make provision beforehand for these occasional revolts. Here and there the contest breaks out into riots.

Now and then the workers are victorious, but only for a time. The real fruit of their battles lies not in the immediate results but in the ever-improved means of communication that are created by modern industry, and that place the workers of different localities in contact with one another. It was just this contact that was needed to centralize the numerous local struggles, all of the same character, into one national struggle between classes. But every class struggle is a political struggle. And that union, to attain which the burghers of the Middle Ages, with their miserable highways, required centuries, the modern proletarians, thanks to railways, achieve in a few years.

This organization of the proletarians into a class, and consequently into a political party, is continually being upset again by the competition between the workers themselves. But it ever rises up again; stronger, firmer, mightier. It compels legislative recognition of particular interests of the workers, by taking advantage of the divisions among the bourgeoisie itself. Thus the ten-hours' bill in England was carried.

Altogether collisions between the classes of the old society further, in many ways, the course of development of the proletariat. The bourgeoisie finds itself involved in a constant battle. At first with the aristocracy; later on, with those portions of the bourgeoisie itself, whose interests have become antagonistic to the progress of industry; at all times with the bourgeoisie of foreign countries. In all these countries it sees itself compelled to appeal to the proletariat, to ask for its help, and thus to drag it into the political arena. The bourgeoisie itself, therefore, supplies the proletariat with its own elements of political and general education, in other words, it furnishes the proletariat with weapons for fighting the bourgeoisie.

Further, as we have already seen, entire sections of the ruling classes are, by the advance of industry, precipitated into the proletariat, or are at least threatened in their conditions of existence. These also supply the proletariat with fresh elements of enlightenment and progress.

Finally, in times when the class struggle nears the decisive hour, the process of dissolution going on within the ruling class, in fact, within the whole range of an old society, assumes such a violent glaring character, that a small section of the ruling class cuts itself adrift, and joins the revolutionary class, the class that holds the future in its hands. Just as, therefore, at an earlier period, a section of the nobility went over to the bourgeoisie, so now a portion of the bourgeoisie goes over to the proletariat, and in particular, a portion of the bourgeois ideologists, who have raised themselves to the level of comprehending theoretically the historical movement as a whole.

Of all the classes that stand face to face with the bourgeoisie today the proletariat alone is a really revolutionary class. The other classes decay and finally disappear in the face of modern industry; the proletariat is its special and essential product.

The lower middle class, the small manufacturer, the shopkeeper, the artisan, the peasant, all these fight against the bourgeoisie to save from extinction their existence as fractions of the middle class. They are therefore not revolutionary, but conservative. Nay, more, they are reactionary, for they try to roll back the wheel of history. If by chance they are revolutionary, they are so only in view of their impending transfer into the proletariat; they thus defend not their present, but their future interests, they desert their own standpoint to place themselves at that of the proletariat.

The "dangerous class," the social scum, that passively rotting class thrown off by the lowest layers of old society, may, here and there, be swept into the movement by a proletarian revolution; its conditions of life, however, prepare it far more for the part of a bribed tool of reactionary intrigue.

In the conditions of the proletariat, those of the old society at large are already virtually swamped. The proletarian is without property; his relation to his wife and children has no longer anything in common with the bourgeois family relations; modern industrial labor, modern subjection to capital, the same in England as in France, in America as in Germany, has stripped him of every trace of national character. Law, morality, religion, are to him so many bourgeois prejudices, behind which lurk in ambush just as many bourgeois interests.

All the preceding classes that got the upper hand sought to fortify their already acquired status by subjecting society at large to their conditions of appropriation. The proletarians cannot become masters of the productive forces of society, except by abolishing their own previous mode of appropriation, and thereby also every other previous mode of appropriation. They have nothing of their own to secure and to fortify; their mission is to destroy all previous securities for, and insurances of, individual property.

All previous historical movements were movements of minorities, or in the interest of minorities. The proletarian movement is the self-conscious, independent movement of the immense majority, in the interest of the immense majority. The proletariat, the lowest stratum of our present society, cannot stir, cannot raise itself up, without the whole super-incumbent strata of official society being sprung into the air.

Though not in substance, yet in form, the struggle of the proletariat with the bourgeoisie is at first a national struggle. The proletariat of each country must, of course, first of all settle matters with its own bourgeoisie.

In depicting the most general phases of the development of the proletariat, we traced the more or less veiled civil war, raging within existing society, up to the point where the war breaks out into open revolution, and where the violent overthrow of the bourgeoisie lays the foundation for the sway of the proletariat.

Hitherto every form of society has been based, as we have already seen, on the antagonism of oppressing and oppressed classes. But in order to oppress a class certain conditions must be assured to it under which it can, at least, continue its slavish existence. The serf, in the period of serfdom, raised himself to membership in the commune, just as the petty bourgeois, under the yoke of feudal absolutism, managed to develop into a bourgeois. The modern laborer, on the contrary, instead of rising with the progress of industry, sinks deeper and deeper below the conditions of existence of his own class. He becomes a pauper and pauperism develops more rapidly than population and wealth. And here it becomes evident that the bourgeoisie is unfit any longer to be the ruling class in society and to impose its conditions of existence upon society as an overriding law. It is unfit to rule because it is incompetent to assure an existence to its slave within his slavery, because it cannot help letting him sink into such a state that it has to feed him instead of being fed by him. Society can no longer live under this bourgeoisie, in other words its existence is no longer compatible with society.

The essential condition for the existence and for the sway of the bourgeois class, is the formation and augmentation of capital; the condition for capital is wage-labor. Wage-labor rests exclusively on competition between the laborers. The advance of industry, whose involuntary promoter is the bourgeoisie, replaces the isolation of the laborers, due to competition, by their revolutionary combination, due to association. The development of modern industry, therefore, cuts from under its feet the very foundation on which the bourgeoisie produces and appropriates products. What the bourgeoisie therefore produces above all, are its own gravediggers. Its fall and the victory of the proletariat are equally inevitable.

II

PROLETARIANS AND COMMUNISTS

In what relation do the Communists stand to the proletarians as a whole?

The Communists do not form a separate party opposed to other working class parties.

They have no interests separate and apart from those of the proletariat as a whole.

They do not set up any sectarian principles of their own by which to shape and mould the proletarian movement.

The Communists are distinguished from the other working class parties by this only: 1. In the national struggles of the proletarians of the different countries, they point out and bring to the front the common interests of the entire proletariat, independently of all nationality. 2. In the various stages of development which the struggle of the working class against the bourgeoisie has to pass through, they always and everywhere represent the interests of the movement as a whole.

The Communists, therefore, are on the one hand, practically, the most advanced and resolute section of the working class parties of every country, that section which pushes forward all others; on the other hand, theoretically, they have over the great mass of the proletariat the advantage of clearly understanding the line of march, the conditions, and the ultimate general results of the proletarian movement.

The immediate aim of the Communists is the same as that of all the other proletarian parties: formation of the proletariat into a class, overthrow of the bourgeois supremacy, conquest of political power by the proletariat.

The theoretical conclusions of the Communists are in no way based on ideas or principles that have been invented, or discovered, by this or that would-be universal reformer.

They merely express, in general terms, actual relations springing from an existing class struggle, from a historical movement going on under our very eyes. The abolition of existing property relations is not at all a distinctive feature of Communism.

All property relations in the past have continually been subject to historical change, consequent upon the change in historical conditions.

The French Revolution, for example, abolished feudal property in favor of bourgeois property.

The distinguishing feature of Communism is not the abolition of property generally, but the abolition of bourgeois property. But modern bourgeois private property is the final and most complete expression of the system of producing and appropriating products, that is based on class antagonisms, on the exploitation of the many by the few.

In this sense the theory of the Communists may be summed up in the single sentence: Abolition of private property.

We Communists have been reproached with the desire of abolishing the right of personally acquiring property as the fruit of a man's own labor, which property is alleged to be the groundwork of all personal freedom, activity, and independence.

Hard-won, self-acquired, self-earned property! Do you mean the property of the petty artisan and of the small peasant, a form of property that preceded the bourgeois form? There is no need to abolish that; the development of industry has to a great extent already destroyed it, and is still destroying it daily.

Or do you mean modern bourgeois private property?

But does wage-labor create any property for the laborer? Not a bit. It creates capital, *i.e.*, that kind of property which exploits wage-labor, and which cannot increase except upon condition of begetting a new supply of wage-labor for fresh exploitation. Property, in its present form, is based on the antagonism of capital and wage-labor. Let us examine both sides of this antagonism.

To be a capitalist, is to have not only a purely personal, but a social *status* in production. Capital is a collective product, and only by the united action of many members, nay, in the last resort, only by the united action of all members of society, can it be set in motion.

Capital is therefore not a personal, it is a social power.

When, therefore, capital is converted into common property, into the property of all members of society, personal property is not thereby transformed into social property. It is only the social character of the property that is changed. It loses its class character.

Let us now take wage-labor.

The average price of wage-labor is the minimum wage, *i.e.*, that quantum of the means of subsistence, which is absolutely requisite to keep the laborer in bare existence as a laborer. What, therefore, the wage-laborer appropriates by means of his labor, merely suffices to prolong and reproduce a bare existence. We by no means intend to abolish this personal appropriation of the products of labor, an appropriation that is made for the maintenance and reproduction of human life, and that leaves no surplus wherewith to command the labor of others. All that we want to do away with, is the miserable character of this appropriation, under which the laborer lives merely to increase capital, and is allowed to live only in so far as the interest of the ruling class requires it.

In bourgeois society living labor is but a means to increase accumulated labor. In Communist society accumulated labor is but a means to widen, to enrich, to promote the existence of the laborer.

In bourgeois society, therefore, the past dominates the present; in Communist society, the present dominates the past. In bourgeois society capital is independent and has individuality, while the living person is dependent and has no individuality.

And the abolition of this state of things is called by the bourgeois: abolition of individuality and freedom! And rightly so. The abolition of bourgeois individuality, bourgeois independence, and bourgeois freedom is undoubtedly aimed at.

By freedom is meant, under the present bourgeois conditions of production, free trade, free selling, and buying.

But if selling and buying disappears, free selling and buying disappears also. This talk about free selling and buying, and all the other "brave words" of our bourgeoisie about freedom in general, have a meaning, if any, only in contrast with restricted selling and buying, with the fettered traders of the Middle Ages, but have no meaning when opposed to the Communistic abolition of buying and selling, of the bourgeois conditions of production, and of the bourgeoisie itself.

You are horrified at our intending to do away with private property. But in your existing society private property is already done away with for nine-tenths of the population; its existence for the few is solely due to its non-existence in the hands of those nine-tenths. You reproach us, therefore, with intending to do away with a form of property, the necessary condition for whose existence is, the non-existence of any property for the immense majority of society.

In one word, you reproach us with intending to do away with your property. Precisely so: that is just what we intend.

From the moment when labor can no longer be converted into capital, money, or rent, into a social power capable of being monopolized, *i.e.*, from the moment when individual property can no longer be transformed into bourgeois property, into capital, from that moment, you say, individuality vanishes!

You must, therefore, confess that by "individual" you mean no other person than the bourgeois, than the middle-class owner of property. This person must, indeed, be swept out of the way, and made impossible.

Communism deprives no man of the power to appropriate the products of society: all that it does is to deprive him of the power to subjugate the labor of others by means of such appropriation.

It has been objected, that upon the abolition of private property all work will cease, and universal laziness will overtake us.

According to this, bourgeois society ought long ago to have gone to the dogs through sheer idleness; for those of its members who work, acquire nothing, and those who acquire anything, do not work. The whole of this objection is but another expression of the tautology: that there can no longer be any wage-labor when there is no longer any capital.

All objections against the communistic mode of producing and appropriating material products, have, in the same way, been urged against the communistic modes of producing and appropriating intellectual products. Just as, to the bourgeois, the disappearance of class property is the disappearance of production itself, so the disappearance of class structure is to him identical with the disappearance of all culture.

That culture, the loss of which he laments, is, for the enormous majority, a mere training to act as a machine.

But don't wrangle with us so long as you apply to our intended abolition of bourgeois property, the standard of your bourgeois notions of freedom, culture, law, etc. Your very ideas are but the outgrowth of the conditions of your bourgeois production and bourgeois property, just as your jurisprudence is but the will of your class made into a law for all, a will, whose essential character and direction are determined by the economical conditions of existence of your class.

The selfish misconception that induces you to transform into eternal laws of nature and of reason, the social forms springing from your present mode of production and form of property—historical relations that rise and disappear in the progress of production—this misconception you share with every ruling class that has preceded you. What you see clearly in the case of ancient property, what you admit in the case of feudal property, you are of course forbidden to admit in the case of your own bourgeois form of property.

Abolition of the family! Even the most radical flare up at this infamous proposal of the Communists.

On what foundation is the present family, the bourgeois family, based? On capital, on private gain. In its completely developed form this family exists only among the bourgeoisie. But this state of things finds its complement in the practical absence of the family among the proletarians and in public prostitution.

The bourgeois family will vanish as a matter of course when its complement vanishes, and both will vanish with the vanishing of capital.

Do you charge us with wanting to stop the exploitation of children by their parents? To this crime we plead guilty.

But, you will say, we destroy the most hallowed of relations, when we replace home education by social.

And your education! Is not that also social and determined by the social conditions under which you educate, by the intervention, direct or indirect, of society by means of schools, etc.? The Communists have not invented the intervention of society in education; they do but seek to alter the character of that intervention, and to rescue education from the influence of the ruling class.

The bourgeois clap-trap about the family and education, about the hallowed co-relation of parent and child becomes all the more disgusting, as, by the action of modern industry, all family ties among the proletarians are torn asunder and their children transformed into simple articles of commerce and instruments of labor.

But you Communists would introduce community of women; screams the whole bourgeoisie in chorus.

The bourgeois sees in his wife a mere instrument of production. He heard that the instruments of production are to be exploited in common, and, naturally, can come to no other conclusion than that the lot of being common to all will likewise fall to the women.

He has not even a suspicion that the real point aimed at is to do away with the status of women as mere instruments of production.

For the rest nothing is more ridiculous than the virtuous indignation of our bourgeois at the community of women which, they pretend, is to be openly and officially established by the Communists. The Communists have no need to introduce community of women; it has existed almost from time immemorial.

Our bourgeois, not content with having the wives and daughters of their proletarians at their disposal, not to speak of common prostitutes, take the greatest pleasure in seducing each other's wives.

Bourgeois marriage is in reality a system of wives in common and thus, at the most, what the Communists might possibly be reproached with, is that they desire to introduce, in substitution for a hypocritically concealed, an openly legalized community of women. For the rest it is self-evident that the abolition of the present system of production must bring with it the abolition of the community of women springing from that system, *i.e.*, of prostitution both public and private.

The Communists are further reproached with desiring to abolish countries and nationality.

The workingmen have no country. We cannot take from them what they have not got. Since the proletariat must first of all acquire political supremacy, must rise to be the leading class of the nation, must constitute itself *the* nation, it is, so far, itself national though not in the bourgeois sense of the word.

National differences and antagonisms between peoples are daily more and more vanishing, owing to the development of the bourgeoisie, to freedom of commerce, to the world's market, to uniformity in the mode of production and in the conditions of life corresponding thereto.

The supremacy of the proletariat will cause them to vanish still faster. United action, of the leading civilized countries at least, is one of the first conditions for the emancipation of the proletariat.

In proportion as the exploitation of one individual by another is put an end to, the exploitation of one nation by another will also be put an end to. In proportion as the antagonism between classes within the nation vanishes, the hostility of one nation to another will come to an end.

The charges against Communism made from a religious, a philosophical, and, generally, from an ideological standpoint, are not deserving of serious examination.

Does it require deep intuition to comprehend that man's ideas, views, and conceptions, in one word, man's consciousness changes with every change in the conditions of his material existence, in his social relations and in his social life?

What else does the history of ideas prove than that intellectual production changes its character in proportion as material production is changed? The ruling ideas of each age have ever been the ideas of its ruling class.

When people speak of ideas that revolutionize society they do but express the fact that within the old society the elements of a new one have been created, and that the dissolution of the old ideas keeps even pace with the dissolution of the old conditions of existence.

When the ancient world was in its last throes, the ancient religions were overcome by Christianity. When Christian ideas succumbed in the eighteenth century to rationalist ideas, feudal society fought its death-battle with the then revolutionary bourgeoisie. The ideas of religious liberty and freedom of conscience merely gave expression to the sway of free competition within the domain of knowledge.

"Undoubtedly," it will be said, "religious, moral, philosophical, and juridical ideas have been modified in the course of historic development. But religion, morality, philosophy, political science, and law, constantly survived this change."

"There are besides, eternal truths, such as Freedom, Justice, etc., that are common to all states of society. But Communism abolishes eternal truths, it abolishes all religion and all morality, instead of constituting them on a new basis; it therefore acts as a contradiction to all past historical experience."

What does this accusation reduce itself to? The history of all past society has consisted in the development of class antagonisms, antagonisms that assumed different forms at different epochs.

But whatever form they may have taken, one fact is common to all past ages, *viz.*, the exploitation of one part of society by the other. No wonder, then, that the social consciousness of past ages, despite all the multiplicity and variety it displays, moves within certain common forms, or general ideas, which cannot completely vanish except with the total disappearance of class antagonisms.

The Communist revolution is the most radical rupture with traditional property relations; no wonder that its development involves the most radical rupture with traditional ideas.

But let us have done with the bourgeois objections to Communism.

We have seen above that the first step in the revolution by the working class is to raise the proletariat to the position of the ruling class, to win the battle of democracy.

The proletariat will use its political supremacy to wrest, by degrees, all capital from the bourgeoisie; to centralize all instruments of production in the hands of the State, *i.e.*, of the proletariat organized as the ruling class; and to increase the total of productive forces as rapidly as possible.

Of course, in the beginning this cannot be effected except by means of despotic inroads on the rights of property and on the conditions of bourgeois production; by means of measures, therefore, which appear economically insufficient and untenable, but which, in the course of the movement, outstrip themselves, necessitate further inroads upon the old social order and are unavoidable as a means of entirely revolutionizing the mode of production.

These measures will of course be different in different countries.

Nevertheless in the most advanced countries the following will be pretty generally applicable:

1.   Abolition of property in land and application of all rents of land to public purposes.

2.   A heavy progressive or graduated income tax.

3.   Abolition of all rights of inheritance.

4.   Confiscation of the property of all emigrants and rebels.

5.   Centralization of credit in the hands of the State, by means of a national bank with State capital and an exclusive monopoly.

6.   Centralization of the means of communication and transport in the hands of the State.

7.   Extension of factories and instruments of production owned by the State; the bringing into cultivation of waste lands, and the improvement of the soil generally in accordance with a common plan.

8.   Equal liability of all to labor. Establishment of industrial armies, especially for agriculture.

9.   Combination of agriculture with manufacturing industries: gradual abolition of the distinction between town and country, by a more equable distribution of the population over the country.

10.   Free education for all children in public schools. Abolition of children's factory labor in its present form. Combination of education with industrial production, etc., etc.

When, in the course of development, class distinctions have disappeared and all production has been concentrated in the hands of a vast association of the whole nation, the public power will lose its political character. Political power, properly so called, is merely the organized power of one class for oppressing another. If the proletariat during its contest with the bourgeoisie is compelled, by the force of circumstances, to organize itself as a class, if, by means of a revolution, it makes itself the ruling class, and, as such, sweeps away by force the old conditions of production, then it will, along with these conditions, have swept away the conditions for the existence of class antagonism, and of classes generally, and will thereby have abolished its own supremacy as a class.

In place of the old bourgeois society with its classes and class antagonisms we shall have an association in which the free development of each is the condition for the free development of all.

Giuseppe Mazzini

Born in Genoa, Giuseppe Mazzini (1805–1872) spent most of his life in exile in France and England. Exile did not, however, prevent Mazzini from devoting much of his life to the Italian unification movement.

But Mazzini was too broad an intellect to limit his efforts to his own country. Rather, he looked beyond the boundaries of Italy to urge the development of an international community in which all people would live together in freedom, equality, and brotherhood. Italy, he believed, should first unite to form one country and then take the lead in developing the wider association of nations of which he dreamed. More a prophet than a practical politician, Mazzini did not immediately affect the course of European history as much as more pragmatic champions of nationalism, such as Otto von Bismarck of Germany. Nevertheless, his influence has not been negligible, for we can see in him a precursor of both Woodrow Wilson and the League of Nations and the United Nations.

Consider the following questions as you study the text below.

1. According to Mazzini, what are the obligations of a citizen to his or her country? What, if anything, should citizens expect in return?

2. In Mazzini's view, what qualities bound the citizens of a country together? Did ethnicity play a role in his definition of country?

The Duties of Man

. . .

Duties to Country

Your first Duties—first, at least, in importance—are, as I have told you, to Humanity. You are *men* before you are *citizens* or *fathers*. If you do not embrace the whole human family in your love, if you do not confess your faith in its unity—consequent on the unity of God—and in the brotherhood of the Peoples who are appointed to reduce that unity to fact—if wherever one of your fellowmen groans, wherever the dignity of human nature is violated by

Joseph Mazzini, *The Duties of Man*, trans. Ella Noyes (London: J. M. Dent & Sons, Ltd., Everyman's Library Edition, 1907), pp. 51–59. Reprinted by permission of J. M. Dent & Sons, Ltd.

falsehood or tyranny, you are not prompt, being able, to succour that wretched one, or do not feel yourself called, being able, to fight for the purpose of relieving the deceived or oppressed—you disobey your law of life, or do not comprehend the religion which will bless the future.

But what can *each* of you, with his isolated powers, *do* for the moral improvement, for the progress of Humanity? You can, from time to time, give sterile expression to your belief: you may, on some rare occasion, perform an act of *charity* to a brother not belonging to your own land, no more. Now, *charity* is not the watchword of the future faith. The watchword of the future faith is *association*, fraternal cooperation towards a common aim, and this is as much superior to *charity* as the work of many uniting to raise with one accord a building for the habitation of all together would be superior to that which you would accomplish by raising a separate hut each for himself, and only helping one another by exchanging stones and bricks and mortar. But divided as you are in language, tendencies, habits, and capacities, you cannot attempt this common work. The *individual* is too weak, and Humanity too vast. *My God*, prays the Breton mariner as he puts out to sea, *protect me, my ship is so little, and Thy ocean so great*! And this prayer sums up the condition of each of you, if no means is found of multiplying your forces and your powers of action indefinitely. But God gave you this means when he gave you a Country, when, like a wise overseer of labour, who distributes the different parts of the work according to the capacity of the workmen, he divided Humanity into distinct groups upon the face of our globe, and thus planted the seeds of nations. Bad governments have disfigured the design of God, which you may see clearly marked out, as far, at least, as regards Europe, by the courses of the great rivers, by the lines of the lofty mountains, and by other geographical conditions; they have disfigured it by conquest, by greed, by jealousy of the just sovereignty of others; disfigured it so much that today there is perhaps no nation except England and France whose confines correspond to this design. They did not, and they do not, recognise any country except their own families and dynasties, the egoism of caste. But the divine design will infallibly be fulfilled. Natural divisions, the innate spontaneous tendencies of the peoples will replace the arbitrary divisions sanctioned by bad governments. The map of Europe will be remade. The Countries of the People will rise, defined by the voice of the free, upon the ruins of the Countries of Kings and privileged castes. Between these Countries there will be harmony and brotherhood. And then the work of Humanity for the general amelioration, for the discovery and application of the real law of life, carried on in associated and distributed according to local capacities, will be accomplished by peaceful and progressive development; then each of you, strong in the affections and in the aid of many millions of men speaking the same language, endowed with the same tendencies, and educated by the same historic tradition, may hope by your personal effort to benefit the whole of Humanity.

To you, who have been born in Italy, God has allotted, as if favouring you specially, the best-defined country in Europe. In other lands, marked by more uncertain or more interrupted limits, questions may arise which the pacific vote of all will one day solve, but which have cost, and will yet perhaps cost, tears and blood; in yours, no. God has stretched round you sublime and indisputable boundaries; on one side the highest mountains of Europe, the Alps; on the other the sea, the immeasurable sea. Take a map of Europe and place one point of a pair of compasses in the north of Italy on Parma; point the other to the mouth of the Var, and describe a semicircle with it in the direction of the Alps; this point, which will fall, when a semicircle is completed, upon the mouth of the Isonzo, will have marked the frontier which God has given you. As far as this frontier your language is spoken and understood; beyond this you have no rights. Sicily, Sardinia, Corsica, and the smaller islands between them and the mainland of Italy belong undeniably to you. Brute force may for a little while contest these frontiers with you, but they have been recognised from of old by the tacit general consent of the peoples; and the day when, rising with one accord for the final trial, you plant your tricoloured flag upon that frontier, the whole of Europe will acclaim re-risen Italy, and receive her into the community of the nations. To this final trial all your efforts must be directed.

Without Country you have neither name, token, voice, nor rights, no admission as brothers into the fellowship of the Peoples. You are the bastards of Humanity. Soldiers without a banner, Israelites among the nations, you will find neither faith nor protection; none will be sureties for you. Do not beguile yourselves with the hope of emancipation from unjust social conditions if you do not first conquer a Country for yourselves; where there is no Country there is no common agreement to which you can appeal; the egoism of self-interest rules alone, and he who has the upper hand keeps it, since there is no common safeguard for the interests of all. Do not be led away by the idea of improving your material conditions without first solving the national question. You cannot do it. Your industrial associations and mutual help societies are useful as a means of educating and disciplining yourselves; as an economic fact they will remain barren until you have an Italy. The economic problem demands, first and foremost, an increase of capital and production; and while your Country is dismembered into separate fragments—while shut off by the barrier of customs and artificial difficulties of every sort, you have only restricted markets open to you—you cannot hope for this increase. Today—do not delude yourselves—you are not the working-class of Italy; you are only fractions of that class; powerless, unequal to the great task which you propose to yourselves. Your emancipation can have no practical beginning until a National Government, understanding the signs of the times, shall, seated in Rome, formulate a Declaration of Principles to be the guide for Italian progress, and shall insert into it these words, *Labour is sacred, and is the source of the wealth of Italy*.

Do not be led astray, then, by hopes of material progress which in your present conditions can only be illusions. Your Country alone, the vast and rich Italian Country, which stretches from the Alps to the farthest limit of Sicily, can fulfil these hopes. You cannot obtain your *rights* except by obeying the commands of *Duty*. Be worthy of them, and you will have them. O my Brothers! love your Country. Our Country is our home, the home which God has given us, placing therein a numerous family which we love and are loved by, and with which we have a more intimate and quicker communion of feeling and thought than with others; a family which by its concentration upon a given spot, and by the homogeneous nature of its elements, is destined for a special kind of activity. Our Country is our field of labour; the products of our activity must go forth from it for the benefit of the whole earth; but the instruments of labour which we can use best and most effectively exist in it, and we may not reject them without being unfaithful to God's purpose and diminishing our own strength. In labouring according to true principles for our Country we are labouring for Humanity; our Country is the fulcrum of the lever which we have to wield for the common good. If we give up this fulcrum we run the risk of becoming useless to our Country and to Humanity. Before *associating* ourselves with the Nations which compose Humanity we must exist as a Nation. There can be no association except among equals; and you have no recognized collective existence.

Humanity is a great army moving to the conquest of unknown lands, against powerful and wary enemies. The Peoples are the different corps and divisions of that army. Each has a post entrusted to it; each a special operation to perform; and the common victory depends on the exactness with which the different operations are carried out. Do not disturb the order of the battle. Do not abandon the banner which God has given you. Wherever you may be, into the midst of whatever people circumstances may have driven you, fight for the liberty of that people if the moment calls for it; but fight as Italians, so that the blood which you shed may win honour and love, not for you only, but for your Country. And may the constant thought of your soul be for Italy, may all the acts of your life be worthy of her, and may the standard beneath which you range yourselves to work for Humanity be Italy's. Do not Say *I*; say *we*. Be every one of you an incarnation of your Country, and feel himself and make himself responsible for his fellow-countrymen; let each one of you learn to act in such a way that in him men shall respect and love his Country.

Your Country is one and indivisible. As the members of a family cannot rejoice at the common table if one of their number is far away, snatched from the affection of his brothers, so you should have no joy or repose as long as a portion of the territory upon which your language is spoken is separated from the Nation.

Your Country is the token of the mission which God has given you to fulfil in Humanity. The faculties, the strength of *all* its sons should be united for the accomplishment of this mission. A certain number of common duties and rights belong to every man who answers to the *Who are you?* of the other peoples, *I am an Italian.* Those duties and those rights cannot be represented except by one *single* authority resulting from your votes. A Country must have, then, a single government. The politicians who call themselves federalists, and who would make Italy into a brotherhood of different states, would dismember the Country, not understanding the idea of Unity. The States into which Italy is divided today are not the creation of our own people; they are the result of the ambitions and calculations of princes or of foreign conquerors, and serve no purpose but to flatter the vanity of local aristocracies for which a narrower sphere than a great Country is necessary. What you, the people, have created, beautified, and consecrated with your affections, with your joys, with your sorrows, and with your blood, is the City and the Commune, not the Province or the State. In the City, in the Commune, where your fathers sleep and where your children will live, where you exercise your faculties and your personal rights, you live out your lives as *individuals.* It is of your City that each of you can say what the Venetians say of theirs: *Venezia la xe nostra: l'avemo fatta nu.*[1] In your City you have need of *liberty* as in your Country you have need of *association.* The Liberty of the Commune and the Unity of the Country—let that, then, be your faith. Do not say Rome and Tuscany, Rome and Lombardy, Rome and Sicily; say Rome and Florence, Rome and Siena, Rome and Leghorn, and so through all the Communes of Italy. Rome for all that represents Italian life; your Commune for whatever represents the *individual* life. All the other divisions are artificial, and are not confirmed by your national tradition.

A Country is a fellowship of free and equal men bound together in a brotherly concord of labour towards a single end. You must make it and maintain it such. A Country is not an aggregation, it is an *association.* There is no true Country without a uniform right. There is no true Country where the uniformity of that right is violated by the existence of caste, privilege, and inequality—where the powers and faculties of a large number of individuals are suppressed or dormant—where there is no common principle accepted, recognised, and developed by all. In such a state of things there can be no Nation, no People, but only a multitude, a fortuitous agglomeration of men whom circumstances have brought together and different circumstances will separate. In the name of your love for your Country you must combat without truce the existence of every privilege, every inequality, upon the soil which has given you birth. One privilege only is lawful—the privilege of Genius when Genius reveals itself in brotherhood with Virtue; but it is a privilege conceded by God and not by men, and when you acknowledge it and follow its inspirations, you acknowledge it freely by the exercise of your own reason and your own choice. Whatever privilege claims your submission in

---

[1]Venice is our own: we have made her.

virtue of force or heredity, or any right which is not a common right, is a usurpation and a tyranny, and you ought to combat it and annihilate it. Your Country should be your Temple. God at the summit, a People of equals at the base. Do not accept any other formula, any other moral law, if you do not want to dishonour your Country and yourselves. Let the secondary laws for the gradual regulation of your existence be the progressive application of this supreme law.

And in order that they should be so, it is necessary that *all* should contribute to the making of them. The laws made by one fraction of the citizens only can never by the nature of things and men do otherwise than reflect the thoughts and inspirations and desires of that fraction; they represent, not the whole country, but a third, a fourth part, a class, a zone of the country. The law must express the general aspiration, promote the good of all, respond to a beat of the nation's heart. The whole nation therefore should be, directly or indirectly, the legislator. By yielding this mission to a few men, you put the egoism of one class in the place of the Country, which is the union of *all* the classes.

A Country is not a mere territory; the particular territory is only its foundation. The Country is the idea which rises upon that foundation; it is the sentiment of love, the sense of fellowship which binds together all the sons of that territory. So long as a single one of your brothers is not represented by his own vote in the development of the national life—so long as a single one vegetates uneducated among the educated—so long as a single one able and willing to work languishes in poverty for want of work—you have not got a Country such as it ought to be, the Country of all and for all. *Votes, education, work* are the three main pillars of the nation; do not rest until your hands have solidly erected them.

And when they have been erected—when you have secured for every one of you food for both body and soul—when freely united, entwining your right hands like brothers round a beloved mother, you advance in beautiful and holy concord towards the development of your faculties and the fulfilment of the Italian mission—remember that that mission is the moral unity of Europe; remember the immense duties which it imposes upon you. Italy is the only land that has twice uttered the great word of unification to the disjoined nations. Twice Rome has been the metropolis, the temple, of the European world; the first time when our conquering eagles traversed the known world from end to end and prepared it for union by introducing civilised institutions; the second time when, after the Northern conquerors had themselves been subdued by the potency of Nature, of great memories and of religious inspiration, the genius of Italy incarnated itself in the Papacy and undertook the solemn mission—abandoned four centuries ago—of preaching the union of souls to the peoples of the Christian world. Today a third mission is dawning for our Italy; as much vaster than those of old as the Italian People, the free and united Country which you are going to found, will be greater and more powerful than Caesars or Popes. The presentiment of this mission agitates Europe and keeps the eye and the thought of the nations chained to Italy.

Your duties to your Country are proportioned to the loftiness of this mission. You have to keep it pure from egoism, uncontaminated by falsehood and by the arts of that political Jesuitism which they call diplomacy.

The government of the country will be based through your labours upon the worship of principles, not upon the idolatrous worship of interests and of opportunity. There are countries in Europe where Liberty is sacred within, but is systematically violated without; peoples who say, *Truth is one thing, utility another; theory is one thing, practice another*. Those countries will have inevitably to expiate their guilt in long isolation, oppression, and anarchy. But you know the mission of our Country, and will pursue another path. Through you Italy will have, with one only God in the heavens, one only truth, one only faith, one only rule of political life upon earth. Upon the edifice, sublimer than Capitol or Vatican, which the people of Italy will raise, you will plant the banner of Liberty and of Association, so that it shines in the sight of all the nations, nor will you lower it ever for terror of despots or lust for the gains of a day. You will have boldness as you have faith. You will speak out aloud to the world, and to those who call themselves the lords of the world, the thought which thrills the heart of Italy. You will never deny the sister nations. The life of the Country shall grow through you in beauty and in strength, free from servile fears and the hesitations of doubt, keeping as its *foundation* the people, as its *rule* the consequences of its principles logically deduced and energetically applied, as its *strength* the strength of all, as its *outcome* the amelioration of all, as its *end* the fulfilment of the mission which God has given it. And because you will be ready to die for Humanity, the life of your Country will be immortal.

William Graham Sumner

For Charles Darwin, the biologist, the theory of evolution was never anything more than a scientific explanation of the origin of biological species. But for many of Darwin's admirers it became the basis for an entirely new way of looking at the universe and everything that has happened in it, particularly since the arrival of *Homo sapiens*. Seizing on the key ideas of the struggle for existence and the survival of the fittest, these writers (who are generally called social Darwinists) found in them concepts capable of explaining the data of morals, politics, economics, sociology, history, and philosophy, as well as those of biology. Although the details of the explanations varied from field to field, in their general outline they were much the same.

In economics—and it was here that social Darwinism had its strongest immediate impact—the theory usually ran along the following lines: Having been victorious in the struggle for existence against other species, humans are now engaged in the same struggle among themselves. The fruits of this struggle lie in social status, which is generally conceived in monetary terms. In other words, the fit become rich and the unfit poor; hence the standard by which the fitness of any individual must be judged is the size of his bank account. Finally, since economic success is the mark of fitness, and since, the argument ran, fitness can be equated with goodness, the rich are not only the highest products of the evolutionary process, but morally they are the best members of society as well. The opposite, of course, holds true for the poor.

Among the most prominent social Darwinists was the American scholar and teacher William Graham Sumner (1840–1910). After a brief career in the ministry, Sumner joined the faculty of Yale University, where he remained for the rest of his life, becoming a figure of the first rank in the intellectual history of our country and a world pioneer in the study of anthropology and sociology.

In the essay that follows Sumner ranges over most of the facets of culture, concentrating on economics and politics. He describes the chief enemy of civilized advance as "the sentimental philosophy," of which socialism offers the prime example.

Consider the following questions as you study the text below.

1. In what ways did Summer deviate from Darwin's theory of evolution? What criticisms might a biologist make of Summer's logic?

2. How would you explain the popularity of social Darwinism in the early twentieth century? To whom did such ideas appeal most? Why?

The Challenge of Facts

Socialism is no new thing. In one form or another it is to be found throughout all history. It arises from an observation of certain harsh facts in the lot of man on earth, the concrete expression of which is poverty and misery. These facts challenge us. It is folly to try to shut our eyes to them. We have first to notice what they are, and then to face them squarely.

Man is born under the necessity of sustaining the existence he has received by an onerous struggle against nature, both to win what is essential to his life and to ward off what is prejudicial to it. He is born under a burden and a necessity. Nature holds what is essential to him, but she offers nothing gratuitously. He may win for his use what she holds, if he can. Only the most meager and inadequate supply for human needs can be obtained directly from nature. There are trees which may be used for fuel and for dwellings, but labor is required to fit them for this use. There are ores in the ground, but labor is necessary to get out the metals and make tools or weapons. For any real satisfaction, labor is necessary to fit the products of nature for human use. In this struggle every individual is under the pressure of the necessities for food, clothing, shelter, fuel, and every individual brings with him more or less energy for the conflict necessary to supply his needs. The relation, therefore, between each man's needs and each man's energy, or "individualism," is the first fact of human life.

.   .   .

The next great fact we have to notice in regard to the struggle of human life is that labor which is spent in a direct struggle with nature is severe in the extreme and is but slightly productive. To subjugate nature, man needs weapons and tools. These, however, cannot be won unless the food and clothing and other prime and direct necessities are supplied in such amount that they can be consumed while tools and weapons are being made, for the tools and weapons themselves satisfy no needs directly. A man who tills the ground with his fingers or with a pointed stick picked up without labor will get a small crop. To fashion even the rudest spade or hoe will cost time, during which the laborer must still eat and drink and wear, but the tool, when obtained, will multiply immensely the power to produce. Such products of labor, used to assist production, have a function so peculiar in the nature of things that we need to distinguish them. We call them capital. A lever is capital, and the advantage of lifting a weight with a lever over lifting it by direct

William Graham Sumner, *The Challenge of Facts*. Published in 1914 but written several years earlier.

exertion is only a feeble illustration of the power of capital in production. The origin of capital lies in the darkness before history, and it is probably impossible for us to imagine the slow and painful steps by which the race began the formation of it. Since then it has gone on rising to higher and higher powers by a ceaseless involution, if I may use a mathematical expression. Capital is labor raised to a higher power by being constantly multiplied into itself. Nature has been more and more subjugated by the human race through the power of capital, and every human being now living shares the improved status of the race to a degree which neither he nor any one else can measure, and for which he pays nothing.

Let us understand this point, because our subject will require future reference to it. It is the most short-sighted ignorance not to see that, in a civilized community, all the advantage of capital except a small fraction is gratuitously enjoyed by the community. For instance, suppose the case of a man utterly destitute of tools, who is trying to till the ground with a pointed stick. He could get something out of it. If now he should obtain a spade with which to till the ground, let us suppose, for illustration, that he could get twenty times as great a produce. Could, then, the owner of a spade in a civilized state demand, as its price, from the man who had no spade, nineteen-twentieths of the produce which could be produced by the use of it? Certainly not. The price of a spade is fixed by the supply and demand of products in the community. A spade is bought for a dollar and the gain from the use of it is an inheritance of knowledge, experience, and skill which every man who lives in a civilized state gets for nothing. What we pay for steam transportation is no trifle, but imagine, if you can, eastern Massachusetts cut off from steam connection with the rest of the world, turnpikes and sailing vessels remaining. The cost of food would rise so high that a quarter of the population would starve to death and another quarter would have to emigrate. Today every man here gets an enormous advantage from the status of a society on a level of steam transportation, telegraph, and machinery, for which he pays nothing.

So far as I have yet spoken, we have before us the struggle of man with nature, but the social problems, strictly speaking, arise at the next step. Each man carries on the struggle to win his support for himself, but there are others by his side engaged in the same struggle. If the stores of nature were unlimited, or if the last unit of the supply she offers could be won as easily as the first, there would be no social problem. If a square mile of land could support an indefinite number of human beings, or if it cost only twice as much labor to get forty bushels of wheat from an acre as to get twenty, we should have no social problem. If a square mile of land could support millions, no one would ever emigrate and there would be no trade or commerce. If it cost only twice as much labor to get forty bushels as twenty, there would be no advance in the arts. The fact is far otherwise. So long as the population is low in proportion to the amount of land, on a given stage of the arts, life is easy and the competition of man with man is weak. When more persons are trying to live on a square mile than it can support, on the existing stage of the arts, life is hard and the competition of man with man is intense. In the former case, industry and prudence may be on a low grade; the penalties are not severe, or certain, or speedy. In the latter case, each individual needs to exert on his own behalf every force, original or acquired, which he can command. In the former case, the average condition will be one of comfort and the population will be all nearly on the average. In the latter case, the average condition will not be one of comfort, but the population will cover wide extremes of comfort and misery. Each will find his place according to his ability and his effort. The former society will be democratic; the latter will be aristocratic.

The constant tendency of population to outstrip the means of subsistence is the force which has distributed population over the world, and produced all advance in civilization. To this day the two means of escape for an overpopulated country are emigration and an advance in the arts. The former wins more land for the same people; the latter makes the same land support more persons. If, however, either of these means opens a chance for an increase of population, it is evident that the advantage so won may be speedily exhausted if the increase takes place. The social difficulty has only undergone a temporary amelioration, and when the conditions of pressure and competition are renewed, misery and poverty reappear. The victims of them are those who have inherited disease and depraved appetites, or have been brought up in vice and ignorance, or have themselves yielded to vice, extravagance, idleness, and imprudence. In the last analysis, therefore, we come back to vice, in its original and hereditary forms, as the correlative of misery and poverty.

The condition for the complete and regular action of the force of competition is liberty. Liberty means the security given to each man that, if he employs his energies to sustain the struggle on behalf of himself and those he cares for, he shall dispose of the produce exclusively as he chooses. It is impossible to know whence any definition or criterion of justice can be derived, if it is not deduced from this view of things; or if it is not the definition of justice that each shall enjoy the fruit of his own labor and self-denial, and of injustice that the idle and the industrious, the self-indulgent and the self-denying, shall share equally in the product. Aside from the *a priori* speculations of philosophers who have tried to make equality an essential element in justice, the human race has recognized, from the earliest times, the above conception of justice as the true one, and has founded upon it the right of property. The right of property, with marriage and the family, gives the right of bequest.

Monogamic marriage, however, is the most exclusive of social institutions. It contains, as essential principles, preference, superiority, selection, devotion. It would not be at all what it is if it were not for these characteristic traits, and it always degenerates when these traits are not present. For instance, if a man should not have a distinct preference for the woman he married, and if he did not select her as superior to others, the marriage would be an imperfect one according to the standard of true monogamic marriage. The family under monogamy, also, is a closed group, having special interests and estimating privacy and reserve as valuable advantages for family development. We grant high prerogatives, in our society, to parents, although our observation teaches us that thousands of human beings are unfit to be parents or to be entrusted with the care of children. It follows, therefore, from the organization of marriage and the family, under monogamy, that great inequalities must exist in a society based on those institutions. The son of wise parents cannot start on a level with the son of foolish ones, and the man who has had no home discipline cannot be equal to the man who has had home discipline. If the contrary were true, we could rid ourselves at once of the wearing labor of inculcating sound morals and manners in our children.

Private property, also, which we have seen to be a feature of society organized in accordance with the natural conditions of the struggle for existence produces inequalities between men. The struggle for existence is aimed against nature. It is from her niggardly hand that we have to wrest the satisfaction for our needs, but our fellow-men are our competitors for the meager supply. Competition, therefore, is a law of nature. Nature is entirely neutral; she submits to him who most energetically and resolutely assails her. She grants her rewards to the fittest, therefore, without regard to other considerations of any kind. If, then, there be liberty, men get from her just in proportion to their works, and their having and enjoying are just in proportion to their being and their doing. Such is the system of nature. If we do not like it, and if we try to amend it, there is only one way in which we can do it. We can take from the better and give to the worse. We can deflect the penalties of those who have done ill and throw them on those who have done better. We can take the rewards from those who have done better and give them to those who have done worse. We shall thus lessen the inequalities. We shall favor the survival of the unfittest, and we shall accomplish this by destroying liberty. Let it be understood that we cannot go outside of this alternative; liberty, inequality, survival of the fittest; not-liberty, equality, survival of the unfittest. The former carries society forward and favors all its best members; the latter carries society downwards and favors all its worst members.

For three hundred years now men have been trying to understand and realize liberty. Liberty is not the right or chance to do what we choose; there is no such liberty as that on earth. No man can do as he chooses: the autocrat of Russia or the King of Dahomey has limits to his arbitrary will; the savage in the wilderness, whom some people think free, is the slave of routine, tradition, and superstitious fears; the civilized man must earn his living, or take care of his property, or concede his own will to the rights and claims of his parents, his wife, his children, and all the persons with whom he is connected by the ties and contracts of civilized life.

What we mean by liberty is civil liberty, or liberty under law; and this means the guarantees of law that a man shall not be interfered with while using his own powers for his own welfare. It is, therefore, a civil and political status; and that nation has the freest institutions in which the guarantees of peace for the laborer and security for the capitalist are the highest. Liberty, therefore, does not by any means do away with the struggle for existence. We might as well try to do away with the need of eating, for that would, in effect, be the same thing. What civil liberty does is to turn the competition of man with man from violence and brute force into an industrial competition under which men vie with one another for the acquisition of material goods by industry, energy, skill, frugality, prudence, temperance, and other industrial virtues. Under this changed order of things the inequalities are not done away with. Nature still grants her rewards of having and enjoying, according to our being and doing, but it is now the man of the highest training and not the man of the heaviest fist who gains the highest reward. It is impossible that the man with capital and the man without capital should be equal. To affirm that they are equal would be to say that a man who has no tool can get as much food out of the ground as the man who has a spade or a plough; or that the man who has no weapon can defend himself as well against hostile beasts or hostile men as the man who has a weapon. If that were so, none of us would work any more. We work and deny ourselves to get capital just because, other things being equal, the man who has it is superior, for attaining all the ends of life, to the man who has it not. Considering the eagerness with which we all seek capital and the estimate we put upon it, either in cherishing it if we have it, or envying others who have it while we have it not, it is very strange what platitudes pass current about it in our society so soon as we begin to generalize about it. If our young people really believed some of the teachings they hear, it would not be amiss to preach them a sermon once in a while to reassure them, setting forth that it is not wicked to be rich, nay even, that it is not wicked to be richer than your neighbor.

It follows from what we have observed that it is the utmost folly to denounce capital. To do so is to undermine civilization, for capital is the first requisite of every social gain, educational, ecclesiastical, political, aesthetic, or other.

It must also be noticed that the popular antithesis between persons and capital is very fallacious. Every law or institution which protects persons at the expense of capital makes it easier for persons to live and to increase the number of consumers of capital while lowering all the motives to prudence and frugality by which capital is created. Hence every such law or institution tends to produce a large population, sunk in misery. All poor laws and all eleemosynary institutions and expenditures have this tendency. On the contrary, all laws and institutions which give security to capital against the interests of other persons than its owners, restrict numbers while preserving the means of subsistence. Hence every such law or institution tends to produce a small society on a high stage of comfort and well-being. It follows that the antithesis commonly thought to exist between the protection of persons and the protection of property is in reality only an antithesis between numbers and quality.

.   .   .

We have now before us the facts of human life out of which the social problem springs. These facts are in many respects hard and stern. It is by strenuous exertion only that each one of us can sustain himself against the destructive forces and the ever recurring needs of life; and the higher the degree to which we seek to carry our development the greater is the proportionate cost of every step. For help in the struggle we can only look back to those in the previous generation who are responsible for our existence. In the competition of life the son of wise and prudent ancestors has immense advantages over the son of vicious and imprudent ones. The man who has capital possesses immeasurable advantages for the struggle of life over him who has none. The more we break down privileges of class, or industry, and establish liberty, the greater will be the inequalities and the more exclusively will the vicious bear the penalties. Poverty and misery will exist in society just so long as vice exists in human nature.

I now go on to notice some modes of trying to deal with this problem. There is a modern philosophy which has never been taught systematically, but which has won the faith of vast masses of people in the modern civilized world. For want of a better name it may be called the sentimental philosophy. It has colored all modern ideas and institutions in politics, religion, education, charity, and industry, and is widely taught in popular literature, novels, and poetry, and in the pulpit. The first proposition of this sentimental philosophy is that nothing is true which is disagreeable. If, therefore, any facts of observation show that life is grim or hard, the sentimental philosophy steps over such facts with a genial platitude, a consoling commonplace, or a gratifying dogma. The effect is to spread an easy optimism, under the influence of which people spare themselves labor and trouble, reflection and forethought, pains and caution—all of which are hard things, and to admit the necessity for which would be to admit that the world is not all made smooth and easy, for us to pass through it surrounded by love, music, and flowers.

Under this philosophy, "progress" has been represented as a steadily increasing and unmixed good; as if the good steadily encroached on the evil without involving any new and other forms of evil; and as if we could plan great steps in progress in our academies and lyceums, and then realize them by resolution. To minds trained to this way of looking at things, any evil which exists is a reproach. We have only to consider it, hold some discussions about it, pass resolutions, and have done with it. Every moment of delay is, therefore, a social crime. It is monstrous to say that misery and poverty are as constant as vice and evil passions of men! People suffer so under misery and poverty! Assuming, therefore, that we can solve all these problems and eradicate all these evils by expending our ingenuity upon them, of course we cannot hasten too soon to do it.

A social philosophy, consonant with this, has also been taught for a century. It could not fail to be popular, for it teaches that ignorance is as good as knowledge, vulgarity as good as refinement, shiftlessness as good as painstaking, shirking as good as faithful striving, poverty as good as wealth, filth as good as cleanliness—in short, that quality goes for nothing in the measurement of men, but only numbers. Culture, knowledge, refinement, skill, and taste cost labor, but we have been taught that they have only individual, not social value, and that socially they are rather drawbacks than otherwise. In public life we are taught to admire roughness, illiteracy, and rowdyism. The ignorant, idle, and shiftless have been taught that they are "the people," that the generalities inculcated at the same time about the dignity, wisdom, and virtue of "the people" are true of them, that they have nothing to learn to be wise, but that, as they stand, they possess a kind of infallibility, and that to their "opinion" the wise must bow. It is not cause for wonder if whole sections of these classes have begun to use the powers and wisdom attributed to them for their interests, as they construe them, and to trample on all the excellence which marks civilization as an obsolete superstition.

Another development of the same philosophy is the doctrine that men come into the world endowed with "natural rights," or as joint inheritors of the "rights of man," which have been "declared" times without number during the last century. The divine rights of man have succeeded to the obsolete divine right of kings. If it is true, then, that a man is born with rights, he comes into the world with claims on somebody besides his parents. Against whom does he hold such rights? There can be no rights against nature or against God. A man may curse his fate because he is born of an inferior race, or with an hereditary disease, or blind, or, as some members of the race seem to do, because they are born females; but they get no answer to their imprecations. But, now, if men have rights by birth, these rights must hold against their fellow-men and must mean that somebody else is to spend his energy to sustain the existence of the persons so born. What then becomes of the natural rights of the one whose energies are to be diverted from his own interests? If it be said that we should all help each other, that means simply that the race as a whole should advance and expand as much and as fast as it can in its career on earth; and the experience on which we are now acting has shown that we shall do this best under liberty and under the organization which we are now developing, by leaving each to exert his energies for his own success. The notion of natural rights is destitute of sense, but it is captivating, and it is the more available on account of its vagueness. It lends itself to the most vicious kind of social dogmatism, for if a man has natural rights, then the reasoning is clear up to the finished socialistic doctrine that a man has a natural right to whatever he needs, and that the measure of his claims is the wishes which he wants fulfilled. If, then, he has need, who is bound to satisfy it for him? Who holds the obligation corresponding to his right? It must be the one who possesses what will satisfy that need, or else the state which can take the possession from those who have earned and saved it, and give it to him who needs it and who, by the hypothesis, has not earned and saved it.

It is with the next step, however, that we come to the complete and ruinous absurdity of this view. If a man may demand from those who have a share of what he needs and has not, may he demand the same also for his wife and for his children, and for how many children? The industrious and prudent man who takes the course of labor and self-denial to secure capital, finds that he must defer marriage, both in order to save and to devote his life to the education of fewer children. The man who can claim a share in another's product has no such restraint. The consequence would be that the industrious and prudent would labor and save, without families, to support the idle and improvident who would increase and multiply, until universal destitution forced a return to the principles of liberty and property; and the man who started with the notion that the world owed him a living would once more find, as he does now, that the world pays him its debt in the state prison.

The most specious application of the dogma of rights is to labor. It is said that every man has a right to work. The world is full of work to be done. Those who are willing to work find that they have three days' work to do in every day that comes. Work is the necessity to which we are born. It is not a right, but an irksome necessity, and men escape it whenever they can get the fruits of labor without it. What they want is the fruits, or wages, not work. But wages are capital which some one has earned and saved. If he and the workman can agree on the terms on which he will part with his capital, there is no more to be said. If not, then the right must be set up in a new form. It is now not a right to work, nor even a right to wages, but a right to a certain rate of wages, and we have simply returned to the old doctrine of spoliation again. It is immaterial whether the demand for wages be addressed to an individual capitalist or to a civil body, for the latter can give no wages which it does not collect by taxes out of the capital of those who have labored and saved.

Another application is in the attempt to fix the hours of labor *per diem* by law. If a man is forbidden to labor over eight hours per day (and the law has no sense or utility for the purposes of those who want it until it takes this form), he is forbidden to exercise so much industry as he may be willing to expend in order to accumulate capital for the improvement of his circumstances.

A century ago there were very few wealthy men except owners of land. The extension of commerce, manufactures, and mining, the introduction of the factory system and machinery, the opening of new countries, and the great discoveries and inventions have created a new middle class, based on wealth, and developed out of the peasants, artisans, unskilled laborers, and small shopkeepers of a century ago. The consequence has been that the chance of acquiring capital and all which depends on capital has opened before classes which formerly passed their lives in a dull round of ignorance and drudgery. This chance has brought with it the same alternative which accompanies every other opportunity offered to mortals. Those who were wise and able to profit by the chance succeeded grandly; those who were negligent or unable to profit by it suffered proportionately. The result has been wide inequalities of wealth within the industrial classes. The net result, however, for all, has been the cheapening of luxuries and a vast extension of physical enjoyment. The appetite for enjoyment has been awakened and nourished in classes which formerly never missed what they never thought of, and it has produced eagerness for material good, discontent, and impatient ambition. This is the reverse side of that eager uprising of the industrial classes which is such a great force in modern life. The chance is opened to advance, by industry, prudence, economy, and emigration, to the possession of capital; but the way is long and tedious. The impatience for enjoyment and the thirst for luxury which we have mentioned are the greatest foes to the accumulation of capital; and there is a still darker side of the picture when we come to notice that those who yield to the impatience to enjoy, but who see others outstrip them, are led to malice and envy. Mobs arise which manifest the most savage and senseless disposition to burn and destroy what they cannot enjoy. We have already had evidence, in more than one country, that such a wild disposition exists and needs only opportunity to burst into activity.

The origin of socialism, which is the extreme development of the sentimental philosophy, lies in the undisputed facts which I described at the outset. The socialist regards this misery as the fault of society. He thinks that we can organize society as we like and that an organization can be devised in which poverty and misery shall disappear. He goes further even than this. He assumes that men have artificially organized society as it now exists. Hence if anything is disagreeable or hard in the present state of society, it follows, on that view, that the task of organizing society has been imperfectly and badly performed, and that it needs to be done over again. These are the assumptions with which the socialist starts, and many socialists seem also to believe that if they can destroy belief in an Almighty God who is supposed to have made the world such as it is, they will then have overthrown the belief that there is a fixed order in human nature and human life which man can scarcely alter at all, and, if at all, only infinitesimally.

The truth is that the social order is fixed by laws of nature precisely analogous to those of the physical order. The most that man can do is by ignorance and self-conceit to mar the operation of social laws. The evils of society are to a great extent the result of the dogmatism and self-interest of statesmen, philosophers, and ecclesiastics who in past time have done just what the socialists now want to do. Instead of studying the natural laws of the social order, they assumed that they could organize society as they chose, they made up their minds what kind of a society they wanted to make, and they planned their little measures for the ends they had resolved upon. It will take centuries of scientific study of the facts of nature to eliminate from human society the mischievous institutions and traditions which the said statesmen, philosophers, and ecclesiastics have introduced into it. Let us not, however, even then delude ourselves with any impossible hopes. The hardships of life would not be eliminated if the laws of nature acted directly and without interference. The task of right living forever changes its form, but let us not imagine that the task will ever reach a final solution or that any race of men on this earth can ever be emancipated from the necessity of industry, prudence, continence, and temperance if they are to pass their lives prosperously. If you believe the contrary you must suppose that some men can come to exist who shall know nothing of old age, disease, and death.

.   .   .

Socialists find it necessary to alter the definition of capital in order to maintain their attacks upon it. Karl Marx, for instance, regards capital as an accumulation of the differences which a merchant makes between his buying price and his selling price. It is, according to him, an accumulation of the differences which the employer gains between what he pays to the employees for making the thing and what he obtains for it from the consumer. In this view of the matter the capitalist employer is a pure parasite, who has fastened on the wage-receiving employee without need or reason and is levying toll on industry. All socialistic writers follow, in different degrees, this conception of capital. If it is true, why do not I levy on some workers somewhere and steal this difference in the product of their labor? Is it because I am more honest or magnanimous than those who are capitalist-employers? I should not trust myself to resist the chance if I had it. Or again, let us ask why, if this conception of the origin of capital is correct, the workmen submit to a pure and unnecessary imposition. If this notion were true, co-operation in production would not need any effort to bring it about; it would take an army to keep it down. The reason why it is not possible for the first comer to start out as an employer of labor is that capital is a prerequisite to all industry. So soon as men pass beyond the stage of life in which they live, like beasts, on the spontaneous fruits of the earth, capital must precede every productive enterprise. It would lead me too far away from my present subject to elaborate this statement as it deserves and perhaps as it needs, but I may say that there is no sound political economy and especially no correct conception of wages which is not based on a complete recognition of the character of capital as necessarily going before every industrial operation. The reason why co-operation in production is exceedingly difficult, and indeed is not possible except in the highest and rarest conditions of education and culture amongst artisans, is that workmen cannot undertake an enterprise without capital, and that capital always means the fruits of prudence and self-denial already accomplished. The capitalist's profits, therefore, are only the reward for the contribution he has made to a joint enterprise which could not go on without him, and his share is as legitimate as that of the handworker.

The socialist assails particularly the institution of bequest or hereditary property, by which some men come into life with special protection and advantage. The right of bequest rests on no other grounds than those of expediency. The love of children is the strongest motive to frugality and to the accumulation of capital. The state guarantees the power of bequest only because it thereby encourages the accumulation of capital on which the welfare of society depends. It is true enough that inherited capital often proves a curse. Wealth is like health, physical strength, education, or anything else which enhances the power of the individual; it is only a chance; its moral character depends entirely upon the use which is made of it. Any force which, when well used, is capable of elevating a man, will, if abused, debase him in the same proportion. This is true of education, which is often and incorrectly vaunted as a positive and purely beneficent instrumentality. An education ill used makes a man only a more mischievous scoundrel, just as an education well used makes him a more efficient, good citizen and producer. So it is with wealth; it is a means to all the higher developments of intellectual and moral culture. A man of inherited wealth can gain in youth all the advantages which are essential to high culture, and which a man who must first earn the capital cannot attain until he is almost past the time of life for profiting by them. If one should believe the newspapers, one would be driven to a philosophy something like this: it is extremely praiseworthy for a man born in poverty to accumulate a fortune; the reason why he wants to secure a fortune is that he wants to secure the position of his children and start them with better advantages than he enjoyed himself; this is a noble desire on his part, but he really ought to doubt and hesitate about so doing because the chances are that he would do far better for his children to leave them poor. The children who inherit his wealth are put under suspicion by it; it creates a presumption against them in all the activities of citizenship.

Now it is no doubt true that the struggle to win a fortune gives strength of character and a practical judgment and efficiency which a man who inherits wealth rarely gets, but hereditary wealth transmitted from generation to generation is the strongest instrument by which we keep up a steadily advancing civilization. In the absence of laws of entail and perpetuity it is inevitable that capital should speedily slip from the hold of the man who is not fit to possess it, back into the great stream of capital, and so find its way into the hands of those who can use it for the benefit of society.

The love of children is an instinct which, as I have said before, grows stronger with advancing civilization. All attacks on capital have, up to this time, been shipwrecked on this instinct. Consequently the most rigorous and logical socialists have always been led sooner or later to attack the family. For, if bequest should be abolished, parents would give their property to their children in their own life-time; and so it becomes a logical necessity to substitute some sort of communistic or socialistic life for family life, and to educate children in masses without the tie of parentage. Every socialistic theory which has been pursued energetically has led out to this consequence. I will not follow up this topic, but it is plain to see that the only equality which could be reached on this course would be that men should be all equal to each other when they were all equal to swine.

Socialists are filled with the enthusiasm of equality. Every scheme of theirs for securing equality has destroyed liberty. The student of political philosophy has the antagonism of equality and liberty constantly forced upon him. Equality of possession or of rights and equality before the law are diametrically opposed to each other. The object of equality before the law is to make the state entirely neutral. The state, under that theory, takes no cognizance of persons. It surrounds all, without distinctions, with the same conditions and guarantees. If it educates one, it educates all—black, white, red, or yellow; Jew or Gentile; native or alien. If it taxes one, it taxes all, by the same system and under the same conditions. If it exempts one from police regulations in home, church, and occupation, it exempts all. From this statement it is at once evident that pure equality before the law is impossible. Some occupations must be subjected to police regulation. Not all can be made subject to militia duty even for the same limited period. The exceptions and special cases furnish the chance for abuse. Equality before the law, however, is one of the cardinal principles of civil liberty, because it leaves each man to run the race of life for himself as best he can. The state stands neutral but benevolent. It does not undertake to aid some and handicap others at the outset in order to offset hereditary advantages and disadvantages, or to make them start equally. Such a notion would belong to the false and spurious theory of equality which is socialistic. If the state should attempt this it would make itself the servant of envy. I am entitled to make the most I can of myself without hindrance from anybody, but I am not entitled to any guarantee that I shall make as much of myself as somebody else makes of himself.

. . .

The newest socialism is, in its method, political. The essential feature of its latest phases is the attempt to use the power of the state to realize its plans and to secure its objects. These objects are to do away with poverty and misery, and there are no socialistic schemes yet proposed, of any sort, which do not, upon analysis, turn out to be projects for curing poverty and misery by making those who have share with those who have not. Whether they are

paper-money schemes, tariff schemes, subsidy schemes, internal improvement schemes, or usury laws, they all have this in common with the most
vulgar of the communistic projects, and the errors of this sort in the past
which have been committed in the interest of the capitalist class now furnish
precedents, illustration, and encouragement for the new category of demands. The latest socialism divides into two phases: one which aims at centralization and despotism—believing that political form more available for
its purposes; the other, the anarchical, which prefers to split up the state into
townships, or "communes," to the same end. The latter furnishes the true etymology and meaning of "communism" in its present use, but all socialism,
in its second stage, merges into a division of property according to the old
sense of communism.

It is impossible to notice socialism as it presents itself at the present moment without pointing out the immense mischief which has been done by
sentimental economists and social philosophers who have thought it their
professional duty, not to investigate and teach the truth, but to dabble in
philanthropy. It is in Germany that this development has been most marked,
and as a consequence of it the judgment and sense of the whole people in regard to political and social questions have been corrupted. It is remarkable
that the country whose learned men have wrought so much for every other
science, especially by virtue of their scientific method and rigorous critical
processes, should have furnished a body of social philosophers without
method, discipline, or severity of scholarship, who have led the nation in
pursuit of whims and dreams and impossible desires. Amongst us there has
been less of it, for our people still possess enough sterling sense to reject sentimental rubbish in its grosser forms, but we have had and still have abundance of the more subtle forms of socialistic doctrine, and these open the
way to the others. We may already see the two developments forming a congenial alliance. We have also our writers and teachers who seem to think that
"the weak" and "the poor" are terms of exact definition; that government exists, in some especial sense, for the sake of the classes so designated; and that
the same classes (whoever they are) have some especial claim on the interest
and attention of the economist and social philosopher. It may be believed
that, in the opinion of these persons, the training of men is the only branch of
human effort in which the labor and care should be spent, not on the best
specimens but on the poorest.

It is a matter of course that a reactionary party should arise to declare
that universal suffrage, popular education, machinery, free trade, and all the
other innovations of the last hundred years are all a mistake. If any one ever
believed that these innovations were so many clear strides towards the mil-
lennium, that they involve no evils or abuses of their own, that they tend to
emancipate mankind from the need for prudence, caution, forethought,
vigilance—in short, from the eternal struggle against evil—it is not strange
that he should be disappointed. If any one ever believed that some "form of

government" could be found which would run itself and turn out the pure results of abstract peace, justice, and righteousness without any trouble to anybody, he may well be dissatisfied. To talk of turning back, however, is only to enhance still further the confusion and danger of our position. The world cannot go back. Its destiny is to go forward and to meet the new problems which are continually arising. Under our so-called progress evil only alters its forms, and we must esteem it a grand advance if we can believe that, on the whole, and over a wide view of human affairs, good has gained a hair's breadth over evil in a century. Popular institutions have their own abuses and dangers just as much as monarchical or aristocratic institutions. We are only just finding out what they are. All the institutions which we have inherited were invented to guard liberty against the encroachments of a powerful monarch or aristocracy, when these classes possessed land and the possession of land was the greatest social power. Institutions must now be devised to guard civil liberty against popular majorities, and this necessity arises first in regard to the protection of property, the first and greatest function of government and element in civil liberty. There is no escape from any dangers involved in this or any other social struggle save in going forward and working out the development. It will cost a struggle and will demand the highest wisdom of this and the next generation. It is very probable that some nations—those, namely, which come up to this problem with the least preparation, with the least intelligent comprehension of the problem, and under the most inefficient leadership—will suffer a severe check in their development and prosperity; it is very probable that in some nations the development may lead through revolution and bloodshed; it is very probable that in some nations the consequence may be a reaction towards arbitrary power. In every view we take of it, it is clear that the general abolition of slavery has only cleared the way for a new social problem of far wider scope and far greater difficulty. It seems to me, in fact, that this must always be the case. The conquest of one difficulty will only open the way to another; the solution of one problem will only bring man face to face with another. Man wins by the fight, not by the victory, and therefore the possibilities of growth are unlimited, for the fight has no end.

The progress which men have made in developing the possibilities of human existence has never been made by jumps and strides. It has never resulted from the schemes of philosophers and reformers. It has never been guided through a set program by the wisdom of any sages, statesmen, or philanthropists. The progress which has been made has been won in minute stages by men who had a definite task before them, and who have dealt with it in detail, as it presented itself, without referring to general principles, or attempting to bring it into logical relations to an *a priori* system. In most cases the agents are unknown and cannot be found. New and better arrangements have grown up imperceptibly by the natural effort of all to make the best of actual circumstances. In this way, no doubt, the new problems arising in our modern society must be solved or must solve themselves. The chief safe-guard and hope of such a development is in the sound instincts and strong sense of the people, which, although it may not reason closely, can reject in-stinctively. If there are laws—and there certainly are such—which permit the acquisition of property without industry, by cunning, force, gambling, swin-dling, favoritism, or corruption, such laws transfer property from those who have earned it to those who have not. Such laws contain the radical vice of socialism. They demand correction and offer an open field for reform be-cause reform would lie in the direction of greater purity and security of the right of property. Whatever assails that right, or goes in the direction of mak-ing it still more uncertain whether the industrious man can dispose of the fruits of his industry for his own interests exclusively, tends directly towards violence, bloodshed, poverty, and misery. If any large section of modern society should rise against the rest for the purpose of attempting any such spoliation, either by violence or through the forms of law, it would destroy civilization as it was destroyed by the irruption of the barbarians into the Roman Empire.

The sound student of sociology can hold out to mankind, as individu-als or as a race, only one hope of better and happier living. That hope lies in an enhancement of the industrial virtues and of the moral forces which thence arise. Industry, self-denial, and temperance are the laws of prosperity for men and states; without them advance in the arts and in wealth means only corruption and decay through luxury and vice. With them progress in the arts and increasing wealth are the prime conditions of an advancing civ-ilization which is sound enough to endure. The power of the human race today over the conditions of prosperous and happy living are sufficient to banish poverty and misery if it were not for folly and vice. The earth does not begin to be populated up to its power to support population on the pres-ent stage of the arts; if the United States were as densely populated as the British Islands, we should have one billion people here. If, therefore, men were willing to set to work with energy and courage to subdue the outlying parts of the earth, all might live in plenty and prosperity. But if they insist on remaining in the slums of great cities or on the borders of an old society, and on a comparatively exhausted soil, there is no device of economist or states-man which can prevent them from falling victims to poverty and misery or from succumbing in the competition of life to those who have greater com-mand of capital. The socialist or philanthropist who nourishes them in their situation and saves them from the distress of it is only cultivating the distress which he pretends to cure.

Catherine Booth

Catherine Booth's (1829–1900) religious devotion was established early on in her life. At age twelve she had already read the Bible eight times. In 1855, she married the Methodist minister William Booth. The two committed themselves to an activist vision of Christianity. In their view, ministers should busy themselves "loosing the chains of injustice, freeing the captive and oppressed, sharing food and home, clothing the naked, and carrying out family responsibilities." In 1864, the couple founded the Christian Mission, an initiative that would develop into the Salvation Army. Catherine Booth died of cancer in 1890, but the organization she helped found and the campaigns for social justice she initiated were carried on by her husband, children, and supporters.

Both Catherine Booth and Henry Mayhew (see selection from *London Labour and the London Poor* in this volume) saw themselves as fighting a war against poverty and injustice. Their approaches, however, could not have been more different. Where Mayhew focused on the accumulation of data and the identification of the social-structural causes of poverty, Booth saw religious awakening as the key to social progress. The selection included here is from a series of public lectures Booth delivered in the 1880s. In them, she attacked "popular Christianity," by which she meant an easy, passive kind of religion in which religious belief was not allowed to interfere with the individual's material comfort or to trouble their conscience. In Booth's opinion, most Britons of her day practiced this sort of Christianity. As you read the passage, pay careful attention to the targets of Booth's attack. According to Booth, who should take primary responsibility for education?

Consider the following questions as you study the text below.

1. In Booth's view, what is the purpose of education? Why did she think that public education failed to fulfill this purpose?

2. Why do you think Booth titled this piece "God of Education"? What harm did she see in education that emphasized intellectual development? What connections did she draw between nineteenth-century education and nineteenth-century science?

God of Education

Everything must bow to the scholastic education of the children. Their very health is sacrificed in hundreds of instances; the whole of the domestic arrangements, the convenience of father and mother and visitors must bow down to this god. The children must be educated, whatever else becomes of them. I touched very briefly on this subject in my address at Exeter Hall on "Family Religion," and some friends seemed to infer that I was against education, whereas I have seldom talked with any one on the subject more profoundly impressed with its importance! I adopted, many years ago, the sentiment of the philosopher Locke, who said that "in nine cases out of ten all the men we meet are what they are for good or for evil, for usefulness or otherwise, by their education." I say I fully believe that, and have acted upon it in training my own family; so you see my quarrel is not with education, but with a certain *kind* of education.

I believe that a child ought to be educated every half-hour of its life— never ought to be left to itself in the sense of not having a recognized influence exerted over its mind. The question is then, What *kind* of education is the right kind to bestow upon children? How ought you to educate them? The same idea which helped us on the question of fashion may help us again here. What should be the great purpose of education? Surely right education must be that which is calculated to help the child to attain the *highest type of its kind*, and to fit it for its highest destiny, You train your horse on that principle. You develop and stengthen it that it may be a perfect creature, having capacity developed for the highest service of which its nature is capable. I say that all right training ought to contemplate this end, and especially with respect to man, God's highest creature. Next comes the question, What *is* the highest type of a man? and the highest destiny of a man? What ought we to aim at? For if the aim is wrong, all our training will be wrong. I say that the highest type of a man is that in which the *soul* rules over the body, in which a purified, ennobled soul rules through an enlightened intelligence, and makes every faculty of the being subservient to the highest purpose, the service of humanity and the service of God! If I understand it, that is the highest type of man and his highest destiny. And it seems to me that all education that falls short of this is a curse rather than a blessing,

The aim of all rightly directed education is to make such men and women, and to fit them for such work, and if it fails of this, I say it is one-sided, unphilosophical, and irreligious, and THAT IS MY QUARREL WITH MODERN EDUCATION. I charge it with being all this, and that is the reason I did not

Catherine Mumford Booth, "Notes of Three Addresses on Household Gods," in *Popular Christianity* (Boston: McDonald, Gill and Co., 1888), pp. 181–90.

educate my children after its theories; I did not believe in them, and the results so far prove dint I was right.

Then first let me look at what ought to be the purpose of education. Most of you, nearly all, I presume, agree as to what I have stated. But the purpose of modern education is anything but this. It is for the most part planned and executed with a view to the aggrandizement or well-being of the individual, looked at in a worldly point of view. Parents look at their boy and say, "Now, what can we do with him?" They have all sorts of aspirations and ambitions for the boy, and they say, "Well, we must educate him, develop his intellect." What for? That he may use it for the service of humanity and the glory of God? Oh no, that never enters their minds. They say, "We will have him educated in order that he may shine in the world. We will have a son who will be able to go to the bar, the senate house, or do anything else that ambition fixes on." The AGGRANDIZEMENT OF THE INDIVIDUAL is the end, not the universal good, and out of this wrong aim arises the undue estimate of mere scholastic education. What would you say of the training of an animal, if it were possible for the trainer to select one or two faculties, and develop and strengthen them to the exclusion, neglect, or extinction of other faculties? Would you say that was right training?

The main idea of modern education is that of the imparting of knowledge. Knowledge is the idol which both the household and the nation to-day are worshipping more largely perhaps than any other, as if progress in knowledge constituted the true progress of man. Oh, if it were so, what a different world we should have to-day; but we know it is quite the contrary. We know that the more knowledge you give to an individual, without giving him a corresponding disposition to use it for good, the more you increase his capacity for mischief. Very often the most learned men live for the worst purposes! But, alas,! the very flower of the youth of our nation is sacrificed to this modern deity. The notion is that our youth must be educated in this mischievous sense; they must be crammed with knowledge; whether it be a curse or a blessing to them, is not the question, *but they must have it*. They must learn the dead languages, and read bad literature, in order to make them like the rest of the world around them, no matter what becomes of their morals; they must be crammed with science,—much of it falsely so called; much of it in embryo, crude and shallow—the shallow theories of minds trying to grasp profound thoughts, and getting lost in the fogs of their own folly, landing the poor pupils on the strand of infidelity and atheism. The intellect, the one faculty of the man, must be strained, and stretched, and crammed, to the utter neglect, and often destruction, of the moral faculties. And when you have done, what have you produced? An enlightened animal, an intellectual monster, who walks abroad, treading under his feet all the tender instincts and most sacred feelings and aspirations of humanity. That is all you have produced; there are thousands such to be seen to-day. Alas! my heart bleeds over the stories I hear all over the land, which I could give you as illustrations of this fact. All this mischief comes of upsetting God's order—cultivating the intellect at the expense of the heart; being at more pains to make our youth clever than to make them GOOD!

This false theory leads to false methods, and hence the deplorable condition of our nation to-day. It leads to the separating from home life our little boys of ten and twelve years of age, and our girls too, alas! sending them away from the tender influences, and what ought to be the grand and noble inspirations of their mothers, to herd with boys of their own age and class, to have their moral nature manipulated by masters, often skeptical or immoral.

Now I say, and will maintain, that the chief end of education is not mere teaching, but INSPIRATION; and if you fail to inspire your pupil with nobleness, disinterested goodness, truth, morality, and religion, not only are all the glorious ends of education lost, but you damn your pupil more deeply than he might have been damned without your education. I ask, Is it not so? Take some of your own sons (alas! I could point to numbers round about) as illustrations of this fact. God has given every child a tutor in his mother, and she is the best and only right tutor for the heart.

I defy you to fill a proper mother's place for influence over the heart. If God were to depute the angel Gabriel, he could not do it. God has tied the child to its mother by such peculiar moral and mental links that no other being could possibly possess. I tell you, mothers here, that if you are good mothers, you are committing the greatest wrong to send away your child from your homes, and I believe this wretched practice is ruining half our nation to-day. God committed the child to its parents to be educated, not to the schoolmaster. You can employ the schoolmaster to teach his head,—and even then you must be very careful of what sort he is, or he will ruin the child; but God committed the child to the parents to be educated, trained— that is taught how to *feel*, *think*, and *act*. And it is to the mother especially belongs the art and the capacity to inspire her boy to love all that is noble and good, and disinterested, and grand in humanity, and to keep on inspiring him until he is strong enough in moral excellence; in other words, strong enough in God's likeness and grace to walk alone. Just as you tend him when he is a baby, and will not leave him to strangers, so, while he is a moral infant, you are to watch and keep and train him until he is able to walk alone. I set my soul on this with regard to my own children, and God has enabled me to do it. I had a great fight over it in many ways, but I said, "I am *determined* to keep my children for God and goodness. They shall have the education that I think likely to help them to be useful to their generation, as far as possible; but I will never sacrifice purity to polish, I will never sacrifice the heart to the head." That was my resolve, and I see no cause to regret it.

I think it was Fenelon who said that "the service of my family is more important than the service of myself, and the service of my nation is more important than the service of my family, and the service of humanity is more important than the service of my nation." That is my opinion. This is God's idea of man's highest vocation: "The Son of Man is come to seek and to save that which was lost." If God's type of manhood had been a being crammed with knowledge to the exclusion of the moral and religious sentiments, Jesus Christ would have been such a man, whereas He was the opposite. He combined all the tenderness, sublime devotion, and self-sacrifice of the woman with the intellect and strength of the man. He was God's model man. That is the type for us. Therefore, for the sake of your children and your own grey hairs, I beseech you to see to it that you train and educate them in His likeness. Alas! I know many parents in this land to-day, who are wringing their hands in anguish for the consequences of a false notion of education; and yet there are tens of thousands more who are making the same experiment, to have the same results.

I was staying in a mansion some time ago, where there was everything that wealth and refinement could procure to make the parents happy. But I thought as I looked at the dear old gentleman—one of the kindly type of man, at whose table you like to sit down because of the genial intercourse and the generous sympathies of his soul towards all humanity—but I thought there seemed to be a gloom over the household. I felt as if he had a sorrowful spirit, though I knew not why. After dinner, when we got into the library, he said, with trembling lips:—

"I wish you could get a word with E——."

I said, "Who is that?"

"My eldest son; do try to get a minute to speak with him."

"Why, what is the matter?" I said.

"I am afraid he has embraced skeptical opinions. I sent him to a professedly Christian school (ah, I thought, the old story!) and then to college, and now I am afraid he is nearly an infidel."

And when I got hold of the young gentleman, I saw that he was just of the type our modern schools produce—self-conceited, self-indulged, proud, vain; a young man who looked down on his father much as an antiquated picture or piece of furniture. Oh, these stories, they break my heart! I felt that this dear old man spent his money on the education of his son, and thought he was doing the best he could for him, to send him to a so-called Christian school and then to a so-called Christian college, and here is the result; and there are thousands of such results!

Yet people send their sons over and over again to these schools and colleges, commit them knowingly to skeptical and infidel teachers—give them over, body, mind, and soul, to them, to go through a process of education which necessitates the putting into their hands of text books containing all manner of idolatrous legends and impure and immoral histories, bringing into their imaginations all manner of profanities and impurities just at the most critical period of their history. And this is all done under the name of "CHRISTIAN EDUCATION."

I could tell you stories that would make you weep almost tears of blood at the consequences of these associations. Don't I know mothers to-day who are wringing their hands in agony, and fathers who are bowed down almost to the grave, broken-hearted, because of them? Add to this education association with troops of godless, lawless, and frequently immoral youths, whom they are sure to have for their companions, and then wonder that youths isolated from their mothers, sisters, and all the refining influences of home life— put into these schools and colleges, and kept there frequently for seven or eight years, and I ask, Can parents be surprised that they receive them back without any principles, without any love for their parents, without any religion, and without any respect for humanity? to walk about and trample under foot the most sacred instincts, and feelings, and aspirations of true manhood and womanhood, and to march over the nation to spread desolation and ruin wherever they go—moral waifs and strays—drifting down the current of humanity, down, down to everlasting shame?

This is the result of modern education falsely so called. I challenge anybody to disprove it. Now then, I say, let every Christian parent in his closet settle before God this matter. What will you make your child? Will you say, "I will be more concerned that he shall be a good, benevolent, holy man, working for the good of his race, than that he shall be one of those intellectual monsters, all head and no heart. I will rather that he should be poor and good than that he should be rich and wicked"? When you come to that you will save your children. But you say, "Well, I must have this position and that position for him, not because of the use he will be to humanity and the glory he will bring to God, but because he will be a bigger man, having social position and influence." Ah! thousands have said that, and their sons have ended in being nobodys—idle, extravagant, spendthrifts, taking all the patrimony of their brothers and sisters to keep them going in their evil courses. Truly "God is not mocked: whatsoever a man soweth, that shall he also reap."

Friedrich Nietzsche

Like Karl Marx, Nietzsche (1844–1900) rejected both the ideals and practices of nineteenth-century European culture. But unlike Marx, he did not do so in order to pave the way for a new classless society; quite the contrary. He claimed that the human race was divided into two basic types, which he called "masters" and "the herd" or "slaves." Unfortunately, he believed, modern society has been dominated by a morality developed by the slaves and exemplified most clearly in democracy and Christianity. His goal was to reverse this historical trend by returning the masters to their rightful eminence. Nietzsche envisioned a new society in which a small aristocratic elite would enjoy an elevated lifestyle provided for by the labors of the rest of humanity, which would be reduced to a machine existence.

The following selection is from Nietzsche's unfinished work *The Will to Power*. The order of sections has been altered slightly.

Consider the following questions as you study the text below.

1. Why was Nietzsche so critical of the late-nineteenth-century social order? What changes would he have made if he could?

2. What role did evolution play in Nietzsche's thought? What qualities did his Overman possess and how were they acquired?

The Will to Power

854. In the era of "universal suffrage," meaning that everyone is able to sit in judgment upon everyone and everything, I am constrained to reestablish the *order of rank*.

855. Power-quanta and nothing but power-quanta determine and distinguish rank.

. . .

866. It is imperative to set forth a counterdirection to the ever-increasing economic exploitation of man and mankind, to the ever more tightly interlocked "machinery" of interests and output. I designate this

Friedrich Nietzsche, *Der Wille zur Macht*, trans. Peter Fuss.

counterdirection *the extraction of man's luxury-surplus*: through it shall be brought to light a stronger kind, a higher type, whose conditions of origin and maintenance shall be other than those of the average man. My concept, my *image* for this type is, as one knows, the word "Overman."[1]

The first direction, which is now fully in view, is marked by conformity, levelling, higher Orientalism, modesty of instinct, contentment with the diminution of man—a kind of *human standstill-level.* Once we achieve, as is unavoidably imminent, collective economic management of the earth, mankind *can* find its meaning as machinery in such service—as a colossal gearbox consisting of ever smaller and ever more finely "adaptable" wheels, characterized by an ever-increasing superfluousness of dominating and ruling elements; as an enormously powerful whole whose component parts represent *minutiae* of power and value.

To counteract this shrinkage and adaptation of men to a specialized utility, one must go in the opposite direction: the production of the *synoptic*, the *all-encompassing*, the *vindicating* man, for whom the mechanization of mankind is a precondition, a foundation upon which he can erect his *higher form of being.*

He needs the *antagonism* of the mass, of the "be-levelled"—the feeling of distance that comes from comparing himself with them. He stands on them, he lives off them. This higher form of *aristocratism* is that of the future. Morally speaking, the machine-collectivity, the solidarity of all wheels, represents a maximum of *human exploitation*; but it presupposes those for whose sake such exploitation would *make sense*. Otherwise it would indeed be nothing but the collective diminution, the *value*-diminution of the human type— a *retrogression* in high style.

It should be apparent that what I am fighting is *economic* optimism: as though the increasing sacrifice of each were necessarily accompanied by an increasing advantage for all. To me just the contrary seems the case: *the sacrifice of each aggregates into a collective loss; man is diminished*, in such a way that one no longer knows *what end* this stupendous process was meant to subserve. A what-for? A *new* what-for? *That's* what mankind requires.

.   .   .

881. With *reference to the order of rank*: What is mediocre about the typical man?—That he fails to comprehend that things necessarily have a *reverse side*; that he combats evils as though they could be dispensed with; that he refuses to take the one with the other—that he would blur and efface the *typical character* of a thing, a state of affairs, a period, a person by sanctioning only part of their qualities and *dismissing* the rest. The "wishfulness" of the

---

[1][Most translators have rendered Nietzsche's *Übermensch* as "Superman" in English; a more accurate and less misleading rendering is "Overman."—*Trans.*]

mediocre is what we others contend with: the *Ideal* conceived as something devoid of anything injurious, evil, dangerous, dubious, or destructive. Our conception is quite the contrary: that with man's every growth his reverse side must also grow, that the *highest* man (granted such a concept is permitted) would be that man who would exhibit *the antithetical character of existence* most vigorously, as his glory and sole vindication. Ordinary men can allow themselves to exhibit this quality of nature only to the smallest degree: increase the many-sidedness of the elements and the tension among antitheses—the preconditions of man's *greatness*—and they soon perish. That man must become better *and* worse: that is my formula for this inevitability.

Most men constitute mere bits and pieces of men; only when they are added together does a man emerge. In this sense there is something fragmentary about whole ages, whole peoples; perhaps it is inherent in the economy of human evolution that man develops only piecemeal. Precisely for this reason we must not fail to recognize that the emergence of the comprehensive man is all that matters, and that the inferior men, the vast majority, are nothing but preludes and rehearsals—an ensemble out of which here and there the *whole man* emerges, the milestoneman, the measure of how far mankind has thus far advanced. It does *not* advance in a straight line; frequently the already achieved type is lost again (for example, notwithstanding three hundred years' exertion, we have failed to measure up to the men of the Renaissance—and Renaissance man in turn fell short of the men of Antiquity).

. . .

874. The deterioration of the rulers and the ruling classes has brought about the greatest mischief in history! Without the Roman Caesars and Roman society the madness of Christianity would never have come to the fore.

When inferior men come to doubt *whether* there are higher men, then there is great danger! Ultimately one discovers that even the inferior, the subjugated, the spiritually impoverished have *virtues*, and that *before God all men are equal: than which no greater nonsense has ever existed on earth!* For eventually the higher men themselves accept as their measure the slaves' standard of virtue—find themselves "prideful," etc., find all their *higher* qualities to be reprehensible.

It was when Nero and Caracalla sat on high that the paradox arose, "the lowest man is *worth more* than the one on high!" And the *image of God* became prevalent which was as *remote* as possible from the image of the Almighty—God on the Cross!

. . .

877. The Revolution made possible Napoleon: that is its justification. For a comparable prize one should long for the anarchic collapse of our entire civilization. Napoleon made possible nationalism: that is his excuse.

The value of a man (leaving aside, and rightly so, morality and immorality, since these concepts do not even begin to touch a man's *worth*) is not to be found in his usefulness; for it persists even if there were no one to whom he could be useful. And why couldn't precisely the man who engenders the most destructive consequences be the summit of the entire human species— so grand, so superior that confronted by him everything would die of envy?

. . .

373. *The origin of moral values.*—Egoism has as much value as the physiological worth of its bearer.

Each individual constitutes the entire evolutionary lineage (he is not, contrary to the moralistic conception of him, merely something that begins with his birth). Should he represent the *ascendancy* of the human lineage, then his value is, in fact, exceptional, and great may be the concern over the maintenance and encouragement of his growth. (It is the concern over the promise of the future which he embodies that gives the fortunate individual so extraordinary a right to egoism.) But should he represent the *descending* lineage, that of degeneration and chronic sickness, then little value accrues to him; and it is a matter of elementary justice that he takes from the fortunate as little space, strength, and sunlight as possible. In this instance society's task is the *suppression of egoism* (it occasionally expresses itself in absurd, pathological, and rebellious forms), be it a question of individuals or of entire degenerated, vestigial strata of mankind. Among such strata, a dogma or religion of "love," of *suppression* of self-affirmation, of patience, suffering, and service, of mutuality in word and deed can be of highest value, even from the point of view of their rulers. For it suppresses feelings of rivalry, resentment, and envy—the all-too-natural feelings of the ill-begotten; it even deifies them by idealizing slavish humility and obedience, subordination, poverty, infirmity, and lowliness. Accordingly, we see why ruling classes (or races) and individuals have always supported the cult of unselfishness, the slave-gospel of the "God on the Cross."

The predominance of an altruistic mode of valuing is the consequence of an instinct-to-failure. At bottom, this value judgment affirms: "I am not worth much,"—a mere physiological value judgment; plainer yet: the feeling of impotence, the dearth of great yea-saying surges of power (in the muscles, nerves, limbs). In accordance with the particular culture of these strata, this value judgment translates itself into a moral or religious judgment (the pre-eminence of religious or moral judgments is always a mark of an inferior culture); it seeks to establish itself out of contexts in which the concept of "value" is already familiar. The interpretation by which the Christian sinner seeks to understand himself is an attempt to *justify* his lack of power and self-assurance: he would rather find himself guilty than feel himself to be bad for no reason; to have need of such interpretations in the first place is already a symptom of decadence. In other instances the misbegotten seeks the reason for it not in his own "guilt" (like the Christian does), but in society (the socialist, the anarchist, the nihilist). Insofar as he feels his condition to be one for which someone *ought* to be guilty, however, he remains the next-of-kin of the Christian, who also believes that he can better endure his negative self-discovery and misbegottenness if he has found someone he can hold *responsible* for it. In both instances, the instinct for *revenge* and *resentment* appears as a means of bearing it, as an instinct of self-preservation—much the same as the predilection for *altruistic* theory and practice. The *hatred of egoism*, be it directed against self (as with the Christian) or other (as with the socialist), reveals itself thereby as a value judgment under the aegis of revenge; yet at the same time as the cunning of self-preservation on the part of the suffering, through an enhancing of their feelings of cooperation and solidarity. Basically, as already indicated, this discharge of resentment in the form of judging, condemning, and punishing egoism (one's own or another's) is nothing but an instinct of self-preservation on the part of the misbegotten. In sum: the cult of altruism is a special form of egoism which, given certain physiological conditions, regularly appears.

When, in righteous indignation, the socialist demands "justice," "equality," "equal rights," he is under pressure of a substandard culture which cannot help him comprehend why he suffers; otherwise regarded, he is amusing himself,—were he better off, he would not dream of making such outcries: he would amuse himself in some other way. Likewise for the Christian: he condemns, calumniates, curses the world—and himself in the bargain. But that is no reason to take his clamor seriously. In both instances we are in the midst of invalids whom crying *benefits*, for whom calumny affords relief.

. ·   .

753. I am averse to (1) socialism, because it dreams naively of "the Good, the True, the Beautiful" and "equal rights" (anarchism too pursues similar ideals, only in a more brutal way); (2) parliamentarianism and the cult of the newspaper, because they are the means by which the herd-animal becomes master.

.   .   .

728. It is part of the very concept of life that it must grow—that it must extend its power and consequently absorb alien forces. Befogged by the narcotic called morality, one speaks of the right of the individual to *defend* himself. By the same token, one ought to speak of the individual's right to *attack*, for *both*—and the second more than the first—are necessities for every living thing: aggressive and defensive egoism are not matters of choice (not to speak of "free will") but the *fatality* of life itself.

In this context it makes no difference whether an individual or a living organism, an aspiring "society," is held in view. At bottom, the right to punish (society's self-defense) was arrived at only through a misuse of the word "right": a right is obtained only by contract, whereas self-defense and self-protection do not rest on a contractual basis. At the very least, and with just as much show of reason, a people should describe its passion for conquest, its lust for power, be it force of arms, trade, commerce, or colonization, as a right—say a growth-right. A society which, definitively and in accordance with its instinct, foreswears war and conquest, is in a state of decline: it is ripe for democracy and rule by shopkeepers.

·   ·   ·

957. It draws near, inexorable, trembling, as frightening as fate—the great task and question, How shall the earth as a whole be administered? And *toward what end* shall mankind as a whole—no longer a mere people, a race—be trained and cultivated?

Legislated morals are the chief means whereby one can cull from man what is suitable to a creative and profound will: provided that such a high order artist-will has power in hand and is able to impose itself over long periods in the form of law-giving, religions, and moralities. To my mind, such men of great achievement, such authentically great men, will be pursued in vain today and probably for a long time to come. They are *lacking*, and will be, until finally, after much disappointment, one begins to understand *why* they are lacking, and that now and for a long time to come nothing impedes their genesis and development with greater hostility than what passes in Europe for "*the* morality"—as though there were and could be no other—the one heretofore described as herd morality, the one which strives with all its might for that common green pasture-land happiness on earth, i.e., security, absence of danger, coziness, ease of life, and, last but not least, "if all goes well," the pious hope of dispensing with all manner of shepherds and bell-wethers. Its two most broadly preached doctrines are called "equality of rights" and "compassion for all suffering"—and suffering itself is thought to be something which must by all means be *got rid of*. That such ideas can still be modern inclines one to a low opinion of modernity. But whoever ponders thoroughly the question where and how the plant Man has hitherto grown up most vigorously cannot help but suppose that this occurred under quite the *contrary* conditions: that the danger of its habitat must be magnified to frightful proportions, its powers of sensation and locomotion must struggle against long hardship and constriction, its will to life must be intensified into an unconditioned will to power and predominance, and that danger, harshness, violence, peril in the street as in the heart, inequality of rights, concealment, stoicism, the art of seduction, deviltry of every kind—in short, that the elevation of the species Man demands the very antithesis of all herdlike wish-fulfillment. A morality with such opposite intentions, seeking to nurture man upwards instead of into the cozy and the mediocre, a morality seeking to nurture a ruling caste—the future *lords of the earth*—must, before it can be promulgated, introduce itself as though in league with prevalent moral law and in the guise of the latter's words and shapes. But that accordingly a number of provisional and diversionary tactics need be discovered and that, whereas the life-span of a man means next to nothing in face of the fulfillment of such protracted tasks and aims, above all else *a new species* must be nurtured, in which the appropriate wills and instincts will be guaranteed duration through many generations—a new ruling species and caste: to envision all this is no easier than to comprehend the lengthy and hard-to-articulate *Etcetera* of its underlying thought. To prepare a *transvaluation of values* for a certain powerful species of men, endowed with the highest intellect and will-power, and to this end liberate him slowly and carefully from a host of repressed and vilified instincts: who ponders this belongs to us, the free spirits. ...

. . .

464. ... But where might I look with any hope at all for my kind of philosophers, or at the very least for *my kind of yearning for new philosophers*? Only where there prevails a *noble* turn of mind, one that believes in slavery and in many gradations of serfdom as being the preconditions of any higher culture; where there prevails a *creative* turn of mind, one that does not postulate the bliss of eternal repose, the "Sabbath of Sabbaths" as the world's destiny, but honors, even in peacetime, the means to new wars; a turn of mind that prescribes laws to the future, one that for the future's sake deals harshly and tyrannically with itself and its time; an unscrupulous, "immoral" turn of mind, determined to nourish towards greatness man's good and evil qualities in equal measure, entrusting itself with the power to give each its proper due—proper in so far as each requires the other. But he who goes in quest of philosophers today, what are his prospects of finding what he seeks? Isn't it likely that even with the best lamp-of-Diogenes to hand, he wanders about day and night in vain? This age has the *contrary* instinct: first and foremost, it wants comfort; secondly, it wants publicity, the bustle and din of the theatre and the dance-hall, so congenial to its county-fair tastes; thirdly, it wants everybody to crawl on his belly in abject submission before the greatest of all lies—its name is "equality of mankind"—and pay homage exclusively to the *equalizing*, the *levelling* virtues. But there, with the advent of the philosopher, as I understand him, is utterly precluded, even though in all innocence this age imagines itself to be conducive to him. Indeed, all the world presently bemoans the evils *earlier* philosophers had to endure, caught as they were between the stake, their guilty conscience, and the presumptuous wisdom of the Church Fathers. But the truth is that just these circumstances afforded far

more *favorable* conditions for a powerful, comprehensive, subtle, and auda-cious mentality than do the circumstances of present-day life. Today, condi-tions favor the appearance of another kind of spirit, that of the demagogue, the actor, perhaps that of the beaver-like, ant-like scholar as well. The superi-or artists, on the other hand, are already in a bad way: aren't nearly all of them being ruined for want of inner discipline? They are no longer being tyrannized from without by Church-or-Court-imposed tablets of absolute value; accordingly, they no longer learn to cultivate their "inner tyrant," their *will*. And what holds true for artists holds true in a higher and more ominous sense for philosophers. Where *are* the free spirits today? Show me a free spirit today!

.   .   .

997. I teach that there are higher and lower men, and that in some cases the existence of entire millennia may be justified by a single individ-ual—that is, a fuller, richer, greater, more whole man, in contrast with count-less incomplete, fragmentary men.

998. The highest men live beyond rulers, free of all bonds; and in the rulers they find their instruments.

999. *Order of rank*: he who *determines* values and directs the will of millennia by directing the highest natures, is the *highest man*.

1000. I think I have fathomed something of what goes on in the soul of the highest man; perhaps anyone who fathoms him entire is doomed: but whoever has glimpsed him must help to make him *possible*.

Fundamental idea: we must take the future as the criterion for all our value appraisals—and not look *behind* us for the laws of our action.

1001. Not "mankind" but the *Overman* is the goal!

Albert Beveridge

What distinguishes the imperialism of the late nineteenth century was that the powers of Europe were seizing their final opportunity to divide the globe among themselves. After Africa and some scattered islands, nothing was left. Hence, the competition took on perhaps a finer edge than it had in earlier times.

Among the most enthusiastic supporters of American imperialism was Albert Beveridge (1862–1927), who served two terms in the United States Senate from the state of Indiana (from 1899 to 1911). Although the reasons he gives in justification of American imperialism in the speech that follows are not such as to be received with much sympathy, or even understanding, today, it is apparent that Beveridge himself took them very seriously. In doing so he was joined by a large number of his fellow-citizens, including many in high places—for example, Presidents William McKinley and Theodore Roosevelt.

Consider the following questions as you study the text below.

1. How did Beveridge justify American imperialism? What role did religion play in his argument?

2. How did Beveridge see America's place in the world? Why did he believe that America had a greater right to territory and power than other nations?

The March of the Flag

It is a noble land that God has given us; a land that can feed and clothe the world; a land whose coastlines would inclose half the countries of Europe; a land set like a sentinel between the two imperial oceans of the globe, a greater England with a nobler destiny.

It is a mighty people that He has planted on this soil; a people sprung from the most masterful blood of history; a people perpetually revitalized by the virile, man-producing working-folk of all the earth; a people imperial by virtue of their power, by right of their institutions, by authority of their Heaven-directed purposes—the propagandists and not the misers of liberty.

Delivered as a campaign speech on September 16, 1898.

It is a glorious history our God has bestowed upon His chosen people; a history heroic with faith in our mission and our future; a history of statesmen who flung the boundaries of the Republic out into unexplored lands and savage wilderness; a history of soldiers who carried the flag across blazing deserts and through the ranks of hostile mountains, even to the gates of sunset; a history of a multiplying people who overran a continent in half a century; a history of prophets who saw the consequences of evils inherited from the past and of martyrs who died to save us from them; a history divinely logical, in the process of whose tremendous reasoning we find ourselves today.

Therefore, in this campaign, the question is larger than a party question. It is an American question. It is a world question. Shall the American people continue their march toward the commercial supremacy of the world? Shall free institutions broaden their blessed reign as the children of liberty wax in strength, until the empire of our principles is established over the hearts of all mankind?

Have we no mission to perform, no duty to discharge to our fellowman? Has God endowed us with gifts beyond our deserts and marked us as the people of His peculiar favor, merely to rot in our own selfishness, as men and nations must, who take cowardice for their companion and self for their deity—as China has, as India has, as Egypt has?

Shall we be as the man who had one talent and hid it, or as he who had ten talents and used them until they grew to riches? And shall we reap the reward that waits on our discharge of our high duty; shall we occupy new markets for what our farmers raise, our factories make, our merchants sell—aye, and please God, new markets for what our ships shall carry?

Hawaii is ours; Puerto Rico is to be ours; at the prayer of her people Cuba finally will be ours; in the islands of the East, even to the gates of Asia, coaling stations are to be ours at the very least; the flag of a liberal government is to float over the Philippines, and may it be the banner that Taylor unfurled in Texas and Fremont carried to the coast.

The Opposition tells us that we ought not to govern a people without their consent. I answer, The rule of liberty that all just government derives its authority from the consent of the governed, applies only to those who are capable of self-government. We govern the Indians without their consent, we govern our territories without their consent, we govern our children without their consent. How do they know what our government would be without their consent? Would not the people of the Philippines prefer the just, humane, civilizing government of this Republic to the savage, bloody rule of pillage and extortion from which we have rescued them?

And, regardless of this formula of words made only for enlightened, self-governing people, do we owe no duty to the world? Shall we turn these peoples back to the reeking hands from which we have taken them? Shall we abandon them, with Germany, England, Japan, hungering for them? Shall we save them from those nations, to give them a self-rule of tragedy?

They ask us how we shall govern these new possessions. I answer: Out of local conditions and the necessities of the case methods of government will grow. If England can govern foreign lands, so can America. If Germany can govern foreign lands, so can America. If they can supervise protectorates, so can America. Why is it more difficult to administer Hawaii than New Mexico or California? Both had a savage and an alien population; both were more remote from the seat of government when they came under our dominion than the Philippines are today.

Will you say by your vote that American ability to govern has decayed; that a century's experience in self-rule has failed of a result? Will you affirm by your vote that you are an infidel to American power and practical sense? Or will you say that ours is the blood of government; ours the heart of dominion; ours the brain and genius of administration? Will you remember that we do but what our fathers did—we but pitch the tents of liberty farther westward, farther southward—we only continue the march of the flag?

The march of the flag! In 1789 the flag of the Republic waved over 4,000,000 souls in thirteen states, and their savage territory which stretched to the Mississippi, to Canada, to the Floridas. The timid minds of that day said that no new territory was needed, and, for the hour, they were right. But Jefferson, through whose intellect the centuries marched; Jefferson, who dreamed of Cuba as an American state; Jefferson, the first Imperialist of the Republic—Jefferson acquired that imperial territory which swept from the Mississippi to the mountains, from Texas to the British possessions, and the march of the flag began!

The infidels to the gospel of liberty raved, but the flag swept on! The title to that noble land out of which Oregon, Washington, Idaho and Montana have been carved was uncertain: Jefferson, strict constructionist of constitutional power though he was, obeyed the Anglo-Saxon impulse within him, whose watchword then and whose watchword throughout the world today is, "Forward!": another empire was added to the Republic, and the march of the flag went on!

Those who deny the power of free institutions to expand urged every argument, and more, that we hear, today; but the people's judgment approved the command of their blood, and the march of the flag went on!

A screen of land from New Orleans to Florida shut us from the Gulf, and over this and the Everglade Peninsula waved the saffron flag of Spain; Andrew Jackson seized both, the American people stood at his back, and, under Monroe, the Floridas came under the dominion of the Republic, and the march of the flag went on! The Cassandras prophesied every prophecy of despair we hear, today, but the march of the flag went on!

Then Texas responded to the bugle calls of liberty, and the march of the flag went on! And, at last, we waged war with Mexico, and the flag swept over the southwest, over peerless California, past the Gate of Gold to Oregon on the north, and from ocean to ocean its folds of glory blazed.

And, now, obeying the same voice that Jefferson heard and obeyed, that Jackson heard and obeyed, that Monroe heard and obeyed, that Seward heard and obeyed, that Grant heard and obeyed, that Harrison heard and obeyed, our President today plants the flag over the islands of the seas, outposts of commerce, citadels of national security, and the march of the flag goes on!

Distance and oceans are no arguments. The fact that all the territory our fathers bought and seized is contiguous, is no argument. In 1819 Florida was farther from New York than Puerto Rico is from Chicago today; Texas, farther from Washington in 1845 than Hawaii is from Boston in 1898; California, more inaccessible in 1847 than the Philippines are now. Gibraltar is farther from London than Havana is from Washington; Melbourne is farther from Liverpool than Manila is from San Francisco.

The ocean does not separate us from lands of our duty and desire—the oceans join us, rivers never to be dredged, canals never to be repaired. Steam joins us; electricity joins us—the very elements are in league with our destiny. Cuba not contiguous? Puerto Rico not contiguous! Hawaii and the Philippines not contiguous! The oceans make them contiguous. And our navy will make them contiguous.

But the Opposition is right—there is a difference. We did not need the western Mississippi Valley when we acquired it, nor Florida, nor Texas, nor California, nor the royal provinces of the far northwest. We had no emigrants to people this imperial wilderness, no money to develop it, even no highways to cover it. No trade awaited us in its savage fastnesses. Our productions were not greater than our trade. There was not one reason for the land-lust of our statesmen from Jefferson to Grant, other than the prophet and the Saxon within them. But, today, we are raising more than we can consume, making more than we can use. Therefore we must find new markets for our produce.

And so, while we did not need the territory taken during the past century at the time it was acquired, we do need what we have taken in 1898, and we need it now. The resources and the commerce of these immensely rich dominions will be increased as much as American energy is greater than Spanish sloth. In Cuba, alone, there are 15,000,000 acres of forest unacquainted with the ax, exhaustless mines of iron, priceless deposits of manganese, millions of dollars' worth of which we must buy, today, from the Black Sea districts. There are millions of acres yet unexplored.

The resources of Puerto Rico have only been trifled with. The riches of the Philippines have hardly been touched by the finger-tips of modern methods. And they produce what we consume, and consume what we produce— the very predestination of reciprocity—a reciprocity "not made with hands, eternal in the heavens." They sell hemp, sugar, cocoanuts, fruits of the trop-ics, timber of price like mahogany; they buy flour, clothing, tools, imple-ments, machinery and all that we can raise and make. Their trade will be ours in time. Do you indorse that policy with your vote?

Cuba is as large as Pennsylvania, and is the richest spot on the globe. Hawaii is as large as New Jersey; Puerto Rico half as large as Hawaii; the Philippines larger than all New England, New York, New Jersey and Delaware combined. Together they are larger than the British Isles, larger than France, larger than Germany, larger than Japan.

If any man tells you that trade depends on cheapness and not on gov-ernment influence, ask him why England does not abandon South Africa, Egypt, India. Why does France seize South China, Germany the vast region whose port is Kaou-chou?

Our trade with Puerto Rico, Hawaii and the Philippines must be as free as between the states of the Union, because they are American territory, while every other nation on earth must pay our tariff before they can com-pete with us. Until Cuba shall ask for annexation, our trade with her will, at the very least, be like the preferential trade of Canada with England. That, and the excellence of our goods and products; that, and the convenience of traffic; that, and the kinship of interests and destiny, will give the monopoly of these markets to the American people.

The commercial supremacy of the Republic means that this Nation is to be the sovereign factor in the peace of the world. For the conflicts of the future are to be conflicts of trade—struggles for markets—commercial wars for existence. And the golden rule of peace is impregnability of position and invincibility of preparedness. So, we see England, the greatest strategist of history, plant her flag and her cannon on Gibraltar, at Quebec, in the Bermu-das, at Vancouver, everywhere.

So Hawaii furnishes us a naval base in the heart of the Pacific; the Ladrones another, a voyage further on; Manila another, at the gates of Asia—Asia, to the trade of whose hundreds of millions American merchants, manu-facturers, farmers, have as good right as those of Germany or France or Russia or England; Asia, whose commerce with the United Kingdom alone amounts to hundreds of millions of dollars every year; Asia, to whom Germany looks to take her surplus products; Asia, whose doors must not be shut against Ameri-can trade. Within five decades the bulk of Oriental commerce will be ours.

No wonder that, in the shadows of coming events so great, free-silver is already a memory. The current of history has swept past that episode. Men understand, today, the greatest commerce of the world must be conducted with the steadiest standard of value and most convenient medium of exchange human ingenuity can devise. Time, that unerring reasoner, has settled the silver question. The American people are tired of talking about money—they want to make it.

· · ·

There are so many real things to be done—canals to be dug, railways to be laid, forests to be felled, cities to be builded, fields to be tilled, markets to be won, ships to be launched, peoples to be saved, civilization to be proclaimed and the flag of liberty flung to the eager air of every sea. Is this an hour to waste upon triflers with nature's laws? Is this a season to give our destiny over to word-mongers and prosperity-wreckers? No! It is an hour to remember our duty to our homes. It is a moment to realize the opportunities fate has opened to us. And so it is an hour for us to stand by the Government.

Wonderfully has God guided us. Yonder at Bunker Hill and Yorktown His providence was above us. At New Orleans and on ensanguined seas His hand sustained us. Abraham Lincoln was His minister and His was the altar of freedom the Nation's soldiers set up on a hundred battle-fields. His power directed Dewey in the East and delivered the Spanish fleet into our hands, as He delivered the elder Armada into the hands of our English sires two centuries ago.[1] The American people can not use a dishonest medium of exchange; it is ours to set the world its example of right and honor. We can not fly from our world duties; it is ours to execute the purpose of a fate that has driven us to be greater than our small intentions. We cannot retreat from any soil where Providence has unfurled our banner; it is ours to save that soil for liberty and civilization.

---

[1][actually in 1588—*Ed.*]

The Cold War was charged by the ever present threat of nuclear exchange. In this 1951 photograph, American troops watch a nuclear explosion during war games conducted at Yucca Flats in Nevada.

THE CONTEMPORARY WORLD

The century began in a peaceful and apparently tranquil way. Indeed, peace had generally reigned for nearly a hundred years, since the end of the Napoleonic Wars early in the nineteenth century. Although there had been some conflicts, those on the international level had been relatively minor and those that had reached a larger scale, like the American Civil War, were internal. Nevertheless, the general tranquillity of the international scene, particularly in Europe, was only apparent, for trouble was brewing beneath the surface. Deep-seated animosities, the legacy of old conflicts, as well as a contest for both political and economic primacy, were a prelude to the struggle that was soon to come. The rise of nation-states in the modern era had engendered fierce feelings of nationalism that were ready to break into open conflict. This was particularly true of the most recently united countries like Germany, which had grown into an economic giant and was chafing at its perceived lack of status among the great powers of Europe.

The period after the first war witnessed three major developments. First was the Communist revolution in Russia, which brought the Tsarist regime to a quick and bloody end. Inspired by the writings of Karl Marx and led by the fiery revolutionary, V. I. Lenin, the Communists seized power and established a new order which, after the destruction of the bourgeoisie by the proletariat, was to usher in a classless society. Thus began a great social, economic, and political experiment whose reverberations were felt through most of the world for the remainder of the century. The second development was the Great Depression, which engulfed most of the world, including the United States, during the decade of the thirties, causing untold want and misery. In Germany the Depression, as well as national resentment over the defeat suffered in the war, spawned the third interwar development—the rise of political extremism. Profiting by a national atmosphere of frustration and helplessness, a young, unscrupulous demagogue, Adolf Hitler, led his National Socialist, or Nazi, party into power, soon turning Germany into a totalitarian state and beginning preparations to overrun Europe. He was joined in this venture by the Fascist leader Benito Mussolini, who had come into power earlier in Italy under somewhat similar circumstances. So the stage was set for World War II.

Although the beginning of this war is usually dated from the German invasion of Poland in September 1939, it had actually been under way since 1931, when Japan, which later joined Germany and Italy in a military coalition known as the Axis, invaded Manchuria. It continued until August 1945, and was brought to an end when American planes dropped atomic bombs on

Hiroshima and Nagasaki. Unlike the first war, in which almost all the fighting occurred in small areas of Europe, this war was worldwide in scope. Although the heaviest fighting took place in Europe—particularly in Russia—and in Asia, no continent escaped. There was extensive combat in northern Africa and even some military activity along the coasts of both North and South America. Finally, a number of small islands in the Pacific Ocean were scenes of heavy battles. No one knows the number of causalties that resulted from the conflict but recent estimates of fatalities range as high as fifty million. A large number of those killed were civilians, who were the victims of mass bombing raids. It is estimated that one American fire-bombing attack on Tokyo, for example, claimed the lives of over one hundred thousand people.

The second World War was accompanied by the most heinous crime in history. Known as the Holocaust, it consisted in the wanton and systematic murder of approximately six million people, most but not all of whom were Jews. These victims were killed mainly by poison gas in specially constructed extermination camps of which Auschwitz in Poland was the most notorious.

When peace finally came in 1945 it proved not to be a real peace. Instead, the "hot" war was replaced by a "cold" war, which was to cast its chill on the world for the next forty years. The cold war was caused by mutual suspicion, misunderstanding, and hostile intent, in approximately equal proportions. The Soviet Union, which had been allied with the Western democracies during the war, was nevertheless deeply suspicious of its wartime partners, with considerable reason. From the very beginning of the revolution in Russia in 1917, the Western powers had opposed the new order, mainly because of their fear that communism would destroy the capitalistic system, and did whatever they could to undermine the Russian experiment. Suspicion fostered misunderstanding; throughout the cold war, each side constantly proclaimed its desire for peace, but the other side interpreted any peaceful overtures made as merely camouflage covering a hostile intent. (And, indeed, there was.) Although both sides were presumably sincere in their desire for peace, each was nevertheless repeatedly maneuvering to secure whatever advantage it could over the other. Although the cold war was by no means the first time that world powers had confronted each other in a hostile stance, it contained an element that made it unique in history. Each side possessed nuclear weapons capable of destroying the other, as well as the ability to deliver these directly on the enemy. Although some analysts maintain that the existence of such destructive weapons preserved the peace, arguing that the knowledge of their existence and the realization that any attack would produce an immediate and devastating counterattack was sufficient to deter the leaders of both sides from employing them, we have firm evidence that during the Cuban missile crisis in 1962, each side was on the brink of ordering a nuclear attack on the other.

The cold war came to an abrupt end with the astonishing collapse of communism and the disintegration of the Soviet Union during the decade of the eighties, an event that, prior to its occurrence, seemed hardly imaginable. Although the causes of this epochal collapse are now beginning to come to light, it will probably be decades before scholars have a full understanding of the reasons for the disintegration of the former Soviet Union.

LOOKING AHEAD

As you learn about twentieth-century Europe, consider the following questions.

1. How would you explain the rise of fascism in the decades following World War I? Why was it most successful in Spain, Italy, and Germany?

2. How did Europe's place in the world change in the aftermath of World War II? How has the relationship among European nations evolved over the course of the last fifty years?

3. With the Cold War over, will Russia finally be integrated into the West? Why or why not?

Bertrand Russell

In his most famous aphorism, Friedrich Nietzsche proclaimed, "God is dead." Hidden beneath the surface of this statement is an important historical fact. During the last hundred years, people in increasing numbers have found themselves unable to accept a world view based on the existence of God.

But if God is banished from the universe, what becomes of religion? Can there be any meaning or value in a universe of blind matter, any significance in human life, so brief and powerless, and soon to be "seized by the silent orders of omnipotent Death"? Can one accept the world view of contemporary science and still find any reason for worship? These are the questions that Bertrand Russell attempted to answer in an essay that some have termed atheistic and others profoundly religious— "A Free Man's Worship."

Bertrand Russell (1872–1970), one of the most eminent intellectual leaders of the twentieth century, was born in Wales. His family was prominent in politics, his grandfather, Lord John Russell, having served as prime minister early in the reign of Queen Victoria. Russell's first scholarly interest, in mathematics, led to the publication in 1910 of *Principia Mathematica* (written in collaboration with A. N. Whitehead), one of the most important books of the century. In the years that followed, Russell wrote more than forty additional books, mainly on philosophy and social and political issues. During World War I, he was imprisoned for his outspoken opposition to the war; later he received considerable notoriety as a result of his leadership in the movement to ban nuclear weapons. He was awarded the Nobel Prize in literature in 1950, in recognition of his long and influential career "as a defender of humanity and freedom of thought."

Consider the following questions as you study the text below.

1. Why did Russell believe that the only moral choice was disbelief in God? Given this position, can we conclude that Russell was an atheist?

2. What did Russell mean by human freedom? What did one need to do in order to be free?

A Free Man's Worship

To Dr. Faustus in his study, Mephistopheles told the history of the Creation, saying:

"The endless praises of the choirs of angels had begun to grow wearisome; for, after all, did he not deserve their praise? Had he not given them endless joy? Would it not be more amusing to obtain undeserved praise, to be worshipped by beings whom he tortured? He smiled inwardly, and resolved that the great drama should be performed.

"For countless ages the hot nebula whirled aimlessly through space. At length it began to take shape, the central mass threw off planets, the planets cooled, boiling seas and burning mountains heaved and tossed, from black masses of cloud hot sheets of rain deluged the barely solid crust. And now the first germ of life grew in the depths of the ocean, and developed rapidly in the fructifying warmth into vast forest trees, huge ferns springing from the damp mould, sea monsters breeding, fighting, devouring, and passing away. And from the monsters, as the play unfolded itself, Man was born, with the power of thought, the knowledge of good and evil, and the cruel thirst for worship. And Man saw that all is passing in this mad, monstrous world, that all is struggling to snatch, at any cost, a few brief moments of life before Death's inexorable decree. And Man said: 'There is a hidden purpose, could we but fathom it, and the purpose is good; for we must reverence something, and in the visible world there is nothing worthy of reverence.' And Man stood aside from the struggle, resolving that God intended harmony to come out of chaos by human efforts. And when he followed the instincts which God had transmitted to him from his ancestry of beasts of prey, he called it Sin, and asked God to forgive him. But he doubted whether he could be justly forgiven, until he invented a divine Plan by which God's wrath was to have been appeased. And seeing the present was bad, he made it yet worse, that thereby the future might be better. And he gave God thanks for the strength that enabled him to forgo even the joys that were possible. And God smiled; and when he saw that Man had become perfect in renunciation and worship, he sent another sun through the sky, which crashed into Man's sun; and all returned again to nebula.

"'Yes,' he murmured, 'it was a good play; I will have it performed again.'"

Such in outline, but even more purposeless, more void of meaning, is the world which Science presents for our belief. Amid such a world, if anywhere, our ideals henceforward must find a home. That Man is the product of causes which had no prevision of the end they were achieving; that his origin, his growth, his hopes and fears, his loves and his beliefs, are but the

Bertrand Russell, "A Free Man's Worship," from *Mysticism and Logic* (London: George Allen & Unwin, Ltd., 1917). Courtesy of George Allen & Unwin, Ltd.

outcome of accidental collocations of atoms; that no fire, no heroism, no intensity of thought and feeling, can preserve an individual life beyond the grave; that all the labours of the ages, all the devotion, all the inspiration, all the noonday brightness of human genius, are destined to extinction in the vast death of the solar system, and that the whole temple of Man's achievement must inevitably be buried beneath the débris of a universe in ruins—all these things, if not quite beyond dispute, are yet so nearly certain, that no philosophy which rejects them can hope to stand. Only within the scaffolding of these truths, only on the firm foundation of unyielding despair, can the soul's habitation henceforth be safely built.

How, in such an alien and inhuman world, can so powerless a creature as Man preserve his aspirations untarnished? A strange mystery it is that Nature, omnipotent but blind, in the revolutions of her secular hurryings through the abysses of space, has brought forth at last a child, subject still to her power, but gifted with sight, with knowledge of good and evil, with the capacity of judging all the works of his unthinking Mother. In spite of Death, the mark and seal of the parental control, Man is yet free, during his brief years, to examine, to criticise, to know, and in imagination to create. To him alone, in the world with which he is acquainted, this freedom belongs; and in this lies his superiority to the resistless forces that control his outward life.

The savage, like ourselves, feels the oppression of his impotence before the powers of Nature; but having in himself nothing that he respects more than Power, he is willing to prostrate himself before his gods, without inquiring whether they are worthy of his worship. Pathetic and very terrible is the long history of cruelty and torture, of degradation and human sacrifice, endured in the hope of placating the jealous gods: surely, the trembling believer thinks, when what is most precious has been freely given, their lust for blood must be appeased, and more will not be required. The religion of Moloch—as such creeds may be generically called—is in essence the cringing submission of the slave, who dare not, even in his heart, allow the thought that his master deserves no adulation. Since the independence of ideals is not yet acknowledged, Power may be freely worshipped, and receive an unlimited respect, despite its wanton infliction of pain.

But gradually, as morality grows bolder, the claim of the ideal world begins to be felt; and worship, if it is not to cease, must be given to gods of another kind than those created by the savage. Some, though they feel the demands of the ideal, will still consciously reject them, still urging that naked Power is worthy of worship. Such is the attitude inculcated in God's answer to Job out of the whirlwind: the divine power and knowledge are paraded, but of the divine goodness there is no hint. Such also is the attitude of those who, in our own day, base their morality upon the struggle for survival, maintaining that the survivors are necessarily the fittest. But others, not content with an answer so repugnant to the moral sense, will adopt the position which we have become accustomed to regard as specially religious, maintaining that, in some hidden manner, the world of fact is really harmonious with the world of ideals. Thus Man creates God, all-powerful and all-good, the mystic unity of what is and what should be.

But the world of fact, after all, is not good; and, in submitting our judgment to it, there is an element of slavishness from which our thoughts must be purged. For in all things it is well to exalt the dignity of Man, by freeing him as far as possible from the tyranny of non-human Power. When we have realised that Power is largely bad, that man, with his knowledge of good and evil, is but a helpless atom in a world which has no such knowledge, the choice is again presented to us: Shall we worship Force, or shall we worship Goodness? Shall our God exist and be evil, or shall he be recognised as the creation of our own conscience?

The answer to this question is very momentous, and affects profoundly our whole morality. The worship of Force, to which Carlyle and Nietzsche and the creed of Militarism have accustomed us, is the result of failure to maintain our own ideals against a hostile universe: it is itself a prostrate submission to evil, a sacrifice of our best to Moloch. If strength indeed is to be respected, let us respect rather the strength of those who refuse that false "recognition of facts" which fails to recognise that facts are often bad. Let us admit that, in the world we know, there are many things that would be better otherwise, and that the ideals to which we do and must adhere are not realised in the realm of matter. Let us preserve our respect for truth, for beauty, for the ideal of perfection which life does not permit us to attain, though none of these things meet with the approval of the unconscious universe. If Power is bad, as it seems to be, let us reject it from our hearts. In this lies Man's true freedom: in determination to worship only the God created by our own love of the good, to respect only the heaven which inspires the insight of our best moments. In action, in desire, we must submit perpetually to the tyranny of outside forces; but in thought, in aspiration, we are free, free from our fellow-men, free from the petty planet on which our bodies impotently crawl, free even, while we live, from the tyranny of death. Let us learn, then, that energy of faith which enables us to live constantly in the vision of the good; and let us descend, in action, into the world of fact, with that vision always before us.

When first the opposition of fact and ideal grows fully visible, a spirit of fiery revolt, of fierce hatred of the gods, seems necessary to the assertion of freedom. To defy with Promethean constancy a hostile universe, to keep its evil always in view, always actively hated, to refuse no pain that the malice of Power can invent, appears to be the duty of all who will not bow before the inevitable. But indignation is still a bondage, for it compels our thoughts to be occupied with an evil world; and in the fierceness of desire from which rebellion springs there is a kind of self-assertion which it is necessary for the wise to overcome. Indignation is a submission of our thoughts, but not of our desires; the Stoic freedom in which wisdom consists is found in the submission of our desires, but not of our thoughts. From the submission of our desires springs the virtue of resignation; from the freedom of our thoughts springs the whole world of art and philosophy, and the vision of beauty by which, at last, we half reconquer the reluctant world. But the vision of beauty is possible only to unfettered contemplation, to thoughts not weighted by the load of eager wishes; and thus Freedom comes only to those who no longer ask of life that it shall yield them any of those personal goods that are subject to the mutations of Time.

Although the necessity of renunciation is evidence of the existence of evil, yet Christianity, in preaching it, has shown a wisdom exceeding that of the Promethean philosophy of rebellion. It must be admitted that, of the things we desire, some, though they prove impossible, are yet real goods; others, however, as ardently longed for, do not form part of a fully purified ideal. The belief that what must be renounced is bad, though sometimes false, is far less often false than untamed passion supposes; and the creed of religion, by providing a reason for proving that it is never false, has been the means of purifying our hopes by the discovery of many austere truths.

But there is in resignation a further good element: even real goods, when they are unattainable, ought not to be fretfully desired. To every man comes, sooner or later, the great renunciation. For the young, there is nothing unattainable; a good thing desired with the whole force of a passionate will, and yet impossible, is to them not credible. Yet, by death, by illness, by poverty, or by the voice of duty, we must learn, each one of us, that the world was not made for us, and that, however beautiful may be the things we crave, Fate may nevertheless forbid them. It is the part of courage, when misfortune comes, to bear without repining the ruin of our hopes, to turn away our thoughts from vain regrets. This degree of submission to Power is not only just and right: it is the very gate of wisdom.

But passive renunciation is not the whole of wisdom; for not by renunciation alone can we build a temple for the worship of our own ideals. Haunting foreshadowings of the temple appear in the realm of imagination, in music, in architecture, in the untroubled kingdom of lyrics, where beauty shines and glows, remote from the touch of sorrow, remote from the fear of change, remote from the failures and disenchantments of the world of fact. In the contemplation of these things the vision of heaven will shape itself in our hearts, giving at once a touchstone to judge the world about us, and an inspiration by which to fashion to our needs whatever is not incapable of serving as a stone in the sacred temple.

Except for those rare spirits that are born without sin, there is a cavern of darkness to be traversed before that temple can be entered. The gate of the cavern is despair, and its floor is paved with the gravestones of abandoned hopes. There Self must die; there the eagerness, the greed of untamed desire must be slain, for only so can the soul be freed from the empire of Fate. But out of the cavern the Gate of Renunciation leads again to the daylight of wisdom, by whose radiance a new insight, a new joy, a new tenderness, shine forth to gladden the pilgrim's heart.

When, without the bitterness of impotent rebellion, we have learnt both to resign ourselves to the outward rule of Fate and to recognise that the non-human world is unworthy of our worship, it becomes possible at last so to transform and refashion the unconscious universe, so to transmute it in the crucible of imagination, that a new image of shining gold replaces the old idol of clay. In all the multiform facts of the world—in the visual shapes of trees and mountains and clouds, in the events of the life of man, even in the very omnipotence of Death—the insight of creative idealism can find the reflection of a beauty which its own thoughts first made. In this way mind asserts its subtle mastery over the thoughtless forces of Nature. The more evil the material with which it deals, the more thwarting to untrained desire, the greater is its achievement in inducing the reluctant rock to yield up its hidden treasures, the prouder its victory in compelling the opposing forces to swell the pageant of its triumph. Of all the arts, Tragedy is the proudest, the most triumphant; for it builds its shining citadel in the very centre of the enemy's country, on the very summit of his highest mountain; from its impregnable watchtowers, his camps and arsenals, his columns and forts, are all revealed; within its walls the free life continues, while the legions of Death and Pain and Despair, and all the servile captains of tyrant Fate, afford the burghers of that dauntless city new spectacles of beauty. Happy those sacred ramparts, thrice happy the dwellers on that all-seeing eminence. Honour to those brave warriors who, through countless ages of warfare, have preserved for us the priceless heritage of liberty, and have kept undefiled by the sacrilegious invaders the home of the unsubdued.

But the beauty of Tragedy does not make visible a quality which, in more or less obvious shapes, is present always and everywhere in life. In the spectacle of Death, in the endurance of intolerable pain, and in the irrevocableness of a vanished past, there is a sacredness, an overpowering awe, a feeling of the vastness of existence, in which, as by some strange marriage of pain, the sufferer is bound to the world by bonds of sorrow. In these moments of insight, we lose all eagerness of temporary desire, all struggling and striving for petty ends, all care for the little trivial things that, to a superficial view, make up the common life of day by day; we see, surrounding the narrow raft illumined by the flickering light of human comradeship, the dark ocean on whose rolling waves we toss for a brief hour; from the great night without, a chill blast breaks in upon our refuge; all the loneliness of humanity and hostile force is concentrated upon the individual soul, which must struggle alone, with what of courage it can command, against the whole weight of a universe that cares nothing for its hopes and fears. Victory, in this struggle with the powers of darkness, is the true baptism into the glorious company of heroes, the true initiation into the overmastering beauty of human existence. From that awful encounter of the soul with the outer world, renunciation, wisdom, and charity are born; and with their birth a new life begins. To take into the inmost shrine of the soul the irresistible forces whose puppets we seem to be—Death and change, the irrevocableness of the past, and the powerlessness of man before the blind hurry of the universe from vanity to vanity—to feel these things and know them is to conquer them.

This is the reason why the Past has such magical power. The beauty of its motionless and silent pictures is like the enchanted purity of late autumn, when the leaves, though one breath would make them fall, still glow against the sky in golden glory. The Past does not change or strive; like Duncan, after life's fitful fever it sleeps well; what was eager and grasping, what was petty and transitory, has faded away, the things that were beautiful and eternal shine out of it like stars in the night. Its beauty, to a soul not worthy of it, is unendurable; but to a soul which has conquered Fate it is the key of religion.

The life of Man, viewed outwardly, is but a small thing in comparison with the forces of Nature. The slave is doomed to worship Time and Fate and Death, because they are greater than anything he finds in himself, and because all his thoughts are of things which they devour. But, great as they are, to think of them greatly, to feel their passionless splendour, is greater still. And such thought makes us free men; we no longer bow before the inevitable in Oriental subjection, but we absorb it, and make it a part of ourselves. To abandon the struggle for private happiness, to expel all eagerness of temporary desire, to burn with passion for eternal things—this is emancipation, and this is the free man's worship. And this liberation is effected by a contemplation of Fate; for Fate itself is subdued by the mind which leaves nothing to be purged by the purifying fire of Time.

United with his fellow-men by the strongest of all ties, the tie of a common doom, the free man finds that a new vision is with him always, shedding over every daily task the light of love. The life of Man is a long march through the night, surrounded by invisible foes, tortured by weariness and pain, towards a goal that few can hope to reach, and where none may tarry long. One by one, as they march, our comrades vanish from our sight, seized by the silent orders of omnipotent Death. Very brief is the time in which we can help them, in which their happiness or misery is decided. Be it ours to shed sunshine on their path, to lighten their sorrows by the balm of sympathy, to give them the pure joy of a never-tiring affection, to strengthen failing courage, to instill faith in hours of despair. Let us not weigh in grudging scales their merits and demerits but let us think only of their need—of the sorrows, the difficulties, perhaps the blindnesses, that make the misery of their lives; let us remember that they are fellow-sufferers in the same darkness, actors in the same tragedy with ourselves. And so, when their day is over, when their good and their evil have become eternal by the immortality of the past, be it ours to feel that, where they suffered, where they failed, no deed of ours was the cause; but whenever a spark of the divine fire kindled in their hearts, we were ready with encouragement, with sympathy, with brave words in which high courage glowed.

Brief and powerless is Man's life; on him and all his race the slow, sure doom falls pitiless and dark. Blind to good and evil, reckless of destruction, omnipotent matter rolls on its relentless way; for Man, condemned today to lose his dearest, tomorrow himself to pass through the gate of darkness, it remains only to cherish, ere yet the blow falls, the lofty thoughts that ennoble his little day; disdaining the coward terrors of the slave of Fate, to worship at the shrine that his own hands have built; undismayed by the empire of chance, to preserve a mind free from the wanton tyranny that rules his outward life; proudly defiant of the irresistible forces that tolerate, for a moment, his knowledge and his condemnation, to sustain alone, a weary but unyielding Atlas, the world that his own ideals have fashioned despite the trampling march of unconscious power.

Sigmund Freud

Sigmund Freud (1856–1939) is the acknowledged founder of the discipline of psychoanalysis, which has become an important feature of twentieth-century culture. But just what is psychoanalysis? In Freud's own view it was primarily a science. As a psychologist Freud was interested in analyzing human nature, in particular the connection between its biological and mental aspects, an undertaking that he conducted largely through the investigation of the "unconscious," or that part of an individual's mental life of which he is not aware. As a doctor, however, Freud was concerned with the health of his patients. Psychoanalysis developed into psychotherapy, which is the method the analyst employs in his attempt to restore his patient to mental health. Early in his career Freud used hypnosis as a therapeutic tool but soon abandoned this and turned to the device of encouraging his patients to speak freely to him with no subjects taboo, a method he called "free-association." This became the standard therapeutic device of the psychoanalytic profession.

The selection that follows is taken from one of Freud's latest works, *An Outline of Psychoanalysis*, which he left unfinished. In it Freud develops perhaps his best-known thesis about the composition of human personality—the idea that each of us is divided into three centers of psychic force: the id, the ego, and the superego. Psychological problems arise when the balance between these forces is upset, the ego losing its control over one of the others. It is the task of the psychoanalyst to help the patient bring his ego, which is that part of him in contact with reality, back into dominance again in the regulation of his life. This, Freud concluded, is always a difficult task because it requires the individual to become able to function rationally, and Freud was, on the whole, pessimistic about the extent of human rationality, believing instead that both on the individual and the societal level irrationality predominates.

Sigmund Freud was born in Moldavia in eastern Europe but moved as a child to Vienna where he lived for eighty years, practicing medicine and psychoanalysis and writing voluminously. In 1937, on the approach of Hitler and the Nazis to Austria, he moved to London, where he died two years later.

Consider the following questions as you study the text below.

1. How did Freud define the id, the ego, and the superego? What was the relationship between these three elements of the psyche?

2. Why must the analyst find out what the patient does not know? How is this task achieved?

An Outline of Psychoanalysis

Chapter One

THE PSYCHICAL APPARATUS

Psychoanalysis makes a basic assumption,[1] the discussion of which falls within the sphere of philosophical thought, but the justification of which lies in its results. We know two things concerning what we call our psyche or mental life: firstly, its bodily organ and scene of action, the brain (or nervous system), and secondly, our acts of consciousness, which are immediate data and cannot be more fully explained by any kind of description. Everything that lies between these two terminal points is unknown to us and, so far as we are aware, there is no direct relation between them. If it existed, it would at the most afford an exact localization of the process of consciousness and would give us no help toward understanding them.

Our two hypotheses start out from these ends or beginnings of our knowledge. The first is concerned with localization. We assume that mental life is the function of an apparatus to which we ascribe the characteristics of being extended in space and of being made up of several portions—which we imagine, that is, as being like a telescope or microscope or something of the sort. The consistent carrying through of a conception of this kind is a scientific novelty, even though some attempts in that direction have been made previously.

We have arrived at our knowledge of this psychical apparatus by studying the individual development of human beings. To the oldest of these mental provinces or agencies we give the name of *id*. It contains everything that is inherited, that is present at birth, that is fixed in the constitution—above all, therefore, the instincts, which originate in the somatic organization and which find their first mental expression in the id in forms unknown to us.[2]

[1][It will be seen that this basic assumption is a double-barrelled one and is sometimes referred to by the author as two separate hypotheses.—*Trans.*]

[2]The oldest portion of the mental apparatus remains the most important throughout life, and it was the first subject of the investigations of psychoanalysis. [Throughout this book the English word *instinct* is, with some misgivings, used to render the German *Trieb*. The sense in which Freud uses the term is, in any case, made clear in the following pages.—*Trans.*]

Under the influence of the real external world which surrounds us, one portion of the id has undergone a special development. From what was originally a cortical layer, provided with organs for receiving stimuli and with apparatus for protection against excessive stimulation, a special organization has arisen which henceforward acts as an intermediary between the id and the external world. This region of our mental life has been given the name of *ego*.

The principal characteristics of the ego are these. In consequence of the relation which was already established between sensory perception and muscular action, the ego is in control of voluntary movement. It has the task of self-preservation. As regards *external* events, it performs that task by becoming aware of the stimuli from without, by storing up experiences of them (in the memory), by avoiding excessive stimuli (through flight), by dealing with moderate stimuli (through adaptation) and, finally, by learning to bring about appropriate modifications in the external world to its own advantage (through activity). As regards *internal* events, in relation to the id, it performs that task by gaining control over the demands of the instincts, by deciding whether they shall be allowed to obtain satisfaction, by postponing that satisfaction to times and circumstances favorable in the external world or by suppressing their excitations completely. Its activities are governed by consideration of the tensions produced by stimuli present within or introduced into it. The raising of these tensions is in general felt as *unpleasure* and their lowering as *pleasure*. It is probable, however, that what is felt as pleasure or unpleasure is not the *absolute* degree of the tensions but something in the rhythm of their changes. The ego pursues pleasure and seeks to avoid unpleasure. An increase in unpleasure which is expected and foreseen is met by a *signal of anxiety*; the occasion of this increase, whether it threatens from without or within, is called a *danger*. From time to time the ego gives up its connection with the external world and withdraws into the state of sleep, in which its organization undergoes far-reaching changes. It may be inferred from the state of sleep that that organization consists in a particular distribution of mental energy.

The long period of childhood, during which the growing human being lives in dependence upon his parents, leaves behind it a precipitate, which forms within his ego a special agency in which this parental influence is prolonged. It has received the name of *superego*. In so far as the superego is differentiated from the ego or opposed to it, it constitutes a third force which the ego must take into account.

Thus an action by the ego is as it should be if it satisfies simultaneously the demands of the id, of the superego, and of reality, that is to say if it is able to reconcile their demands with one another. The details of the relation between the ego and the superego become completely intelligible if they are carried back to the child's attitude toward his parents. The parents' influence naturally includes not merely the personalities of the parents themselves but also the racial, national, and family traditions handed on through them as well as the demands of the immediate social *milieu* which they represent. In the same way, an individual's superego in the course of his development takes over contributions from later successors and substitutes of his parents, such as teachers, admired figures in public life, or high social ideals. It will be seen that, in spite of their fundamental difference, the id and the superego have one thing in common: they both represent the influences of the past (the id the influence of heredity, the superego essentially the influence of what is taken over from other people), whereas the ego is principally determined by the individual's own experience, that is to say by accidental and current events.

This general pattern of a psychical apparatus may be supposed to apply equally to the higher animals which resemble man mentally. A superego must be presumed to be present whenever, as in the case of man, there is a long period of dependence in childhood. The assumption of a distinction between ego and id cannot be avoided.

Animal psychology has not yet taken in hand the interesting problem which is here presented.

Chapter Two

THE THEORY OF THE INSTINCTS

The power of the id expresses the true purpose of the individual organism's life. This consists in the satisfaction of its innate needs. No such purpose as that of keeping itself alive or of protecting itself from dangers by means of anxiety can be attributed to the id. That is the business of the ego, which is also concerned with discovering the most favorable and least perilous method of obtaining satisfaction, taking the external world into account. The superego may bring fresh needs to the fore, but its chief function remains the *limitation* of satisfactions.

The forces which we assume to exist behind the tensions caused by the needs of the id are called *instincts*. They represent the somatic demands upon mental life. Though they are the ultimate cause of all activity, they are by nature conservative; the state, whatever it may be, which a living thing has reached, gives rise to a tendency to reestablish that state so soon as it has been abandoned. It is possible to distinguish an indeterminate number of instincts and in common practice this is in fact done. For us, however, the important question arises whether we may not be able to derive all of these various instincts from a few fundamental ones. We have found that instincts can change their aim (by displacement) and also that they can replace one another—the energy of one instinct passing over to another. This latter process is still insufficiently understood. After long doubts and vacillations we have decided to assume the existence of only two basic instincts, *Eros* and *the destructive instinct*. (The contrast between the instincts of self-preservation and of the preservation of the species, as well as the contrast between ego-love and object-love, fall within the bounds of Eros.) The aim of the first of these basic instincts is to establish ever greater unities and to preserve them thus—in short, to bind together; the aim of the second, on the contrary, is to undo connections and so to destroy things. We may suppose that the final aim of the destructive instinct is to reduce living things to an inorganic state. For this reason we also call it the *death instinct*. If we suppose that living things appeared later than inanimate ones and arose out of them, then the death instinct agrees with the formula that we have stated, to the effect that instincts tend toward a return to an earlier state. We are unable to apply the formula to Eros (the love instinct). That would be to imply that living substance had once been a unity but had subsequently been torn apart and was now tending toward reunion.[3]

In biological functions the two basic instincts work against each other or combine with each other. Thus, the act of eating is a destruction of the object with the final aim of incorporating it, and the sexual act is an act of aggression having as its purpose the most intimate union. The interaction of the two basic instincts with and against each other gives rise to the whole variegation of the phenomena of life.

. . .

Chapter Six

THE TECHNIQUE OF PSYCHOANALYSIS

A dream, then, is a psychosis, with all the absurdities, delusions, and illusions of a psychosis. No doubt it is a psychosis which has only a short duration, which is harmless and even performs a useful function, which is brought about with the subject's consent and is ended by an act of his will. Nevertheless it is a psychosis, and we learn from it that even so deep-going a modification of mental life as this can be undone and can give place to normal functioning. Is it too bold, then, to hope that it must also be possible to submit the dreaded spontaneous illnesses of the mind to our control and bring about their cure?

We already possess much knowledge preliminary to such an undertaking. We have postulated that it is the ego's task to meet the demands of the three forces upon which it is dependent—reality, the id, and the superego—

---

[3]Something of the sort has been imagined by poets, but nothing like it is known to us from the actual history of living substances.

and meanwhile to preserve its own organization and maintain its own autonomy. The necessary condition for the pathological states we have mentioned can only be a relative or absolute weakening of the ego which prevents it from performing its tasks. The severest demand upon the ego is probably the keeping down of the instinctual claims of the id, and for this end the ego is obliged to maintain great expenditures of energy upon anticathexes. But the claims made by the superego, too, may become so powerful and so remorseless that the ego may be crippled, as it were, for its other tasks. We may suspect that, in the economic conflicts which now arise, the id and the superego often make common cause against the hard-pressed ego, which, in order to retain its normal state, clings on to reality. But if the other two are too strong, they may succeed in loosening the organization of the ego and altering it so that its proper relation to reality is disturbed or even abolished. We have seen it happen in dreams: when the ego is detached from the reality of the external world, then, under the influence of the external world, it slips down into psychosis.

Our plan of cure is based upon these views. The ego has been weakened by the internal conflict; we must come to its aid. The position is like a civil war which can only be decided by the help of an ally from without. The analytical physician and the weakened ego of the patient, basing themselves upon the real external world, are to combine against the enemies, the instinctual demands of the id, and the moral demands of the superego. We form a pact with each other. The patient's sick ego promises us the most complete candor, promises, that is, to put at our disposal all of the material which his self-perception provides; we, on the other hand, assure him of the strictest discretion and put at his service our experience in interpreting material that has been influenced by the unconscious. Our knowledge shall compensate for his ignorance and shall give his ego once more mastery over the lost provinces of his mental life. This pact constitutes the analytic situation.

No sooner have we taken this step than we meet with a first disappointment, a first warning against complacency. If the patient's ego is to be a useful ally in our common work, it must, however hard it may be pressed by the hostile powers, have retained a certain degree of coherence, a fragment at least understanding for the demands of reality. But this is not to be expected from the ego of a psychotic; it cannot carry out a pact of this sort, indeed it can scarcely engage in it. It will very soon toss us away and the help we offer it, to join the portions of the external world that no longer mean anything to it. Thus we learn that we must renounce the idea of trying our plan of cure upon psychotics—renounce it forever, perhaps, or only for the moment, until we have discovered some other plan better suited for that purpose.

But there is another class of psychological patients who evidently resemble the psychotics very closely, the immense number of sufferers from severe neuroses. The causes as well as the pathogenic mechanisms of their illness must be the same or at least very similar. Their ego, however, has proved more resistant and has become less disorganized. Many of them, in spite of their troubles and of their consequent inadequacy, are none the less able to maintain their position in real life. It may be that these neurotics will show themselves ready to accept our help. We will confine our interest to them and see how far and by what means we can "cure" them.

We conclude our pact then with the neurotics: complete candor on one side, strict discretion on the other. This looks as though we were aiming at the post of a secular father confessor. But there is a great difference, for what we want to hear from our patient is not only what he knows and conceals from other people, but what he does *not* know. With this end in view we give him a more detailed definition of what we mean by candor. We impose upon him the *fundamental rule* of analysis, which is henceforward to govern his behavior to us. He must tell us not only what he can say intentionally and willingly, what will give him relief like a confession, but everything else besides that his self-observation presents him with—everything that comes into his head, even if it is *disagreeable* to say it, even if it seems *unimportant* or positively *meaningless*. If he can succeed after this injunction in putting his self-criticism out of action, he will provide us with a mass of material—thoughts, ideas, recollections—which already lie under the influence of the unconscious, which are often its direct derivatives, and which thus put us in a position to conjecture the nature of his repressed unconscious material and to extend, by the information we give him, his ego's knowledge of his unconscious.

Vladimir Ilyich Lenin

The history of communism presents one of the major anomalies of the modern world. In their writings, Marx and Engels always assumed that the revolution and the consequent ushering in of the classless society would occur first in the most advanced industrial countries of Europe— England, France, and Germany. Russia, still slumbering in a state of archaic semifeudalism, was almost the last place in the world in which they expected their ideas to bear fruit. Nevertheless, it was Russia, rather than western Europe, that embraced communism. The reasons for this unforeseen historical development obviously are numerous and highly complex. Yet, important among them is the personal career of Vladimir Ilyich Lenin[1] (1870–1924). Lenin revised the Marxist theory to fit conditions in Russia and then led the bitter struggle, both against the existing regime and against rival revolutionaries and reformers, that resulted in 1917 in the victory of his version of Marxism in Russia.

The first of the two following selections, taken from a pamphlet entitled *What Is to Be Done?* (1902), contains Lenin's most significant departure from Marx—namely, his views on the nature and function of "the party." Leon Trotsky (1877–1940), Lenin's famous brother-revolutionary, made the following prophecy about Lenin's views on the party: "The organization of the Party takes the place of the Party itself; the Central Committee takes the place of the organization; and finally the dictator takes the place of the Central Committee." The second selection is from Lenin's most important work, *State and Revolution*, written during the revolution of 1917 in Russia. Ostensibly a commentary on Marxist doctrine, it became a detailed statement of Lenin's personal views regarding the political and social organization that was to follow the revolution.

Consider the following questions as you study the text below.

1. According to Lenin, what was the difference between an "organization of workers" and an "organization of revolutionaries"? Why was this difference critical to his approach to revolution?

2. According to Lenin, what must happen before the state can "wither away"? What role did revolutionaries play in this process?

---

[1]Born Vladimir Ilyich Ulyanov.

What Is to Be Done?

. . .

The history of all countries shows that the working class, exclusively by its own effort, is able to develop only trade union consciousness, *i.e*, it may itself realise the necessity for combining in unions, for fighting against the employers and for striving to compel the government to pass necessary labour legislation, etc. The theory of socialism, however, grew out of the philosophic, historical and economic theories that were elaborated by the educated representatives of the propertied classes, the intellectuals. According to their social status, the founders of modern scientific socialism, Marx and Engels, themselves belonged to the bourgeois intelligentsia. Similarly, in Russia, the theoretical doctrine of Social-Democracy arose quite independently of the spontaneous growth of the labour movement; it arose as a natural and inevitable outcome of the development of ideas among the revolutionary socialist intelligentsia. At the time of which we are speaking, *i.e.*, the middle of the nineties, this doctrine not only represented the completely formulated programme of the Emancipation of Labour group, but had already won the adherence of the majority of the revolutionary youth in Russia.

. . .

It is only natural that a Social-Democrat, who conceives the political struggle as being identical with the "economic struggle against the employers and the government," should conceive of an "organisation of revolutionaries" as being more or less identical with an "organisation of workers." And this, in fact, is what actually happens; so that when we talk about organisation, we literally talk in different tongues. I recall a conversation I once had with a fairly consistent Economist, with whom I had not been previously acquainted. We were discussing the pamphlet *Who Will Make the Political Revolution?* and we were very soon agreed that the principal defect in that brochure was that it ignored the question of organisation. We were beginning to think that we were in complete agreement with each other—but as the conversation proceeded, it became clear that we were talking of different things. My interlocutor accused the author of the brochure just mentioned of ignoring strike funds, mutual aid societies, etc.;

V. I. Lenin, "What Is to Be Done?" *Lenin: Collected Works* (London: Lawrence and Wishart Ltd., 1961), Vol. 5, pp. 375–76, 451–53, 464–67.

whereas I had in mind an organisation of revolutionaries as an essential factor in "making" the political revolution. After that became clear, I hardly remember a single question of importance upon which I was in agreement with that Economist!

What was the source of our disagreement? The fact that on questions of organisation and politics the Economists are forever lapsing from Social-Democracy into trade unionism. The political struggle carried on by the Social-Democrats is far more extensive and complex than the economic struggle the workers carry on against the employers and the government. Similarly (and indeed for that reason), the organisation of a revolutionary Social-Democratic Party must inevitably *differ* from the organisations of the workers designed for the latter struggle. A workers' organisation must in the first place be a trade organisation; secondly, it must be as wide as possible; and thirdly, it must be as public as conditions will allow (here, and further on, of course, I have only autocratic Russia in mind). On the other hand, the organisations of revolutionaries must consist first and foremost of people whose profession is that of a revolutionary (that is why I speak of organisations of *revolutionaries*, meaning revolutionary Social-Democrats). In view of this common feature of the members of such an organisation, *all distinctions as between workers and intellectuals*, and certainly distinctions of trade and profession, must be obliterated. Such an organisation must of necessity be not too extensive and as secret as possible.

.   .   .

I assert: (1) that no movement can be durable without a stable organisation of leaders to maintain continuity; (2) that the more widely the masses are spontaneously drawn into the struggle and form the basis of the movement and participate in it, the more necessary is it to have such an organisation, and the more stable must it be (for it is much easier for demogogues to sidetrack the more backward sections of the masses); (3) that the organisation must consist chiefly of persons engaged in revolutionary activities as a profession; (4) that in a country with an autocratic government, the more we *restrict* the membership of this organisation to persons who are engaged in revolutionary activities as a profession and who have been professionally trained in the art of combating the political police, the more difficult will it be to catch the organisation, and (5) the *wider* will be the circle of men and women of the working class or of other classes of society able to join the movement and perform active work in it.

.   .   .

The active and widespread participation of the masses will not suffer; on the contrary, it will benefit by the fact that a "dozen" experienced revolutionaries, no less professionally trained than the police, will centralise all the secret side of the work—prepare leaflets, work out approximate plans and appoint bodies of leaders for each urban district, for each factory district and to each educational institution, etc. (I know that exception will be taken to my "undemocratic" views, but I shall reply to this altogether unintelligent objection later on.) The centralisation of the more secret functions in an organisation of revolutionaries will not diminish, but rather increase the extent and the quality of the activity of a large number of other organisations intended for wide membership and which, therefore, can be as loose and as public as possible, for example, trade unions, workers' circles for self-education and the reading of illegal literature, and socialist and also democratic circles for *all other sections of the population,* etc., etc. We must have *as large a number as possible* of such organisations having the widest possible variety of functions, but it is absurd and dangerous to *confuse those with organisations of revolutionaries,* to erase the line of demarcation between them, to dim still more the masses' already incredibly hazy appreciation of the fact that in order to "serve" the mass movement we must have people who will devote themselves exclusively to Social-Democratic activities, and that such people must *train* themselves patiently and steadfastly to be professional revolutionaries.

Aye, this appreciation has become incredibly dim. The most grievous sin we have committed in regard to organisation is that *by our primitiveness we have lowered the prestige of revolutionaries in Russia.* A man who is weak and vacillating on theoretical questions, who has a narrow outlook, who makes excuses for his own slackness on the ground that the masses are awakening spontaneously, who resembles a trade union secretary more than a people's tribune, who is unable to conceive of a broad and bold plan, who is incapable of inspiring even his opponents with respect for himself, and who is inexperienced and clumsy in his own professional art—the art of combating the political police—such a man is not a revolutionary but a wretched amateur!

Let no active worker take offense at these frank remarks, for as far as insufficient training is concerned, I apply them first and foremost to myself. I used to work in a circle that set itself great and all-embracing tasks; and every member of that circle suffered to the point of torture from the realisation that we were proving ourselves to be amateurs at a moment in history when we might have been able to say, paraphrasing a well-known epigram: "Give us an organisation of revolutionaries, and we shall overturn the whole of Russia!"

State and Revolution

Chapter I

CLASS SOCIETY AND THE STATE

. . .

4. *The "Withering Away" of the State and Violent Revolution.* Engels' words regarding the "withering away" of the state enjoy such popularity, they are so often quoted, and they show so clearly the essence of the usual adulteration by means of which Marxism is made to look like opportunism, that we must dwell on them in detail. Let us quote the whole passage from which they are taken.

> *The proletariat seizes state power, and then transforms the means of production into state property. But in doing this, it puts an end to itself as the proletariat, it puts an end to all class differences and class antagonisms, it puts an end also to the state as the state. Former society, moving in class antagonisms, had need of the state, that is, an organisation of the exploiting class at each period for the maintenance of its external conditions of production; therefore, in particular, for the forcible holding down of the exploited class in the conditions of oppression (slavery, bondage or serfdom, wage-labour) determined by the existing mode of production. The state was the official representative of society as a whole, its embodiment in a visible corporate body; but it was this only in so far as it was the state of that class which itself, in its epoch, represented society as a whole: in ancient times, the state of the slave-owning citizens; in the Middle Ages, of the feudal nobility; in our epoch, of the bourgeoisie. When ultimately it becomes really representative of society as a whole, it makes itself superfluous. As soon as there is no longer any class of society to be held in subjection; as soon as, along with class domination and the struggle for individual existence based on the former anarchy of production, the collisions and excesses arising from these have also been abolished, there is nothing more to be repressed, and a special repressive force, a state, is no longer necessary. The first act in which the state really comes forward as the representative of society as a whole—the seizure of the means of production in the name of society—is at the same time its last independent act as a state. The interference of a state power in social relations becomes superfluous in one sphere after another, and then becomes dormant of itself. Government over persons is replaced by the administration of things and the direction of the processes of production.*

V. I. Lenin, *State and Revolution* (New York: International Publishers Co., Inc., 1932), pp. 15–17, 20, 70–75, 78–85. By permission of International Publishers Co., Inc.

The state is not "abolished," it withers away. *It is from this standpoint that we must appraise the phrase "people's free state"—both its justification at times for agitational purposes, and its ultimate scientific inadequacy—and also the demand of the so-called Anarchists that the state should be abolished overnight.*

Without fear of committing an error, it may be said that of this argument by Engels so singularly rich in ideas, only one point has become an integral part of Socialist thought among modern Socialist parties, namely, that, unlike the Anarchist doctrine of the "abolition" of the state, according to Marx the state "withers away." To emasculate Marxism in such a manner is to reduce it to opportunism, for such an "interpretation" only leaves the hazy conception of a slow, even, gradual change, free from leaps and storms, free from revolution. The current popular conception, if one may say so, of the "withering away" of the state undoubtedly means a slurring over, if not a negation, of revolution.

Yet, such an "interpretation" is the crudest distortion of Marxism, which is advantageous only to the bourgeoisie; in point of theory, it is based on a disregard for the most important circumstances and considerations pointed out in the very passage summarising Engels' ideas, which we have just quoted in full.

In the first place, Engels at the very outset of his argument says that, in assuming state power, the proletariat by that very act "puts an end to the state as the state." One is "not accustomed" to reflect on what this really means. Generally, it is either ignored altogether, or it is considered as a piece of "Hegelian weakness" on Engels' part. As a matter of fact, however, these words express succinctly the experience of one of the greatest proletarian revolutions—the Paris Commune of 1871, of which we shall speak in greater detail in its proper place. As a matter of fact, Engels speaks here of the destruction of the bourgeois state by the proletarian revolution, while the words about its withering away refer to the remains of *proletarian* statehood *after* the Socialist revolution. The bourgeois state does not "wither away," according to Engels, but is "put an end to" by the proletariat in the course of the revolution. What withers away after the revolution is the proletarian state or semistate.

Secondly, the state is a "special repressive force." This splendid and extremely profound definition of Engels' is given by him here with complete lucidity. It follows from this that the "special repressive force" of the bourgeoisie for the suppression of the proletariat, of the millions of workers by a handful of the rich, must be replaced by a "special repressive force" of the proletariat for the suppression of the bourgeoisie (the dictatorship of the proletariat). It is just this that constitutes the destruction of "the state as the state." It is just as that constitutes the "act" of "the seizure of the means of production in the name of society." And it is obvious that such a substitution of one (proletarian) "special repressive force" for another (bourgeois) "special repressive force" can in no way take place in the form of a "withering away."

Thirdly, as to the "withering away" or, more expressively and colour-fully, as to the state "becoming dormant," Engels refers quite clearly and definitely to the period *after* "the seizure of the means of production [by the state] in the name of society," that is, *after* the Socialist revolution. We all know that the political form of the "state" at that time is complete democracy. But it never enters the head of any of the opportunists who shamelessly distort Marx that when Engels speaks here of the state "withering away," of "becoming dormant," he speaks of *democracy*. At first sight this seems very strange. But it is "unintelligible" only to one who has not reflected on the fact that democracy is *also* a state and that, consequently, democracy will also disappear when the state disappears. The bourgeois state can only be "put an end to" by a revolution. The state in general, *i.e.*, most complete democracy, can only "wither away."

. . .

The replacement of the bourgeois by the proletarian state is impossible without a violent revolution. The abolition of the proletarian state, *i.e.*, of all states, is only possible through "withering away."

. . .

Chapter V

THE ECONOMIC BASE OF THE WITHERING AWAY OF THE STATE

1.   Formulation of the Question by Marx.

. . .

The whole theory of Marx is an application of the theory of evolution—in its most consistent, complete, well-considered and fruitful form—to modern capitalism. It was natural for Marx to raise the question of applying this theory both to the *coming* collapse of capitalism and to the *future* evolution of *future* Communism.

On the basis of what *data* can the future evolution of future Communism be considered?

On the basis of the fact that *it has its origin* in capitalism, that it develops historically from capitalism, that it is the result of the action of a social force to which capitalism *has given birth*. There is no shadow of an attempt on Marx's part to conjure up a Utopia, to make idle guesses about that which cannot be known. Marx treats the question of Communism in the same way as a naturalist would treat the question of the evolution of, say, a new biological species, if he knew that such and such was its origin, and such and such the direction in which it changed.

. . .

The first fact that has been established with complete exactness by the whole theory of evolution, by science as a whole—a fact which the Utopians forgot, and which is forgotten by the present-day opportunists who are afraid of the Socialist revolution—is that, historically, there must undoubtedly be a special state or epoch of *transition* from capitalism to Communism.

2. *Transition from Capitalism to Communism.* Marx continues:

> *Between capitalist and Communist society lies the period of the revolutionary transformation of the former into the latter. To this also corresponds a political transition period, in which the state can be no other than the revolutionary dictatorship of the proletariat.*

This conclusion Marx bases on an analysis of the role played by the proletariat in modern capitalist society, on the data concerning the evolution of this society, and on the irreconcilability of the opposing interests of the proletariat and the bourgeoisie.

Earlier the question was put thus: to attain its emancipation, the proletariat must overthrow the bourgeoisie, conquer political power and establish its own revolutionary dictatorship.

Now the question is put somewhat differently: the transition from capitalist society, developing towards Communism, towards a Communist society, is impossible without a "political transition period," and the state in this period can only be the revolutionary dictatorship of the proletariat.

What, then, is the relation of this dictatorship to democracy?

We have seen that the *Communist Manifesto* simply places side by side the two ideas: the "transformation of the proletariat into the ruling class" and the "establishment of democracy." On the basis of all that has been said above, one can define more exactly how democracy changes in the transition from capitalism to Communism.

In capitalist society, under the conditions most favourable to its development, we have more or less complete democracy in the democratic republic. But this democracy is always bound by the narrow framework of capitalist exploitation, and consequently always remains, in reality, a democracy for the minority, only for the possessing classes, only for the rich. Freedom in capitalist society always remains just about the same as it was in the ancient Greek republics: freedom for the slave-owners. The modern wage-slaves, owing to the conditions of capitalist exploitation, are so much crushed by want and poverty that "democracy is nothing to them," "politics is nothing to them"; that, in the ordinary peaceful course of events, the majority of the population is debarred from participating in social and political life.

The correctness of this statement is perhaps most clearly proved by Germany, just because in this state constitutional legality lasted and remained stable for a remarkably long time—for nearly half a century (1871–1914)—and because Social-Democracy in Germany during that time was able to achieve far more than in other countries in "utilising legality," and was able to organise into a political party a larger proportion of the working class than anywhere in the world.

What, then, is this largest proportion of politically conscious and active wage-slaves that has so far been observed in capitalist society? One million members of the Social-Democratic party—out of fifteen million wage-workers. Three million organised in trade unions—out of fifteen million.

Democracy for an insignificant minority, democracy for the rich—that is the democracy of capitalist society. If we look more closely into the mechanism of capitalist democracy, everywhere, both in the "petty"—so-called petty—details of the suffrage (residential qualification, exclusion of women, etc.), and in the technique of the representative institutions, in the actual obstacles to the right of assembly (public buildings are not for "beggars"!), in the purely capitalist organisation of the daily press, etc., etc.—on all sides we see restriction after restriction upon democracy. These restrictions, exceptions, exclusions, obstacles for the poor, seem slight, especially in the eyes of one who has himself never known want and has never been in close contact with the oppressed classes in their mass life (and nine-tenths, if not ninety-nine hundredths, of the bourgeois publicists and politicians are of this class), but in their sum total these restrictions exclude and squeeze out the poor from politics and from an active share in democracy.

Marx splendidly grasped this *essence* of capitalist democracy, when, in analysing the experience of the Commune, he said that the oppressed were allowed, once every few years, to decide which particular representatives of the oppressing class should be in parliament to represent and repress them!

But from this capitalist democracy—inevitably narrow, subtly rejecting the poor, and therefore hypocritical and false to the core—progress does not march onward, simply, smoothly and directly, to "greater and greater democracy," as the liberal professors and petty-bourgeois opportunists would have us believe. No, progress marches onward, *i.e.*, towards Communism, through the dictatorship of the proletariat; it cannot do otherwise, for there is no one else and no other way to *break the resistance* of the capitalist exploiters.

But the dictatorship of the proletariat—*i.e.*, the organisation of the vanguard of the oppressed as the ruling class for the purpose of crushing the oppressors—cannot produce merely an expansion of democracy. *Together* with an immense expansion of democracy which *for the first time* becomes democracy for the poor, democracy for the people, and not democracy for the rich folk, the dictatorship of the proletariat produces a series of restrictions of liberty in the case of the oppressors, the exploiters, the capitalists. We must crush them in order to free humanity from wage-slavery; their resistance must be broken by force; it is clear that where there is suppression there is also violence, there is no liberty, no democracy.

Engels expressed this splendidly in his letter to Bebel when he said, as the reader will remember, that "as long as the proletariat still *needs* the state, it needs it not in the interests of freedom, but for the purpose of crushing its antagonists; and as soon as it becomes possible to speak of freedom, then the state, as such, ceases to exist."

Democracy for the vast majority of the people, and suppression by force, *i.e.*, exclusion from democracy, of the exploiters and oppressors of the people—this is the modification of democracy during the *transition* from capitalism to Communism.

Only in Communist society, when the resistance of the capitalists has been completely broken, when the capitalists have disappeared, when there are no classes (*i.e.*, there is no difference between the members of society in their relation to the social means of production), *only then* "the state ceases to exist," and *it becomes possible to speak of freedom*. Only then a really full democracy, a democracy without any exceptions, will be possible and will be realised. And only then will democracy itself begin to *wither away* due to the simple fact that, freed from capitalist slavery, from the untold horrors, savagery, absurdities, and infamies of capitalist exploitation, people will gradually *become accustomed* to the observance of the elementary rules of social life that have been known for centuries and repeated for thousands of years in all school books; they will become accustomed to observing them without force, without compulsion, without subordination, without the *special apparatus* for compulsion which is called the state.

The expression "the state *withers away*," is very well chosen, for it indicates both the gradual and the elemental nature of the process. Only habit can, and undoubtedly will, have such an effect; for we see around us millions of times how readily people get accustomed to observe the necessary rules of life in common, if there is no exploitation, if there is nothing that causes indignation, that calls forth protest and revolt and has to be *suppressed*.

Thus, in capitalist society, we have a democracy that is curtailed, poor, false; a democracy only for the rich, for the minority. The dictatorship of the proletariat, the period of transition to Communism, will, for the first time, produce democracy for the people, for the majority, side by side with the necessary suppression of the minority—the exploiters. Communism alone is capable of giving a really complete democracy, and the more complete it is the more quickly will it become unnecessary and wither away of itself.

In other words: under capitalism we have a state in the proper sense of the word, that is, special machinery for the suppression of one class by another, and of the majority by the minority at that. Naturally, for the successful discharge of such a task as the systematic suppression by the exploiting minority of the exploited majority, the greatest ferocity and savagery of suppression are required, seas of blood are required, through which mankind is marching in slavery, serfdom, and wage-labor.

Again, during the *transition* from capitalism to Communism, suppression is *still* necessary; but it is the suppression of the minority of exploiters by the majority of exploited. A special apparatus, special machinery for suppression, the "state," is *still* necessary, but this is now a transitional state, no longer a state in the usual sense, for the suppression of the minority of exploiters, by the majority of the wage-slaves of *yesterday*, is a matter comparatively so easy, simple and natural that it will cost far less bloodshed than the suppression of the risings of slaves, serfs or wage laborers, and will cost mankind far less. This is compatible with the diffusion of democracy among such an overwhelming majority of the population, that the need for *special machinery* of suppression will begin to disappear. The exploiters are, naturally, unable to suppress the people without a most complex machinery for performing this task; but *the people* can suppress the exploiters even with very simple "machinery," almost without any "machinery," without any special apparatus, by the simple *organisation of the armed masses* (such as the Soviets of Workers' and Soldiers' Deputies, we may remark, anticipating a little).

Finally, only Communism renders the state absolutely unnecessary, for there is *no one* to be suppressed—"no one" in the sense of a *class*, in the sense of a systematic struggle with a definite section of the population. We are not Utopians, and we do not in the least deny the possibility and inevitability of excesses on the part of *individual persons*, nor the need to suppress *such* excesses. But, in the first place, no special machinery, no special apparatus of repression is needed for this; this will be done by the armed people itself, as simply and as readily as any crowd of civilised people, even in modern society, parts a pair of combatants or does not allow a woman to be outraged. And, secondly, we know that the fundamental social cause of excesses which consist in violating the rules of social life is the exploitation of the masses, their want and their poverty. With the removal of this chief cause, excesses will inevitably begin to *"wither away."* We do not know how quickly and in what succession, but we know that they will wither away. With their withering away, the state will also *wither away*.

Without going into Utopias, Marx defined more fully what can *now* be defined regarding this future, namely, the difference between the lower and higher phases (degrees, stages) of Communist society.

.   .   .

Marx continues:

4.   *Higher Phase of Communist Society.*

    In a higher phase of Communist society, when the enslaving subordination of individuals in the division of labour has disappeared, and with it also the antagonism between mental and physical labour; when labour has become not only a means of living, but itself the first necessity of life; when, along with the all-round development of individuals, the productive forces too have grown, and all the springs of social wealth are flowing more freely—it is only at that stage that it will be possible to pass completely beyond the narrow horizon of bourgeois rights, and for society to inscribe on its banners: from each according to his ability; to each according to his needs!

Only now can we appreciate the full correctness of Engels' remarks in which he mercilessly ridiculed all the absurdity of combining the words "freedom" and "state." While the state exists there is no freedom. When there is freedom, there will be no state.

The economic basis for the complete withering away of the state is that high stage of development of Communism when the antagonism between mental and physical labour disappears, that is to say, when one of the principal sources of modern *social* inequality disappears—a source, moreover, which it is impossible to remove immediately by the mere conversion of the means of production into public property, by the mere expropriation of the capitalists.

This expropriation will make a gigantic development of the productive forces *possible*. And seeing how incredibly, even now, capitalism *retards* this development, how much progress could be made even on the basis of modern technique at the level it has reached, we have a right to say, with the fullest confidence, that the expropriation of the capitalists will inevitably result in a gigantic development of the productive forces of human society. But how rapidly this development will go forward, how soon it will reach the point of breaking away from the division of labour, of removing the antagonism between mental and physical labour, of transforming work into the "first necessity of life"—this we do not and *cannot* know.

Consequently, we have a right to speak solely of the inevitable withering away of the state, emphasising the protracted nature of this process and its dependence upon the rapidity of development of the *higher phase of* Communism; leaving quite open the question of lengths of time, or the concrete forms of withering away, since material for the solution of such questions is *not available*.

The state will be able to wither away completely when society has realised the rule: "From each according to his ability; to each according to his needs"; *i.e.*, when people have become accustomed to observe the fundamental rules of social life, and their labour is so productive, that they voluntarily work *according to their ability*. "The narrow horizon of bourgeois rights," which compels one to calculate, with the hard-heartedness of a Shylock, whether he has not worked half an hour more than another, whether he is not getting less pay than another—this narrow horizon will then be left behind. There will then be no need for any exact calculation by society of the quantity of products to be distributed to each of its members; each will take freely "according to his needs."

. . .

What is generally called Socialism was termed by Marx the "first" or lower phase of Communist society. In so far as the means of production became *public* property, the word "Communism" is also applicable here, providing we do not forget that it is *not* full Communism. The great significance of Marx's elucidations consists of this: that here, too, he consistently applied materialist dialectics, the doctrine of evolution, looking upon Communism as something which evolves *out* of capitalism. Instead of artificial, "elaborate," scholastic definitions and profitless disquisitions on the meaning of words (what Socialism is, what Communism is), Marx gives an analysis of what may be called stages in the economic ripeness of Communism.

In its first phase or first stage Communism *cannot* as yet be economically ripe and entirely free of all tradition and of all taint of capitalism. Hence the interesting phenomenon of Communism retaining, in its first phase, "the narrow horizon of bourgeois rights." Bourgeois rights, with respect to distribution of articles of *consumption*, inevitably presupposes, of course, the existence of the *bourgeois state*, for rights are nothing without an apparatus capable of *enforcing* the observance of the rights.

Consequently, for a certain time not only bourgeois rights, but even the bourgeois state remains under Communism, without the bourgeoisie!

This may look like a paradox, or simply a dialectical puzzle for which Marxism is often blamed by people who would not make the least effort to study its extraordinarily profound content.

But, as a matter of fact, the old surviving in the new confronts us in life at every step, in nature as well as in society. Marx did not smuggle a scrap of "bourgeois" rights into Communism of his own accord; he indicated what is economically and politically inevitable in a society issuing *from the womb* of capitalism.

Democracy is of great importance for the working class in its struggle for freedom against the capitalists. But democracy is by no means a limit one may not overstep; it is only one of the stages in the course of development from feudalism to capitalism, and from capitalism to Communism.

Democracy means equality. The great significance of the struggle of the proletariat for equality, and the significance of equality as a slogan, are apparent, if we correctly interpret it as meaning the abolition of *classes*. But democracy means only *formal* equality. Immediately after the attainment of equality for all members of society *in respect of* the ownership of the means of production, that is, of equality of labour and equality of wages, there will inevitably arise before humanity the question of going further from formal equality to real equality, *i.e.*, to realising the rule, "From each according to his ability; to each according to his needs." By what stages, by means of what practical measures humanity will proceed to this higher aim—this we do not and cannot know. But it is important to realise how infinitely mendacious is the usual bourgeois presentation of Socialism as something lifeless, petrified, fixed once for all, whereas in reality, it is *only* with Socialism that there will commence a rapid, genuine, real mass advance, in which first the *majority* and then the whole of the population will take part—an advance in all domains of social and individual life.

Democracy is a form of the state—one of its varieties. Consequently, like every other state, it consists in organised, systematic application of force against human beings. This on the one hand. On the other hand, however, it signifies the formal recognition of the equality of all citizens, the equal right of all to determine the structure and administration of the state. This, in turn, is connected with the fact that, at a certain stage in the development of democracy, it first rallies the proletariat as a revolutionary class against capitalism, and gives it an opportunity to crush, to smash to bits, to wipe off the face of the earth the bourgeois state machinery—even its republican variety: the standing army, the police, and bureaucracy; then it substitutes for all this a *more* democratic, but still a state machinery in the shape of armed masses of workers, which becomes transformed into universal participation of the people in the militia.

Here "quantity turns into quality": *such* a degree of democracy is bound up with the abandonment of the framework of bourgeois society, and the beginning of its Socialist reconstruction. If *every one* really takes part in the administration of the state, capitalism cannot retain its hold. In its turn, capitalism, as it develops, itself creates *prerequisites* for "every one" *to be able* really to take part in the administration of the state. Among such prerequisites are: universal literacy, already realised in most of the advanced capitalist countries, then the "training and disciplining" of millions of workers by the huge, complex, and socialised apparatus of the post-office, the railways, the big factories, large-scale commerce, banking, etc., etc.

With such *economic* prerequisites it is perfectly possible, immediately, within twenty-four hours after the overthrow of the capitalists and bureaucrats, to replace them, in the control of production and distribution, in the business of *control* of labour and products, by the armed workers, by the whole people in arms. (The question of control and accounting must not be confused with the question of the scientifically educated staff of engineers, agronomists, and so on. These gentlemen work today, obeying the capitalists; they will work even better tomorrow, obeying the armed workers.)

Accounting and control,—these are the *chief* things necessary for the organising and correct functioning of the *first phase* of Communist society. *All* citizens are here transformed into hired employees of the state, which is made up of the armed workers. *All* citizens become employees and workers of *one* national state "syndicate." All that is required is that they should work equally, should regularly do their share of work, and should receive equal pay. The accounting and control necessary for this have been *simplified* by capitalism to the utmost, till they have become the extraordinarily simple operations of watching, recording and issuing receipts, within the reach of anybody who can read and write and knows the first four rules of arithmetic.[1]

When the *majority* of the people begin everywhere to keep such accounts and maintain such control over the capitalists (now converted into employees) and over the intellectual gentry, who still retain capitalist habits, this control will really become universal, general, national; and there will be no way of getting away from it, there will be "nowhere to go."

The whole of society will have become one office and one factory, with equal work and equal pay.

But this "factory" discipline, which the proletariat will extend to the whole of society after the defeat of the capitalists and the overthrow of the exploiters, is by no means our ideal, or our final aim. It is but a *foothold* necessary for the radical cleansing of society of all the hideousness and foulness of capitalist exploitation, *in order to advance further*.

From the moment when all members of society, or even only the overwhelming majority, have learned how to govern the state *themselves*, have taken this business into their own hands, have "established" control over the insignificant minority of capitalists, over the gentry with capitalist leanings, and the workers thoroughly demoralised by capitalism—from this moment the need for any government begins to disappear. The more complete the democracy, the nearer the moment when it begins to be unnecessary. The more democratic the "state" consisting of armed workers, which is "no longer a state in the proper sense of the word," the more rapidly does *every* state begin to wither away.

For when *all* have learned to manage, and independently are actually managing by themselves social production, keeping accounts, controlling the idlers, the gentlefolk, the swindlers and similar "guardians of capitalist traditions," then the escape from this national accounting and control will inevitably become so increasingly difficult, such a rare exception, and will probably be accompanied by such swift and severe punishment (for armed workers are men of practical life, not sentimental intellectuals, and they will scarcely allow any one to trifle with them), that very soon the *necessity* of observing the simple, fundamental rules of everyday social life in common will have become a *habit*.

The door will then be wide open for the transition from the first phase of Communist society to its higher phase, and along with it to the complete withering away of the state.

---

[1]When most of the functions of the state are reduced to this accounting and control by the workers themselves, then it ceases to be a "political state," and the "public functions will lose their political character and be transformed into simple administrative functions."

W. E. B. Du Bois

W. E. B. Du Bois's (1868–1963) life was defined by the struggle of African Americans for an equal place in American society. Born just three years after the end of the Civil War, Du Bois lived to witness the civil rights movements of the 1950s and 1960s. The first African American to receive a doctorate from Harvard, Du Bois founded the National Association for the Advancement of Colored People (NAACP) and was the editor of its journal *Crisis*. Du Bois did not see the cause of civil rights for African Americans as a problem of interest to that group alone. Rather, Du Bois believed that racism was a poison that had infected all of American society. As he stated in his foreword to *The Souls of Black Folk*, "the problem of the Twentieth Century, is the problem of the color-line."

The Souls of Black Folk, from which the excerpt included here was taken, was Du Bois's effort to show his readers "the strange meaning of being black ... at the dawning of the Twentieth Century." In the section that follows entitled "Of the Sorrow Songs," Du Bois sketched the meaning and importance of African-American folksongs to American life as a whole. As you read the passage, pay close attention to Du Bois's vision of American history. What version of American history was he implicitly critiquing? What were the implications of his rhetorical question, "Would America have been America without her Negro People"?

Consider the following questions as you study the text below.

1. According to Du Bois, how should African-American folksong be interpreted? In his view, what light did such songs shed on American history?

2. How did Du Bois respond to the assertion that the status of African Americans in the early twentieth century was a simple reflection of racial inferiority? Why was he unconvinced by contemporary notions of historical progress?

The Souls of Black Folk

I walk through the churchyard To lay this body down;
I know moon-rise, I know star-rise;
I walk in the moonlight, I walk in the starlight;
I'll lie in the grave and stretch out my arms,
I'll go to judgment in the evening of the day,
And my soul and thy soul shall meet that day, When I lay this body down.

NEGRO SONG.

They that walked in darkness sang songs in the olden days—Sorrow Songs—for they were weary at heart. And so before each thought that I have written in this book I have set a phrase, a haunting echo of these weird old songs in which the soul of the black slave spoke to men. Ever since I was a child these songs have stirred me strangely. They came out of the South unknown to me, one by one, and yet at once I knew them as of me and of mine. Then in after years when I came to Nashville I saw the great temple builded of these songs towering over the pale city. To me Jubilee Hall seemed ever made of the songs themselves, and its bricks were red with the blood and dust of toil. Out of them rose for me morning, noon, and night, bursts of wonderful melody, full of the voices of my brothers and sisters, full of the voices of the past.

Little of beauty has America given the world save the rude grandeur God himself stamped on her bosom; the human spirit in this new world has expressed itself in vigor and ingenuity rather than in beauty. And so by fateful chance the Negro folk-song—the rhythmic cry of the slave—stands to-day not simply as the sole American music, but as the most beautiful expression of human experience born this side the seas. It has been neglected, it has been, and is, half despised, and above all it has been persistently mistaken and misunderstood; but notwithstanding, it still remains as the singular spiritual heritage of the nation and the greatest gift of the Negro people. ...

W. E. B. Du Bois, *The Souls of Black Folk* (Chicago: A. C. McClurg, 1903).

What are these songs, and what do they mean? I know little of music and can say nothing in technical phrase, but I know something of men, and knowing them, I know that these songs are the articulate message of the slave to the world. They tell us in these eager days that life was joyous to the black slave, careless and happy. I can easily believe this of some, of many. But not all the past South, though it rose from the dead, can gainsay the heart-touching witness of these songs. They are the music of an unhappy people, of the children of disappointment; they tell of death and suffering and unvoiced longing toward a truer world, of misty wanderings and hidden ways.

The songs are indeed the siftings of centuries; the music is far more ancient than the words, and in it we can trace here and there signs of development. My grandfather's grandmother was seized by an evil Dutch trader two centuries ago; and coming to the valleys of the Hudson and Housatonic, black, little, and lithe, she shivered and shrank in the harsh north winds, looked longingly at the hills, and often crooned a heathen melody to the child between her knees, thus:

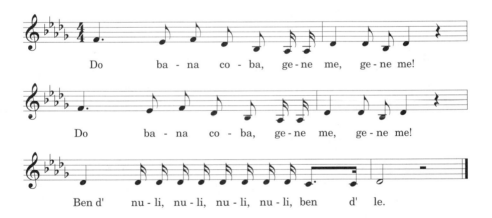

The child sang it to his children and they to their children's children, and so two hundred years it has travelled down to us and we sing it to our children, knowing as little as our fathers what its words may mean, but knowing well the meaning of its music.

This was primitive African music; it may be seen in larger form in the strange chant which heralds "The Coming of John":

"You may bury me in the East,
You may bury me in the West,
But I'll hear the trumpet sound in that morning,"
—the voice of exile. ...

Through all the sorrow of the Sorrow Songs there breathes a hope—a faith in the ultimate justice of things. The minor cadences of despair change often to triumph and calm confidence. Sometimes it is faith in life, sometimes a faith in death, sometimes assurance of boundless justice in some fair world beyond. But whichever it is, the meaning is always clear: that sometime, somewhere, men will judge men by their souls and not by their skins. Is such a hope justified? Do the Sorrow Songs sing true?

The silently growing assumption of this age is that the probation of races is past, and that the backward races of to-day are of proven inefficiency and not worth the saving. Such an assumption is the arrogance of peoples irreverent toward Time and ignorant of the deeds of men. A thousand years ago such an assumption, easily possible, would have made it difficult for the Teuton to prove his right to life. Two thousand years ago such dogmatism, readily welcome, would have scouted the idea of blond races ever leading civilization. So wofully unorganized is sociological knowledge that the meaning of progress, the meaning of "swift" and "slow" in human doing, and the limits of human perfectability, are veiled, unanswered sphinxes on the shores of science. Why should Æschylus have sung two thousand years before Shakespeare was born? Why has civilization flourished in Europe, and flickered, flamed, and died in Africa? So long as the world stands meekly dumb before such questions, shall this nation proclaim its ignorance and unhallowed prejudices by denying freedom of opportunity to those who brought the Sorrow Songs to the Seats of the Mighty?

Your country? How came it yours? Before the Pilgrims landed we were here. Here we have brought our three gifts and mingled them with yours: a gift of story and song—soft, stirring melody in an ill-harmonized and unmelodious land; the gift of sweat and brawn to beat back the wilderness, conquer the soil, and lay the foundations of this vast economic empire two hundred years earlier than your weak hands could have done it; the third, a gift of the Spirit. Around us the history of the land has centred for thrice a hundred years; out of the nation's heart we have called all that was best to throttle and subdue all that was worst; fire and blood, prayer and sacrifice, have billowed over this people, and they have found peace only in the altars of the God of Right. Nor has our gift of the Spirit been merely passive. Actively we have woven ourselves with the very warp and woof of this nation,—we fought their battles, shared their sorrow, mingled our blood with theirs, and generation after generation have pleaded with a headstrong, careless people to despise not Justice, Mercy, and Truth, lest the nation be smitten with a curse. Our song, our toil, our cheer, and warning have been given to this nation in blood-brotherhood. Are not these gifts worth the giving? Is not this work and striving? Would America have been America without her Negro people?

Even so is the hope that sang in the songs of my fathers well sung. If somewhere in this whirl and chaos of things there dwells Eternal Good, pitiful yet masterful, then anon in His good time America shall rend the Veil and the prisoned shall go free. Free, free as the sunshine trickling down the morning into these high windows of mine, free as yonder fresh young voices welling up to me from the caverns of brick and mortar below—swelling with song, instinct with life, tremulous treble and darkening bass. My children, my little children, are singing to the sunshine, and thus they sing:

And the traveller girds himself, and sets his face toward the Morning, and goes his way.

Marquis Childs

The Wall Street stock-market crash on Black Thursday (October 24, 1929) marked a major turning point in American history. The Roaring Twenties came to an abrupt and dramatic end and a new era—the Great Depression—was ushered in. Although the Depression lasted approximately a decade and engulfed the entire world, its worst years in the United States coincided with the administration of President Herbert Hoover (1929—1933). The magnitude of the worldwide economic collapse is clearly revealed in the statistics: It is estimated that between 1929 and 1932, total world production decreased by 38 percent and international trade fell by two thirds. During the same years, the national income of the United States declined from $85 billion to $37 billion. Although everyone was affected to some extent, those who suffered most were the "little people," particularly small farmers and industrial workers. Unemployment became massive and chronic: During the depths of the Depression in the United States alone, thirteen million workers out of a labor force of approximately fifty million were without jobs. Worse still, the unemployed remained without work not simply for weeks or months but in many cases for several years. In our great cities the bread line and the soup kitchen became familiar sights.

Estimates of the total economic loss caused by the depression have ranged as high as $200 billion (equivalent to several trillion dollars in today's money). Less easily calculable but more lastingly important was the harm caused by human suffering, loss of self-respect, and increasing disillusionment with democratic institutions. Although democracy survived the Depression in America, in Europe it was not so fortunate. Of crucial importance was the collapse of the Weimar Republic in Germany and the rise to power of Adolf Hitler and the Nazis, which in turn helped set in motion a series of events that culminated in World War II.

To illustrate the Great Depression we have chosen a brief but vivid description of its effects on a typical midwestern town, written by the social and political commentator Marquis Childs (1903—1990). The title of the selection is derived from that of Sinclair Lewis's well-known novel about American small-town life at the beginning of the twenties—*Main Street*.

Consider the following questions as you study the text below.

1. Describe Childs's vision of small town morality. In his view, what impact did the Depression have on social mores?

2. Does Childs offer any hope for the future? What did he hope his readers would take away from "Main Street Ten Years After"?

Main Street Ten Years After

The casual visitor viewing Melrose for the first time in four years would observe few changes. There are the current phenomena of the depression, empty stores, For Rent signs, smokeless factories, closing-out sales. But on a fine summer evening, an endless procession of cars, and many of them are new, passes out along Washington Boulevard to the Spring Valley Highway. And on any Saturday afternoon, the group waiting to drive off from the first tee at the country club is apparently as large as ever, as jovial, as well fed, as carefree. There is, however, a startling disparity between this familiar surface and what is really happening as a result of the depression.

This town of nineteen thousand, located in a rich farming community, might be anywhere in the Middle West, Minnesota, Ohio, Iowa, Illinois. Along with the other Main Streets, it had its boom, a whole series of booms. There was the War, with fat contracts for the steel-castings company and the wire-cloth factory. It was in 1924 that Main Street was made Main Avenue, paved drives were put through Sunset Park, the new half-million-dollar high school was finished and the Kiwanis public golf links and swimming pool were opened. Then came the stock-market boom.

The majority in Melrose were not lured away from rock-ribbed safety—savings banks and real-estate bonds. The collapse of the banks and the bonds the bankers sold was the immediate cause of the deflation in Melrose. School teachers, insurance salesmen, small wage earners, dentists, retired farmers, saw life savings disappear, security vanish. An entire generation, with striking exceptions, has been stripped; and not by some remote force a thousand miles away but, so the reasoning is, by the man who used to live in the big house on the corner of South Main Avenue and Washington Boulevard.

What is surprising is the passive resignation with which the blow has been accepted; this awful pretense that seeks to conceal the mortal wound, to carry on as though it were still the best possible of all worlds. Before the depression, one of the principal pleasures was to discover how much one's neighbor was spending; now the game is to find out how much he has lost and how he is standing his losses. This curiosity is almost a form of psychopathology; sympathy is all too often an ill concealed form of triumph, a kind of "Thank God, someone is worse off than we are."

Marquis Childs, "Main Street Ten Years After," *New Republic*, 73 (1932–33), 263–65.

The First National Bank of Melrose was the first to go. There was no warning; in the middle of the banking day the doors were closed by the examiners. It was one of the oldest banks in the state, regarded as a branch of the United States Treasury. Within two or three hours everyone knew of the disaster. Depositors, stunned and disbelieving, gathered in small groups to read the notice on the door. There were wild rumors. It was said that Mr. Johnson, the new president, had fled to Canada with his blonde secretary. Someone brought a report that the closing was only temporary, someone else spread word that there would be nothing left for the depositors. The other three banks, forewarned, withstood heavy runs.

There was little public lamentation. The most shocking example was old Mrs. Gearman. She beat with her fists upon the closed plate-glass doors and screamed and sobbed without restraint. She had in a savings account the $2,000 from her husband's insurance and $963 she had saved over a period of twenty-five-years from making rag rugs. Nothing was left but charity. For a week neighbors did not see her. A policeman found her sitting in the middle of the kitchen of her small, scrubbed house. They took her to the insane asylum a few days afterward.

Others were more successful in concealing the tragic extent of their losses. For fifty-two years Amy Blanshard taught the fourth grade. Her sister kept house for her. They lived in the upper half of the old Blanshard home, renting the lower half. Amy had more than $11,000 in a savings account in the First National Bank. On a salary which was never more than a thousand dollars a year, it is plain what heroic economies this must have required. As a direct result of the closing, twelve families, most of them elderly couples, were forced onto the county. School children had on deposit about $25,000 in small accounts; these were repaid in full before any other claims "to retain the faith of the youngest generation in our banks."

There were charges and countercharges. It was said that all the directors withdrew their deposits before the bank failed and that more important businessmen were warned, too. In the first bitter reaction there was talk of criminal prosecution against one director, Davis, who according to rumor, succeeded in tapping the bank before it collapsed, for a sum greater than the amount of his stock. There was a public meeting in the armory which ended on a note of reassurance from President Johnson. There would be sufficient assets to cover virtually the entire amount on deposit at the time of the bank's closing. Gradually the whispered rumors were forgotten.

"Do you see any of the bankers themselves ruined?" Jeffery Fagan demands, with fire in his eye. (He dropped $17,000.) "They're still riding around in their big cars. I can remember the day when it was the banker that went to the poorhouse and the depositors got their money. It takes about as much brains and honesty to run a bank now as it used to take to run a peanut stand." This last is a concise expression of opinion in Melrose. The spectacle of the Davises whizzing about in their expensive car is not one to cheer the losers. Reason has no part in this reaction; the fact that the capitalization of the bank was absurdly low and Davis' share of the stock only a small percentage of the total of deposits is not considered. What no one can forget is that only 31 percent of the deposits were paid after a delay of eight months. The prospect for a further dividend is slight.

The collapse of the Merchants' Bank and Trust Company was less spectacular. It had long been weak, and when a plan to merge it with the Melrose National Bank failed, it wilted away. There were other calamities to take public attention. One was the failure of the Ryder Furniture and Carpet Company. Like the First National Bank, it had been regarded as a Gibraltar of stability. Edward Ryder represented the third generation in the business; the Ryder store occupied one of the four principal corners at Main and Washington. After the grand closing-out sale, people were not slow to discover that the Ryders had nothing left. The bank got the property, tore down the old building and put up a new one that is occupied by a chain clothing store.

The Ryders themselves offered a more complex problem which no one undertook to solve. The envious said they had long lived beyond their means and it served them right. Mrs. Ryder sold Chevrolets until she exhausted the roster of her friends. The town watched them slip from one subterfuge to another, recalling with little charity the days when the Ryders went on Mediterranean cruises and Bermudan holidays. They lost their home on South Main Avenue. For a time, an aged aunt sent money for apartment rent. When this failed, the Ryders took refuge in a friend's third floor. There were stories. People said that while she ate at the Busy Bee Cafe, he waited outside in the car and she brought out what she could in a paper napkin; that for three days he lived on peanuts from a penny slot machine. He grows thinner and grayer; she tries to maintain the surface pretense.

Perhaps the most appalling blow of all was reserved for early in 1932. R. William McSwirtle was in more ways than one the town's leading citizen. The Melrose National Bank was long known as McSwirtle's bank. He was the personification of the small-town Middle Western banker, gray, respectable, shiny, with cold, fish-colored eyes concealed behind pince-nez, and a pompous smile. The very sight of this pious man was for a long time enough to reassure depositors. He was the chief angel of the Episcopal Church. Not a young boy in the past thirty years has escaped hearing R. William's famous lecture, "Banks and the Churches."

But there were rumors about his bank all through the fall and winter of 1931. The women of the town drew most assurance from the fact that the McSwirtle household was maintained on the same scale as before. R. William certainly tried. He even fought off another threatening run. But the end was close at hand. Early in March of this year The Melrose Advocate announced he had resigned as president of the bank, because of ill health, but would continue in an advisory capacity. Two days later the bank failed and R. William left for parts unknown.

It developed that he had looted the bank of some $300,000. In addition he had extracted about $100,000 from various personal accounts. He had managed the finances of a number of persons of comparatively large income: Dr. Maxwell, the leading surgeon; a half-dozen of the more prosperous professors at Cremona College; old Mrs. Tompkins. Shock followed upon shock until it seemed that God himself had fallen from his throne. Mrs. McSwirtle, Dorothy and young Ted had signed for R. William a number of mysterious papers which proved to be promissory notes. The late neo-Georgian home on South Main Avenue, Dorothy's undyed sealskin coat, the new Packard convertible coupe, everything melted away and the McSwirtles sought shelter with relatives in Decatur.

It is impossible to convey the blasting effect this had upon Melrose. The City National, the only remaining bank, promptly called a thirty-day moratorium on deposits above $100 and convinced the town that, as is true today, it would be possible to pay off every depositor in full in cash. "But," the president added grimly, "we wouldn't have any bank left." Two of the directors of this bank died of nervous strain. ...

Even to maintain a pretense of the old standard has become a desperate kind of endurance contest for many. A number have succumbed; they have given up, withdrawing from the social and economic life of the town in a kind of living death, pariahs, outcasts, disregarded in even the humblest councils. Their condition is more fortunate than that of those who still struggle. It is, in a sense, as though the whole town were entrenched behind a false front. How much longer they will be able to hold out is a question that no one dares to ask—openly. There is now little consolation in knowing that Chestnut Springs, with all its banks and all its furniture factories closed, is in a worse condition. With the majority, the battle is too grim for such easy consolations. There is small solace in the plight of the Fergusons next door; their condition is prophetic. What will happen next spring Melrose does not venture to guess; next month is too close at hand.

John Dewey

For the first half of the twentieth century, the American intellectual scene was dominated by the figure of John Dewey (1859–1952). Born of a family whose roots reached back to the early colonial days of New England, Dewey became interested in philosophy while attending the University of Vermont. After finishing college, he entered graduate school at Johns Hopkins University to study for his doctorate in philosophy. There, as almost everywhere else in late-nineteenth-century America, the dominant philosophy was the absolute idealism of Hegel. Although Dewey accepted Hegelian idealism for a time, he soon gave it up in favor of the pragmatic philosophy of the great American philosopher William James (1842–1910).

Pragmatism, as developed first by James and later more fully by Dewey, was an attempt to find a basis for philosophy in the experimental method employed by the empirical sciences. During the preceding three hundred years, scientists had achieved phenomenal results through experimentation. Dewey believed that the use of this same method could lead to similar advances in every field of intellectual endeavor. This conviction became the foundation for Dewey's pragmatic philosophy, which rested on two basic theses: (1) that the truth or validity of any hypothesis depends on the results it produces when it is put into practice; and therefore, (2) that experimental verification is the ideal method for attaining truth and hence for solving problems in all areas of life and thought.

In the selection that follows, Dewey uses the theory of pragmatism to attack one of the great issues of contemporary politics. The problem with which he is concerned is evident from the title of the book from which the selection is taken, *Liberalism and Social Action*. Historically, the liberal movement (particularly with such writers as John Locke and Jeremy Bentham) had stood for a minimum of social action by government agencies. Even John Stuart Mill, though he had begun to have doubts, still believed that the liberty of the individual must be preserved from the encroachment of government. But Dewey, writing in the middle of the Great Depression of the thirties, recognized that the policy of laissez-faire was no longer viable in the twentieth century. The problem, as he saw it, was this: How can one preserve the human liberty in which liberals believe, yet admit the need for society to act on behalf of its members? His answer is reproduced in the following selection, taken from the final chapter of his book.

Consider the following questions as you study the text below.

1. Compare and contrast Dewey and Marx's definition of the word "revolution." Why did Dewey believe that revolution was a constant process?

2. For Dewey, what was the purpose of the social and economic order? How could a rational and productive order be achieved?

Liberalism and Social Action

. . .

RENASCENT LIBERALISM

Nothing is blinder than the supposition that we live in a society and world so static that either nothing new will happen or else it will happen because of the use of violence. Social change is here as a fact, a fact having multifarious forms and marked in intensity. Changes that are revolutionary in effect are in process in every phase of life. Transformations in the family, the church, the school, in science and art, in economic and political relations, are occurring so swiftly that imagination is baffled in attempt to lay hold of them. Flux does not have to be created. But it does have to be directed. It has to be so controlled that it will move to some end in accordance with the principles of life, since life itself is development. Liberalism is committed to an end that is at once enduring and flexible: the liberation of individuals so that realization of their capacities may be the law of their life. It is committed to the use of freed intelligence as the method of directing change. In any case, civilization is faced with the problem of uniting the changes that are going on into a coherent pattern of social organization. The liberal spirit is marked by its own picture of the pattern that is required: a social organization that will make possible effective liberty and opportunity for personal growth in mind and spirit in all individuals. Its present need is recognition that established material security is a prerequisite of the ends which it cherishes, so that, the basis of life being secure, individuals may actively share in the wealth of cultural resources that now exist and may contribute, each in his own way, to their further enrichment.

The fact of change has been so continual and so intense that it overwhelms our minds. We are bewildered by the spectacle of its rapidity, scope and intensity. It is not surprising that men have protected themselves from the impact of such vast change by resorting to what psychoanalysis has taught us to call rationalizations, in other words, protective fantasies. The Victorian idea that change is a part of an evolution that necessarily leads through successive stages to some preordained divine far-off event is one rationalization. The conception of a sudden, complete, almost catastrophic, transformation, to be brought about by the victory of the proletariat over the class now dominant, is a similar rationalization. But men have met the impact of change in the realm of actuality, mostly by drift and by temporary, usually incoherent, improvisations. Liberalism, like every theory of life, has suffered from the state of confused uncertainty that is the lot of a world suffering from rapid and varied change for which there is no intellectual and moral preparation.

Because of this lack of mental and moral preparation the impact of swiftly moving changes produced, as I have just said, confusion, uncertainty, and drift. Change in patterns of belief, desire and purpose has lagged behind the modification of the external conditions under which men associate. Industrial habits have changed most rapidly; there has followed at considerable distance, change in political relations; alterations in legal relations and methods have lagged even more, while changes in the institutions that deal most directly with patterns of thought and belief have taken place to the least extent. This fact defines the primary, though not by any means the ultimate, responsibility of a liberalism that intends to be a vital force. Its work is first of all education, in the broadest sense of that term. Schooling is a part of the work of education, but education in its full meaning includes all the influences that go to form the attitudes and dispositions (of desire as well as of belief), which constitute dominant habits of mind and character.

.   .   .

When, then, I say that the first object of a renascent liberalism is education, I mean that its task is to aid in producing the habits of mind and character, the intellectual and moral patterns, that are somewhere near even with the actual movements of events. It is, I repeat, the split between the latter as they have externally occurred and the ways of desiring, thinking, and of putting emotion and purpose into execution that is the basic cause of present confusion in mind and paralysis in action. The educational task cannot be accomplished merely by working upon men's minds, without action that effects actual change in institutions. The idea that dispositions and attitudes can be altered by merely "moral" means conceived of as something that goes on wholly inside of persons is itself one of the old patterns that has to be changed. Thought, desire and purpose exist in a constant give and take of interaction with environing conditions. But resolute thought is the first step in that change of action that will itself carry further the needed change in patterns of mind and character.

In short, liberalism must now become radical, meaning by "radical" perception of the necessity of thoroughgoing changes in the setup of institutions and corresponding activity to bring the changes to pass. For the gulf between what the actual situation makes possible and the actual state itself is so great that it cannot be bridged by piecemeal policies undertaken *ad hoc*. The process of producing the changes will be, in any case, a gradual one. But "reforms" that deal now with this abuse and now with that without having a social goal based upon an inclusive plan, differ entirely from effort at reforming, in its literal sense, the institutional scheme of things. The liberals of more than a century ago were denounced in their time as subversive radicals, and only when the new economic order was established did they become apologists for the *status quo* or else content with social patchwork. If radicalism be defined as perception of need for radical change, then today any liberalism which is not also radicalism is irrelevant and doomed.

But radicalism also means, in the minds of many, both supporters and opponents, dependence upon use of violence as the main method of effecting drastic changes. Here the liberal parts company. For he is committed to the organization of intelligent action as the chief method. Any frank discussion of the issue must recognize the extent to which those who decry the use of any violence are themselves willing to resort to violence and are ready to put their will into operation. Their fundamental objection is to change in the economic institution that now exists, and for its maintenance they resort to the use of the force that is placed in their hands by this very institution. They do not need to advocate the use of force; their only need is to employ it. Force, rather than intelligence, is built into the procedures of the existing social system, regularly as coercion, in times of crisis as overt violence. The legal system, conspicuously in its penal aspect, more subtly in civil practice, rests upon coercion. Wars are the methods recurrently used in settlement of disputes between nations. One school of radicals dwells upon the fact that in the past the transfer of power in one society has either been accomplished by or attended with violence. But what we need to realize is that physical force is used, at least in the form of coercion, in the very set-up of our society. That the competitive system, which was thought of by early liberals as the means by which the latent abilities of individuals were to be evoked and directed into socially useful channels, is now in fact a state of scarcely disguised battle hardly needs to be dwelt upon. That the control of the means of production by the few in legal possession operates as a standing agency of coercion of the many, may need emphasis in statement, but is surely evident to one who is willing to observe and honestly report the existing scene. It is foolish to regard the political state as the only agency now endowed with coercive power. Its exercise of this power is pale in contrast with that exercised by concentrated and organized property interests.

It is not surprising in view of our standing dependence upon the use of coercive force that at every time of crisis coercion breaks out into open violence. In this country, with its tradition of violence fostered by frontier conditions and by the conditions under which immigration went on during the greater part of our history, resort to violence is especially recurrent on the part of those who are in power. In times of imminent change, our verbal and sentimental worship of the Constitution, with its guarantees of civil liberties of expression, publication and assemblage, readily goes overboard. Often the officials of the law are the worst offenders, acting as agents of some power that rules the economic life of a community. What is said about the value of free speech as a safety valve is then forgotten with the utmost of ease: a comment, perhaps, upon the weakness of the defense of freedom of expression that values it simply as a means of blowing-off steam.

It is not pleasant to face the extent to which, as matter of fact, coercive and violent force is relied upon in the present social system as a means of social control. It is much more agreeable to evade the fact. But unless the fact is acknowledged as a fact in its full depth and breadth, the meaning of dependence upon intelligence as the alternative method of social direction will not be grasped. Failure in acknowledgment signifies, among other things, failure to realize that those who propagate the dogma of dependence upon force have the sanction of much that is already entrenched in the existing system. They would but turn the use of it to opposite ends. The assumption that the method of intelligence already rules and that those who urge the use of violence are introducing a new element into the social picture may not be hypocritical but it is unintelligently unaware of what is actually involved in intelligence as an alternative method of social action.

. . .

Intelligence in politics when it is identified with discussion means reliance upon symbols. The invention of language is probably the greatest single invention achieved by humanity. The development of political forms that promote the use of symbols in place of arbitrary power was another great invention. The nineteenth-century establishment of parliamentary institutions, written constitutions and the suffrage as means of political rule, is a tribute to the power of symbols. But symbols are significant only in connection with realities behind them. No intelligent observer can deny, I think, that they are often used in party politics as a substitute for realities instead of as means of contact with them. Popular literacy, in connection with the telegraph, cheap postage and the printing press, has enormously multiplied the number of those influenced. That which we term education has done a good deal to generate habits that put symbols in the place of realities. The forms of popular government make necessary the elaborate use of words to influence political action. "Propaganda" is the inevitable consequence of the combination of these influences and it extends to every area of life. Words not only take the place of realities but are themselves debauched. Decline in the prestige of suffrage and of parliamentary government is intimately associated with the belief, manifest in practice even if not expressed in words, that intelligence is an individual possession to be reached by means of verbal persuasion.

This fact suggests, by way of contrast, the genuine meaning of intelligence in connection with public opinion, sentiment and action. The crisis in democracy demands the substitution of the intelligence that is exemplified in scientific procedure for the kind of intelligence that is now accepted. The need for this change is not exhausted in the demand for greater honesty and impartiality, even though these qualities be now corrupted by discussion carried on mainly for purposes of party supremacy and for imposition of some special but concealed interest. These qualities need to be restored. But the need goes further. The social use of intelligence would remain deficient even if these moral traits were exalted, and yet intelligence continued to be identified simply with discussion and persuasion, necessary as are these things. Approximation to use of scientific method in investigation and of the engineering mind in the invention and projection of far-reaching social plans is demanded. The habit of considering social realities in terms of cause and effect and social policies in terms of means and consequences is still inchoate. The contrast between the state of intelligence in politics and in the physical control of nature is to be taken literally. What has happened in this latter is the outstanding demonstration of the meaning of organized intelligence. The combined effect of science and technology has released more productive energies in a bare hundred years than stands to the credit of prior human history in its entirety. Productively it has multiplied nine million times in the last generation alone. The prophetic vision of Francis Bacon of subjugation of the energies of nature through change in methods of inquiry has well-nigh been realized. The stationary engine, the locomotive, the dynamo, the motor car, turbine, telegraph, telephone, radio and moving picture are not the products of either isolated individual minds nor of the particular economic regime called capitalism. They are the fruit of methods that first penetrated to the working causalities of nature and then utilized the resulting knowledge in bold imaginative ventures of invention and construction.

We hear a great deal in these days about class conflict. The past history of man is held up to us as almost exclusively a record of struggles between classes, ending in the victory of a class that had been oppressed and the transfer of power to it. It is difficult to avoid reading the past in terms of the contemporary scene. Indeed, fundamentally it is impossible to avoid this course. With a certain proviso, it is highly important that we are compelled to follow this path. For the past as past is gone, save for esthetic enjoyment and refreshment, while the present is with us. Knowledge of the past is significant only as it deepens and extends our understanding of the present. Yet there is a proviso. We must grasp the things that are most important in the present when we turn to the past and not allow ourselves to be misled by secondary phenomena no matter how intense and immediately urgent they are. Viewed from this standpoint, the rise of scientific method and of technology based upon it is the genuinely active force in producing the vast complex of changes the world is now undergoing, not the class struggle whose spirit and method are opposed to science. If we lay hold upon the causal force exercised by this embodiment of intelligence we shall know where to turn for the means of directing further change.

When I say that scientific method and technology have been the active force in producing the revolutionary transformations society is undergoing, I do not imply no other forces have been at work to arrest, deflect and corrupt their operation. Rather this fact is positively implied. At this point, indeed, is located the conflict that underlies the confusions and uncertainties of the present scene. The conflict is between institutions and habits originating in the pre-scientific and pre-technological age and the new forces generated by science and technology. The application of science, to a considerable degree, even its own growth, has been conditioned by the system to which the name of capitalism is given, a rough designation of a complex of political and legal arrangements centering about a particular mode of economic relations. Because of the conditioning of science and technology by this setting, the second and humanly most important part of Bacon's prediction has so far largely missed realization. The conquest of natural energies has not accrued to the betterment of the common human estate in anything like the degree he anticipated.

Because of conditions that were set by the legal institutions and the moral ideas existing when the scientific and industrial revolutions came into being, the chief usufruct of the latter has been appropriated by a relatively small class. Industrial entrepreneurs have reaped out of all proportion to what they sowed. By obtaining private ownership of the means of production and exchange they deflected a considerable share of the results of increased productivity to their private pockets. This appropriation was not the fruit of criminal conspiracy or of sinister intent. It was sanctioned not only by legal institutions of age-long standing but by the entire prevailing moral code. The institution of private property long antedated feudal times. It is the institution with which men have lived, with few exceptions, since the dawn of civilization. Its existence has deeply impressed itself upon mankind's moral conceptions. Moreover, the new industrial forces tended to break down many of the rigid class barriers that had been in force, and to give to millions a new outlook and inspire a new hope;—especially in this country with no feudal background and no fixed class system.

Since the legal institutions and the patterns of mind characteristic of ages of civilization still endure, there exists the conflict that brings confusion

308 The Contemporary World

into every phase of present life. The problem of bringing into being a new social orientation and organization is, when reduced to its ultimates, the problem of using the new resources of production, made possible by the advance
of physical science, for social ends, for what Bentham called the greatest
good of the greatest number. Institutional relationships fixed in the pre-scientific age stand in the way of accomplishing this great transformation. Lag
in mental and moral patterns provides the bulwark of the older institutions;
in expressing the past they still express present beliefs, outlooks and purposes. Here is the place where the problem of liberalism centers today.

. . .

It is true that in this country, because of the interpretations made by
courts of a written constitution, our political institutions are unusually in-
flexible. It is also true, as well as even more important (because it is a factor
in causing this rigidity) that our institutions, democratic in form, tend to
favor in substance a privileged plutocracy. Nevertheless, it is sheer defeatism
to assume in advance of actual trial that democratic political institutions are
incapable either of further development or of constructive social application.
Even as they now exist, the forms of representative government are poten-
tially capable of expressing the public will when that assumes anything like
unification. And there is nothing inherent in them that forbids their supple-
mentation by political agencies that represent definitely economic social
interests, like those of producers and consumers.

The final argument in behalf of the use of intelligence is that as are the
means used so are the actual ends achieved—that is, the consequences. I
know of no greater fallacy than the claim of those who hold to the dogma of
the necessity of brute force that its use will be the method of calling genuine
democracy into existence—of which they profess themselves the simon-pure
adherents. It requires an unusually credulous faith in the Hegelian dialectic
of opposites to think that all of a sudden the use of force by a class will be
transmuted into a democratic classless society. Force breeds counterforce;
the Newtonian law of action and reaction still holds in physics, and violence
is physical. To profess democracy as an ultimate ideal and the suppression of
democracy as a means to the ideal may be possible in a country that has
never known even rudimentary democracy, but when professed in a country
that has anything of a genuine democratic spirit in its traditions, it signifies
desire for possession and retention of power by a class, whether that class be
called Fascist or Proletarian. In the light of what happens in nondemocratic
countries, it is pertinent to ask whether the rule of a class signifies the dictatorship of the majority, or dictatorship over the chosen class by a minority
party; whether dissenters are allowed even within the class the party claims
to represent; and whether the development of literature and the other arts
proceeds according to a formula prescribed by a party in conformity with a

doctrinaire dogma of history and of infallible leadership, or whether artists are free from regimentation? Until these questions are satisfactorily answered, it is permissible to look with considerable suspicion upon those who assert that suppression of democracy is the road to the adequate establishment of genuine democracy. The one exception—and that apparent rather than real—to dependence upon organized intelligence as the method for directing social change is found when society through an authorized majority has entered upon the path of social experimentation leading to great social change, and a minority refuses by force to permit the method of intelligent action to go into effect. Then force may be intelligently employed to subdue and disarm the recalcitrant minority.

There may be some who think I am unduly dignifying a position held by a comparatively small group by taking their arguments as seriously as I have done. But their position serves to bring into strong relief the alternatives before us. It makes clear the meaning of renascent liberalism. The alternatives are continuation of drift with attendant improvisations to meet special emergencies; dependence upon violence; dependence upon socially organized intelligence. The first two alternatives, however, are not mutually exclusive, for if things are allowed to drift, the result may be some sort of social change effected by the use of force, whether so planned or not. Upon the whole, the recent policy of liberalism has been to further "social legislation"; that is, measures which add performance of social services to the older functions of government. The value of this addition is not to be despised. It marks a decided move away from *laissez-faire* liberalism, and has considerable importance in educating the public mind to a realization of the possibilities of organized social control. It has helped to develop some of the techniques that in any case will be needed in a socialized economy. But the cause of liberalism will be lost for a considerable period if it is not prepared to go further and socialize the forces of production, now at hand, so that the liberty of individuals will be supported by the very structure of economic organization.

The ultimate place of economic organization in human life is to assure the secure basis for an ordered expression of individual capacity and for the satisfaction of the needs of man in non-economic directions. The effort of mankind in connection with material production belongs, as I said earlier, among interests and activities that are, relatively speaking, routine in character, "routine" being defined as that which, without absorbing attention and energy, provides a constant basis for liberation of the values of intellectual, esthetic and companionship life. Every significant religious and moral teacher and prophet has asserted that the material is instrumental to the good life. Nominally at least, this idea is accepted by every civilized community. The transfer of the burden of material production from human muscles and brain to steam, electricity and chemical processes now makes possible the effective actualization of this idea. Needs, wants and desires are always the moving force in generating creative action. When these wants are compelled by force of conditions to be directed for the most part, among the mass of mankind, into obtaining the means of subsistence, what should be a means becomes perforce an end in itself. Up to the present the new mechanical forces of production, which are the means of emancipation from this state of affairs, have been employed to intensify and exaggerate the reversal of the true relation between means and ends. Humanly speaking, I do not see how it would have been possible to avoid an epoch having this character. But its perpetuation is the cause of the continually growing social chaos and strife. Its termination cannot be effected by preaching to individuals that they should place spiritual ends above material means. It can be brought about by organized social reconstruction that puts the results of the mechanism of abundance at the free disposal of individuals. The actual corrosive "material-ism" of our times does not proceed from science. It springs from the notion, sedulously cultivated by the class in power, that the creative capacities of in-dividuals can be evoked and developed only in a struggle for material pos-sessions and material gain. We either should surrender our professed belief in the supremacy of ideal and spiritual values and accommodate our beliefs to the predominant material orientation, or we should through organized en-deavor institute the socialized economy of material security and plenty that will release human energy for pursuit of higher values.

Since liberation of the capacities of individuals for free, self-initiated expression is an essential part of the creed of liberalism, liberalism that is sin-cere must will the means that condition the achieving of its ends. Regimen-tation of material and mechanical forces is the only way by which the mass of individuals can be released from regimentation and consequent suppres-sion of their cultural possibilities. The eclipse of liberalism is due to the fact that it has not faced the alternatives and adopted the means upon which re-alization of its professed aims depends. Liberalism can be true to its ideals only as it takes the course that leads to their attainment. The notion that organized social control of economic forces lies outside the historic path of liberalism shows that liberalism is still impeded by remnants of its earlier *laissez-faire* phase, with its opposition of society and the individual. The thing which now dampens liberal ardor and paralyzes its efforts is the con-ception that liberty and development of individuality as ends exclude the use of organized social effort as means. Earlier liberalism regarded the sepa-rate and competing economic action of individuals as the means of social well-being as the end. We must reverse the perspective and see that social-ized economy is the means of free individual development as the end.

That liberals are divided in outlook and endeavor while reactionaries are held together by community of interests and the ties of custom is well-nigh a commonplace. Organization of standpoint and belief among liberals can be achieved only in and by unity of endeavor. Organized unity of action attended by consensus of beliefs will come about in the degree in which so-cial control of economic forces is made the goal of liberal action. The greatest educational power, the greatest force in shaping the dispositions and attitudes of individuals, is the social medium in which they live. The medium that now lies closest to us is that of unified action for the inclusive end of a socialized economy. The attainment of a state of society in which a basis of material security will release the powers of individuals for cultural expression is not the work of a day. But by concentrating upon the task of securing a socialized economy as the ground and medium for release of the impulses and capacities men agree to call ideal, the now scattered and often conflicting activities of liberals can be brought to effective unity.

It is no part of my task to outline in detail a program for renascent liberalism. But the question of "what is to be done" cannot be ignored. Ideas must be organized, and this organization implies an organization of individuals who hold these ideas and whose faith is ready to translate itself into action. Translation into action signifies that the general creed of liberalism be formulated as a concrete program of action. It is in organization for action that liberals are weak, and without this organization there is danger that democratic ideals may go by default. Democracy has been a fighting faith. When its ideals are reinforced by those of scientific method and experimental intelligence, it cannot be that it is incapable of evoking discipline, ardor, and organization. To narrow the issue for the future to a struggle between Fascism and Communism is to invite a catastrophe that may carry civilization down in the struggle. Vital and courageous democratic liberalism is the one force that can surely avoid such a disastrous narrowing of the issue. I for one do not believe that Americans living in the tradition of Jefferson and Lincoln will weaken and give up without a whole-hearted effort to make democracy a living reality. This, I repeat, involves organization.

The question cannot be answered by argument. Experimental method means experiment, and the question can be answered only by trying, by organized effort. The reasons for making the trial are not abstract or recondite. They are found in the confusion, uncertainty and conflict that mark the modern world. The reasons for thinking that the effort if made will be successful are also not abstract and remote. They lie in what the method of experimental and cooperative intelligence has already accomplished in subduing to potential human use the energies of physical nature. In material production, the method of intelligence is now the established rule; to abandon it would be to revert to savagery. The task is to go on, and not backward, until the method of intelligence and experimental control is the rule in social relations and social direction. Either we take this road or we admit that the problem of social organization in behalf of human liberty and the flowering of human capacities is insoluble.

It would be fantastic folly to ignore or to belittle the obstacles that stand in the way. But what has taken place, also against great odds, in the scientific and industrial revolutions, is an accomplished fact; the way is marked out. It may be that the way will remain untrodden. If so, the future holds the menace of confusion moving into chaos, a chaos that will be externally masked for a time by an organization of force, coercive and violent, in which the liberties of men will all but disappear. Even so, the cause of liberty of the human spirit, the cause of opportunity of human beings for full development of their powers, the cause for which liberalism enduringly stands, is too precious and too ingrained in the human constitution to be forever obscured. Intelligence after millions of years of errancy has found itself as a method, and it will not be lost forever in the blackness of night. The business of liberalism is to bend every energy and exhibit every courage so that these precious goods may not even be temporarily lost but be intensified and expanded here and now.

The Fascist State

Late in 1923 Adolf Hitler (1889–1945) led an uprising in Munich against the government of Bavaria. Known as the "beer hall putsch" because of its point of origin, the insurrection was quickly subdued by the authorities. Hitler was captured, tried, and sentenced to prison. While serving his sentence he wrote *Mein Kampf* (*My Struggle*). It is a strange book, coming from the pen of the man who would later become dictator of Germany and then, after launching the most destructive war in human history, master of most of Europe. Long and rambling, the book is a collection of personal reminiscences, interpretations of history, analyses of the current political situation, pseudoscience, and plans for the future of Europe. Permeating it are Hitler's views on the nature and importance of race, including his claims about the superiority of people he referred to (without any clear definition) as "Aryans." Arrayed against the Aryans were a variety of "inferior" races, of whom the lowest, in his mind, were the Jews. The evidence we have makes it fairly clear that Hitler's virulent anti-Semitism grew out of his experiences as a young, and unsuccessful, artist living in Vienna before the first world war.

After he gained control of Germany in 1933, Hitler and his government persecuted the Jews. His attack on them culminated during the second world war with the Holocaust. Given the code-title "the final solution of the Jewish question," the Holocaust was to be the systematic extermination of the Jewish race (as well as other "inferior" groups such as gypsies). Hitler put his close friend and political lieutenant, Heinrich Himmler (1900–1945), in charge of the Holocaust. Among the many posts he held, Himmler was the head of the SS (*Shutzstaffeln*, or Guard Detachments) of the Nazi party, a large paramilitary organization that included the dreaded Gestapo, or Secret Police, and also provided the personnel for the extermination camps set up to destroy European Jewry. The largest of these camps was established at Auschwitz-Birkenau, deep in the Polish countryside. Of the Jews murdered by the Nazis in the Holocaust, a number estimated to be nearly six million people, nearly one third were put to death at Auschwitz. Rudolf Hoess (1900–1947), an ardent Nazi with previous experience in several concentration camps, was chosen as first commandant of Auschwitz. In that capacity he was directly responsible for the extermination program of the camp. After the war he went into hiding but was later captured by the British army and turned over to the Polish government for prosecution. While he was in prison awaiting trial he wrote his *Autobiography*.

The first of the two selections that follow is taken from Hitler's *Mein Kampf*. In it the author sets forth his racist views, particularly as these apply to the Jewish people. The second selection is from Hoess's *Autobiography*; it gives a factual, yet vivid account of the extermination process as it was actually carried out at Auschwitz, by the man who was directing the operation. Hitler died at the end of April 1945, committing suicide in his underground bunker in the center of Berlin, as Russian troops were overrunning the city. Himmler committed suicide a few days later, after being captured by British troops as he was attempting to escape from Germany into Denmark. Hoess was executed by the Polish government in 1947.

Consider the following questions as you study the text below.

1. What "natural laws" were Hitler's arguments built on? What connections did he make between nation and race?

2. What connections do you see between the arguments presented in *Mein Kampf* and the policies described by Rudolf Hoess? Besides Hitler, in your opinion, who shares responsibility for the Holocaust?

Mein Kampf

XI. Nation and Race

There are some truths which are so obvious that for this very reason they are not seen or at least not recognized by ordinary people. They sometimes pass by such truisms as though blind and are most astonished when someone suddenly discovers what everyone really ought to know. Columbus's eggs lie around by the hundreds of thousands, but Columbuses are met with less frequently.

Thus men without exception wander about in the garden of Nature; they imagine that they know practically everything and yet with few exceptions pass blindly by one of the more patent principles of Nature's rule: the inner segregation of the species of all living beings on this earth.

Adolf Hitler, *Mein Kampf*, trans. Ralph Manheim (Boston: Houghton Mifflin Company, 1943; London: Hurst & Blackett, Ltd.). Copyright 1943 by Houghton Mifflin Company. Reprinted by permission of Houghton Mifflin Company and Hutchinson Publishing Group, Ltd.

Even the most superficial observation shows that Nature's restricted form of propagation and increase is an almost rigid basic law of all the innumerable forms of expression of her vital urge. Every animal mates only with a member of the same species. The titmouse seeks the titmouse, the finch the finch, the stork the stork, the field mouse the field mouse, the dormouse the dormouse, the wolf the she-wolf, etc.

Only unusual circumstances can change this, primarily the compulsion of captivity or any other cause that makes it impossible to mate within the same species. But then Nature begins to resist this with all possible means, and her most visible protest consists either in refusing further capacity for propagation to bastards or in limiting the fertility of later offspring; in most cases, however, she takes away the power of resistance to disease or hostile attacks.

This is only too natural.

Any crossing of two beings not at exactly the same level produces a medium between the level of the two parents. This means: the offspring will probably stand higher than the racially lower parent, but not as high as the higher one. Consequently, it will later succumb in the struggle against the higher level. Such mating is contrary to the will of Nature for a higher breeding of all life. The precondition for this does not lie in associating superior and inferior, but in the total victory of the former. The stronger must dominate and not blend with the weaker, thus sacrificing his own greatness. Only the born weakling can view this as cruel, but he after all is only a weak and limited man; for if this law did not prevail, any conceivable higher development of organic living beings would be unthinkable.

The consequence of this racial purity, universally valid in Nature, is not only the sharp outward delimitation of the various races, but their uniform character in themselves. The fox is always a fox, the goose a goose, the tiger a tiger, etc., and the difference can lie at most in the varying measure of force, strength, intelligence, dexterity, endurance, etc., of the individual specimens. But you will never find a fox who in his inner attitude might, for example, show humanitarian tendencies toward geese, as similarly there is no cat with a friendly inclination toward mice.

Therefore, here, too, the struggle among themselves arises less from inner aversion than from hunger and love. In both cases, Nature looks on calmly, with satisfaction, in fact. In the struggle for daily bread all those who are weak and sickly or less determined succumb, while the struggle of the males for the female grants the right or opportunity to propagate only to the healthiest. And struggle is always a means for improving a species' health and power of resistance and, therefore, a cause of its higher development.

If the process were different, all further and higher development would cease and the opposite would occur. For, since the inferior always predominates numerically over the best, if both had the same possibility of preserving life and propagating, the inferior would multiply so much more rapidly that in the end the best would inevitably be driven into the background, unless a correction of this state of affairs were undertaken. Nature does just this by subjecting the weaker part to such severe living conditions that by them alone the number is limited, and by not permitting the remainder to increase promiscuously, but making a new and ruthless choice according to strength and health.

No more than Nature desires the mating of weaker with stronger individuals, even less does she desire the blending of a higher with a lower race, since, if she did, her whole work of higher breeding, over perhaps hundreds of thousands of years, might be ruined with one blow.

Historical experience offers countless proofs of this. It shows with terrifying clarity that in every mingling of Aryan blood with that of lower peoples the result was the end of the cultured people. North America, whose population consists in by far the largest part of Germanic elements who mixed but little with the lower colored peoples, shows a different humanity and culture from Central and South America, where the predominantly Latin immigrants often mixed with the aborigines on a large scale. By this one example, we can clearly and distinctly recognize the effect of racial mixture. The Germanic inhabitant of the American continent, who has remained racially pure and unmixed, rose to be master of the continent; he will remain the master as long as he does not fall a victim to defilement of the blood.

The result of all racial crossing is therefore in brief always the following:

(a) Lowering of the level of the higher race;
(b) Physical and intellectual regression and hence the beginning of a slowly but surely progressing sickness.

To bring about such a development is, then, nothing else but to sin against the will of the eternal creator. ...

Everything we admire on this earth today—science and art, technology and inventions—is only the creative product of a few peoples and originally perhaps of one race. On them depends the existence of this whole culture. If they perish, the beauty of this earth will sink into the grave with them.

However much the soil, for example, can influence men, the result of the influence will always be different depending on the races in question. The low fertility of a living space may spur the one race to the highest achievements; in others it will only be the cause of bitterest poverty and final undernourishment with all its consequences. The inner nature of peoples is always determining for the manner in which outward influences will be effective. What leads the one to starvation trains the other to hard work.

All great cultures of the past perished only because the originally creative race died out from blood poisoning.

The ultimate cause of such a decline was their forgetting that all culture depends on men and not conversely; hence that to preserve a certain culture the man who creates it must be preserved. This preservation is bound up with the rigid law of necessity and the right to victory of the best and stronger in this world.

Those who want to live, let them fight, and those who do not want to fight in this world of eternal struggle do not deserve to live.

Even if this were hard—that is how it is! Assuredly, however, by far the harder fate is that which strikes the man who thinks he can overcome Nature, but in the last analysis only mocks her. Distress, misfortune, and diseases are her answer.

The man who misjudges and disregards the racial laws actually forfeits the happiness that seems destined to be his. He thwarts the triumphal march of the best race and hence also the precondition for all human progress, and remains, in consequence, burdened with all the sensibility of man, in the animal realm of helpless misery.

It is idle to argue which race or races were the original representative of human culture and hence the real founders of all that we sum up under the word "humanity." It is simpler to raise this question with regard to the present, and here an easy, clear answer results. All the human culture, all the results of art, science, and technology that we see before us today, are almost exclusively the creative product of the Aryan. This very fact admits of the not unfounded inference that he alone was the founder of all higher humanity, therefore representing the prototype of all that we understand by the word "man." He is the Prometheus of mankind from whose bright forehead the divine spark of genius has sprung at all times, forever kindling anew that fire of knowledge which illumined the night of silent mysteries and thus caused man to climb the path to mastery over the other beings of this earth. Exclude him—and perhaps after a thousand years darkness will again descend on the earth, human culture will pass, and the world turn to a desert.

If we were to divide mankind into three groups, the founders of culture, the bearers of culture, the destroyers of culture, only the Aryan could be considered as the representative of the first group. From him originate the foundations and walls of all human creation, and only the outward form and color are determined by the changing traits of character of the various peoples. He provides the mightiest building stones and plans for all human progress and only the execution corresponds to the nature of the varying men and races. ...

The question of the inner causes of the Aryan's importance can be answered to the effect that they are to be sought less in a natural instinct of self-preservation than in the special type of its expression. The will to live, subjectively viewed, is everywhere equal and different only in the form of its actual expression. In the most primitive living creatures the instinct of self-preservation does not go beyond concern for their own ego. Egoism, as we designate this urge, goes so far that it even embraces time; the moment itself claims everything, granting nothing to the coming hours. In this condition the animal lives only for himself, seeks food only for his present hunger, and fights only for his own life. As long as the instinct of self-preservation expresses itself in this way, every basis is lacking for the formation of a group, even the most primitive form of family. Even a community between male and female, beyond pure mating, demands an extension of the instinct of self-preservation, since concern and struggle for the ego are now directed toward the second party; the male sometimes seeks food for the female, too, but for the most part both seek nourishment for the young. Nearly always one comes to the defense of the other, and thus the first, though infinitely simple, forms of a sense of sacrifice result. As soon as this sense extends beyond the narrow limits of the family, the basis for the formation of larger organisms and finally formal states is created.

In the lowest peoples of the earth this quality is present only to a very slight extent, so that often they do not go beyond the formation of the family. The greater the readiness to subordinate purely personal interests, the higher rises the ability to establish comprehensive communities.

This self-sacrificing will to give one's personal labor and if necessary one's own life for others is most strongly developed in the Aryan. The Aryan is not greatest in his mental qualities as such, but in the extent of his willingness to put all his abilities in the service of the community. In him the instinct of self-preservation has reached the noblest form, since he willingly subordinates his own ego to the life of the community and, if the hour demands, even sacrifices it.

Not in his intellectual gift lies the source of the Aryan's capacity for creating and building culture. If he had just this alone, he could only act destructively, in no case could he organize; for the innermost essence of all organization requires that the individual renounce putting forward his personal opinion and interests and sacrifice both in favor of a larger group. Only by way of this general community does he again recover his share. Now, for example, he no longer works directly for himself, but with his activity articulates himself with the community, not only for his own advantage, but for the advantage of all. The most wonderful elucidation of this attitude is provided by his word "work," by which he does not mean an activity for maintaining life in itself, but exclusively a creative effort that does not conflict with the interests of the community. Otherwise he designates human activity, in so far as it serves the instinct of self-preservation without consideration for his fellow men, as theft, usury, robbery, burglary, etc.

This state of mind, which subordinates the interests in the ego to the conservation of the community, is really the first premise for every truly human culture. From it alone can arise all the great works of mankind, which bring the founder little reward, but the richest blessings to posterity. Yes, from it alone can we understand how so many are able to bear up faithfully under a scanty life which imposes on them nothing but poverty and frugality, but gives the community the foundation of its existence. Every worker, every peasant, every inventor, official, etc., who works without ever being able to achieve any happiness or prosperity for himself, is a representative of his lofty idea, even if the deeper meaning of his activity remains hidden in him.

What applies to work as the foundation of human sustenance and all human progress is true to an even greater degree for the defense of man and his culture. In giving one's own life for the existence of the community lies the crown of all sense of sacrifice. It is this alone that prevents what human hands have built from being overthrown by human hands or destroyed by Nature.

Our own German language possesses a word which magnificently designates this kind of activity: *Pflichterfüllung* (fulfillment of duty); it means not to be self-sufficient but to serve the community.

The basic attitude from which such activity arises, we call—to distinguish it from egoism and selfishness—idealism. By this we understand only the individual's capacity to make sacrifices for the community, for his fellow men.

How necessary it is to keep realizing that idealism does not represent a superfluous expression of emotion, but that in truth it has been, is, and will be, the premise for what we designate as human culture, yes, that it alone created the concept of "man." It is to this inner attitude that the Aryan owes his position in this world, and to it the world owes man; for it alone formed from pure spirit the creative force which, by a unique pairing of the brutal fist and the intellectual genius, created the monuments of human culture.

Without his idealistic attitude all, even the most dazzling faculties of the intellect, would remain mere intellect as such—outward appearance without inner value, and never creative force.

But, since true idealism is nothing but the subordination of the interests and life of the individual to the community, and this in turn is the precondition for the creation of organizational forms of all kinds, it corresponds in its innermost depths to the ultimate will of Nature. It alone leads men to voluntary recognition of the privilege of force and strength, and thus makes them into a dust particle of that order which shapes and forms the whole universe.

The purest idealism is unconsciously equivalent to the deepest knowledge.

How correct this is, and how little true idealism has to do with playful flights of the imagination, can be seen at once if we let the unspoiled child, a healthy boy, for example, judge. The same boy who feels like throwing up when he hears the tirades of a pacifist "idealist" is ready to give his young life for the ideal of his nationality.

Here the instinct of knowledge unconsciously obeys the deeper necessity of the preservation of the species, if necessary at the cost of the individual, and protests against the visions of the pacifist windbag who in reality is nothing but a cowardly, though camouflaged, egoist, transgressing the laws of development; for development requires willingness on the part of the

individual to sacrifice himself for the community, and not the sickly imagin-
ings of cowardly know-it-alls and critics of Nature.

Especially, therefore, at times when the ideal attitude threatens to disappear, we can at once recognize a diminution of that force which forms the
community and thus creates the premises of culture. As soon as egoism becomes the ruler of a people, the bands of order are loosened and in the chase
after their own happiness men fall from heaven into a real hell.

Yes, even posterity forgets the men who have only served their own advantage and praises the heroes who have renounced their own happiness.

The mightiest counterpart to the Aryan is represented by the Jew. In
hardly any people in the world is the instinct of self-preservation developed
more strongly than in the so-called "chosen." Of this, the mere fact of the
survival of this race may be considered the best proof. Where is the people
which in the last two thousand years has been exposed to so slight changes
of inner disposition, character, etc., as the Jewish people? What people, finally, has gone through greater upheavals than this one—and nevertheless is-
sued from the mightiest catastrophes of mankind unchanged? What an
infinitely tough will to live and preserve the species speaks from these facts!

The mental qualities of the Jew have been schooled in the course of
many centuries. Today he passes as "smart," and this in a certain sense he
has been at all times. But his intelligence is not the result of his own development, but of visual instruction through foreigners. For the human mind cannot climb to the top without steps; for every step upward he needs the
foundation of the past, and this in the comprehensive sense in which it can
be revealed only in general culture. All thinking is based only in small part
on man's own knowledge, and mostly on the experience of the time that has
preceded. The general cultural level provides the individual man, without
his noticing it as a rule, with such a profusion of preliminary knowledge
that, thus armed, he can more easily take further steps of his own. The boy of
today, for example, grows up among a truly vast number of technical acquisitions of the last centuries, so that he takes for granted and no longer pays
attention to much that a hundred years ago was a riddle to even the greatest
minds, although for following and understanding our progress in the field in
question it is of decisive importance to him. If a very genius from the twenties of the past century should suddenly leave his grave today, it would be
harder for him even intellectually to find his way in the present era than for
an average boy of fifteen today. For he would lack all the infinite preliminary
education which our present contemporary unconsciously, so to speak, as-
similates while growing up amidst the manifestation of our present general
civilization.

Since the Jew—for reasons which will at once become apparent—was
never in possession of a culture of his own, the foundations of his intellectual work were always provided by others. His intellect at all times developed
through the cultural world surrounding him.

The reverse process never took place.

For if the Jewish people's instinct of self-preservation is not smaller but larger than that of other peoples, if his intellectual faculties can easily arouse the impression that they are equal to the intellectual gifts of other races, he lacks completely the most essential requirement for a cultured people, the idealistic attitude.

In the Jewish people the will to self-sacrifice does not go beyond the individual's naked instinct of self-preservation. Their apparently great sense of solidarity is based on the very primitive herd instinct that is seen in many other living creatures in this world. It is a noteworthy fact that the herd instinct leads to mutual support only as long as a common danger makes this seem useful or inevitable. The same pack of wolves which has just fallen on its prey together disintegrates when hunger abates into its individual beasts. The same is true of horses which try to defend themselves against an assailant in a body, but scatter again as soon as the danger is past.

It is similar with the Jew. His sense of sacrifice is only apparent. It exists only as long as the existence of the individual makes it absolutely necessary. However, as soon as the common enemy is conquered, the danger threatening all averted and the booty hidden, the apparent harmony of the Jews among themselves ceases, again making way for their old causal tendencies. The Jew is only united when a common danger forces him to be or a common booty entices him; if these two grounds are lacking, the qualities of the crassest egoism come into their own, and in the twinkling of an eye the united people turns into a horde of rats, fighting bloodily among themselves.

If the Jews were alone in this world, they would stifle in filth and offal; they would try to get ahead of one another in hate-filled struggle and exterminate one another, in so far as the absolute absence of all sense of self-sacrifice, expressing itself in their cowardice, did not turn battle into comedy here too.

So it is absolutely wrong to infer any ideal sense of sacrifice in the Jews from the fact that they stand together in struggle, or, better expressed, in the plundering of their fellow men.

Here again the Jew is led by nothing but the naked egoism of the individual.

That is why the Jewish state—which should be the living organism for preserving and increasing a race—is completely unlimited as to territory. For a state formation to have a definite spatial setting always presupposes an idealistic attitude on the part of the state-race, and especially a correct interpretation of the concept of work. In the exact measure in which this attitude is lacking any attempt at forming, even of preserving, a spatially delimited state fails. And thus the basis on which alone culture can arise is lacking.

Hence the Jewish people, despite all apparent intellectual qualities, is without any true culture, and especially without any true culture of its own. For what sham culture the Jew today possesses is the property of other peoples, and for the most part it is ruined in his hands.

In judging the Jewish people's attitude on the question of human culture, the most essential characteristic we must always bear in mind is that there has never been a Jewish art and accordingly there is none today either; that above all the two queens of all the arts, architecture and music, owe nothing original to the Jews. What they do accomplish in the field of art is either patchwork or intellectual theft. Thus, the Jews lack those qualities which distinguish the races that are creative and hence culturally blessed.

To what an extent the Jew takes over foreign culture, imitating or rather ruining it, can be seen from the fact that he is mostly found in the art which seems to require the least original invention, the art of acting. But even here, in reality, he is only a "juggler," or rather an ape; for even here he lacks the last touch that is required for real greatness; even here he is not the creative genius, but a superficial imitator, and all the twists and tricks that he uses are powerless to conceal the inner lifelessness of his creative gift. Here the Jewish press most lovingly helps him along by raising such a roar of hosannahs about even the most mediocre bungler, just so long as he is a Jew, that the rest of the world actually ends up by thinking that they have an artist before them, while in truth it is only a pitiful comedian.

No, the Jew possesses no culture-creating force of any sort, since the idealism, without which there is no true higher development of man, is not present in him and never was present. Hence his intellect will never have a constructive effect, but will be destructive, and in very rare cases perhaps will at most be stimulating, but then as the prototype of the "force which always wants evil and nevertheless creates good." [1] Not through him does any progress of mankind occur, but in spite of him.

. . .

Autobiography of Rudolf Hoess

The Final Solution of the Jewish Question in Auschwitz Concentration Camp

In the summer of 1941, I cannot remember the exact date, I was suddenly summoned to the Reichsführer SS [Heinrich Himmler], directly by his adjutant's office. Contrary to his usual custom, Himmler received me without his adjutant being present and said in effect:

Trans. C. Fitzgibbow.

[1]Goethe's *Faust*, lines 1336–37: Mephistopheles to Faust.

The Führer [Hitler] has ordered that the Jewish question be solved once and for all and that we, the SS, are to implement that order.

The existing extermination centres in the east are not in a position to carry out the large actions which are anticipated. I have therefore earmarked Auschwitz for this purpose, both because of its good position as regards communications and because the area can easily be isolated and camouflaged. At first I thought of calling in a senior SS officer for this job, but I changed my mind in order to avoid difficulties concerning the terms of reference. I have now decided to entrust this task to you. It is difficult and onerous and calls for complete devotion notwithstanding the difficulties that may arise. You will learn further details from Sturmbannführer Eichmann[1] of the Reich Security Head Office who will call on you in the immediate future.

The departments concerned will be notified by me in due course. You will treat this order as absolutely secret, even from your superiors. After you talk with Eichmann you will immediately forward to me the plans of the projected installations.

The Jews are the sworn enemies of the German people and must be eradicated. Every Jew that we can lay our hands on is to be destroyed now during the war, without exception. If we cannot now obliterate the biological basis of Jewry, the Jews will one day destroy the German people.

On receiving these grave instructions I returned forthwith to Auschwitz, without reporting to my superior at Oranienburg.

Shortly afterwards Eichmann came to Auschwitz and disclosed to me the plans for the operations as they affected the various countries concerned.

. . .

I cannot say on what date the extermination of the Jews began. Probably it was in September 1941, but it may not have been until January 1942. The Jews from Upper Silesia were the first to be dealt with. These Jews were arrested by the Kattowitz Police Unit and taken in drafts by train to a siding on the west side of the Auschwitz-Dziedzice railway line where they were unloaded. So far as I can remember, these drafts never consisted of more than 1,000 prisoners.

On the platform the Jews were taken over from the police by a detachment from the camp and were brought by the commander of the protective custody camp in two sections to the bunker, as the extermination building was called.

---

[1][Adolf Eichmann, the official who directed the Nazi extermination program under Himmler, escaped after the war to Argentina where he was captured in 1961 by Israeli secret agents, returned to Israel, tried, and executed for his crimes.—*Ed.*]

Their luggage was left on the platform, whence it was taken to the sorting office called Canada situated between the DAW [a factory using slave labor to produce armaments] and the timber-yard.

The Jews were made to undress near the bunker, after they had been told that they had to go into the rooms (as they were also called) in order to be deloused.

All the rooms, there were five of them, were filled at the same time, the gas-proof doors were then screwed up and the contents of the gas containers discharged into the rooms through special vents.

After half an hour the doors were reopened (there were two doors in each room), the dead bodies were taken out, and brought to the pits in small trolleys which ran on rails.

The victims' clothing was taken in lorries to the sorting office. The whole operation, including assistance given during undressing, the filling of the bunker, the emptying of the bunker, the removal of the corpses, as well as the preparation and filling up of the mass graves, was carried out by a special detachment of Jews, who were separately accommodated and who, in accordance with Eichmann's orders, were themselves liquidated after every big action.

While the first transports were being disposed of, Eichmann arrived with an order from the Reichsführer SS stating that the gold teeth were to be removed from the corpses and the hair cut from the women. This job was also undertaken by the special detachment.

The extermination process was at that time carried out under the supervision of the commander of the protective custody camp or the *Rapportführer*. Those who were too ill to be brought into the gas-chambers were shot in the back of the neck by a small-calibre weapon.

An SS doctor also had to be present. The trained disinfectors were responsible for discharging the gas into the gas chamber.

During the spring of 1942 the actions were comparatively small, but the transports increased in the summer, and we were compelled to construct a further extermination building. The peasant farmstead west of the future site of crematoria III and IV was selected and made ready. Two huts near Bunker I and three near Bunker II were erected, in which the victims undressed. Bunker II was the larger and could hold about 1,200 people.

During the summer of 1942 the bodies were still being placed in the mass graves. Towards the end of the summer, however, we started to burn them; at first on wood pyres bearing some 2,000 corpses, and later in pits together with bodies previously buried. In the early days oil refuse was poured on the bodies, but later methanol was used. Bodies were burnt in pits, day and night, continuously.

By the end of November all the mass graves had been emptied. The number of corpses in the mass graves amounted to 107,000.

. . .

It became apparent during the first cremation in the open air that in the long run it would not be possible to continue in that manner. During bad weather or when a strong wind was blowing, the stench of burning flesh was carried for many miles and caused the whole neighbourhood to talk about the burning of Jews, despite official counterpropaganda. It is true that all members of the SS detailed for the extermination were bound to the strictest secrecy over the whole operation, but, as later SS legal proceedings showed, this was not always observed. Even the most severe punishment was not able to stop their love of gossip.

Moreover the air defense services protested against the fires which could be seen from great distances at night. Nevertheless, burnings had to go on, even at night, unless further transports were to be refused. The schedule of individual operations, fixed at a conference by the Ministry of Communications, had to be rigidly adhered to in order to avoid, for military reasons, obstruction and confusion on the railways concerned. These reasons led to the energetic planning and eventual construction of the two large crematoria, and in 1943 to the building of two further smaller installations. Yet another one was planned, which would far exceed the others in size, but it was never completed.

·   ·   ·

During previous interrogations I have put the number of Jews who arrived in Auschwitz for extermination at two and a half millions. This figure was supplied by Eichmann who gave it to my superior officer, Gruppenführer Glucks, when he was ordered to make a report to the Reichsführer SS shortly before Berlin was surrounded. Eichmann, and his permanent deputy Gunther, were the only ones who possessed the necessary information on which to calculate the total number destroyed. In accordance with orders given by the Reichsführer SS, after every large action all evidence in Auschwitz on which a calculation of the number of victims might be based had to be burnt.

As head of Department DI I personally destroyed every bit of evidence which could be found in my office. The heads of other offices did the same.

According to Eichmann, the Reichsführer SS and the Reich Security Head Office also had all their data destroyed.

Only his personal notes could give the required information. It is possible that, owing to the negligence of some department or other, a few isolated documents, teleprinter messages, or wireless messages have been left undestroyed, but they could not give sufficient information on which to make a calculation.

I myself never knew the total number and I have nothing to help me make an estimate of it.

·   ·   ·

"Action Reinhardt" was the code name given to the collection, sorting and utilisation of all articles which were acquired as the result of the transports of Jews and their extermination.

Any member of the SS who laid hands on this Jewish property was by order of the Reichsführer SS, punished with death.

Valuables worth many millions of pounds were seized.

An immense amount of property was stolen by members of the SS and by the police, and also by prisoners, civilian employees and railway personnel. A great deal of this still lies hidden and buried in the Auschwitz-Birkenau camp area.

When the Jewish transports unloaded on arrival, their luggage was left on the platform until all the Jews had been taken to the extermination buildings or into the camp. During the early days all the luggage would then be brought by a transport detachment to the sorting office, Canada I, where it would be sorted and disinfected. The clothing of those who had been gassed in bunkers I and II or in crematoria I to IV was also brought to the sorting office.

By 1942 Canada I could no longer keep up with the sorting. Although new huts and sheds were constantly being added and prisoners were sorting day and night, and although the number of persons employed was constantly stepped up and several trucks (often as many as twenty) were loaded daily with the items sorted out, the piles of unsorted luggage went on mounting up. So in 1942, the construction of Canada II warehouse was begun at the west end of building sector II of Birkenau. A start was also made on the erection of extermination buildings and a bath house for the new arrivals. Thirty newly built huts were crammed to capacity immediately after completion, while mountains of unsorted effects piled up between them. In spite of the augmented labour gangs, it was out of the question to complete the job during the course of the individual actions, which always took from four to six weeks. Only during the longer intervals was it possible to achieve some semblance of order.

Clothing and footwear were examined for hidden valuables (although only cursorily in view of the quantities involved) and then stored or handed over to the camp to complete the inmates' clothing. Later on, it was also sent to other camps. A considerable part of the clothing was passed to welfare organisations for resettlers and later for victims of air raids. Large and important munition plants received considerable quantities for their foreign workers.

Blankets and mattresses, etc., were also sent to the welfare organisations. In so far as the camp required articles of this nature they were retained to complete their inventory, but other camps also received large consignments.

Valuables were taken over by a special section of the camp command and sorted out by experts, and a similar procedure was followed with the money that was found.

The jewellery was usually of great value, particularly if its Jewish owners came from the west; precious stones worth thousands of pounds, priceless gold and platinum watches set with diamonds, rings, earrings and necklaces of great rarity. Currency from all countries amounted to many thousands of pounds. Often tens of thousands of pounds in value, mostly in thousand dollar notes, were found on single individuals. Every possible hiding place in their clothes and luggage and on their bodies was made use of.

When the sorting out process that followed each major operation had been completed, the valuables and money were packed into trunks and taken by lorry to the Economic Administration Head Office in Berlin and thence to the Reichsbank, where a special department dealt exclusively with items taken during actions against the Jews. Eichmann told me on one occasion that the jewellery and currency were sold in Switzerland, and that the entire Swiss jewellery market was dominated by these sales.

.   .   .

The extermination process in Auschwitz took place as follows:

Jews selected for gassing were taken as quietly as possible to the crematoria, the men being separated from the women. In the undressing room, prisoners of the special detachment, detailed for this purpose, would tell them in their own language that they were going to be bathed and deloused, that they must leave their clothes neatly together and above all remember where they had put them, so that they would be able to find them again quickly after delousing. The prisoners of the special detachment had the greatest interest in seeing that the operation proceeded smoothly and quickly. After undressing, the Jews went into the gas-chambers, which were furnished with showers and water pipes and gave a realistic impression of a bath house.

The women went in first with their children, followed by the men who were always the fewer in number. This part of the operation nearly always went smoothly, for the prisoners of the special detachment would calm those who betrayed any anxiety or who perhaps had some inkling of their fate. As an additional precaution these prisoners of the special detachment and an SS man always remained in the chamber until the last moment.

The door would now be quickly screwed up and the gas immediately discharged by the waiting disinfectors through vents in the ceilings of the gas-chambers, down a shaft that led to the floor. This ensured the rapid distribution of the gas. It could be observed through the peep-hole in the door that those who were standing nearest to the induction vents were killed at once. It can be said that about one-third died straight away. The remainder staggered about and began to scream and struggle for air. The screaming, however, soon changed to the death rattle and in a few minutes all lay still. After twenty minutes at the latest no movement could be discerned. The time required for the gas to have effect varied according to the weather, and depended on whether it was damp or dry, cold or warm. It also depended on the quality of the gas, which was never exactly the same, and on the composition of the transports which might contain a high proportion of healthy Jews, or old and sick, or children. The victims became unconscious after a few minutes, according to their distance from the intake shaft. Those who screamed and those who were old or sick or weak, or the small children, died quicker than those who were healthy or young.

The door was opened half an hour after the induction of the gas, and the ventilation switched on. Work was immediately begun on removing the corpses. There was no noticeable change in the bodies and no sign of convulsions or discoloration. Only after the bodies had been left lying for some time, that is to say after several hours, did the usual death stains appear in the places where they had lain. Soiling through opening of the bowels was also rare. There were no signs of wounding of any kind. The faces showed no distortion.

The special detachment now set about removing the gold teeth and cutting the hair from the women. After this, the bodies were taken up by lift and laid in front of the ovens, which had meanwhile been stoked up. Depending on the size of the bodies, up to three corpses could be put into one oven retort at the same time. The time required for cremation also depended on this, but on an average it took twenty minutes. As previously stated, crematoria I and II could cremate about 2,000 bodies in twenty-four hours, but a higher number was not possible without causing damage to the installations. Numbers III and IV should have been able to cremate 1,500 bodies in twenty-four hours, but, as far as I know, these figures were never attained.

During the period when the fires were kept burning continuously, without a break, the ashes fell through the grates and were constantly removed and crushed to powder. The ashes were taken in lorries to the Vistula [River], where they immediately *drifted away* and dissolved.

.   .   .

Many of the women hid their babies among the piles of clothing. The men of the Special Detachment were particularly on the look-out for this, and would speak words of encouragement to the woman until they had persuaded her to take the child with her. The women believed that the disinfectant might be bad for their smaller children, hence their efforts to conceal them.

The smaller children usually cried because of the strangeness of being undressed in this fashion, but when their mothers or members of the Special Detachment comforted them, they became calm and entered the gas-chambers, playing or joking with one another and carrying their toys.

I noticed that women who either guessed or knew what awaited them nevertheless found the courage to joke with the children to encourage them, despite the mortal terror visible in their own eyes.

One woman approached me as she walked past and, pointing to her four children who were manfully helping the smallest ones over the rough ground, whispered:

"How can you bring yourself to kill such beautiful, darling children? Have you no heart at all?"

One old man, as he passed by me, hissed:

"Germany will pay a heavy penance for this mass murder of the Jews." His eyes glowed with hatred as he said this. Nevertheless he walked calmly into the gas-chamber, without worrying about the others.

One young woman caught my attention particularly as she ran busily hither and thither, helping the smallest children and the old women to undress. During the selection she had had two small children with her, and her agitated behaviour and appearance had brought her to my notice at once. She did not look in the least like a Jewess. Now her children were no longer with her. She waited until the end, helping the women who were not undressed and who had several children with them, encouraging them and calming the children. She went with the very last ones into the gas-chamber. Standing at the doorway, she said:

"I knew all the time that we were being brought to Auschwitz to be gassed. When the selection took place I avoided being put with the able-bodied ones, as I wished to look after the children. I wanted to go through it all, fully conscious of what was happening. I hope that it will be quick. Goodbye!"

From time to time women would suddenly give the most terrible shrieks while undressing, or tear their hair, or scream like maniacs. These were immediately led away behind the building and shot in the back of the neck with a small-calibre weapon.

It sometimes happened that, as the men of the Special Detachment left the gas-chamber, the women would suddenly realize what was happening, and would call down every imaginable curse upon our heads.

I remember, too, a woman who tried to throw her children out of the gas-chamber, just as the door was closing. Weeping she called out:

"At least let my precious children live."

Resistance

Justina's Diary was written by Gusta Dawidson-Draenger, a leader of Akiva, a Zionist youth movement committed to resistance to the Nazis. According to a witness at the trial of Adolf Eichmann, *Justina's Diary* was written while Dawidson-Draenger was in prison. It was written on toilet paper stolen for her by fellow prisoners. Although Dawidson-Draenger managed to escape from this particular imprisonment, she was subsequently recaptured and executed.

The *Diary* was written at a time when it had become clear to many that the Nazis intended nothing less than the extermination of Europe's Jews. Nonetheless, the choice to resist was not an easy one. Resistors faced an opponent with vastly superior resources and weapons. Moreover, the Nazis punished the Jewish communities collectively for individual acts of resistance. Perhaps most important, in order to resist one had to come to terms with the reality that resistance almost certainly meant death and that resistance movements had absolutely no chance of succeeding, if what was meant by success was military defeat of the Nazis. As you read the diary entry that follows, pay close attention to the author's feelings about joining the resistance. What did she mean when she declared that she and her fellow resistors "were free"? Of what were they free? What was the price of this freedom?

Consider the following questions as you study the text below.

1. Why was it so important to the resistors to form a "family"? How did they express their familial solidarity?

2. What did Dolek mean when he declared to his fellow resistors that "Whoever desires to live, let him not seek life among us"? How would you resolve the apparent contradiction between the resistors' desire to strike back at their enemies and their fatalistic attitudes about their own deaths?

Justina's Diary

They were free. Their last links with everyday life were broken. Thus, after this "action," those who had still hesitated to leave behind a younger brother, an only sister, aging parents, suddenly felt free to plunge into the maelstrom of [underground] work; it was a feeling of freedom which sprouted out of the rubble of shattered family life. That itself proved difficult for those who embraced the cause only after all feeling was gone. For questions arose, questions that pierced like pangs of conscience: Why was I not willing to commit myself sooner? Why was death necessary before I could feel free to act? These questions penetrated deeper and deeper into the hearts of many and whenever one or another found himself behind prison walls, he spent long hours searching for the answers.

Now, however, thrown into the whirlpool of work, they could not worry about it for long: there was no time for contemplation. But pain gnawed at the hearts with such intensity that people demanded work as a last resort. One after another, they volunteered, and there were assignments for all, without delay.

It was the end of October. The fall season was exceptionally beautiful. The leaves retained their fresh greenness for a long time. The sun gilded the earth, its rays warmed the air. But these were only days of grace. At any moment the sky could turn gray and heavy rain start pounding the ground. Rainy, muddy autumn loomed just ahead. One had to expect a change in weather at any moment. After two difficult experiences in the woods, they knew that this was not the time to seek a new field of operations: it was too late in the year. Spring was the time for a new start. Now it was autumn, with winter to follow, which would undoubtedly thwart their newly started efforts.

A new concept was born. Here they were stuck in the capital. Surely targets for their activity could be found nearby. Without building a large secret organization in the forests, they could operate right where they were. Even their smallest act would reach the nerve center of the authorities. To damage the essential cogs of the machine—this was to become their goal. There, in the woods, partisan actions could only be carried out with larger detachments; a mere handful would hardly be effective. Here, however, every act carried out singly or in pairs would cause the authorities to feel uneasy, more than uneasy. It was important to shake them up by daring self-assurance; to make them realize that they did not exercise their bestial rule over a soulless mass, that the downtrodden people had awakened, had suffered enough, and that the long awaited springtime of nations was coming.

"From Justina's Diary: Resistance in Cracow," in *A Holocaust Reader*, ed. Lucy S. Dawidowicz (New York: Behrman House, 1976), pp. 340–47. Reprinted by permission of Behrman House.

Here and there voices of reason argued that the vigilance of the rulers must not be aroused, that it was more important to muster one's strength and create the impression that nothing was happening, that every suspicious sign must be suppressed at the roots. Yet such behavior was not for them. How could they be certain that they would live to see the spring? They brushed against death every day. They could never know whether they might escape its reach. Thus they were forced to act, so as to make the enemy feel their rebellion. They decided to transfer their activities to Cracow and later to the other larger cities.

Even within the district so much needed to be done! Within the ghetto the traitors had to be dealt with—those who for a few pieces of silver or for a self-serving promise of survival would sell their own brothers. Among them were those who had the murder of hundreds of Jews on their conscience. For an entire year the populace had dreaded the mass arrests conducted at night, when the police went from house to house and collected innocent people, according to perfidiously drawn lists, people who were killed off within a few days. They promised themselves to get first the head, and then his helpers.

They decided to leave one base of operations within the ghetto, another on the outside. Contact points were established in all larger cities along the Cracow-Lemberg lines. Cracow itself was surrounded with a network of suburban apartments. The leadership was slowly moving out of Cracow. It was high time: their names were abroad in the entire district. The news that it was they who dispatched people to the forests was being spread from person to person. Their names were almost invariably spoken with reverence, with charged emotion, because their names became the expression of a new idea of freedom to which people clung with all their hearts. But at the same time their names had reached the ears of the wrong people as well. They became quite well known to the Jewish police which really served the authorities better than it did its own people. …

The leadership was again complete. The operations continued at full speed. People had strictly defined tasks which they pursued from morning till night—intelligence gathering, liaison work, technical matters, or specific assignments. Everyone was always totally absorbed by this effort. And so, exhausted, pursued, they rushed home late in the evening, crossing the threshold with joy in their hearts. It was the last home of their lives, the last place in which all human sentiments rose once again like a tall bright flame. Such was their need for mutual love, such was the constant longing for the warmh of life together that whenever one hearth was extinguished, they immediately kindled another, even more potent than the one they had lost. The storms of war kept blowing out their fires, but time and again their old desire to stay together would be awakened. …

The leadership suddenly became swamped with work which pinned them in place. They worked without stopping: one assignment followed another. Even though all stood ready to work, they were still shorthanded.

They operated simultaneously in different places. They believed that the tactic of parallel concurrent strikes in different sections had a shattering effect on the authorities. The greater the shock, the greater their zeal to continue. These were truly unusual times for them.

But the shreds of personal feelings were never fully extinguished. There was always an ember left in one's heart, a small flame of feeling remained in the depths of one's soul. When they reassembled after a difficult assignment, this small flame burned stronger and higher; a new fire of brotherly togetherness was lit. Young people remained alone, without parents or family, with few belongings, usually in a sparsely furnished one-room apartment. The remaining belongings of the deported parents had to be sold or otherwise disposed of when one got ready to leave.

Someone had an idea: to establish a "liquidation place"—that was what it was called. It was organized in the apartment of Szymek, whose parents had been deported. Here the young people brought everything they possessed: linens, clothing, shoes, valuables—all that could be useful to others or that could be sold for the common good. After all items were assembled and sorted, the "liquidation" process began. Every one registered his needs and received the items he required. Thus people's personal belongings became communal property. … A joint treasury was established, and a communal kitchen soon followed. Slowly the feeling of homelessness began to disappear. The missing warmth of the parental home was replaced by a new warmth, one based, not on bonds of blood, but on bonds of the spirit.

They gathered at mealtimes, and those were the most joyful times of the day. The next step came when they all moved in together into a small two-room apartment, and this became their home. It was on the ground floor, entered by way of a large, long anteroom. Even before one reached the door, the cheerful sound of youthful voices within could be heard. One opened the door and was immediately in the warm circle of happy laughter and animated talk. Elsa invariably stood busy at the kitchen stove. She was forever cooking, washing, ordering people about, complaining. She was like a worried mother whose chores were never finished—coal bricks to be cut, water to be fetched, the fire refused to burn—and the children, always giving trouble. And all the while the children circled the stove in a tight group, hands on their hips, and scoffed at their angry mother. … She devoted her entire being to that kitchen. … She liked neatness above all. She swept, scrubbed the floor, cleaned incessantly. People always upset her work, but she was never angry. She did not know how to be angry. Abashed, she only smiled and rather than scold, she shyly asked, "Clean your shoes before you enter the room. Please understand." Then she grabbed the broom and swept the floor again. She kept busy at it all day long.

Szymek played an important part here. First of all, he was the official tenant of the place. He rather liked this role; he looked into every corner observing everybody at work, hands in his pockets. Having surveyed all the activities, he would move away dissatisfied, saying "What a mess it is here! What a horrible mess!" Szymek and Noli were in charge of the supplies. They reigned over the wardrobes and fitted out the people with whatever was needed. They had a lot of fun with it. Various old-fashioned pieces of apparel, relics of an older age, which found their way to the "liquidation place," caused much merriment and laughter.

The life of the entire movement was concentrated here. Whoever came to Cracow made certain to visit the district so as to come to No. 13 and meet people, no matter what the difficulties. ... The residents and the visitors, those who had been together for years and those who for years had longed for one another, met here. How did these oppressed people generate so much joy? Perhaps it was that they felt that once they left this place at No. 13, their last family nest would be gone. Or they may have felt that this environment was not only their last home, but also the last focal point of national life, the last assemblage of their own people, among whom they could be themselves.

So they tried to absorb all national values, revive old traditions; they tried to live in the specific atmosphere of traditional Jewish life. Dolek visited frequently. The whole crowd would gather around him, and that evening a more solemn, more profound mood would prevail. There was an unexplained beauty in the room. These unusual evenings, festive and charged with emotion, were indelibly impressed on the memories of all those who experienced them.

The apartment became more and more crowded. More people came, and though many left for new assignments, still more arrived to take their place. During the day the door was in constant motion. At night it was difficult to find space for all. Two beds would be placed side by side, and people slept crosswise, six or seven together. Sleeping places were improvised on the floor, on chairs; every nook and cranny would be used for sleeping. Living conditions were poor, the most primitive comforts were lacking, but no one would willingly part with these hardships, which were dearer to them than the greatest luxuries, the most affluent life.

At that time the apartment at No. 13 was the base for all underground activities. Toward evening, groups of two or three left stealthily, some to take action against traitors and informers within the ghetto, others to seek arms on the outside. A minute before the curfew they returned, out of breath, at times triumphant, at times mortified at having failed, though they had so nearly succeeded. Frequently they miraculously eluded the police. At times it seemed the bullets passed right over their heads, that only a timely turn of the head had saved them.

One of the most beautiful evenings was arranged in Anka's honor. It was the ushering in of the Sabbath. The preparations for the celebration lasted fully two days. All were waiting for it impatiently: it was to start at dusk on Friday and last until daybreak the following morning. This tradition has been maintained in the movement for many years. From the grayness of a weekday one is suddenly plunged into a festive mood. In religious concentration one anticipates the moment when the candles will flame into light in the festively decorated room. The girls in white blouses, the boys in white wide-collared shirts took their places around the table, covered with a white cloth. First a moment of silence, then a strong burst of song, greeting the Sabbath. Eyes gleamed in the candlelight. Strong emotions were reflected in those wide-open black pupils. Another spirit animated them, purer and better. This is the way it had always been, for years and years. In a quiet village, in the noisy city, high up in the mountains, among the factory smokestacks, they had come to greet the Sabbath with the same song, with the same emotions. And today it was the last time together. They had no presentiment of disaster. They were so happy! Song followed song, the ringing notes binding them more tightly and strongly together! In the midst of this happiness that filled them to overflowing, from out of somewhere came its epithet: it was *our* last supper. The name caught on, it was remembered. Thenceforth that evening was never referred to otherwise.

Dolek sat at the end of the table and around him were all the dear faces, radiant, friendly, brave, and so very, very close. They sat crowded together. The room had been filled long since, and new guests kept arriving. Room had to be made for all. In a corner, Martusia, wide-eyed, staring at Dolek, at the radiant faces, at the flaming candles. This was her first Sabbath away from home. She left Tomaszów a few days ago, when the "action" had already started, aware that she might never again see her parents. They were so young in spirit! Her father, saying good-bye to her, told her, "Too bad I am not a few years younger. I would certainly have gone with you!" Maria took those words along and kept them in her heart, her dearest memento of her father. Now she kept thinking of them all the time.

Her home was no more! There the "action" most likely caught her father, her mother, her younger sister. She is alone, all alone in the world. Only seventeen, her eyes wide, she scans the room. She does not feel pain, she does not long for her lost home, for her childhood, for that carefree girlhood which has gone forever. Here is her place, among this youthful company. She feels happy in the crowded room. It is so good to listen to Dolek's words. She has known him for a long time. She feels that today he speaks in quite a different way from the past. Power used to resonate in his words, creative force which summoned faith in life and love of it. Tonight his words forebode the inevitable end which they must confront with dignity.

It was as if he felt death approaching, because he spoke frequently about it. He did not believe that they could survive and he did not want others to believe it. He did not want to delude himself. He wanted all those who undertook the underground work to realize that the end was near. Even now he dropped his hard words into the festive mood:

"There is no return from our journey. We march along the road to death, remember that! Whoever desires to live, let him not seek life among us. We are at the end. But our end is not the dusk. Our end is death, which a strong man steps forward to confront. I feel that this is our last communal ushering in of the Sabbath. We will have to leave the ghetto. There is too much commotion around us. This week we will start dismantling our cozy center at No. 13. Another phase of our life will be over. But we must not regret anything. This is the way it must be."

The windows were gray with dawn, when this, our last supper came to an end.

The Atomic Age

Although heavy fighting had been waged on the mainland of Asia since the Japanese invasion of Manchuria in 1931, the beginning of World War II is usually dated from September 1, 1939, when Nazi Germany launched its surprise attack on Poland. Unlike World War I, in which hostilities were generally confined to relatively small areas of Europe, World War II was virtually global in extent. Land, sea, and aerial combat spread throughout most of Europe, large areas of Asia and Africa, along the coastlines of both North and South America, and on innumerable islands scattered across the Pacific Ocean. The United States entered the war following the Japanese surprise attack on the Pacific Fleet at Pearl Harbor, Hawaii, on December 7, 1941. The war finally came to an end, first with the German collapse in May 1945, and then the Japanese surrender three months later, following the American atomic bomb attacks on Hiroshima and Nagasaki.

The bomb had been developed over several years by American scientists and engineers working in great secrecy under the code name "Manhattan Project." It had been tested only once—in the desert of New Mexico—before being released over Hiroshima. The decision to drop the bomb in Japan, probably the most awesome decision ever to face a human being, was made by President Harry S Truman.

It is difficult to describe in words the effects of the atomic explosions over the two Japanese cities. Nevertheless, the following selection, although written largely in factual, unemotional terms, succeeds in capturing something of the essence not only of the material destruction wreaked but also of the human suffering, both physical and psychological, of the victims of the attacks. It is taken from a report prepared shortly after the war by a team of American investigators who visited both cities, examined the effects of the bombing, and questioned many survivors of the attacks.

Consider the following questions as you study the text below.

1. In your opinion, was the use of the atomic bomb necessary? In what ways was this weapon different from the conventional bombs that had been used throughout the war?

2. Do the authors of the report seem aware of the historical importance of the atomic bomb? What was the purpose of the report?

The Effects of Atomic Bombs on Hiroshima and Nagasaki

I. Introduction

The available facts about the power of the atomic bomb as a military weapon lie in the story of what it did at Hiroshima and Nagasaki. Many of these facts have been published, in official and unofficial form, but mingled with distortions or errors. The United States Strategic Bombing Survey, therefore, in partial fulfillment of the mission for which it was established, has put together in these pages a fairly full account of just what the atomic bombs did at Hiroshima and Nagasaki. Together with an explanation of how the bomb achieved these effects, this report states the extent and nature of the damage, the casualties, and the political repercussions from the two attacks. The basis is the observation, measurement, and analysis of the Survey's investigators. The conjecture that is necessary for understanding of the complex phenomena and for applying the findings to the problems of defense of the United States is clearly labelled.

When the atomic bombs fell, the United States Strategic Bombing Survey was completing a study of the effects of strategic bombing on Germany's ability and will to resist. A similar study of the effects of strategic bombing on Japan was being planned. The news of the dropping of the atomic bomb gave a new urgency to this project, for a study of the air war against Japan clearly involved new weapons and new possibilities of concentration of attack that might qualify or even change the conclusions and recommendations of the Survey as to the effectiveness of air power. The directors of the Survey, therefore, decided to examine exhaustively the effects of the atomic bombs, in order that the full impact on Japan and the implications of their results could be confidently analyzed. Teams of experts were selected to study the scenes of the bombings from the special points of emphasis of physical damage, civilian defense, morale, casualties, community life, utilities and transportation, various industries, and the general economic and political repercussions. In all, more than 110 men—engineers, architects, fire experts, economists, doctors, photographers, draftsmen—participated in the field study at each city, over a period of 10 weeks from October to December, 1945. Their detailed studies are now being published.

.   .   .

The Effects of Atomic Bombs on Hiroshima and Nagasaki (Washington, D.C.: U.S. Government Printing Office, 1946).

II. The Effects of the Atomic Bombing

A. THE ATTACKS AND DAMAGE

1. *The attacks.*   A single atomic bomb, the first weapon of its type ever used against a target, exploded over the city of Hiroshima at 0815 on the morning of 6 August 1945. Most of the industrial workers had already reported to work, but many workers were enroute and nearly all the school children and some industrial employees were at work in the open on the program of building removal to provide firebreaks and disperse valuables to the country. The attack came 45 minutes after the "all clear" had been sounded from a previous alert. Because of the lack of warning and the populace's indifference to small groups of planes, the explosion came as an almost complete surprise, and the people had not taken shelter. Many were caught in the open, and most of the rest in flimsily constructed homes or commercial establishments.

The bomb exploded slightly northwest of the center of the city. Because of this accuracy and the flat terrain and circular shape of the city, Hiroshima was uniformly and extensively devastated. Practically the entire densely or moderately built-up portion of the city was leveled by blast and swept by fire. A "fire-storm," a phenomenon which has occurred infrequently in other conflagrations, developed in Hiroshima: fires springing up almost simultaneously over the wide flat area around the center of the city drew in air from all directions. The inrush of air easily overcame the natural ground wind, which had a velocity of only about 5 miles per hour. The "fire-wind" attained a maximum velocity of 30 to 40 miles per hour 2 to 3 hours after the explosion. The "fire-wind" and the symmetry of the built-up center of the city gave a roughly circular shape to the 4.4 square miles which were almost completely burned out.

The surprise, the collapse of many buildings, and the conflagration contributed to an unprecedented casualty rate. Seventy to eighty thousand people were killed, or missing and presumed dead, and an equal number were injured. ...

At Nagasaki, 3 days later, the city was scarcely more prepared, though vague references to the Hiroshima disaster had appeared in the newspaper of 8 August. From the Nagasaki Prefectural Report on the bombing, something of the shock of the explosion can be inferred:

> *The day was clear with not very much wind—an ordinary midsummer's day. The strain of continuous air attack on the city's population and the severity of the summer had vitiated enthusiastic air raid precautions. Previously, a general alert had been sounded at 0748, with a raid alert at 0750; this was canceled at 0830, and the alertness of the people was dissipated by a great feeling of relief.*

The city remained on the warning alert, but when two B-29s were again sighted coming in the raid signal was not given immediately; the bomb was dropped at 1102 and the raid signal was given a few minutes later, at 1109. Thus only about 400 people were in the city's tunnel shelters, which were adequate for about 30 percent of the population.

> *When the atomic bomb exploded, an intense flash was observed first, as though a large amount of magnesium had been ignited, and the scene grew hazy with white smoke. At the same time at the center of the explosion, and a short while later in other areas, a tremendous roaring sound was heard and a crushing blast wave and intense heat were felt. The people of Nagasaki, even those who lived on the outer edge of the blast, all felt as though they had sustained a direct hit, and the whole city suffered damage such as would have resulted from direct hits everywhere by ordinary bombs.*
>
> *The zero area, where the damage was most severe, was almost completely wiped out and for a short while after the explosion no reports came out of that area. People who were in comparatively damaged areas reported their condition under the impression that they had received a direct hit. If such a great amount of damage could be wreaked by a near miss, then the power of the atomic bomb is unbelievably great.*

In Nagasaki, no fire-storm arose, and the uneven terrain of the city confined the maximum intensity of damage to the valley over which the bomb exploded. The area of nearly complete devastation was thus much smaller; only about 1.8 square miles. Casualties were lower also; between 35,000 and 40,000 were killed, and about the same number injured. People in the tunnel shelters escaped injury, unless exposed in the entrance shaft.

·   ·   ·

Hiroshima before the war was the seventh largest city in Japan, with a population of over 340,000, and was the principal administrative and commercial center of the southwestern part of the country. As the headquarters of the Second Army and of the Chugoku Regional Army, it was one of the most important military command stations in Japan, the site of one of the largest military supply depots, and the foremost military shipping point for both troops and supplies. Its shipping activities had virtually ceased by the time of the attack, however, because of sinkings and the mining of the Inland Sea. It had been relatively unimportant industrially before the war, ranking only twelfth, but during the war new plants were built that increased its significance. These factories were not concentrated, but spread over the outskirts of the city; this location, we shall see, accounts for the slight industrial damage.

The impact of the atomic bomb shattered the normal fabric of community life and disrupted the organizations for handling the disaster. In the 30 percent of the population killed and the additional 30 percent seriously injured were included corresponding proportions of the civic authorities and rescue groups. A mass flight from the city took place, as persons sought safety from the conflagration and a place for shelter and food. Within 24 hours, however, people were streaming back by the thousands in search of relatives and friends and to determine the extent of their property loss. Road blocks had to be set up along all routes leading into the city, to keep curious and unauthorized people out. The bulk of the dehoused population found refuge in the surrounding countryside; within the city the food supply was short and shelter virtually nonexistent.

On 7 August, the commander of the Second Army assumed general command of the counter-measures, and all military units and facilities in the area were mobilized for relief purposes. Army buildings on the periphery of the city provided shelter and emergency hospital space, and dispersed Army supplies supplemented the slight amounts of food and clothing that had escaped destruction. The need far exceeded what could be made available. Surviving civilians assisted; although casualties in both groups had been heavy, 190 policemen and over 2,000 members of the Civilian Defense Corps reported for duty on 7 August.

The status of medical facilities and personnel dramatically illustrates the difficulties facing authorities. Of more than 200 doctors in Hiroshima before the attack, over 90 percent were casualties and only about 30 physicians were able to perform their normal duties a month after the raid. Out of 1,780 nurses, 1,654 were killed or injured. Though some stocks of supplies had been dispersed, many were destroyed. Only three out of 45 civilian hospitals could be used, and two large Army hospitals were rendered unusable. Those within 3,000 feet of group zero were totally destroyed, and the mortality rate of the occupants was practically 100 percent. Two large hospitals of reinforced concrete construction were located 4,900 feet from ground zero. The basic structures remained erect but there was such severe interior damage that neither was able to resume operation as a hospital for some time and the casualty rate was approximately 90 percent, due primarily to falling plaster, flying glass, and fire. Hospitals and clinics beyond 7,000 feet, though often remaining standing, were badly damaged and contained many casualties from flying glass or other missiles.

With such elimination of facilities and personnel, the lack of care and rescue activities at the time of the disaster is understandable; still, the eyewitness account of Father Siemes[1] shows how this lack of first-aid contributed to the seriousness of casualties. At the improvised first-aid stations, he reports:

[1]German-born Jesuit professor at Jochi University, Tokyo; in the Hiroshima area when the bomb fell.

> *... Iodine is applied to the wounds but they are left uncleansed. Neither ointment nor other therapeutic agents are available. Those that have been brought in are laid on the floor and no one can give them any further care. What could one do when all means are lacking? Among the passersby, there are many who are uninjured. In a purposeless, insensate manner, distraught by the magnitude of the disaster, most of them rush by and none conceives the thought of organizing help on his own initiative. They are concerned only with the welfare of their own families— in the official aid stations and hospitals, a good third or half of those that had been brought in died. They lay about there almost without care, and a very high percentage succumbed. Everything was lacking, doctors, assistants, dressings, drugs, etc. ...*

Effective medical help had to be sent in from the outside, and arrived only after a considerable delay.

Fire-fighting and rescue units were equally stripped of men and equipment. Father Siemes reports that 30 hours elapsed before any organized rescue parties were observed. In Hiroshima, only 16 pieces of fire-fighting equipment were available for fighting the conflagration, three of them borrowed. However, it is unlikely that any public fire department in the world, even without damage to equipment or casualties to personnel, could have prevented development of a conflagration in Hiroshima, or combatted it with success at more than a few locations along its perimeter. The total fire damage would not have been much different.

When the atomic bomb fell, Nagasaki was comparatively intact. Because the most intense destruction was confined to the Urukami Valley, the impact of the bomb on the city as a whole was less shattering than at Hiroshima. In addition, no fire-storm occurred; indeed, a shift in wind direction helped control the fires. Medical personnel and facilities were hard-hit, however. Over 80 percent of the city's hospital beds and the Medical College were located within 3,000 feet of the center of the explosion, and were completely gutted by fire; buildings of wooden construction were destroyed by fire and blast. The mortality rate in this group of buildings was between 75 and 80 percent. Exact casualty figures for medical personnel are unknown, but the city seems to have fared better than Hiroshima: 120 doctors were at work on 1 November, about one-half of the preraid roster. Casualties were undoubtedly high: 600 out of 850 medical students at the Nagasaki Medical College were killed and most of the others injured; and of the 20 faculty members, 12 were killed and 4 others injured.

·   ·   ·

The city's repair facilities were completely disorganized by the atomic bomb, so that with the single exception of shutting off water to the affected areas no repairs were made to roads, bridges, water mains, or transportation installations by city forces. The prefecture took full responsibility for such restoration as was accomplished, delegating to the scattered city help the task of assisting in relief of victims. There were only 3 survivors of 115 employees of the street car company, and as late as the middle of November 1945 no cars were running. A week after the explosion, the water works officials made an effort to supply water to persons attempting to live in the bombed-out areas, but the leakage was so great that the effort was abandoned. It fell to the prefecture, therefore, to institute recovery measures even in those streets normally the responsibility of the city. Of the entire public works construction group covering the Nagasaki city area, only three members appeared for work and a week was required to locate and notify other survivors. On the morning of 10 August, police rescue units and workers from the Kawaminami shipbuilding works began the imperative task of clearing the Omura-Nagasaki pike, which was impassable for 8,000 feet. A path 6 1/2 feet wide was cleared despite the intense heat from smouldering fires, and by 15 August had been widened to permit two-way traffic. No trucks, only rakes and shovels, were available for clearing the streets, which were filled with tile, bricks, stone, corrugated iron, machinery, plaster, and stucco. Street areas affected by blast and not by fire were littered with wood. Throughout the devastated area, all wounded had to be carried by stretcher, since no motor vehicles were able to proceed through the cluttered streets for several days. The plan for debris removal required clearance of a few streets leading to the main highway; but there were frequent delays caused by the heat of smouldering fires and by calls for relief work. The debris was simply raked and shoveled off the streets. By 20 August the job was considered complete. The streets were not materially damaged by the bomb nor were the surface or the abutments of the concrete bridges, but many of the wooden bridges were totally or partially destroyed by fire.

Under the circumstances—fire, flight of entire families, destruction of official records, mass cremation—identification of dead and the accurate count of casualties was impossible. As at Hiroshima, the season of the year made rapid disposal of bodies imperative, and mass cremation and mass burial were resorted to in the days immediately after the attack. Despite the absence of sanitary measures, no epidemics broke out here. The dysentery rate rose from 25 per 100,000 to 125 per 100,000. A census taken on 1 November 1945 found a population of 142,700 in the city.

At Nagasaki, the scale of destruction was greater than at Hiroshima, though the actual area destroyed was smaller because of the terrain and the point of fall of the bomb. The Nagasaki Prefectural Report described vividly the impress of the bomb on the city and its inhabitants:

> *Within a radius of 1 kilometer from ground zero, men and animals died almost instantaneously from the tremendous blast pressure and heat; houses and other structures were smashed, crushed and scattered;*

and fires broke out. The strong complex steel members of the structures of the Mitsubishi Steel Works were bent and twisted like jelly and the roofs of the reinforced concrete National Schools were crumpled and collapsed, indicating a force beyond imagination. Trees of all sizes lost their branches or were uprooted or broken off at the trunk.

Outside a radius of 1 kilometer and within a radius of 2 kilometers from ground zero, some men and animals died instantly from the great blast and heat, but the great majority were seriously or superficially injured. Houses and other structures were completely destroyed while fires broke out everywhere. Trees were uprooted and withered by the heat.

Outside a radius of 2 kilometers and within a radius of 4 kilometers from ground zero, men and animals suffered various degrees of injury from window glass and other fragments scattered about by the blast and many were burned by the intense heat. Dwelling and other structures were half damaged by blast.

Outside a radius of 4 kilometers and within a radius of 8 kilometers from ground zero, living creatures were injured by materials blown about by the blast; the majority were only superficially wounded. Houses were half or only partially damaged.

While the conflagration with its uniformly burnt-out area caught the attention of Hiroshima, the blast effects, with their resemblance to the aftermath of a hurricane, were most striking at Nagasaki. Concrete buildings had their sides facing the blast stove in like boxes. Long lines of steel-framed factory sheds, over a mile from ground zero, leaned their skeletons away from the explosion. Blast resistant objects such as telephone poles leaned away from the center of the explosion; on the surrounding hills trees were blown down within considerable areas. Although there was no general conflagration, fires contributed to the total damage in nearly all concrete structures. Evidence of primary fire is more frequent than at Hiroshima.

. . .

B. GENERAL EFFECTS

1. *Casualties.* The most striking result of the atomic bombs was the great number of casualties. The exact number of dead and injured will never be known because of the confusion after the explosions. Persons unaccounted for might have been burned beyond recognition in the falling buildings, disposed of in one of the mass cremations of the first week of recovery, or driven out of the city to die or recover without any record remaining. No sure count of even the preraid population existed. Because of the decline in activity in the two port cities, the constant threat of incendiary raids, and the formal evacuation programs of the Government, an unknown number of the

inhabitants had either drifted away from the cities or been removed according to plan. In this uncertain situation, estimates of casualties have generally ranged between 100,000 and 180,000 for Hiroshima, and between 50,000 and 100,000 for Nagasaki. The Survey believes the dead at Hiroshima to have been between 70,000 and 80,000 with an equal number injured; at Nagasaki over 35,000 dead and somewhat more than that injured seems the most plausible estimate.

Most of the immediate casualties did not differ from those caused by incendiary or high-explosive raids. The outstanding difference was the presence of radiation effects, which became unmistakable about a week after the bombing. At the time of impact, however, the causes of death and injury were flash burns, secondary effects of blast and falling debris, and burns from blazing buildings. No records are available that give the relative importance of the various types of injury, especially for those who died immediately after the explosion. Indeed, many of these people undoubtedly died several times over, theoretically, since each was subjected to several injuries, any one of which would have been fatal.

Radiation disease. The radiation effects upon survivors resulted from the gamma rays liberated by the fission process rather than from induced radio-activity or the lingering radio-activity of deposits of primary fission products. Both at Nagasaki and at Hiroshima, pockets of radio-activity have been detected where fission products were directly deposited, but the degree of activity in these areas was insufficient to produce casualties. Similarly, induced radio-activity from the interaction of neutrons with matter caused no authenticated fatalities. But the effects of gamma rays—here used in a general sense to include all penetrating high-frequency radiations and neutrons that caused injury—are well established, even though the Allies had no observers in the affected areas for several weeks after the explosions.

Our understanding of radiation casualties is not complete. In part the deficiency is in our basic knowledge of how radiation effects animal tissue.

According to the Japanese, those individuals very near the center of the explosion but not affected by flash burns or secondary injuries became ill within 2 or 3 days. Bloody diarrhea followed, and the victims expired, some within 2 to 3 days after the onset and the majority within a week. Autopsies showed remarkable changes in the blood picture—almost complete absence of white blood cells, and deterioration of bone marrow. Mucous membranes of the throat, lungs, stomach, and the intestines showed acute inflammation.

The majority of the radiation cases, who were at greater distances, did not show severe symptoms until 1 to 4 weeks after the explosion, though many felt weak and listless on the following day. After a day or two of mild nausea and vomiting, the appetite improved and the person felt quite well until symptoms reappeared at a later date. In the opinion of some Japanese physicians, those who rested or subjected themselves to less physical exertion showed a longer delay before the onset of subsequent symptoms.

The first signs of recurrence were loss of appetite, lassitude, and general discomfort. Inflammation of the gums, mouth, and pharynx appeared next. Within 12 to 48 hours, fever became evident. In many instances it reached only 100° Fahrenheit and remained for only a few days. In other cases, the temperature went as high as 104° or 106° Fahrenheit. The degree of fever apparently had a direct relation to the degree of exposure to radiation. Once developed, the fever was usually well sustained, and in those cases terminating fatally it continued high until the end. If the fever subsided, the patient usually showed a rapid disappearance of other symptoms and soon regained his feeling of good health. The other symptoms commonly seen were shortage of white corpuscles, loss of hair, inflammation and gangrene of the gums, inflammation of the mouth and pharynx, ulceration of the lower gastro-intestinal tract, small livid spots (petechiae) resulting from escape of blood into the tissues of the skin or mucous membrane, and larger hemorrhages of gums, nose and skin.

Loss of hair usually began about 2 weeks after the bomb explosion, though in a few instances it is reported to have begun as early as 4 to 5 days afterward. The areas were involved in the following order of frequency with variations depending on the degree of exposure: scalp, armpits, beard, pubic region, and eyebrows. Complete baldness was rare. Microscopic study of the body areas involved has shown atrophy of the hair follicles. In those patients who survived after 2 months, however, the hair has commenced to regrow. An interesting but unconfirmed report has it that loss of the hair was less marked in persons with grey hair than in those with dark hair. ...

The effects of the bomb on pregnant women are marked, however. Of women in various stages of pregnancy who were within 3,000 feet of ground zero, all known cases have had miscarriages. Even up to 6,500 feet they have had miscarriages or premature infants who died shortly after birth. In the group between 6,500 and 10,000 feet, about one-third have given birth to apparently normal children. Two months after the explosion, the city's total incidence of miscarriages, abortions, and premature birth was 27 percent as compared with a normal rate of 6 percent. Since other factors than radiation contributed to this increased rate, a period of years will be required to learn the ultimate effects of mass radiation upon reproduction.

Treatment of victims by the Japanese was limited by the lack of medical supplies and facilities. Their therapy consisted of small amounts of vitamins, liver extract, and an occasional blood transfusion. Allied doctors used penicillin and plasma with beneficial effects. Liver extract seemed to benefit the few patients on whom it was used: It was given in small frequent doses when available. A large percentage of the cases died of secondary disease, such as septic bronchopneumonia or tuberculosis, as a result of lowered resistance. Deaths from radiation began about a week after exposure and reached a peak in 3 to 4 weeks. They had practically ceased to occur after 7 to 8 weeks.

Unfortunately, no exact definition of the killing power of radiation can yet be given, nor a satisfactory account of the sort and thickness of concrete or earth that will shield people. From the definitive report of the Joint Commission will come more nearly accurate statements on these matters. In the meanwhile the awesome lethal effects of the atomic bomb and the insidious additional peril of the gamma rays speak for themselves.

.   .   .

2. *Morale.* As might be expected, the primary reaction to the bomb was fear—uncontrolled terror, strengthened by the sheer horror of the destruction and suffering witnessed and experienced by the survivors. Between one-half and two-thirds of those interviewed in the Hiroshima and Nagasaki areas confessed having such reactions, not just for the moment but for some time. As two survivors put it:

> *Whenever a plane was seen after that, people would rush into their shelters; they went in and out so much that they did not have time to eat. They were so nervous they could not work.*
>
> *After the atomic bomb fell, I just couldn't stay home. I would cook, but while cooking I would always be watching out and worrying whether an atomic bomb would fall near me.*

The behavior of the living immediately after the bombings, as described earlier, clearly shows the state of shock that hindered rescue efforts. A Nagasaki survivor illustrates succinctly the mood of survivors:

> *All I saw was the flash and I felt my body get warm and then I saw everything flying around. My grandmother was hit on the head by a flying piece of roof and she was bleeding. … I became hysterical seeing my grandmother bleeding and we just ran around without knowing what to do.*
>
> *I was working at the office. I was talking to a friend at the window. I saw the whole city in a red flame, then I ducked. The pieces of the glass hit my back and face. My dress was torn off by the glass. Then I got up and ran to the mountain where the good shelter was.*

The two typical impulses were these: Aimless, even hysterical activity or flight from the city to shelter and food.

The United Nations

Just as World War I had spawned the League of Nations, so World War II gave birth to the United Nations. Planning for the international organization to preserve world peace began early in the war, during a number of conferences among the nations fighting against Axis aggression, and the United Nations came into being with the signing of its Charter by fifty-one countries in June 1945, following an organizing conference held in San Francisco, even before the war against Japan had been concluded. Later the United Nations established its permanent headquarters in New York City. The United States, rather than rejecting the United Nations, as it had the League of Nations a quarter-century before, took a strong lead in its formation and operation.

In establishing the United Nations its founders attempted to profit from the experience of the League of Nations and, in particular, to avoid the major weaknesses of the earlier international organization. To some extent they were successful in that endeavor. Recognizing the impotence of the League against major powers that engaged in acts violating world peace, the Charter of the United Nations empowered the Security Council (composed of representatives of eleven member nations) to impose both economic and military sanctions against countries that engaged in acts of aggression. This power has been invoked on several occasions and has in some cases proved effective. A notable example occurred in 1950, when North Korea invaded the Republic of Korea. The Security Council immediately met, asked that the fighting be stopped and, when North Korea did not respond, authorized the deployment of troops to the area. Sixteen member nations joined in the military effort, the result being the Korean War, which came to an end in 1953 when North Korea and the United Nations signed an armistice, the North Koreans relinquishing the territory they had occupied following their act of aggression. In a number of other instances the United Nations has proved effective in preventing or controlling warfare. Nevertheless, even though more successful than the League of Nations, it was for decades frustrated by a basic weakness in its constitution. This appears in Article 27 of the Charter, which stipulates the voting procedures of the Security Council. The Council, although composed of members from eleven countries, has had five members—from China, France, Great Britain, the United States, and the former USSR—who sat permanently on it. Furthermore, the Council can take substantive action only with the approval of all five of these members. Thus, any one of the great powers could exercise a veto on the Security Council. And, during the long decades of the "cold war," this veto power was constantly exercised by one or other of the opposing sides, mainly by the USSR. But now, with the collapse of communism in Eastern Europe and the disintegration of the Soviet Union, the cold war has apparently come to an end and there has been a surge of hope about the future of the United Nations and its ability to act as a deterrent to aggression and a preserver of world peace in the years ahead.

The selection that follows contains the first 51 Articles (out of a total of 111) of the Charter of the United Nations.

Consider the following questions as you study the text below.

1. Has the United Nations been an effective force for peace in the years since World War II? What role do you see the United Nations playing in the near future?

2. Why has the General Assembly diminished in importance over the last several decades? In your opinion, should the members of the Security Council continue to have veto power?

Charter of the United Nations[1]

WE THE PEOPLES OF THE UNITED NATIONS DETERMINED

to save succeeding generations from the scourge of war, which twice in our lifetime has brought untold sorrow to mankind, and

to reaffirm faith in fundamental human rights, in the dignity and worth of the human person, in the equal rights of men and women and of nations large and small, and

to establish conditions under which justice and respect for the obligations arising from treaties and other sources of international law can be maintained, and

to promote social progress and better standards of life in larger freedom,

---

[1]Amendments to Articles 23 and 27 of the Charter of the United Nations, adopted by the General Assembly on 17 December 1963, came into force on 31 August 1965.

The Amendment to Article 23 enlarged the Security Council from 11 to 15 members.

The amended Article 27 provided that decisions of the Security Council on procedural matters shall be made by an affirmative vote of nine members (formerly seven) and on all other matters by an affirmative vote of nine members (formerly seven), including the concurring votes of the five permanent members of the Security Council.

AND FOR THESE ENDS

to practice tolerance and live together in peace with one another as good
    neighbours, and
to unite our strength to maintain international peace and security, and
to ensure by the acceptance of principles and the institution of methods, that
    armed force shall not be used, save in the common interest, and
to employ international machinery for the promotion of the economic and
    social advancement of all peoples,

HAVE RESOLVED TO COMBINE OUR EFFORTS
TO ACCOMPLISH THESE AIMS

Accordingly, our respective Governments, through representatives assem-
    bled in the city of San Francisco, who have exhibited their full powers
    found to be in good and due form, have agreed to the present Charter
    of the United Nations and do hereby establish an international organi-
    zation to be known as the United Nations.

Chapter I

PURPOSES AND PRINCIPLES

Article 1   The Purposes of the United Nations are:
    1.   To maintain international peace and security, and to that end: to
take effective collective measures for the prevention and removal of threats
to the peace, and for the suppression of acts of aggression or other breaches
of the peace, and to bring about by peaceful means, and in conformity with
the principles of justice and international law, adjustment or settlement of international disputes or situations which might lead to a breach of the peace;
    2.   To develop friendly relations among nations based on respect for
the principle of equal rights and self-determination of peoples, and to take
other appropriate measures to strengthen universal peace;
    3.   To achieve international cooperation in solving international prob-
lems of an economic, social, cultural or humanitarian character, and in promoting and encouraging respect for human rights and for fundamental
freedoms for all without distinction as to race, sex, language, or religion; and
    4.   To be a centre for harmonizing the actions of nations in the attain-
ment of these common ends.
    Article 2   The Organization and its Members, in pursuit of the Purposes
stated in Article 1, shall act in accordance with the following Principles.
    1.   The Organization is based on the principle of the sovereign
equality of all its Members.

2. All Members, in order to ensure to all of them the rights and benefits resulting from membership, shall fulfil in good faith the obligations assumed by them in accordance with the present Charter.

3. All Members shall settle their international disputes by peaceful means in such a manner that international peace and security, and justice, are not endangered.

4. All Members shall refrain in their international relations from the threat or use of force against the territorial integrity or political independence of any state, or in any other manner inconsistent with the Purposes of the United Nations.

5. All Members shall give the United Nations every assistance in any action it takes in accordance with the present Charter, and shall refrain from giving assistance to any state against which the United Nations is taking preventive or enforcement action.

6. The Organization shall ensure that states which are not Members of the United Nations act in accordance with these Principles so far as may be necessary for the maintenance of international peace and security.

7. Nothing contained in the present Charter shall authorize the United Nations to intervene in matters which are essentially within the domestic jurisdiction of any state or shall require the Members to submit such matters to settlement under the present Charter; but this principle shall not prejudice the application of enforcement measures under Chapter VII.

Chapter II

MEMBERSHIP

Article 3   The original Members of the United Nations shall be the states which, having participated in the United Nations Conference on International Organization at San Francisco, or having previously signed the Declaration by United Nations of 1 January 1942, sign the present Charter and ratify it in accordance with Article 110.

Article 4   1.   Membership to the United Nations is open to all other peaceloving states which accept the obligations contained in the present Charter and, in the judgment of the Organization, are able and willing to carry out these obligations.

2. The admission of any such state to membership in the United Nations will be effected by a decision of the General Assembly upon the recommendation of the Security Council.

Article 5   A member of the United Nations against which preventive or enforcement action has been taken by the Security Council may be suspended from the exercise of the rights and privileges of membership by the General Assembly upon the recommendation of the Security Council. The exercise of these rights and privileges may be restored by the Security Council.

Article 6   A member of the United Nations which has persistently violated the Principles contained in the present Charter may be expelled from the Organization by the General Assembly upon the recommendation of the Security Council.

Chapter III

ORGANS

Article 7   1.   There are established as the principal organs of the United Nations: a General Assembly, a Security Council, an Economic and Social Council, a Trusteeship Council, an International Court of Justice, and a Secretariat.

2.   Such subsidiary organs as may be found necessary may be established in accordance with the present Charter.

Article 8   The United Nations shall place no restrictions on the eligibility of men and women to participate in any capacity and under conditions of equality in its principal and subsidiary organs.

Chapter IV

THE GENERAL ASSEMBLY

Composition

Article 9   1.   The General Assembly shall consist of all the members of the United Nations.

2.   Each Member shall have not more than five representatives in the General Assembly.

Functions and Powers

Article 10   The General Assembly may discuss any questions or any matters within the scope of the present Charter or relating to the powers and functions of any organs provided for in the present Charter, and except as provided in Article 12, may make recommendations to the Members of the United Nations or to the Security Council or to both on any such questions or matters.

Article 11   1.   The General Assembly may consider the general principles of cooperation in the maintenance of international peace and security, including the principles governing disarmament and the regulation of armaments, and may make recommendations with regard to such principles to the Members or to the Security Council or to both.

2. The General Assembly may discuss any questions relating to the maintenance of international peace and security brought before it by any Member of the United Nations, or by the Security Council, or by a state which is not a Member of the United Nations in accordance with Article 35, paragraph 2, and, except as provided in Article 12, may make recommendations with regard to any such question to the state or states concerned or to the Security Council or to both. Any such question on which action is necessary shall be referred to the Security Council by the General Assembly either before or after discussion.

3. The General Assembly may call the attention of the Security Council to situations which are likely to endanger international peace and security.

4. The powers of the General Assembly set forth in this Article shall not limit the general scope of Article 10.

Article 12   1.   While the Security Council is exercising in respect of any dispute or situation the functions assigned to it in the present Charter, the General Assembly shall not make any recommendation with regard to that dispute or situation unless the Security Council so requests.

2. The Secretary-General, with the Security Council, shall notify the General Assembly at each session of any matters relative to the maintenance of international peace and security which are being dealt with by the Security Council and shall similarly notify the General Assembly or the Members of the United Nations if the General Assembly is not in session, immediately the Security Council ceases to deal with such matters.

Article 13   1.   The General Assembly shall initiate studies and make recommendations for the purpose of:

a. promoting international cooperation in the political field and encouraging the progressive development of international law and its codification;
b. promoting international cooperation in the economic, social, cultural, educational, and health fields, and assisting in the realization of human rights and fundamental freedoms for all without distinction as to race, sex, language, or religion.

2. The further responsibilities, functions and powers of the General Assembly with respect to matters mentioned in paragraph 1b above are set forth in Chapters IX and X.

Article 14   Subject to the provisions of Article 12, the General Assembly may recommend measures for the peaceful adjustment of any situation, regardless of origin, which it deems likely to impair the general welfare or friendly relations among nations, including situations resulting from a violation of the provisions of the present Charter setting forth the Purposes and Principles of the United Nations.

Article 15   1.   The General Assembly shall receive and consider annual and special reports from the Security Council; these reports shall include an account of the measures that the Security Council has decided upon or taken to maintain international peace and security.

2.   The General Assembly shall receive and consider reports from the other organs of the United Nations.

Article 16   The General Assembly shall perform such functions with respect to the international trusteeship system as are assigned to it under Chapters XII and XIII, including the approval of the trusteeship agreements for areas not designed as strategic.

Article 17   1.   The General Assembly shall consider and approve the budget of the Organization.

2.   The expenses of the Organization shall be borne by the Members as apportioned by the General Assembly.

3.   The General Assembly shall consider and approve any financial and budgetary arrangements with specialized agencies referred to in Article 57 and shall examine the administrative budgets of such specialized agencies with a view to making recommendations to the agencies concerned.

Voting

Article 18   1.   Each member of the General Assembly shall have one vote.

2.   Decisions of the General Assembly on important questions shall be made by a two-thirds majority of the members present and voting. These questions shall include: recommendations with respect to the maintenance of international peace and security, the election of the nonpermanent members of the Security Council, the election of the members of the Economic and Social Council, the election of members of the Trusteeship Council in accordance with paragraph 1c of Article 86, the admission of new members to the United Nations, the suspension of the rights and privileges of membership, the expulsion of Members, questions relating to the operation of the trusteeship system, and budgetary questions.

3.   Decisions on other questions including the determination of additional categories of questions to be decided by a two-thirds majority, shall be made by a majority of the members present and voting.

Article 19   A member of the United Nations which is in arrears in the payment of its financial contributions to the Organization shall have no vote in the General Assembly if the amount of its arrears equals or exceeds the amount of the contributions due from it for the preceding two full years. The General Assembly may, nevertheless, permit such a Member to vote if it is satisfied that the failure to pay is due to conditions beyond the control of the Member.

Procedure

Article 20   The General Assembly shall meet in regular annual sessions and in such special sessions as occasion may require. Special sessions shall be convoked by the Secretary-General at the request of the Security Council or of a majority of the Members of the United Nations.

Article 21   The General Assembly shall adopt its own rules of procedure. It shall elect its President for each session.

Article 22   The General Assembly may establish such subsidiary organs as it deems necessary for the performance of its functions.

Chapter V

THE SECURITY COUNCIL

Composition

Article 23   1.   The Security Council shall consist of fifteen members of the United Nations. The Republic of China, France, the Union of Soviet Socialist Republics, the United Kingdom of Great Britain and Northern Ireland, and the United States of America shall be permanent members of the Security Council. The General Assembly shall elect ten other Members of the United Nations to be nonpermanent members of the Security Council, due regard being specially paid, in the first instance to the contribution of Members of the United Nations to the maintenance of international peace and security and to the other purposes of the Organization, and also to equitable geographical distribution.

2.   The nonpermanent members of the Security Council shall be elected for a term of two years. In the first election of the nonpermanent members after the increase of the membership of the Security Council from eleven to fifteen, two of the four additional members shall be chosen for a term of one year. A retiring member shall not be eligible for immediate re-election.

3.   Each member of the Security Council shall have one representative.

Functions and Powers

Article 24   1.   In order to ensure prompt and effective action by the United Nations, its Members confer on the Security Council primary responsibility for the maintenance of international peace and security, and agree that in carrying out its duties under this responsibility the Security Council acts on their behalf.

2.   In discharging these duties the Security Council shall act in accordance with the Purposes and Principles of the United Nations. The specific

powers granted to the Security Council for the discharge of these duties are laid down in Chapters VI, VII, VIII, and XII.

3. The Security Council shall submit annual and, when necessary, special reports to the General Assembly for its consideration.

Article 25   The Members of the United Nations agree to accept and carry out the decisions of the Security Council in accordance with the present Charter.

Article 26   In order to promote the establishment and maintenance of international peace and security with the least diversion for armaments of the world's human economic resources, the Security Council shall be responsible for formulating, with the assistance of the Military Staff Committee referred to in Article 47, plans to be submitted to the Members of the United Nations for the establishment of a system for the regulation of armaments.

Voting

Article 27   1.   Each member of the Security Council shall have one vote.

2.   Decisions of the Security Council on procedural matters shall be made by an affirmative vote of nine members.

3.   Decisions of the Security Council on all other matters shall be made by an affirmative vote of nine members including the concurring votes of the permanent members; provided that, in decisions under Chapter VI, and under paragraph 3 of Article 52, a party to a dispute shall abstain from voting.

Procedure

Article 28   1.   The Security Council shall be so organized as to be able to function continuously. Each member of the Security Council shall for this purpose be represented at all times at the seat of the Organization.

2.   The Security Council shall hold periodic meetings at which each of its members may, if it so desires, be represented by a member of the government or by some other specially designated representative.

3.   The Security Council may hold meetings at such places other than the seat of the Organization as in its judgment will best facilitate its work.

Article 29   The Security Council may establish such subsidiary organs as it deems necessary for the performance of its functions.

Article 30   The Security Council shall adopt its own rules of procedure, including the method of selecting its President.

Article 31   Any Member of the United Nations which is not a member of the Security Council may participate, without vote, in the discussion of any question brought before the Security Council whenever the latter considers that the interests of that Member are specially affected.

Article 32   Any Member of the United Nations which is not a member of the Security Council or any state which is not a Member of the United

Nations, if it is a party to a dispute under consideration by the Security Council, shall be invited to participate, without vote, in the discussion relating to the dispute. The Security Council shall lay down such conditions as it deems just for the participation of such a state which is not a Member of the United Nations.

Chapter VI

PACIFIC SETTLEMENT OF DISPUTES

Article 33   1.   The parties to any dispute, the continuance of which is likely to endanger the maintenance of international peace and security, shall, first of all, seek a solution by negotiation, enquiry, mediation, conciliation, arbitration, judicial settlement, resort to regional agencies or arrangements, or other peaceful means of their own choice.

2.   The Security Council shall, when it deems necessary, call upon the parties to settle their dispute by such means.

Article 34   The Security Council may investigate any dispute, or any situation which might lead to international friction or give rise to a dispute, in order to determine whether the continuance of the dispute or situation is likely to endanger the maintenance of international peace and security.

Article 35   1.   Any Member of the United Nations may bring any dispute, or any situation of the nature referred to in Article 34, to the attention of the Security Council or of the General Assembly.

2.   A state which is not a Member of the United Nations may bring to the attention of the Security Council or of the General Assembly any dispute to which it is a party if it accepts in advance, for the purposes of the dispute, the obligations of pacific settlement provided in the present Charter.

3.   The proceedings of the General Assembly in respect of matters brought to its attention under this Article will be subject to the provisions of Articles 11 and 12.

Article 36   1.   The Security Council may, at any stage of a dispute of the nature referred to in Article 33 or of a situation of like nature, recommend appropriate procedures or methods of adjustment.

2.   The Security Council should take into consideration any procedures for the settlement of the dispute which have already been adopted by the parties.

3.   In making recommendations under this Article the Security Council should also take into consideration that legal disputes should as a general rule be referred by the parties to the International Court of Justice in accordance with the provisions of the Statute of the Court.

Article 37   1.   Should the parties to a dispute of the nature referred to in Article 33 fail to settle it by the means indicated in that Article, they shall refer it to the Security Council.

2.   If the Security Council deems that the continuance of the dispute is in fact likely to endanger the maintenance of international peace and security, it shall decide whether to take action under Article 36 or to recommend such terms of settlement as it may consider appropriate.

Article 38   Without prejudice to the provisions of Articles 33 to 37, the Security Council may, if all the parties to any dispute so request, make recommendations to the parties with a view to a pacific settlement of the dispute.

Chapter VII

ACTION WITH RESPECT TO THREATS TO THE PEACE, BREACHES OF THE PEACE, AND ACTS OF AGGRESSION

Article 39   The Security Council shall determine the existence of any threat to the peace, breach of the peace, or act of aggression and shall make recommendations, or decide what measures shall be taken in accordance with Articles 41 and 42, to maintain or restore international peace and security.

Article 40   In order to prevent an aggravation of the situation, the Security Council may, before making the recommendations or deciding upon the measures provided for in Article 39, call upon the parties concerned to comply with such provisional measures as it deems necessary or desirable. Such provisional measures shall be without prejudice to the rights, claims, or position of the parties concerned. The Security Council shall duly take account of failure to comply with such provisional measures.

Article 41   The Security Council may decide what measures not involving the use of armed forces are to be employed to give effect to its decisions, and it may call upon the Members of the United Nations to apply such measures. These may include complete or partial interruption of economic relations and of rail, sea, air, postal, telegraphic, radio, and other means of communication, and the severance of diplomatic relations.

Article 42   Should the Security Council consider that measures provided for in Article 41 would be inadequate or have proved to be inadequate, it may take such action by air, sea, or land forces as may be necessary to maintain or restore international peace and security. Such action may include demonstrations, blockade, and other operations by air, sea, or land forces of Members of the United Nations.

Article 43   1.   All Members of the United Nations, in order to contribute to the maintenance of international peace and security, undertake to make available to the Security Council, on its call and in accordance with a special agreement or agreements, armed forces, assistance, and facilities, including rights of passage, necessary for the purpose of maintaining international peace and security.

2.   Such agreement or agreements shall govern the numbers and types of forces, the degree of readiness and general location, and the nature of the facilities and assistance to be provided.

3.   The agreement or agreements shall be negotiated as soon as possible on the initiative of the Security Council. They shall be concluded between the Security Council and Members or between the Security Council and groups of Members and shall be subject to ratification by the signatory states in accordance with their respective constitutional processes.

Article 44   When the Security Council has decided to use force it shall, before calling upon a Member not represented on it to provide armed forces in fulfillment of the obligations assumed under Article 43, invite that Member, if the Member so desires, to participate in the decisions of the Security Council concerning the employment of contingents of that Member's armed forces.

Article 45   In order to enable the United Nations to take urgent military measures, Members shall hold immediately available national airforce contingents for combined international enforcement action. The strength and degree of readiness of these contingents and plans for their combined action shall be determined, within the limits laid down in the special agreement or agreements referred to in Article 43, by the Security Council with the assistance of the Military Staff Committee.

Article 46   Plans for the application of armed force shall be made by the Security Council with the assistance of the Military Staff Committee.

Article 47   1.   There shall be established a Military Staff Committee to advise and assist the Security Council on all questions relating to the Security Council's military requirements for the maintenance of international peace and security, the employment and command of forces placed at its disposal, the regulation of armaments, and possible disarmament.

2.   The Military Staff Committee shall consist of the Chiefs of Staff, of the permanent members of the Security Council or their representatives. Any Member of the United Nations not permanently represented on the Committee shall be invited by the Committee to be associated with it when the efficient discharge of the Committee's responsibilities requires the participation of that Member in its work.

3.   The Military Staff Committee shall be responsible under the Security Council for the strategic direction of any armed forces placed at the disposal of the Security Council. Questions relating to the command of such forces shall be worked out subsequently.

4.   The Military Staff Committee, with the authorization of the Security Council and after consultation with appropriate regional agencies, may establish regional subcommittees.

Article 48   1.   The action required to carry out the decisions of the Security Council for the maintenance of international peace and security shall be taken by all the Members of the United Nations or by some of them, as the Security Council may determine.

2.   Such decisions shall be carried out by the Members of the United Nations directly and through their action in the appropriate international agencies of which they are members.

Article 49   The Members of the United Nations shall join in affording mutual assistance in carrying out the measures decided upon by the Security Council.

Article 50   If preventive or enforcement measures against any state are taken by the Security Council, any other state, whether a Member of the United Nations or not, which finds itself confronted with special economic problems arising from the carrying out of those measures shall have the right to consult the Security Council with regard to a solution of those problems.

Article 51   Nothing in the present Charter shall impair the inherent right of individual or collective self-defence if an armed attack occurs against a Member of the United Nations until the Security Council has taken measures necessary to maintain international peace and security. Measures taken by Members in the exercise of this right of self-defence shall be immediately reported to the Security Council and shall not in any way affect the authority and responsibility of the Security Council under the present Charter to take at any time such action as it deems necessary in order to maintain or restore international peace and security.

Simone de Beauvoir

Simone de Beauvoir (1908–1986) was a leading member of the French intellectual and literary elite through much of the twentieth century. Many of her writings—novels, essays, and memoirs—are based on the philosophy of existentialism, as expressed in the work of Jean-Paul Sartre, her intimate friend. In the final chapter of *The Second Sex*, from which the following selection is taken, de Beauvoir scathingly describes the relationship between the sexes in the world of her times, then concludes by sketching ways in which a new society can emerge in which men and women can live together in freedom and equality.

Consider the following questions as you study the text below.

1. According to de Beauvoir, who is to blame for the oppression of women? What must happen before this oppression can be eliminated?

2. According to de Beauvoir, why did the Soviet Union fail to achieve the promise of equality of men and women? What more should have been done?

The Second Sex

Society, being codified by man, decrees that woman is inferior: she can do away with this inferiority only by destroying the male's superiority. She sets about mutilating, dominating man, she contradicts him, she denies his truth and his values. But in doing this she is only defending herself; it was neither a changeless essence nor a mistaken choice that doomed her to immanence, to inferiority. They were imposed upon her. All oppression creates a state of war. And this is no exception. The existent who is regarded as inessential cannot fail to demand the reestablishment of her sovereignty.

Today the combat takes a different shape; instead of wishing to put man in a prison, woman endeavors to escape from one; she no longer seeks to drag him into the realms of immanence but to emerge, herself, into the light of transcendence. Now the attitude of the males creates a new conflict: it is with a bad grace that the man lets her go. He is very well pleased to

From *The Second Sex*, by Simone de Beauvoir, trans. H. M. Parshley. Copyright 1952 by Alfred A. Knopf, Inc. Reprinted by permission of Alfred A. Knopf, Inc., and the Estate of Simone de Beauvoir.

remain the sovereign subject, the absolute superior, the essential being; he refuses to accept his companion as an equal in any concrete way. She replies to his lack of confidence in her by assuming an aggressive attitude. It is no longer a question of a war between individuals each shut up in his or her sphere: a caste claiming its rights goes over the top and it is resisted by the privileged caste. Here two transcendences are face to face; instead of displaying mutual recognition, each free being wishes to dominate the other.

This difference of attitude is manifest on the sexual plane as on the spiritual plane. The "feminine" woman in making herself prey tries to reduce man, also, to her carnal passivity; she occupies herself in catching him in her trap, in enchaining him by means of the desire she arouses in him in submissively making herself a thing. The emancipated woman, on the contrary, wants to be active, a taker, and refuses the passivity man means to impose on her.

.   .   .

The quarrel will go on as long as men and women fail to recognize each other as peers; that is to say, as long as femininity is perpetuated as such. Which sex is the more eager to maintain it? Woman, who is being emancipated from it, wishes none the less to retain its privileges; and man, in that case, wants her to assume its limitations. "It is easier to accuse one sex than to excuse the other," says Montaigne.[1] It is vain to apportion praise and blame. The truth is that if the vicious circle is so hard to break, it is because the two sexes are each the victim at once of the other and of itself. Between two adversaries confronting each other in their pure liberty, an agreement could be easily reached: the more so as the war profits neither. But the complexity of the whole affair derives from the fact that each camp is giving aid and comfort to the enemy; woman is pursuing a dream of submission, man a dream of identification. Want of authenticity does not pay: each blames the other for the unhappiness he or she has incurred in yielding to the temptations of the easy way; what man and woman loathe in each other is the shattering frustration of each one's own bad faith and baseness.

We have seen why men enslaved women in the first place; the devaluation of femininity has been a necessary step in human evolution, but it might have led to collaboration between the two sexes; oppression is to be explained by the tendency of the existent to flee from himself by means of identification with the other, whom he oppresses to that end. In each individual man that tendency exists today; and the vast majority yield to it. The husband wants to find himself in his wife, the lover in his mistress, in the form of a stone image; he is seeking in her the myth of his virility, of his sovereignty, of his immediate reality. "My husband never goes to the movies,"

[1][French essayist (1533–1592)—*Ed.*]

says his wife, and the dubious masculine opinion is graved in the marble of eternity. But he is himself the slave of his double: what an effort to build up an image in which he is always in danger! In spite of everything his success in this depends upon the capricious freedom of women: he must constantly try to keep this propitious to him. Man is concerned with the effort to appear male, important, superior; he pretends so as to get pretense in return; he, too, is aggressive, uneasy; he feels hostility for women because he is afraid of them, he is afraid of them because he is afraid of the personage, the image, with which he identifies himself. What time and strength he squanders in liquidating, sublimating, transferring complexes, in talking about women, in seducing them, in fearing them! He would be liberated himself in their liberation. But this is precisely what he dreads. And so he obstinately persists in the mystifications intended to keep woman in her chains.

That she is being tricked, many men have realized. "What a misfortune to be a woman! And yet the misfortune, when one is a woman, is at bottom not to comprehend that it is one," says Kierkegaard.[2] For a long time there have been efforts to disguise this misfortune. For example, guardianship has been done away with: women have been given "protectors," and if they are invested with the rights of the old-time guardians, it is in woman's own interest. To forbid her working, to keep her at home, is to defend her against herself and to assure her happiness. We have seen what poetic veils are thrown over her monotonous burdens of housekeeping and maternity: in exchange for her liberty she has received the false treasures of her "femininity." Balzac[3] illustrates this maneuver very well in counseling man to treat her as a slave while persuading her that she is a queen. Less cynical, many men try to convince themselves that she is really privileged. There are American sociologists who seriously teach today the theory of "low-class gain." In France, also, it has often been proclaimed—although in a less scientific manner—that the workers are very fortunate in not being obliged to "keep up appearances" and still more so the bums who can dress in rags and sleep on the sidewalks, pleasures forbidden to the Count de Beaumont and the Wendels. Like the carefree wretches gaily scratching at their vermin, like the merry Negroes laughing under the lash and those joyous Tunisian Arabs burying their starved children with a smile, woman enjoys that incomparable privilege: irresponsibility. Free from troublesome burdens and cares, she obviously has "the better part." But it is disturbing that with an obstinate

---

[2]*In Vino Veritas.* He says further: "Politeness is pleasing—essentially—to woman, and the fact that she accepts it without hesitation is explained by nature's care for the weaker, for the unfavored being, and for one to whom an illusion means more than a material compensation. But this illusion, precisely, is fatal to her. ... To feel oneself freed from distress thanks to something imaginary, to be the dupe of something imaginary, is that not a still deeper mockery? ... Woman is very far from being *verwahrlost* (neglected), but in another sense she is, since she can never free herself from the illusion that nature has used to console her."

[3][French novelist (1799–1850)—*Ed.*]

perversity—connected no doubt with original sin—down through the centuries and in all countries, the people who have the better part are always crying to their benefactors: "It is too much! I will be satisfied with yours!" But the munificent capitalists, the generous colonists, the superb males, stick to their guns: "Keep the better part, hold on to it!"

It must be admitted that the males find in woman more complicity than the oppressor usually finds in the oppressed. And in bad faith they take authorization from this to declare that she has *desired* the destiny they have imposed on her. We have seen that all the main features of her training combine to bar her from the roads of revolt and adventure. Society in general—beginning with her respected parents—lies to her by praising the lofty values of love, devotion, the gift of herself, and then concealing from her the fact that neither lover nor husband nor yet her children will be inclined to accept the burdensome charge of all that. She cheerfully believes these lies because they invite her to follow the easy slope: in this others commit their worst crime against her; throughout her life from childhood on, they damage and corrupt her by designating as her true vocation this submission, which is the temptation of every existent in the anxiety of liberty. If a child is taught idleness by being amused all day long and never being led to study, or shown its usefulness, it will hardly be said, when he grows up, that he chose to be incapable and ignorant; yet this is how woman is brought up, without ever being impressed with the necessity of taking charge of her own existence. So she readily lets herself come to count on the protection, love, assistance, and supervision of others, she lets herself be fascinated with the hope of self-realization without *doing* anything. She does wrong in yielding to the temptation; but man is in no position to blame her, since he has led her into the temptation. When conflict arises between them, each will hold the other responsible for the situation; she will reproach him with having made her what she is: "No one taught me to reason or to earn my own living"; he will reproach her with having accepted the consequences. "You don't know anything, you are an incompetent," and so on. Each sex thinks it can justify itself by taking the offensive; but the wrongs done by one do not make the other innocent.

The innumerable conflicts that set men and women against one another come from the fact that neither is prepared to assume all the consequences of this situation which the one has offered and the other accepted. The doubtful concept of "equality in inequality," which the one uses to mask his despotism and the other to mask her cowardice, does not stand the test of experience: in their exchanges, woman appeals to the theoretical equality she has been guaranteed, and man the concrete inequality that exists. The result is that in every association an endless debate goes on concerning the ambiguous meaning of the words *give* and *take*: she complains of giving her all, he protests that she takes his all. Woman has to learn that exchanges—it is a fundamental law of political economy—are based on the value the merchandise offered has for the buyer, and not for the seller: she has been deceived in being persuaded that her worth is priceless. The truth is that for man she is an amusement, a pleasure, company, an inessential boon; he is for her the meaning, the justification of her existence. The exchange, therefore, is not of two items of equal value.

This inequality will be especially brought out in the fact that the time they spend together—which fallaciously seems to be the same time—does not have the same value for both partners. During the evening the lover spends with his mistress he could be doing something of advantage to his career, seeing friends, cultivating business relationships, seeking recreation; for a man normally integrated in society, time is a positive value: money, reputation, pleasure. For the idle, bored woman, on the contrary, it is a burden she wishes to get rid of; when she succeeds in killing time, it is a benefit to her: the man's presence is pure profit. In a liaison what most clearly interests the man, in many cases, is the sexual benefit he gets from it: if need be, he can be content to spend no more time with his mistress than is required for the sexual act; but—with exceptions—what she, on her part, wants is to kill all the excess time she has on her hands; and—like the storekeeper who will not sell potatoes unless the customer will take turnips also—she will not yield her body unless her lover will take hours of conversation and "going out" into the bargain. A balance is reached if, on the whole, the cost does not seem too high to the man, and this depends, of course, on the strength of his desire and the importance he gives to what is to be sacrificed. But if the woman demands—offers—too much time, she becomes wholly intrusive, like the river overflowing its banks, and the man will prefer to have nothing rather than too much. Then she reduces her demands; but very often the balance is reached at the cost of a double tension: she feels that the man has "had" her at a bargain, and he thinks her price is too high. This analysis, of course, is put in somewhat humorous terms; but—except for those affairs of jealous and exclusive passion in which the man wants total possession of the woman—this conflict constantly appears in cases of affection, desire, and even love. He always has "other things to do" with his time; whereas she has time to burn; and he considers much of the time she gives him not as a gift but as a burden.

As a rule he consents to assume the burden because he knows very well that he is on the privileged side, he has a bad conscience; and if he is of reasonable good will he tries to compensate for the inequality by being generous. He prides himself on his compassion, however, and at the first clash he treats the woman as ungrateful and thinks, with some irritation: "I'm too good to her." She feels she is behaving like a beggar when she is convinced of the high value of her gifts, and that humiliates her.

Here we find the explanation of the cruelty that woman often shows she is capable of practicing; she has a good conscience because she is on the unprivileged side; she feels she is under no obligation to deal gently with the favored caste, and her only thought is to defend herself. She will even be very happy if she has occasion to show her resentment to a lover who has not been able to satisfy all her demands: since he does not give her enough, she takes savage delight in taking back everything from him. At this point the wounded lover suddenly discovers the value *in toto* of a liaison each moment of which he held more or less in contempt: he is ready to promise her everything, even though he will feel exploited again when he has to make good. He accuses his mistress of blackmailing him: she calls him stingy; both feel wronged.

Once again it is useless to apportion blame and excuses: justice can never be done in the midst of injustice. A colonial administrator has no possibility of acting rightly toward the natives, nor a general toward his soldiers; the only solution is to be neither colonist nor military chief; but a man could not prevent himself from being a man. So there he is, culpable in spite of himself and laboring under the effects of a fault he did not himself commit; and here she is, victim and shrew in spite of herself. Sometimes he rebels and becomes cruel, but then he makes himself an accomplice of the injustice, and the fault becomes really his. Sometimes he lets himself be annihilated, devoured, by his demanding victim; but in that case he feels duped. Often he stops at a compromise that at once belittles him and leaves him ill at ease. A well-disposed man will be more tortured by the situation than the woman herself: in a sense it is always better to be on the side of the vanquished; but if she is well-disposed also, incapable of self-sufficiency, reluctant to crush the man with the weight of her destiny, she struggles in hopeless confusion.

In daily life we meet with an abundance of these cases which are incapable of satisfactory solution because they are determined by unsatisfactory conditions. A man who is compelled to go on materially and morally supporting a woman whom he no longer loves feels he is victimized; but if he abandons without resources the woman who has pledged her whole life to him, she will be quite as unjustly victimized. The evil originates not in the perversity of individuals—and bad faith first appears when each blames the other—it originates rather in a situation against which all individual action is powerless. Women are "clinging," they are a dead weight, and they suffer for it; the point is that their situation is like that of a parasite sucking out the living strength of another organism. Let them be provided with living strength of their own, let them have the means to attack the world and wrest from it their own subsistence, and their dependence will be abolished—that of man also. There is no doubt that both men and women will profit greatly from the new situation.

A world where men and women would be equal is easy to visualize, for that precisely is what the Soviet Revolution *promised*: women raised and trained exactly like men were to work under the same conditions[4] and for

---

[4]That certain too laborious occupations were to be closed to women is not in contradiction to this project. Even among men there is an increasing effort to obtain adaptation to profession; their varying physical and mental capacities limit their possibilities of choice; what is asked is that, in any case, no line of sex or caste be drawn.

the same wages. Erotic liberty was to be recognized by custom, but the sexual act was not to be considered a "service" to be paid for; woman was to be *obliged* to provide herself with other ways of earning a living; marriage was to be based on a free agreement that the spouses could break at will; maternity was to be voluntary, which meant that contraception and abortion were to be authorized and that, on the other hand, all mothers and their children were to have exactly the same rights, in or out of marriage; pregnancy leaves were to be paid for by the State, which would assume charge of the children, signifying not that they would be *taken away* from their parents, but that they would not be *abandoned* to them.

But is it enough to change laws, institutions, customs, public opinion, and the whole social context, for men and women to become truly equal? "Women will always be women," say the skeptics. Other seers prophesy that in casting off their femininity they will not succeed in changing themselves into men and they will become monsters. This would be to admit that the woman of today is a creation of nature; it must be repeated once more that in human society nothing is natural and that woman, like much else, is a product elaborated by civilization. The intervention of others in her destiny is fundamental: if this action took a different direction, it would produce a quite different result. Woman is determined not by her hormones or by mysterious instincts, but by the manner in which her body and her relation to the world are modified through the action of others than herself. The abyss that separates the adolescent boy and girl has been deliberately opened out between them since earliest childhood; later on, woman could not be other than what she *was made*, and that past was bound to shadow her for life. If we appreciate its influence, we see clearly that her destiny is not predetermined for all eternity.

We must not believe, certainly, that a change in woman's economic condition alone is enough to transform her, though this factor has been and remains the basic factor in her evolution; but until it has brought about the moral, social, cultural, and other consequences that it promises and requires, the new woman cannot appear. At this moment they have been realized nowhere, in Russia no more than in France or the United States; and this explains why the woman of today is torn between the past and the future. She appears most often as a "true woman" disguised as a man, and she feels herself as ill at ease in her flesh as in her masculine garb. She must shed her old skin and cut her own new clothes. This she could do only through a social evolution. No single educator could fashion a *female human being* today who would be the exact homologue of the *male human being*; if she is raised like a boy, the young girl feels she is an oddity and thereby she is given a new kind of sex specification. Stendhal[5] understood this when he said: "The forest must be planted all at once." But if we imagine, on the contrary, a society in

[5][Pen name of Marie Henri Beyle, French Novelist (1783–1842)—*Ed.*]

which the equality of the sexes would be concretely realized, this equality would find new expression in each individual.

If the little girl were brought up from the first with the same demands and rewards, the same severity and the same freedom, as her brothers, taking part in the same studies, the same games, promised the same future, surrounded with women and men who seemed to her undoubted equals, the meanings of the castration complex and of the Œdipus complex would be profoundly modified. Assuming on the same basis as the father the material and moral responsibility of the couple, the mother would enjoy the same lasting prestige; the child would perceive around her an androgynous world and not a masculine world. Were she emotionally more attracted to her father—which is not even sure—her love for him would be tinged with a will to emulation and not a feeling of powerlessness; she would not be oriented toward passivity. Authorized to test her powers in work and sports, competing actively with the boys, she would not find the absence of the penis—compensated by the promise of a child—enough to give rise to an inferiority complex; correlatively, the boy would not have a superiority complex if it were not instilled into him and if he looked up to women with as much respect as to men.[6] The little girl would not seek sterile compensation in narcissism and dreaming, she would not take her fate for granted; she would be interested in what she was *doing*, she would throw herself without reserve into undertakings.

I have already pointed out how much easier the transformation of puberty would be if she looked beyond it, like the boys, toward a free adult future: menstruation horrifies her only because it is an abrupt descent into femininity. She would also take her young eroticism in much more tranquil fashion if she did not feel a frightened disgust for her destiny as a whole; coherent sexual information would do much to help her over this crisis. And thanks to coeducational schooling, the august mystery of Man would have no occasion to enter her mind: it would be eliminated by everyday familiarity and open rivalry.

Objections raised against this system always imply respect for sexual taboos; but the effort to inhibit all sex curiosity and pleasure in the child is quite useless; one succeeds only in creating repressions, obsessions, neuroses. The excessive sentimentality, homosexual fervors, and platonic crushes of adolescent girls, with all their train of silliness and frivolity, are much more injurious than a little childish sex play and a few definite sex experiences. It would be beneficial above all for the young girl not to be influenced against taking charge herself of her own existence, for then she would not

---

[6]I knew a little boy of eight who lived with his mother, aunt, and grandmother, all independent and active women, and his weak old half-crippled grandfather. He had a crushing inferiority complex in regard to the feminine sex, although he made efforts to combat it. At school he scorned comrades and teachers because they were miserable males.

seek a demigod in the male—merely a comrade, a friend, a partner. Eroticism and love would take on the nature of free transcendence and not that of resignation; she could experience them as a relation between equals. There is no intention, of course, to remove by a stroke of the pen all the difficulties that the child has to overcome in changing into an adult; the most intelligent, the most tolerant education could not relieve the child of experiencing things for herself; what could be asked is that obstacles should not be piled gratuitously in her path. Progress is already shown by the fact that "vicious" little girls are no longer cauterized with a red-hot iron. Psychoanalysis has given parents some instruction, but the conditions under which, at the present time, the sexual training and initiation of woman are accomplished are so deplorable that none of the objections advanced against the idea of a radical change could be considered valid. It is not a question of abolishing in woman the contingencies and miseries of the human condition, but of giving her the means for transcending them.

Woman is the victim of no mysterious fatality; the peculiarities that identify her as specifically a woman get their importance from the significance placed upon them. They can be surmounted, in the future, when they are regarded in new perspectives. Thus, as we have seen, through her erotic experience woman feels—and often detests—the domination of the male; but this is no reason to conclude that her ovaries condemn her to live forever on her knees. Virile aggressiveness seems like a lordly privilege only within a system that in its entirety conspires to affirm masculine sovereignty; and woman *feels* herself profoundly passive in the sexual act only because she already *thinks* of herself as such. Many modern women who lay claim to their dignity as human beings still envisage their erotic life from the standpoint of a tradition of slavery: since it seems to them humiliating to lie beneath the man, to be penetrated by him, they grow tense in frigidity. But if the reality were different, the meaning expressed symbolically in amorous gestures and postures would be different, too: a woman who pays and dominates her lover can, for example, take pride in her superb idleness and consider that she is enslaving the male who is actively exerting himself. And here and now there are many sexually well-balanced couples whose notions of victory and defeat are giving place to the idea of an exchange.

As a matter of fact, man, like woman, is flesh, therefore passive, the plaything of his hormones and of the species, the restless prey of his desires. And she, like him, in the midst of the carnal fever, is a consenting, a voluntary gift, an activity; they live out in their several fashions the strange ambiguity of existence made body. In those combats where they think they confront one another, it is really against the self that each one struggles, projecting into the partner that part of the self which is repudiated; instead of living out the ambiguities of their situation, each tries to make the other bear the abjection and tries to reserve the honor for the self. If, however, both should assume the ambiguity with a clear-sighted modesty, correlative of an authentic pride, they would see each other as equals and would live out their erotic drama in amity. The fact that we are human beings is infinitely more important than all the peculiarities that distinguish human beings from one another; it is never the given that confers superiorities: "virtue," as the ancients called it, is defined at the level of "that which depends on us." In both sexes is played out the same drama of the flesh and the spirit, of finitude and transcendence; both are gnawed away by time and laid in wait for by death, they have the same essential need for one another; and they can gain from their liberty the same glory. If they were to taste it, they would no longer be tempted to dispute fallacious privileges, and fraternity between them could then come into existence.

I shall be told that all this is utopian fancy, because woman cannot be "made over" unless society has first made her really the equal of man. Conservatives have never failed in such circumstances to refer to that vicious circle; history, however, does not revolve. If a caste is kept in a state of inferiority, no doubt it remains inferior; but liberty can break the circle. Let the Negroes vote and they become worthy of having the vote; let woman be given responsibilities and she is able to assume them. The fact is that oppressors cannot be expected to make a move of gratuitous generosity; but at one time the revolt of the oppressed, at another time even the very evolution of the privileged caste itself, creates new situations; thus men have been led, in their own interest, to give partial emancipation to women: it remains only for women to continue their ascent, and the successes they are obtaining are an encouragement for them to do so. It seems almost certain that sooner or later they will arrive at complete economic and social equality, which will bring about an inner metamorphosis.

However this may be, there will be some to object that if such a world is possible it is not desirable. When woman is "the same" as her male, life will lose its salt and spice. This argument, also, has lost its novelty: those interested in perpetuating present conditions are always in tears about the marvelous past that is about to disappear, without having so much as a smile for the young future. It is quite true that doing away with the slave trade meant death to the great plantations, magnificent with azaleas and camellias, it meant ruin to the whole refined Southern civilization. The attics of time have received its rare old laces along with the clear pure voices of the Sistine *castrati*,[7] and there is a certain "feminine charm" that is also on the way to the same dusty repository. I agree that he would be a barbarian indeed who failed to appreciate exquisite flowers, rare lace, the crystal-clear voice of the eunuch, and feminine charm.

.   .   .

---

[7]Eunuchs were long used in the male choirs of the Sistine Chapel in Rome, until the practice was forbidden by Pope Leo XIII in 1880. The operation of castration caused the boy's soprano voice to be retained into adulthood, and it was performed for this purpose.—*Trans.*

And it is true that the evolution now in progress threatens more than feminine charm alone: in beginning to exist for herself, woman will relinquish the function as double and mediator to which she owes her privileged place in the masculine universe; to man, caught between the silence of nature and the demanding presence of other free beings, a creature who is at once his like and a passive thing seems a great treasure. The guise in which he conceives his companion may be mythical, but the experiences for which she is the source or the pretext are none the less real: there are hardly any more precious, more intimate, more ardent. There is no denying that feminine dependence, inferiority, woe, give women their special character; assuredly woman's autonomy, if it spares men many troubles, will also deny them many conveniences; assuredly there are certain forms of the sexual adventure which will be lost in the world of tomorrow. But this does not mean that love, happiness, poetry, dream, will be banished from it.

Let us not forget that our lack of imagination always depopulates the future; for us it is only an abstraction; each one of us secretly deplores the absence there of the one who was himself. But the humanity of tomorrow will be living in its flesh and in its conscious liberty; that time will be its present and it will in turn prefer it. New relations of flesh and sentiment of which we have no conception will arise between the sexes; already, indeed, there have appeared between men and women friendships, rivalries, complicities, comradeships—chaste or sensual—which past centuries could not have conceived. To mention one point, nothing could seem to me more debatable than the opinion that dooms the new world to uniformity and hence to boredom. I fail to see that this present world is free from boredom or that liberty ever creates uniformity.

To begin with, there will always be certain differences between man and woman; her eroticism, and therefore her sexual world, have a special form of their own and therefore cannot fail to engender a sensuality, a sensitivity, of a special nature. This means that her relations to her own body, to that of the male, to the child, will never be identical with those the male bears to his own body, to that of the female, and to the child; those who make much of "equality in difference" could not with good grace refuse to grant me the possible existence of differences in equality. Then again, it is institutions that create uniformity. Young and pretty, the slaves of the harem are always the same in the sultan's embrace; Christianity gave eroticism its savor of sin and legend when it endowed the human female with a soul; if society restores her sovereign individuality to woman, it will not therefore destroy the power of love's embrace to move the heart.

It is nonsense to assert that revelry, vice, ecstasy, passion, would become impossible if man and woman were equal in concrete matters; the contradictions that put the flesh in opposition to the spirit, the instant to time, the swoon of immanence to the challenge of transcendence, the absolute of pleasure to the nothingness of forgetting, will never be resolved; in sexuality will always be materialized the tension, the anguish, the joy, the frustration, and the triumph of existence. To emancipate woman is to refuse to confine her to the relations she bears to man, not to deny them to her; let her have her independent existence and she will continue none the less to exist for him also: mutually recognizing each other as subject, each will yet remain for the other an *other*. The reciprocity of their relations will not do away with the miracles—desire, possession, love, dream, adventure—worked by the division of human beings into two separate categories; and the words that move us—giving, conquering, uniting—will not lose their meaning. On the contrary, when we abolish the slavery of half of humanity, together with the whole system of hypocrisy that it implies, then the "division" of humanity will reveal its genuine significance and the human couple will find its true form.

Frantz Fanon

Much has been written in recent years about the evils of racism. What distinguishes the work of Frantz Fanon (1925–1961) is his ability to penetrate beyond the level simply of moral outrage to probe deeply into its causes and, more particularly, its effects on the people who are its victims. In defining racism as the "shameless exploitation of one group of men by another which has reached a higher state of technical development," Fanon shifts his analysis away from older biological and physical attempts at explanation to broader economic and technological causes. Because it permeates the society in which it exists, racism leads to fundamental modifications in its culture. Traditional relationships and styles of life are broken down, leaving the victimized people disoriented, caught between two diverse patterns of culture with no sense of belonging to either. The results are psychological disturbances for the individual and social instability for the group.

Frantz Fanon was well equipped to undertake an analysis of both colonialism and racism. As a member of the National Liberation Front he participated actively in the bloody struggle that led to the liberation of Algeria from French colonial rule in the fifties. And as a practicing psychiatrist he studied at close hand the effects of racism on the minds and personalities of multitudes of its victims in northern Africa. In the last five years of his short life Fanon devoted most of his time and energies to the liberation of Africa as a whole and its eventual unification. The essay "Racism and Culture" was originally delivered as an address before the first Congress of Negro Writers and Artists, held in Paris in 1956.

Consider the following questions as you study the text below.

1. In Fanon's view, what are causes of racism? Is it possible to rid a society of racism? How?

2. Why did Fanon see a logical connection between racism and colonization? What implications did he draw from this observation?

Racism and Culture

The unilaterally decreed normative value of certain cultures deserves our careful attention. One of the paradoxes immediately encountered is the rebound of egocentric, sociocentric definitions.

There is first affirmed the existence of human groups having no culture; then of a hierarchy of cultures; and finally, the concept of cultural relativity.

We have here the whole range from overall negation to singular and specific recognition. It is precisely this fragmented and bloody history that we must sketch on the level of cultural anthropology.

There are, we must say, certain constellations of institutions, established by particular men, in the framework of precise geographical areas, which at a given moment have undergone a direct and sudden assault of different cultural patterns. The technical, generally advanced development of the social group that has thus appeared enables it to set up an organized domination. The enterprise of deculturation turns out to be the negative of a more gigantic work of economic, and even biological, enslavement.

The doctrine of cultural hierarchy is thus but one aspect of a systematized hierarchization implacably pursued.

The modern theory of the absence of cortical integration of colonial peoples is the anatomicpsychological counterpart of this doctrine. The apparation of racism is not fundamentally determining. Racism is not the whole but the most visible, the most day-to-day and, not to mince matters, the crudest element of a given structure.

To study the relations of racism and culture is to raise the question of their reciprocal action. If culture is the combination of motor and mental behavior patterns arising from the encounter of man with nature and with his fellow-man, it can be said that racism is indeed a cultural element. There are thus cultures with racism and cultures without racism.

This precise cultural element, however, has not become encysted. Racism has not managed to harden. It has had to renew itself, to adapt itself, to change its appearance. It has had to undergo the fate of the cultural whole that informed it.

The vulgar, primitive, over-simple racism purported to find in biology—the Scriptures having proved insufficient—the material basis of the doctrine. It would be tedious to recall the efforts then undertaken: the comparative form of the skulls, the quantity and the configuration of the folds of the brain, the characteristics of the cell layers of the cortex, the dimensions of the vertebrae, the microscopic appearance of the epiderm, etc. ...

Intellectual and emotional primitivism appeared as a banal consequence, a recognition of existence.

Such affirmations, crude and massive, give way to a more refined argument. Here and there, however, an occasional relapse is to be noted. Thus the "emotional instability of the Negro," the "subcritical integration of the Arab," "the quasi-generic culpability of the Jew" are data that one comes upon among a few contemporary writers. The monograph by J. Carothers, for example, sponsored by the World Health Organization, invokes "scientific arguments" in support of a physiological lobotomy of the African Negro.

These old-fashioned positions tend in any case to disappear. This racism that aspires to be rational, individual, genotypically and phenotypically determined, becomes transformed into cultural racism. The object of racism is no longer the individual man but a certain form of existing. At the extreme, such terms as "message" and "cultural style" are resorted to. "Occidental values" oddly blend with the already famous appeal to the fight of the "cross against the crescent."

The morphological equation, to be sure, has not totally disappeared, but events of the past thirty years have shaken the most solidly anchored convictions, upset the checkerboard, restructured a great number of relationships.

The memory of Nazism, the common wretchedness of different men, the common enslavement of extensive social groups, the apparition of "European colonies," in other words the institution of a colonial system in the very heart of Europe, the growing awareness of workers in the colonizing and racist countries, the evolution of techniques, all this has deeply modified the problem and the manner of approaching it.

We must look for the consequences of this racism on the cultural level.

Racism, as we have seen, is only one element of a vaster whole: that of the systematized oppression of a people. How does an oppressing people behave? Here we rediscover constants.

We witness the destruction of cultural values, of ways of life. Language, dress, techniques, are devalorized. How can one account for this constant? Psychologists, who tend to explain everything by movements of the psyche, claim to discover this behavior on the level of contacts between individuals: the criticism of an original hat, of a way of speaking, of walking. ...

Such attempts deliberately leave out of account the special character of the colonial situation. In reality the nations that undertake a colonial war have no concern for the confrontation of cultures. War is a gigantic business and every approach must be governed by this datum. The enslavement, in the strictest sense, of the native population is the prime necessity.

For this its systems of reference have to be broken. Expropriation, spoliation, raids, objective murder, are matched by the sacking of cultural patterns, or at least condition such sacking. The social panorama is destructured; values are flouted, crushed, emptied.

The lines of force, having crumpled, no longer give direction. In their stead a new system of values is imposed, not proposed but affirmed, by the heavy weight of cannons and sabers.

The setting up of the colonial system does not of itself bring about the death of the native culture. Historic observation reveals, on the contrary, that the aim sought is rather a continued agony than a total disappearance of the preexisting culture. This culture, once living and open to the future, becomes closed, fixed in the colonial status, caught in the yoke of oppression. Both present and mummified, it testifies against its members. It defines them in fact without appeal. The cultural mummification leads to a mummification of individual thinking. The apathy so universally noted among colonial peoples is but the logical consequence of this operation. The reproach of inertia constantly directed at "the native" is utterly dishonest. As though it were possible for a man to evolve otherwise than within the framework of a culture that recognizes him and that he decides to assume.

Thus we witness the setting up of archaic, inert institutions, functioning under the oppressor's supervision and patterned like a caricature of formerly fertile institutions.

These bodies appear to embody respect for tradition, the cultural specificities, the personality of the subjugated people. This pseudorespect in fact is tantamount to the most utter contempt, to the most elaborate sadism. The characteristic of a culture is to be open, permeated by spontaneous, generous, fertile lines of force. The appointment of "reliable men" to execute certain gestures is a deception that deceives no one. Thus the Kabyle *djemaas* named by the French authority are not recognized by the natives. They are matched by another *djemaa* democratically elected. And naturally the second as a rule dictates to the first what his conduct should be.

The constantly affirmed concern with "respecting the culture of the native populations" accordingly does not signify taking into consideration the values borne by the culture, incarnated by men. Rather, this behavior betrays a determination to objectify, to confine, to imprison, to harden. Phrases such as "I know them," "that's the way they are," show this maximum objectification successfully achieved. I can think of gestures and thoughts that define these men.

Exoticism is one of the forms of this simplification. It allows no cultural confrontation. There is on the one hand a culture in which qualities of dynamism, of growth, of depth can be recognized. As against this, we find characteristics, curiosities, things, never a structure.

Thus in an initial phase the occupant establishes his domination, massively affirms his superiority. The social group, militarily and economically subjugated, is dehumanized in accordance with a polydimensional method.

Exploitation, tortures, raids, racism, collective liquidations, rational oppression take turns at different levels in order literally to make of the native an object in the hands of the occupying nation.

This object man, without means of existing, without a *raison d'être*, is broken in the very depth of his substance. The desire to live, to continue, becomes more and more indecisive, more and more phantomlike. It is at this stage that the well-known guilt complex appears. In his first novels, Wright [American writer] gives a very detailed description of it.

Progressively, however, the evolution of techniques of production, the industrialization, limited though it is, of the subjugated countries, the increasingly necessary existence of collaborators, impose a new attitude upon the occupant. The complexity of the means of production, the evolution of economic relations inevitably involving the evolution of ideologies, unbalance the system. Vulgar racism in its biological form corresponds to the period of crude exploitation of man's arms and legs. The perfecting of the means of production inevitably brings about the camouflage of the techniques by which man is exploited, hence of the forms of racism.

It is therefore not as a result of the evolution of people's minds that racism loses its virulence. No inner revolution can explain this necessity for racism to seek more subtle forms to evolve. On all sides men become free, putting an end to the lethargy to which oppression and racism had condemned them.

In the very heart of the "civilized nations" the workers finally discover that the exploitation of man, at the root of a system, assumes different faces. At this stage racism no longer dares appear without disguise. It is unsure of itself. In an ever greater number of circumstances the racist takes to cover. He who claimed to "sense," to "see through" those others, finds himself to be a target, looked at, judged. The racist's purpose has become a purpose haunted by bad conscience. He can find salvation only in a passion-driven commitment such as is found in certain psychoses. And having defined the symptomatology of such passion-charged deliria is not the least of Professor Baruk's merits.

Racism is never a super-added element discovered by chance in the course of the investigation of the cultural data of a group. The social constellation, the cultural whole, are deeply modified by the existence of racism.

It is a common saying nowadays that racism is a plague of humanity. But we must not content ourselves with such a phrase. We must tirelessly look for the repercussions of racism at all levels of sociability. The importance of the racist problem in contemporary American literature is significant. The Negro in motion pictures, the Negro and folklore, the Jew and children's stories, the Jew in the café, are inexhaustible themes.

Racism, to come back to America, haunts and vitiates American culture. And this dialectical gangrene is exacerbated by the coming to awareness and the determination of millions of Negroes and Jews to fight this racism by which they are victimized.

This passion-charged, irrational, groundless phase, when one examines it, reveals a frightful visage. The movement of groups, the liberation, in certain parts of the world, of men previously kept down, make for a more and more precarious equilibrium. Rather unexpectedly, the racist group points accusingly to a manifestation of racism among the oppressed. The "intellectual primitivism" of the period of exploitation gives way to the "medieval, in fact prehistoric fanaticism" of the period of the liberation.

For a time it looked as though racism had disappeared. This soul-soothing, unreal impression was simply the consequence of the evolution of forms of exploitation. Psychologists spoke of a prejudice having become unconscious. The truth is that the rigor of the system made the daily affirmation of a superiority superfluous. The need to appeal to various degrees of approval and support, to the native's cooperation, modified relations in a less crude, more subtle, more "cultivated" direction. It was not rare, in fact, to see a "democratic and humane" ideology at this state. The commercial undertaking of enslavement, of cultural destruction, progressively gave way to a verbal mystification.

The interesting thing about this evolution is that racism was taken as a topic of meditation, sometimes even as a publicity technique.

Thus the blues—"the black slave lament"—was offered up for the admiration of the oppressors. This modicum of stylized oppression is the exploiter's and the racist's rightful due. Without oppression and without racism you have no blues. The end of racism would sound the knell of great Negro music. …

As the all-too-famous Toynbee might say, the blues are the slave's response to the challenge of oppression.

Still today, for many men, even colored, Armstrong's music has a real meaning only in this perspective.

Racism bloats and disfigures the face of the culture that practices it. Literature, the plastic arts, songs for shopgirls, proverbs, habits, patterns, whether they set out to attack it or to vulgarize it, restore racism. This means that a social group, a country, a civilization, cannot be unconsciously racist.

We say once again that racism is not an accidental discovery. It is not a hidden, dissimulated element. No superhuman efforts are needed to bring it out.

Racism stares one in the face for it so happens that it belongs in a characteristic whole: that of the shameless exploitation of one group of men by another which has reached a higher stage of technical development. This is why military and economic oppression generally precedes, makes possible, and legitimizes racism.

The habit of considering racism as a mental quirk, as a psychological flaw, must be abandoned.

But the men who are a prey to racism, the enslaved, exploited, weakened social group—how do they behave? What are their defense mechanisms?

What attitudes do we discover here?

In an initial phase we have seen the occupying power legitimizing its domination by scientific arguments, the "inferior race" being denied on the basis of race. Because no other solution is left it, the racialized social group tries to imitate the oppressor and thereby to deracialize itself. The "inferior race" denies itself as a different race. It shares with the "superior race" the convictions, doctrines, and other attitudes concerning it.

Having witnessed the liquidation of its systems of reference, the collapse of its cultural patterns, the native can only recognize with the occupant that "God is not on his side." The oppressor, through the inclusive and frightening character of his authority, manages to impose on the native new ways of seeing, and in particular a pejorative judgment with respect to his original forms of existing.

This event, which is commonly designated as alienation, is naturally very important. It is found in the official texts under the name of assimilation.

Now this alienation is never wholly successful. Whether or not it is because the oppressor quantitatively and qualitatively limits the evolution, unforeseen, disparate phenomena manifest themselves.

The inferiorized group had admitted, since the force of reasoning was implacable, that its misfortunes resulted directly from its racial and cultural characteristics.

Guilt and inferiority are the usual consequences of this dialectic. The oppressed then tries to escape these, on the one hand by proclaiming his total and unconditional adoption of the new cultural models, and on the other, by pronouncing an irreversible condemnation of his own cultural style.[1]

Yet the necessity that the oppressor encounters at a given point to dissimulate the forms of exploitation does not lead to the disappearance of this exploitation. The more elaborate, less crude economic relations require a daily coating, but the alienation at this level remains frightful.

Having judged, condemned, abandoned his cultural forms, his language, his food habits, his sexual behavior, his way of sitting down, of resting, of laughing, of enjoying himself, the oppressed *flings himself* upon the imposed culture with the desperation of a drowning man.

Developing his technical knowledge in contact with more and more perfected machines, entering into the dynamic circuit of industrial production, meeting men from remote regions in the framework of the concentration of capital, that is to say, on the job, discovering the assembly line, the team, production "time," in other words yield per hour, the oppressed is shocked to find that he continues to be the object of racism and contempt.

---

[1] A little-studied phenomenon sometimes appears at this stage. Intellectuals, students, belonging to the dominant group, make "scientific" studies of the dominated society, its art, its ethical universe.

In the universities the rare colonized intellectuals find their own cultural system being revealed to them. It even happens that scholars of the colonizing countries grow enthusiastic over this or that specific feature. The concepts of purity, naïveté, innocence appear. The native intellectual's vigilance must here be doubly on the alert.

It is at this level that racism is treated as a question of persons. "There are a few hopeless racists, but you must admit that on the whole the population likes. …"

With time all this will disappear.

This is the country where there is the least amount of race prejudice. …

Films on race prejudice, poems on race prejudice, messages on race prejudice. …

Spectacular and futile condemnations of race prejudice. In reality, a colonial country is a racist country. If in England, in Belgium, or in France, despite the democratic principles affirmed by these respective nations, there are still racists, it is these racists who, in their opposition to the country as a whole, are logically consistent.

It is not possible to enslave men without logically making them inferior through and through. And racism is only the emotional, affective, sometimes intellectual explanation of this inferiorization.

The racist in a culture with racism is therefore normal. He has achieved a perfect harmony of economic relations and ideology. The idea that one forms of man, to be sure, is never totally dependent on economic relations, in other words—and this must not be forgotten—on relations existing historically and geographically among men and groups. An ever greater number of members belonging to racist societies are taking a position. They are dedicating themselves to a world in which racism would be impossible. But everyone is not up to this kind of objectivity, this abstraction, this solemn commitment. One cannot with impunity require of a man that he be against "the prejudices of his group."

And, we repeat, every colonialist group is racist.

"Acculturized" and deculturized at one and the same time, the oppressed continues to come up against racism. He finds this sequel illogical, what he has left behind him inexplicable, without motive, incorrect. His knowledge, the appropriation of precise and complicated techniques, sometimes his intellectual superiority as compared to a greater number of racists, lead him to qualify the racist world as passion-charged. He perceives that the racist atmosphere impregnates all the elements of the social life. The sense of an overwhelming injustice is correspondingly very strong. Forgetting racism as a consequence, one concentrates on racism as cause. Campaigns of deintoxication are launched. Appeal is made to the sense of humanity, to love, to respect for the supreme values. …

Race prejudice in fact obeys a flawless logic. A country that lives, draws its substance from the exploitation of other peoples, makes those peoples inferior. Race prejudice applied to those peoples is normal.

Racism is therefore not a constant of the human spirit.

It is, as we have seen, a disposition fitting into a well-defined system. And anti-Jewish prejudice is not different from anti-Negro prejudice. A society has race prejudice or it has not. There are no degrees of prejudice. One cannot say that a given country is racist but that lynchings or extermination camps are not to be found there. The truth is that all that and still other things exist on the horizon. These virtualities, these latencies circulate, carried by the life-stream of psychoaffective, economic relations. ...

Discovering the futility of his alienation, his progressive deprivation, the inferiorized individual, after this phase of deculturation, of extraneousness, comes back to his original positions.

This culture, abandoned, sloughed off, rejected, despised, becomes for the inferiorized an object of passionate attachment. There is a very marked kind of overvaluation that is psychologically closely linked to the craving for forgiveness.

But behind this simplifying analysis there is indeed the intuition experienced by the inferiorized of having discovered a spontaneous truth. This is a psychological datum that is part of the texture of History and of Truth.

Because the inferiorized rediscovers a style that had once been devalorized, what he does is in fact to cultivate culture. Such a caricature of cultural existence would indicate, if it were necessary, that culture must be lived, and cannot be fragmented. It cannot be had piecemeal.

Yet the oppressed goes into ecstasies over each rediscovery. The wonder is permanent. Having formerly emigrated from his culture, the native today explores it with ardor. It is a continual honeymoon. Formerly inferiorized, he is now in a state of grace.

Not with impunity, however, does one undergo domination. The culture of the enslaved people is sclerosed, dying. No life any longer circulates in it. Or more precisely, the only existing life is dissimulated. The population that normally assumes here and there a few fragments of life, which continues to attach dynamic meanings to institutions, is an anonymous population. In a colonial system these are the traditionalists.

The former emigré, by the sudden ambiguity of his behavior, causes consternation. To the anonymity of the traditionalist he opposes a vehement and aggressive exhibitionism.

The state of grace and aggressiveness are the two constants found at this stage. Aggressiveness being the passion-charged mechanism making it possible to escape the sting of paradox.

Because the former emigré is in possession of precise techniques, because his level of action is in the framework of relations that are already complex, these rediscoveries assume an irrationsl aspect. There is an hiatus, a discrepancy between intellectual development, technical appropriation, highly differentiated modes of thinking and of logic, on the one hand, and a "simple pure" emotional basis on the other. ...

Rediscovering tradition, living it as a defense mechanism, as a symbol of purity, of salvation, the decultured individual leaves the impression that the mediation takes vengeance by substantializing itself. This falling back on archaic positions having no relation to technical development is paradoxical.

The institutions thus valorized no longer correspond to the elaborate methods of action already mastered.

The culture put into capsules, which has vegetated since the foreign domination, is revalorized. It is not reconceived, grasped anew, dynamized from within. It is shouted. And this headlong, unstructured, verbal revalorization conceals paradoxical attitudes.

It is at this point that the incorrigible character of the inferiorized is brought out for mention. Arab doctors sleep on the ground, spit all over the place, etc. …

Negro intellectuals consult a sorcerer before making a decision, etc. …

"Collaborating" intellectuals try to justify their new attitude. The customs, traditions, beliefs, formerly denied and passed over in silence are violently valorized and affirmed.

Tradition is no longer scoffed at by the group. The group no longer runs away from itself. The sense of the past is rediscovered, the worship of ancestors resumed. …

The past, becoming henceforth a constellation of values, becomes identified with the Truth.

This rediscovery, this absolute valorization almost in defiance of reality, objectively indefensible, assumes an incomparable and subjective importance. On emerging from these passionate espousals, the native will have decided, "with full knowledge of what is involved," to fight all forms of exploitation and of alienation of man. At this same time, the occupant, on the other hand, multiplies appeals to assimilation, then to integration, to community.

The native's hand-to-hand struggle with his culture is too solemn, too abrupt an operation to tolerate the slightest slip-up. No neologism can mask the new certainty: the plunge into the chasm of the past is the condition and the source of freedom.

The logical end of this will to struggle is the total liberation of the national territory. In order to achieve this liberation, the inferiorized man brings all his resources into play, all his acquisitions, the old and the new, his own and those of the occupant.

The struggle is at once total, absolute. But then race prejudice is hardly found to appear.

At the time of imposing his domination, in order to justify slavery, the oppressor had invoked scientific argument. There is nothing of the kind here.

A people that undertakes a struggle for liberation rarely legitimizes race prejudice. Even in the course of acute periods of insurrectional armed struggle one never witnesses the recourse to biological justifications.

The struggle of the inferiorized is situated on a markedly more human level. The perspectives are radically new. The opposition is the henceforth classical one of the struggles of conquest and of liberation.

In the course of struggle the dominating nation tries to revive racist arguments but the elaboration of racism proves more and more ineffective.

There is talk of fanaticism, of primitive attitudes in the face of death, but once again the now crumbling mechanism no longer responds. Those who were once unbudgeable, the constitutional cowards, the timid, the eternally inferiorized, stiffen and emerge bristling.

The occupant is bewildered.

The end of race prejudice begins with a sudden incomprehension.

The occupant's spasmed and rigid culture, now liberated, opens at last to the culture of people who have really become brothers. The two cultures can affront each other, enrich each other.

In conclusion, universality resides in this decision to recognize and accept the reciprocal relativism of different cultures, once the colonial status is irreversibly excluded.

Alma-Ata Declaration

The most important, dramatic, and unexpected political event of the late twentieth century was the recent disintegration of the Union of Soviet Socialist Republics, an event that took experts on Soviet affairs almost completely by surprise. The general opinion, nurtured in the West through the decades as far back as the time of Stalin, was that the Soviet Union was a monolithic state, completely under the control of its political leaders and the Communist party. It was also widely believed that this system was not only tolerated, but actively supported, by the people of the Soviet Union. Under these circumstances, Western experts generally agreed, significant political change in the USSR in the forseeable future was hardly within the realm of possibility.

The process of disintegration, which culminated in the Alma-Ata Declaration reproduced in the selection below, began in the Baltic states of Estonia, Latvia, and Lithuania, which had been forcibly absorbed into the USSR in 1940 during World War II and never felt themselves a real part of the Soviet system. Separatism then spread elsewhere in the vast Soviet domains, as different regions joined—for ethnic, religious, economic, and political reasons—the exodus from control by the Kremlin. The leaders of eleven Republics, all previous members of the Soviet Union, met on December 21, 1991, in the remote city of Alma-Ata (not far from the border of China) where they promulgated and signed the declaration that follows, creating a Commonwealth of Independent States and declaring the death of the Union of Soviet Socialist Republics.

Consider the following questions as you study the text below.

1. How would you explain the collapse of the Soviet Union? What alternative alliances are emerging to take its place?

2. How much progress has been made toward the development of democracy in the former Soviet republics? In your opinion, was the signatories' stated intention of building democratic states sincere?

Alma-Ata Declaration

The following independent states—the Azerbaidzhan Republic, the Republic of Armenia, the Republic of Belarus, the Republic of Kazakhstan, the Republic of Kyrgyzstan, the Republic of Moldova, the Russian Federation (RSFSR), the Republic of Tadzhikistan, Turkmenistan, the Republic of Uzbekistan and Ukraine,

Seeking to build democratic states based on the rule of law, states the relations among which will be developed on the basis of mutual recognition of and respect for state sovereignty and sovereign equality, the inalienable right of self-determination, the principles of equality and noninterference in internal affairs, the renunciation of the use of force and the threat of force and of economic or any other means of pressure, the peaceful settlement of disputes, respect for human rights and liberties, including the rights of national minorities, and the conscientious fulfillment of obligations and other generally recognized principles and norms of international law;

Recognizing and respecting one another's territorial integrity and the inviolability of existing borders;

Believing that the strengthening of relations of friendship, good-neighborliness and mutually advantageous cooperation, which have deep historical roots, corresponds to the fundamental interests of the peoples and serves the cause of peace and security;

Aware of their responsibility for preserving civil peace and concord among nationalities;

Adhering to the goals and principles of the Agreement on the Creation of a Commonwealth of Independent States,

Declare the following:

Cooperation among the members of the Commonwealth will be carried out on the principle of equality, through coordinating institutions formed on a parity basis and operating in accordance with a procedure determined by agreements among the members of the Commonwealth, which is neither a state nor a suprastate formation.

With a view to ensuring international strategic stability and security, the joint command of military-strategic forces and unified control over nuclear weapons will be preserved; the parties will respect one another's aspirations to achieve the status of nuclear-weapon-free and/or neutral states.

The Commonwealth of Independent States is open, with the consent of all its members, for accession by member-states of the former USSR, as well as by other states that share the goals and principles of the Commonwealth.

Alma-Ata Declaration, from *The Current Digest of the Soviet Press*, Vol. XLIII, No. 51 (January 22, 1992). Courtesy of *The Current Digest of the Soviet Press*.

Commitment to cooperation in the formation and development of a common economic space and of all-European and Eurasian markets is confirmed.

With the formation of the Commonwealth of Independent States, the Union of Soviet Socialist Republics ceases to exist.

The member-states of the Commonwealth, in accordance with their constitutional procedures, guarantee the fulfillment of the international obligations stemming from the treaties and agreements of the former USSR.

The member-states of the Commonwealth pledge to unswervingly observe the principles of this Declaration.—[signed] A. MUTALIBOV, President of the Azerbaidzhan Republic; L. TER-PETROSYAN, President of the Republic of Armenia; S. SHUSHKEVICH, Chairman of the Supreme Soviet of the Republic of Belarus; N. NAZARBAYEV, President of the Republic of Kazakhstan; A. AKAYEV, President of the Republic of Kyrgyzstan; M. SNEGUR, President of the Republic of Moldova; B. YELTSIN, President of the Russian Federation (RSFSR); R. NABIYEV, President of the Republic of Tadzhikistan; S. NIYAZOV, President of Turkmenistan; I. KARIMOV, President of the Republic of Uzbekistan; and L. KRAVCHUK, President of Ukraine.

Alma-Ata, Dec. 21, 1991.